Dismantling the Patriarchy, Bit by Bit

Dismantling the Patriarchy, Bit by Bit

Art, Feminism, and Digital Technology

Judith K. Brodsky

BLOOMSBURY VISUAL ARTS
LONDON • NEW YORK • OXFORD • NEW DELHI • SYDNEY

BLOOMSBURY VISUAL ARTS
Bloomsbury Publishing Plc
50 Bedford Square, London, WC1B 3DP, UK
1385 Broadway, New York, NY 10018, USA
29 Earlsfort Terrace, Dublin 2, Ireland

BLOOMSBURY, BLOOMSBURY VISUAL ARTS and the Diana logo are trademarks of
Bloomsbury Publishing Plc

First published in Great Britain 2022

Cover design by Toby Way
Cover Image: Adrianne Wortzel, photograph of the back of one of the stripped
Elmo dolls used for Battle of the Pyramids (2008). Courtesy of the artist.

A catalogue record for this book is available from the British Library.

A catalog record for this book is available from the Library of Congress.

ISBN: HB: 978-1-3502-4348-4
ePDF: 978-1-3502-4349-1
eBook: 978-1-3502-4350-7

Typeset by RefineCatch Limited, Bungay, Suffolk
Printed and bound in Great Britain

Contents

Plates

Preface

This book came into being as a result of a session I chaired on feminist and transgender digital artists at the 2014 College Art Association Annual Conference just after organizing an exhibition on the same subject at Rutgers with my longtime colleague and collaborator, Dr. Ferris Olin. I was collaborating also at the time on a project documenting feminist digital artists with Muriel Magenta, a professor at Arizona State University, who is a pioneer in the development of digital art. My panelists included important digital artists like Magenta, Claudia Hart, and Zach Blas along with art historians like Sophie Landres who was revising the history of the collaboration between Nam June Paik and Charlotte Moorman. Anna Coatman, then an acquiring editor for I.B. Tauris, was in the audience and after the session asked me if I would be interested in doing a book on the history of feminist digital artists. I was excited by the prospect, but had to delay because of a prior book commitment. In 2018 I was ready to begin, and proceeded to spend two years researching and writing this book, which, I believe, is the first book linking the Feminist Art Movement with the development of digital art.

I was somewhat overwhelmed by how much had happened in the field since 2014. It hasn't been easy to capture the growth and the variety of contemporary feminist digital art in a comprehensive conceptual framework.

I want to acknowledge two people who have helped me do that. The first person is my husband, Michael Curtis, a Rutgers University retired political science professor and the author of over thirty-five books, who, at ninety-seven, is still writing and who made many helpful suggestions as he read various versions of the manuscript, and also listened to me patiently when I wanted to talk about parts of the manuscript with which I was having difficulties.

The second is Dr. Ferris Olin, also, like me, a retired Rutgers professor, who has been my longtime collaborator in feminist art. We did one of the first projects to focus on documenting the careers of older women artists, founded the Rutgers University Institute for Women and Art, and mounted many exhibitions of feminist artists such as the multilocation *The Fertile Crescent*, one of the first US exhibitions of women artists from the Middle East, and an exhibition titled *How American Women Artists Invented Postmodernism* (2005) which brought together twenty artists who had been pioneers in the Feminist Art Movement during the 1970s, including many who are no longer with us such as Mary Beth Edelson, Rachel Rosenthal, Miriam Schapiro, Carolee Schneemann, Sylvia Sleigh, Nancy Spero, May Stevens, and June Wayne. Ferris also has documented the history of the Rutgers Center for Innovative Print and Paper, which I established in 1986, in preparation for a catalogue raisonné and retrospective exhibition, neither of which is yet a reality but will be eventually. This is the first major project that I've done without Ferris as my collaborator for many years. However, we developed many of the ideas in this book together over the years, and Ferris read and commented on the manuscript in its first state.

I also want to thank my grandson, Jake Brodsky, a graduate of Brown University's Department of Modern Culture and Media, a center for experimental writing, who introduced me to hypertext literature; my stepson, Anthony Curtis, an intellectual property lawyer with a PhD in electrical engineering who, in his youth, played video games, for reading through and commenting on the chapter on video games; my step-granddaughter, Paula Curtis, PhD, a Japanese culture scholar, who read through and commented on the chapter on Japanese Feminism, Video Games, and Anime; and my step-granddaughter, Isabel Curtis, who taught me so much about the continuing impact of manga and anime on the current young generation.

In the course of editing, I was also in touch with several individuals to clarify or confirm details about the concepts or lives of artists in the book. I want, in particular, to thank Laurens Schwartz, son of the artist Lillian Schwartz. I owe Elizabeth A. Napier a deep debt of gratitude for helping me prepare the manuscript for publication. Her intelligence, wide knowledge, and careful work were especially important in editing the footnotes and bibliography, preparing the index, and reading over the manuscript several times to correct for lack of clarity, abbreviated nomenclature, repetition, and other errors.

Several books were key to developing a conceptual framework for a very complicated subject: Judy Malloy's *Women, Art, and Technology* (2003); Christiane Paul's *Digital Art* (2008) and *A Companion to Digital Art* (2016); Judy Wajcman's *Feminism Confronts Technology* (2000); *New Media Futures*, edited by Donna Cox, Ellen Sandor, and Janine Fron (2018); *White Heat Cold Logic: British Computer Art 1960–1980* (2008), edited by Paul Brown, Charlie Gere, Nicholas Lambert, and Catherine Mason; *Hybrid Practices: Art in Collaboration with*

Science and Technology in the Long 1960s, edited by David Cateforis, Steven Duval, and Shepherd Steiner, particularly, the chapter by Anne Collins Goodyear (2019); Susan Napier's *Anime, from Akira to Howl's Moving Castle* (2001); and *Processed Lives: Gender and Technology in Everyday Life*, edited by Melodie Calvert and Jennifer Terry (2005). There are many other books, essays, and articles I read that were also important to my research, but too many to list here—please see my bibliography.

Finally, I would like to thank the superb professionals at Bloomsbury who worked with me on the publication: Arts and Culture editor, April Peake; assistant editor, Yvonne Thouroude; Barbara Cohen Bastos, Sue Littleford, copy editor, Merv Honeywood at RefineCatch.

Abbreviations

AI	artificial intelligence
BIPOC	Black, indigenous, people of color
CalArts	California Institute of the Arts
CAVS	Center for Advanced Visual Studies, MIT
ERICA	ERato Intelligent Conversational Android
E.A.T.	Experiments in Art and Technology
FSW	Feminist Studio Workshop
LC	Laboria Cuboniks
LGBTQI	lesbian, gay, bisexual, transgender, queer, and intersex
MFA	master of fine arts
MIT	Massachusetts Institute of Technology
MoMA	Museum of Modern Art New York
NASA	National Aeronautics and Space Administration
NGO	nongovernmental organization
NT	New Tendencies
UCLA	University of California, Los Angeles
VR	virtual reality
WCA	Women's Caucus for Art

Introduction

This book is about how digital artists are transforming technology under the impact of feminist theory. It documents the history and contemporary practice of such artists in one volume for the first time. But it goes even further to show how they have made significant contributions to the aesthetic and practice of digital art and have altered digital technology itself.

The birth of digital technology in the late 1960s as a medium for artmaking is often linked to the rise of the Conceptual Art Movement. This book proposes a second link, the rise of the Feminist Art Movement. The 1960s and 1970s generation of feminist artists both repurposed traditional art disciplines and sought out new art forms to express an aesthetic based on women's experience. They began to explore the new field of what was then electronic technology. When one looks at the history of digital technology and art through the lens of feminism, a picture emerges in which feminist art theory played an important role in the development of digital artmaking and also had influence on digital technology itself, helping to free technology from the limitations imposed by its origins in a patriarchal context and transforming it into an accessible way of apprehending the world for people everywhere. Furthermore, the innovations of digital artists influenced by feminist theory have enhanced the effectiveness in the delivery of feminist messages exponentially.

How feminism is defined in this book is crucial. Feminism evolved in the 1960s and 1970s among mostly white women, both heterosexual and lesbian, the majority either American or European, as a social justice movement to accord women parity with men in all areas of society. Despite its radical assault on patriarchal male privilege, it quickly became critiqued as mired (even if unconsciously) in a continuation of colonialism, privileging whiteness and heteronormative gender definitions as universals for all humanity. Postcolonialism, queer, and critical race theory recognized the basis of feminism as a social justice movement but transformed it to become inclusive of gender fluidity, race, power, and oppression in general. It became an intersectional movement and is used as such in this book.

Even while rejecting patriarchal binary definitions of gender, the task of restoring women's history and elevating women to their rightful place in history must continue. Women's abilities, skills, and contributions to society are still undervalued and often invisible in the postcolonialist world. We are still discovering so many areas where work is needed on the recognition of women. One of those areas is in the realm of technology.

Women? Technology? The words repel each other with magnetic force. For millennia, technology was considered a male domain, the result of cultural stereotyping that men create knowledge and women do not. The assumption that technology belongs to men has resulted in burying the record of women's participation in the old technologies and continuing to render invisible women's participation in the digital era.

Women artists have suffered the same dismissal. Only since the Feminist Art Movement of the 1970s has women's art been taken seriously, and the contribution of women artists to image-making in popular culture is still rarely explored. Even as women artists started to be recognized, women artists in fields like architecture, design, sound, or media, all of which require technology, continued to suffer a double disregard based on their gender and their choice of medium.

The transformation of technology to digital began in the later 1960s when computers became generally available. Many artists embarked on using computers not only in traditional fields, but also to create new forms of artmaking. The term "new media" came into use and the growth of digital art over the last fifty years has been so great that the term is now obsolete. Yet, despite the expanding literature on women artists, there are few women included in the various histories of digital art. More often, there are none whereas even a small amount of research shows that women artists were among the first to become involved in digital artmaking and have played an important role in the development of digital art.

The origins of digital technology are inherently patriarchal as defined by masculinism. Masculinism, the basis of the patriarchal society, is a hierarchy in which white heterosexual males are dominant, exercising power over women, the LGBTQI population, indigenous groups, and people of color, oppressing otherness and elevating the authority of the white heteronormative male sphere to enforce its beliefs and codes of behavior on everyone else. Power and domination, the basic characteristics of masculinism, were embedded in the origins of digital technology. The internet, for instance, originated as a weapon developed by the scientific community on behalf of the United States government to help the allies win the Second World War (1941–5). Although by the end of the second decade of the twenty-first century, access to the internet was no longer limited to the West and was embedded in the culture of the world, it still retained the nature of its origin as shown by how it has been used by terrorists. Furthermore, digital technology still belongs mostly to the powerful. It remains unavailable to poor populations—including most of the people who live in the rural areas of postcolonial Africa and Asia.

This survey of pre-digital and digital art as practiced by artists influenced by feminist theory is weighted toward the United States, England, and Japan because digital technology originated in these economically developed countries and artists living in them had access to electronic media and computers. Restrictive social, political, and economic conditions in the rest of the world meant little access to advanced technology for most individuals, let alone for artists who were concerned with feminist, queer, and critical race theory. Nevertheless, an attempt has been made to document at least some of these artists, primarily those who have had the opportunity to live and work at times in the United States and Western Europe. Undoubtedly, there are many more, but more research on the ground in other countries is needed to bring them to light. Furthermore, even in the Western countries and Japan, additional research is needed to document the contributions of artists of color and other underrepresented groups to the history of digital art.

In contrast to masculinism, feminism envisions a society that is inclusive and nonhierarchical. Under the umbrella of feminist theory, many artists are shaping a different kind of technology, breaking down patriarchal codes and substituting new paradigms of technology that are more suited to an equitable society such as using computers for the benefit of the community rather than to wage war. The practitioners of digitally based art in this book may not call themselves feminist, but their work can be described as feminist because their work fits the principles of feminism.

Like the history of digital technology, the history of art until recently was also masculinist, its structure and theories based on patriarchal stereotypes formulated in the Western colonialist era. Creativity belonged in the male sphere. Women could not be great artists because of their gender. Feminist art historians did more than insert women artists back into art history; they challenged the Western patriarchal assumptions that only white men from a European background could be artists so successfully that art history has begun to abandon its Western colonialist and white bias, encompassing the work of cis heteronormative and lesbian artists, trans artists, artists of color, and artists from societies formerly considered "primitive."

Art history was also masculinist in its system of hierarchies. "High art" included painting, sculpture, and architecture. Forms of artmaking like weaving were associated with women and denigrated as "craft" rather than art. Illustration, design, fashion, all the forms of art that exist outside the museum, were not considered art, nor were the visual forms of popular culture—comics, animations, films, television. That division was already breaking down but was accelerated by the emergence of digital technology. Mobile devices and the internet have multiplied visual images exponentially, and the proliferation of software enables anyone to create "art." For the most part, the digital forms of the dramatic arts such as film and television and the increasingly popular use of sound are beyond the scope of this book, but consideration of video games and anime are included because they have had so much impact on visual representation throughout the world.

Technological art is complex. It ranges from video, animation, design, sculpture that is kinetic or envisioned through 3-D computer modeling, painting that originates through preliminary computer work, to installations and performances that use mechanical electrical devices. By the beginning of the twenty-first century, all technological art was digitally based, but during the last four decades of the twentieth century, video and photography were analog forms of media and the technological elements in performances or installations were simple plug-in applications. Often projects involved various kinds of technology. Artists did not make the distinction between the old and new technology as digital began to overtake earlier forms of technology. What was important was the fact that, whether analog or digital, it did not carry the weight of art of the past with its restrictions, conventions, and associations with binary patriarchal values.

Each of the following chapters addresses a different aspect of how artists are reformulating digital technology as an art practice that both questions masculinist systems of knowledge and establishes it as an art practice that is nonhierarchic and inclusive.

Chapter 1 recapitulates the history of the development of digital technology itself starting with Ada Lovelace, the nineteenth-century mathematician who first conceived of the capacities of the modern computer. The history of video art is said to begin with Nam June Paik in 1965; but feminist artists like Joan Jonas were exploring video at the very same time. Nam June Paik, himself, was collaborating with Charlotte Moorman, but as Jennifer Chan has pointed out, she is described as "a woman cellist" while he is described as "the father of video." Miriam Schapiro was one of the first artists to create a series of paintings based on computer formulations. Lillian Schwartz, working at Bell Telephone Laboratories, undertook some of the first efforts to establish a digital aesthetics.

During the 1960s, dance, visual art, and music were intertwined with electronic media in New York City performances like those mounted by Billy Klüver's Experiments in Art and Technology (E.A.T.). Several women artists were influential figures in this movement like Simone Forti, Yvonne Rainer, and Carolee Schneemann. On the West Coast, Lynn Hershman Leeson was experimenting with electronically wired sculptures. Artists in other countries became interested in digital technology. Zagreb, London, and Paris were centers of development, and the first major exhibitions of technological art were held in London and New York.

Chapter 2 documents how women artists in the 1970s contributed to innovations that improved digital technology itself, as well as employing digital technology in their art practices. The Middle West was a center of experimentation due to the involvement of the University of Illinois, Urbana, in the development of a computer in the first generation of supercomputers, the ILLIAC (Illinois Automatic Computer), which exponentially increased the capacity of computers up to that time. Women artists who were students and had access to the ILLIAC at Illinois went to Chicago and elsewhere to continue their studies and to teach, bringing their enthusiasm for digital art with them. This chapter also makes the connection between the use of video art and the Feminist Art Movement which exploded in the 1970s. Laurie Anderson, Dara Birnbaum, and Martha Rosler are examples of influential feminist artists who turned to media. Not only was their content feminist, but also they made innovations in the medium itself. During the 1970s, one of the first internet artworks was produced by Vera Frenkel in Canada, and Joan Brigham and Harriet Casdin at the Center for Advanced Visual Studies, Massachusetts Institute of Technology were the key artists in the collaborative digital sculpture, *Centerbeam*, seen first at *documenta* 6, Kassel, Germany. *documenta* 6 was extraordinary in featuring women artists who used digital technology. In addition to the women artists and engineers involved in creating Centerbeam (several besides Brigham and Casdin), Laurie Anderson, Valie Export, Joan Jonas, Friederike Pezold, and Chantel Ackerman all participated in *documenta* 6.

Chapter 3 tells the story of artists who sought to alter the binary system which is the basis for computer technology. They worked either to eliminate the binary or to make it a positive attribute. No matter how complex the result may seem, computers operate through a string of on/off commands, paralleling the heteronormative structure of the patriarchal society, which is also binary, the opposition of self/other, male/female, master/slave, dark/light. Rather than viewing the binary as oppositional, feminist artists, responding to theories put forth by Donna Haraway and Sadie Plant, began to think of the zero (the "off" position) as opportunity to build a new meaning that would subvert the binary. Calling themselves cyberfeminists, the most radical of the early collectives were VNS Matrix and Old Boys Network, and later, the Laboria Cuboniks. More recently, Legacy Russell argued that the "glitch," ordinarily treated as an error in transmission of electronic data, should instead be considered an "erratum," providing the opening for inclusion of queer, Black, and other peoples who do not conform to the heteronormative profile of the patriarchal society.

Chapter 4 covers how the invention of the World Wide Web led to a profusion of websites devoted to feminist activism. Feminist collectives like subRosa, founded by Faith Wilding and Hyla Willis, used digital technology to focus on such issues as restoring control of reproduction to women rather than allowing it to be regulated by the government. Johanna Burai, while still at art school in Sweden, exposed the racism of search engines like Google. Tensions arose among cyberfeminists about whether to use digital technology to foment revolution or for networking to empower women.

Chapter 5 explores how language has been used to disrupt the masculinism of digital technology. Having discovered projection of language into public space, thanks to a commission from the New York Public Art Fund, Jenny Holzer continued to use digital projection of her words to fight against patriarchal domination. An even more radical use of language is the innovation of hypertext literature in the work of such feminist artists as Judy Malloy. Rather than the conventional linear structure of prose to which we are all accustomed in the patriarchal society, which gives the author power over how the reader moves through the text, hypertext literature is built out of links on websites. The reader has choice over which links to access, transferring the power of structuring the narrative to individual readers, who then are no longer subject to patriarchal domination.

Chapter 6 shows how queer and transgender artists like Zach Blas, micha cárdenas, Vaginal Davis, Juliana Huxtable, and Xandra Ibarra have adopted feminist interrogation of the patriarchal society and are using their art to disrupt and subvert patriarchal social structures by creating new technical paradigms that break borders of disciplines, turn static mediums into time-based art, disrupt the separation of the offline world from the virtual world; and create alternate social structures in which everyone can take his/her/their place as a first-class citizen. The Feminist Studio Workshop at the Woman's Building, Los Angeles was an early center for lesbian studies and video experimentation.

As described in Chapter 7, women artists like Lynn Hershman Leeson pioneered the device of the avatar and used it to protest sexism and racism, at first in live performance by artists such as Betsy Damon, and Eleanor Antin, but then through video and the internet where they can reach audiences on a much larger scale. This chapter also documents how the avatar is used for its capacity to convey queerness along with race (Howardena Pindell and Adrian Piper were early users of video to make art about racism), and how it is particularly suited to social networking as in the work of Ann Hirsch, LaTurbo Avedon, and Amalia Ulman.

Chapter 8 traces the gradual elimination of the representation of the female body. The chapter starts with the history of feminist artists of the 1970s such as Joan Semmel and Alice Neel, who attempted to disrupt the male gaze by such devices as inverting the gaze and depicting the male nude in the same manner as traditional female nudes. But feminist artists of the 1980s like Cindy Sherman rejected that effort as essentialist. It served only to reinforce the male gaze. The 1980s also saw African American women artists like Lorna Simpson address the absence of the Black female body in representation. Representation of the body had to be abandoned altogether as it is in the work of Mona Hatoum. Digital technology provided the final nails for the coffin of the body. The distinction between the physical body and the digital body disappeared. The body became a set of pixels rather than an offline body as demonstrated by Hito Steyerl in her video, *How Not to Be Seen: A Fucking Didactic Educational .MOV File.*

Chapter 9 examines the intersection of feminist theory and patriarchal epistemology. The fact that artists like Laurie Anderson, Diane Burko, Ellen K. Levy, and Addie Wagenknecht, who identify as female address scientific issues is enough by itself to rend the fabric of patriarchal stereotypes, given the traditional skepticism in the heteronormative society for women's ability to understand science. But the artists referred to in this chapter go further, questioning the hierarchy that places human beings above animals (Kathy High, Patricia Piccinini), interrogating digital colonialism in which technologically advanced countries impose their culture on others via the internet (Morehshin Allahyari), and querying the validity of genetic and facial recognition (Heather Dewey-Hagborg).

The subject of Chapter 10 is how the dominant heteronormative culture uses surveillance to maintain power. Artists in this chapter identify and question several different kinds of surveillance include enforcement of ideals of beauty through capitalist modes of marketing, rendering as inferiors, the people who don't meet those standards (Brenda Oelbaum, Laura Schrager, Shawné Michaelain Holloway). Surveillance can also mean government surveillance of citizens in their daily activities (Shu Lea Cheang, Suzanne Treister, Jill Magid,

Laura Poitras), or the surveillance in facial recognition and DNA analysis (Heather Dewey-Hagborg).

Chapters 11 and 12 examine video gaming and its global impact on popular culture as well as on digital artists. The first of the two chapters shows how women have been involved in the video-gaming world as players and designers from the start and are contributing new approaches that are more compatible with feminist principles of community, gender equality, and diversity (Anna Anthropy, Dona Bailey, Natalie Bookchin, Brenda Brathwaite, Mattie Brice, Mary Flanagan, Claudia Hart, Brenda Laurel). Chapter 12 looks at the impact of Japanese anime culture on digital art worldwide aesthetically and as an acceptable alternative to American culture which is viewed as imperialistic by many postcolonial countries (Chiho Aoshima, Mariko Mori, Yoshiko Shimada, Aya Takano, Naoko Takeuchi).

Chapters 13 and 14 are about artists whose practice consists in creating robots (Erin Gee, Heidi Kumao, Adrianne Wortzel), virtual reality (VR) installations (Janicza Bravo, Zara Houshmand, Hyphen-Labs, Nonny de la Peña, Tamiko Thiel, Milica Zec), and augmented reality (AR) projects (Nancy Baker Cahill, Sarah Drury, Hana Iverson, Les Liens Invisibles, Manifest.AR, Teri Rueb). Using AI, Stephanie Dinkins explores racism and Karen Palmer, the impact of empathy on judgment. Aware of how digital personal assistants like Alexa or Siri are given female voices, feminist artists have created robots or designed machines that expose the bias of artificial intelligence (AI) (Anna Rüst). Augmented reality is being used increasingly for public art projects, particularly projects addressing environmental concerns (Grimanesa Amorós, Amy Balkin, Sophia Brueckner, HeHe, Laurie Palmer, Andrea Polli). Another area of analysis is the speculation that feminist artists may have been drawn to VR which is an immersive digital environment and AR which merges the offline and virtual worlds out of wanting to create Utopian worlds in place of the patriarchal one of oppression (Evelyn Hriberšek).

Finally, a concluding chapter summarizes the contributions feminist digital artists have made to advance feminist principles as well adding new concepts to digital technology and visual art.

1

Reinserting Women into the History of Digital Art

Pioneer Feminist Artists

Women's ideas and imagination have been crucial to the development of old and new technologies including digital devices and tools. Hypatia was a fourth century CE mathematician who lived in Alexandria, Egypt, at that time the intellectual center of the Roman Empire. She wrote the equations for conic sections, thus expanding Euclidean geometry but the story goes that she was also executed for daring to be a female mathematician. Many centuries later, Émilie du Châtelet, usually just known as a friend of Voltaire, translated Newton's *Principia* into French with her own notes of explanation added anonymously. It was published posthumously in 1759 after her death from childbirth. Another French woman, Nicole-Reine Lepaute, worked with Alexis-Claude Clairaut and Joseph-Jérôme Lefrançais de Laland throughout 1757, to predict the date of the return of Halley's Comet.[1]

Ada Lovelace (1815–52) has now been given her due as the genius who developed the algorithms that until recently were credited to Charles Babbage. Inspired by the Jacquard loom, which used punched cards to produce intricate woven designs mechanically, he invented the Analytical Engine, the hardware that has been called the first modern computer. He envisioned the Engine as being able to process information beyond weaving designs, including words and numbers, but it was Lovelace's equations that made the Engine work. Ada Lovelace was born Augusta Ada Byron, the only legitimate child of Annabella Milbanke and the poet, Lord Byron. In tribute to her work, Lovelace is often referred to as the first programmer.[2]

The term, "computers," was first applied to women, and the history of women computers in the nineteenth century shows how women's work in technology came to be considered as unimportant as the women themselves. With the Industrial Revolution fully underway after the Civil War, scientific research and technological innovation exploded. More workers were needed to handle the profusion of data that poured out, just as clerical work began to be considered appropriate for women. This data required classification and organization if it were to be useful, but as monotonous, mind-numbing clerical work, it was considered inappropriate for male scientists.

At Harvard University, Edward Pickering, the director of the observatory, in 1881 hired his housemaid to do the busy work of compiling the overwhelming amount of data that had been collected. In turn, that housemaid, Williamina Fleming, hired dozens of women to work in the observatory. The women were actually called "computers." Women's colleges had been established so there were trained female mathematicians available, but, despite their education, they were expected to marry and become homemakers. They were having trouble finding jobs worthy of their education and could be hired for much less than their male colleagues. Fleming herself worked for thirty-six years in the observatory. Her team of more than eighty women discovered and cataloged over 10,000 stars as well as other astronomical entities. Thus, women entered the field of pre-digital technology as drones to do the work that was beneath the dignity of men.[3]

The categorization of both pre-digital and digital technology as belonging in the male sphere persisted after the Second World War despite the hundreds of women who were involved in information technology during the war years. The British women who worked at Bletchley Park and helped to break the Nazi codes are now recognized thanks to a popular BBC television series, but the six women, Kathleen McNulty Mauchly Antonelli, Jean Jennings Bartik, Frances Elizabeth Snyder Holberton, Marlyn Wescoff Meltzer, Frances Bilas Spence, and Ruth Lichterman Teitelbaum, who programmed the ENIAC (Electronic Numerical Integrator and Computer), the first all-electronic computer in the United States (although George Stibitz at Bell Telephone Laboratories had earlier built a prototype) were not. They are now recognized, but when the ENIAC was first introduced in 1946, only the male directors of the project were cited.[4]

Two women who helped to advance digital technology around the middle of the twentieth century were Grace Murray Hopper, a Rear Admiral in the US Navy during the Second World War, and Radia Perlman. Hopper is credited with the creation of some of the basics of modern computing, particularly her work on compiling, by which programming is translated via a digital processor and Random Access Memory (RAM) into a language that the computer can read. Perlman's work led to a feature that makes the internet work so well. She developed the Spanning Tree Protocol (STP) which makes it possible for the internet to deliver data reliably through multiple links that provide automatic alternatives if an active link fails. The STP Protocol also disables the links that are not being used, thus leaving a single clear path between the source and the receiver of the data involved.[5]

These few examples show the variety and significance of women's contributions to pre-digital and digital technology. Just as these and hundreds of other women were crucial to technological advancement itself, women artists have been pioneers in shaping the field of technological art. It should be noted that using accurate nomenclature is difficult in describing the various kinds of technology used by artists on the path to the digital artmaking of today. Electronic media, analog, and pre-digital cover most art practices. But the point is that all of it leads to contemporary digital art.

In the United States (and beyond), Nam June Paik was a major force in legitimatizing the use of technology in art. But not usually acknowledged is the fact that, at the same time (the mid-1960s), American women artists also began to assimilate technology into their art practices. Originally from South Korea, Nam June Paik began collaborating with the New York-based cellist, Charlotte Moorman, in 1965 shortly after he moved to New York. American artist, Lillian Schwartz, who lived in New Jersey, began to experiment with creating kinetic sculptures around the same time. Some universities began to acquire computers in the 1960s, and women artists connected to various institutions were among the first to explore their potential for artmaking. Miriam Schapiro developed compositions for her paintings on computers at the University of California, San Diego; Colette Bangert drew on a digital plotter at the University of Kansas in 1967; and Vera Molnár began drawing on the computer in 1968 at the Université de Paris IV (Sorbonne Nouvelle).[6]

Miriam Schapiro (Plate 1) made hard-edge abstract paintings in the late 1960s between her earlier abstract expressionist period and the art that led to her becoming known as one of the founders of the Feminist Art Movement in the 1970s. Schapiro moved from New York to California in 1965 when her husband, artist and art critic Paul Brach, was invited by the University of California, San Diego, to initiate an art department. When they moved to San Diego, Schapiro met David Nabilof, a physicist at the campus and with his help began to use the computer to create compositions for her paintings. Her involvement in 1965 is simultaneous with Nam June Paik's exploration of newly developing technologies such as robotics and electronic media. Schapiro's use of the computer is situated within the tradition of drawing, but it was also revolutionary: through the program she was using, she could turn the form in the original drawing around and see what it would look like from another perspective. Without the use of the computer, Schapiro would have had to build the form itself so that she could see what it would look like from different angles. It was three-dimensional computer modeling before computer-aided design software programs for non-computer scientists were developed.[7]

Kansas City artist Colette Bangert used a digital plotter (the plotter is a printer that uses lines to connect dots), at the University of Kansas in 1967 to make landscape drawings. The university was given a plotter, and her husband, a mathematician and supervisor of applications programming at the University of Kansas Computation Center, was asked to test it. Together they began to experiment graphically and create drawings, which they signed together. The repetition and chance elements of the plotter paralleled how Bangert conceived of landscape forms. Her interest in relating digital technology to nature was a major contribution to developing a variety of computer image making possibilities.[8]

An example of the excitement around computers in the 1960s is an experiment at San José State University. In 1963, Joan Shogren, an artist working as a secretary in the Chemistry Department, which had an IBM 1620, suggested to graduate student, Jim Larson, that "a computer should be able to design a picture." Shogren and Dr. Ralph Fessenden, assistant professor of chemistry, fed into the computer what they considered the principles of good design. The computer output was a series of 1,600 numbers from zero to five arranged in patterns. At that point, humans took over and arbitrarily assigned colors to the numbers (much as at the end of the second decade of the twenty-first century, arbitrary colors are still being assigned to computer images of the cosmos), creating an abstract image made up of rectangles of varying sizes.[9]

Another woman pioneer in digital art, Grace Hertlein had the opportunity to use computers at the School of the Art Institute of Chicago while she was an undergraduate student in the late 1960s. One of her digital images was first shown in 1969 at the Fall Joint Computer Conference, Las Vegas. Hertlein's work was known in Europe and she was one of twenty artists invited to be in an exhibition in Zagreb in 1973. Katherine Nash, at the University of Minnesota, was one of the first artists to use software to create her images. During the early days of computer art, artists had to do coding—in other words creating algorithms from scratch rather than having a software program that they could use. Nash along with Richard Williams created ART 1, to introduce art students to coding.[10]

One of the important feminist ambitions is to counteract the patriarchal belief that women are passive and acted upon, rather than having their own agency. According to several revisionist feminist art historians, Charlotte

Moorman (Plate 2) exemplifies the connection between technology and the representation of agency in the female body. Until recently, Moorman was primarily known for the legal hullabaloo that arose as a result of her bare-breasted cello performance in one of her collaborations with Nam June Paik. She was arrested for indecent exposure after a 1967 performance of Nam June Paik's *Opera Sextronique* at the Film-Makers Cooperative on West Forty-First Street in Times Square in which she appeared topless with electric propellers pasted to her nipples. Both Moorman and Paik were arrested and spent the night in jail at The Tombs, on Centre Street. There were no charges against Paik, but Moorman was charged, tried, and convicted.

Feminist art historians argue that the perception of Moorman as passively performing at Nam June Paik's direction stemmed from masculinist objectification of women's bodies which made it hard for critics to get past her nude body, particularly when it was sexualized parts of her body, her breasts, that were on display. Prior to the research on Moorman's papers, it was always assumed that Nam June Paik was responsible for conceiving the performances. Instead, according to Moorman's own papers, she was an equal partner in planning as well as execution. Her performances should be seen as female agency dominating technology rather than passively accepting it.[11]

Moorman's and Nam June Paik's collaboration is typical of the 1960s avant-garde in New York when dance, visual art, music, and conceptual art groups as diverse as Fluxus and Judson Dance Theater were merging the arts into an interdisciplinary mix and experimenting with technology. The excitement and energy of the space race with its new emphasis on science resulted in artists seeing the creativity of scientists as parallel to their own creativity. As Western artists in the sixteenth century experimented with the new medium of printmaking, in the nineteenth century with the arrival of photography, and then in the twentieth century with film, artists in the 1960s were attracted to the possibilities offered by the new technologies. Many were drawn to John Cage, among them Yoko Ono, whose contributions to conceptual and feminist art, obscured for many decades by her relationship to John Lennon, have now been acknowledged. Yoko Ono, primarily a performance artist, experimented with film, producing a dozen, among them *Bottoms* (*Film No. 4*, 1966–7) consisting only of views of buttocks, the vertical and horizonal creases dividing the screen and often looking as if they are close-ups of two people speaking to each other.

Experiments in Art and Technology (E.A.T.), one of the most influential of such groups, was founded by visual artist Robert Rauschenberg, performance artist Robert Whitman, Billy Klüver (born Johan Wilhelm Klüver, Monaco), and

Fred Waldhauer. The latter two were engineers at Bell Telephone Laboratories. Klüver first became involved with the burgeoning group of performance avant-garde artists in the early 1960s when he helped Jean Tinguely with aspects of the self-destructing sculpture that Tinguely created for the Museum of Modern Art (MoMA) garden.

Performance artists increasingly experimented with technology. According to the oral history of Julie Martin, who became an important figure in E.A.T.'s structure (she married Klüver and later led E.A.T.), Klüver was the one who introduced the concept of collaboration between artists and engineers to Rauschenberg and Whitman and explained how it might contribute to the arts, and at the same time to engineering which he believed would also benefit from the collaboration.[12]

Although not well documented, women artists played a significant role in E.A.T. The influential innovative choreographer Simone Forti was living in New York in the early 1960s. At the time she was married to the artist Robert Morris, and the two became integral figures in the New York avant-garde scene. Forti and Morris separated in 1962 and she first lived with, and then married, Robert Whitman. Although Whitman asked her to forego her career and raise a family, she played an active role in E.A.T.'s productions, suggesting that she contributed more to E.A.T. than previously believed. The choreographer Yvonne Rainer, also known later for her feminist films, was another woman whose role in E.A.T. should be acknowledged more fully.[13]

Other New York artists besides those in E.A.T. were enthusiastic about interaction between artists and engineers. The performance artist, Carolee Schneemann, was an early user of electronic technology. In *Snows*, an anti-Vietnam War performance which premiered in New York in 1967, Schneemann, with the help of E.A.T., wired the seats of the Martinique Theater so that the audience's responses triggered various light and sound effects.[14]

Lillian Schwartz was an extraordinary individual, an accomplished artist in traditional media who was already experimenting with creating art through pre-digital technology when she had the opportunity to be artist in residence (the only one ever) at the Bell Telephone Laboratories (Bell Labs) in Murray Hill, New Jersey. When she was invited to the Labs in 1968 she developed digital programs geared for engineering into ones that could be used to create art.

From childhood, Schwartz was an art prodigy. By age twelve, she was using professional tools her brother brought to her from Disney Studios. She painted both the figure and abstractly. She also studied media. While stationed in occupied Japan after the Second World War, she recovered from polio-induced paralysis by learning Chinese brushwork and studying the production of cloisonné. After settling in New Jersey, she continued to study traditional art disciplines but always pushed each medium to its extreme via palettes, materials, different types of perspective. In 1960, she was allowed to use a plastic factory and created sculptures using rods to draw abstract art inside the cooling acrylic which she later reshaped by using a saw and gluing on other plastic objects.

She was involved in many of the various avant-garde New York movements of the 1960s, and her kinetic sculpture was included in one of the first major exhibitions to focus on technology in art, *The Machine as seen at the end of the mechanical age* (MoMA, New York, 1968). It was organized and curated by Pontus Hultén, who had known Billy Klüver since their early adulthood when both were living in Sweden. Hultén's concept was to review the history of the machine as visualized by artists from the time of Leonardo and to conclude with an array of projects that were selected from a competition organized by E.A.T. requiring that artists collaborate with engineers on the projects (E.A.T. called them electronogists and technologists). Nine projects were chosen from the submissions, along with a tenth which was a collaboration between Robert Rauschenberg and Klüver. Among the nine projects selected from the competition three of the artists were women: Lucy Jackson Young, Lillian Schwartz, and Robin Parkinson. In the historical section, the only woman was Marian Zazeela, who collaborated with her husband, the composer/musician La Monte Young. They were included because of their integration of sound and light in an installation titled *Dream House*. Young composed the music, and Zazeela the display of lights that paralleled and provided a visual experience to accompany the music. Zazeela is the first artist to explore the potential of programming electric light.[15]

Schwartz's project was a kinetic sculpture, *Proxima Centauri*. It consisted of a large, polished black tower. Inside were wood shelves for holding a slide projector, red light, ripple tank, mirror, motors, and input wiring from sensor pads placed around the base of the box to detect pressure from a viewer. The slides were hand painted using a technique for distorting the 2-D image so that when it was projected onto the dome, the image became a 3-D abstraction. To fulfill the E.A.T. requirements Schwartz was assigned an electrician who said he needed to take her designs with him in order to study the technical plans, which included wiring. Schwartz could have wired the sculpture in a day: she grew up during the Great Depression. Her father died while she was a child, leaving twelve siblings. But poverty led her to paint abstract images on the house's walls when wallpaper peeled off, and she learned to rewire lamps. The electrician had not even begun wiring when Hultén, Klüver, and curators from MoMA appeared. Her son,

Laurens, had to climb into the box and control the light and tank, raise the dome, and start the projector. The electrician eventually wired the sculpture and per E.A.T. requirements was given co-credit. The MoMA exhibition became a traveling show. At the second museum, the wiring caused an electrical fire. The replacement was built and wired by Schwartz. Years later, the electrician tried to blackmail her for millions stating that her diagrams which he still had, were his.

Schwartz came to Bell Labs through meeting Leon Harmon who was a perceptualist engineer at the renowned Bell Labs. At the opening reception of *The Machine as seen at the end of the mechanical age*, he was fascinated by *Proxima* and met Schwartz. They immediately became involved in a discussion of the physiology of vision, perception, science, and art. He invited her to the Labs in 1968, resulting in a relationship with Bell Labs that lasted for four decades.

She began by working with punch cards to make drawings on the computer. Her first such work, a drawing titled *Head* (Plate 3a) was created first on graph paper and then translated into the holes on a punch card which was then fed into the computer. What emerged was an electronic tape which Schwartz transferred into microfilm and enlarged for use in a silk screen. After this groundbreaking, but relatively simple innovation based on the punch card technology that was the basis for the first modern computers, Schwartz turned to developing techniques with which she began to generate her legacy, a series of abstract animated films that opened new possibilities for image-making and were influential and emulated internationally (Plate 3b).

Her animated films have soundtracks created through working with the composers who came to Bell Labs to experiment with Max Mathews, the pioneer in the development of computer-generated music, who directed the Acoustical and Behavioral Research Center at Bell Labs from 1962 to 1985. Schwartz additionally contributed to scientific research in such areas as visual and color perception, and sound. She created databases on the palettes and structures of paintings, sculptures, and graphics to analyze the choices of artists and to investigate the creative process itself. She made very important contributions to digital art analysis, and restoration, particularly in Italian Renaissance painting and fresco. Her legacy is enormous. She has received major honors for her work as the pioneer in animation, virtual reality, multimedia, and other innovations using digital technology. Her films were shown and won awards at the Venice Biennale, Zagreb, Cannes, and the National Academy of Television Arts and Sciences as well as receiving Emmy nominations and awards.[16]

Through her innovations and the quality of her work, Schwartz established computer art as a visual artmaking field despite being a woman in a field that was dominated by men. In using computers to make art, she, like other digital artists, should be given more due in mainstream art history as pioneers in what is now becoming a major art practice in the twenty-first century.

In looking at the work they generated using pre-digital and digital technology, it is hard to say whether Schapiro, Schwartz, Molnár, or Bangert were thinking of their work as feminist. Although their involvement in technology itself may be considered important in revising art history to include women, and although Schapiro later emerged as a founder of the Feminist Art Movement, it may have been the novelty of a technology-based art practice that appealed to them as more open to their ideas than the traditional modes of artmaking like painting and sculpture that were so firmly embedded in the history of Western patriarchy as male art practices.

Nothing in their work itself suggests feminist themes. However, other women artists who, if not yet declaring themselves as feminist, were clearly using technology, at first pre-digital and then digital, to express protofeminist concepts. Joan Jonas was one of the first woman artists who found electronic media a medium conducive to exploring her female identity. Her first venture into electronic media was the 1968 film, *Wind*, in which she filmed a performance of women on a beach—a performance which had protofeminist overtones. But she quickly moved into video, her primary medium for the rest of her career. As soon as the Portapak, the first lightweight, portable video camera, was invented in 1967, she acquired one. She said she was drawn to video over film because video provided her with an intimacy that film could not. With film, she felt distanced from the art she was making, but with the accessibility, ease, and immediacy of video the work of art and she merged into one, enabling her to communicate more directly with her audience. *Organic Honey's Visual Telepathy*, her first video, produced in 1972, is based on the feminist concept that gender is constructed rather than innate. In it she uses mirrors combined with her appearance as herself and as a masked double whose name is Organic Honey, creating an ambiguity about who is the real woman and what is only illusion.[17]

Lynn Hershman Leeson also began experimenting with electronic media in the late 1960s. Hershman Leeson began working on a series of sculptures that she titled *Breathing Machines*. She created them by first casting her own face and then dressing the casts up with different wigs and makeup. The electronic element of these sculptures was the addition of sensors and sound so that when viewers passed by, breaths, sighs, and speech emanated from the sculptures. When one was selected for exhibition at the San Francisco Museum of Modern Art, it was subsequently withdrawn from exhibition because sound was not considered appropriate for a visual arts exhibition. Hershman Leeson's goals in the *Breathing Machines* were very complex. In addition to expressing a female identity, Hershman Leeson evoked the Civil Rights Movement through painting the faces black. She also may have been referring to cloning and to the intersection of science and humanity through her use of the casting technique, itself.[18]

By the mid-1960s, the use of technology was expanding among the avant-garde collaborative groups in East and West Europe as well as North America, characterized by conceptual and political radicalism along with interdisciplinary interaction between artists and scientists. E.A.T. was an enormous influence. By 1969 it had two thousand artists and as many engineer members. Artists from around the world asked to start E.A.T. offshoots in their own cities, or else they founded their own groups, two examples of which were the Research Center Art, Technology, and Society, formed in Amsterdam in 1967, and the Computer Arts Society, London, founded in 1968 to "encourage the creative use of computers."[19] The first exhibitions featuring electronic media, along with other pre-digital technology and early computer-assisted art, were held, artists sought out interaction with computer scientists, along with access to computers, and international conferences became the venues for theoretical acceptance of digital technology as a legitimate means of artmaking. There seems to have been much less resistance to the computer as a tool for artmaking than was the case in the United States.[20]

A group called New Tendencies (NT) was established as early as 1961 in Zagreb. NT started with an exhibition and ended up becoming an umbrella for the nascent computer arts community around the world as a result of its activities that served as a bridge and site for political and philosophical interaction between East and West artists during the Cold War. The initial focus of the artists involved in NT was on experimenting with new forms of artmaking—anti-emotional and theoretical, such as Conceptual Art, Op Art, and Minimalism. Inevitably, when computers became more available in the middle of the 1960s, many of the artists involved in NT were attracted to experimentation in digital media. Their activity culminated in an international conference in 1969.

Rarely are women mentioned in the documentation of NT, and yet women artists were involved throughout the later second half of the decade. There were no women artists in the first two NT exhibitions. But the third included Marina Apollonio, Lucia Di Luciano, and Grazia Varisco, all from Italy where they were members of experimental collaborative groups; Helga Philipp from Vienna; Bridget Riley, London; and Marianne Aue, Amsterdam.[21]

Another center for early computer art was the Technische Hochschule Stuttgart, renamed Universität Stuttgart in 1967. Max Bense, a philosopher and physicist who was interested in the intersection of mathematics and art, particularly concrete poetry, and an influential semiotics scholar, founded an institute called the Studiengalerie des Studium Generale in 1958, the mission of which was to conduct research and mount exhibitions of art based on algorithmic sources. *Computer-grafik*, an exhibition of the work of his student, Georg Nees, was one of the first exhibitions of algorithmic derived art in Europe. Held in 1965, the exhibition was the occasion for the publication of a brochure listing Bense and Neese as authors, titled *Projekte generativer Ästhetik* [The Projects of Generative Aesthetics]. The brochure explained Bense's concepts and contained six of Nees's computer-generated drawings. The gallery closed in 1978, having presented ninety-one exhibitions. Georg Nees received the first doctorate in computer art. Bense was also the mentor of Frieder Nake, another of the earliest computer artists.[22]

It was Bense who suggested to the curator, Jasia Reichardt, that she mount an exhibition on art and technology. That landmark exhibition heralded the arrival of technology as an accepted art form (to be discussed further toward the end of this chapter). The members of Max Bense's group were all male, as identified so far. It's hard to believe that no women were involved. However, there was an active female artist organization in Stuttgart, GEDOK, and at least one woman architect, Grit Bauer-Revellio, so it is likely future research may unearth German women who were technology art pioneers.[23]

While the use of technology in American artmaking grew out of the radical performance/Fluxus movement of the 1960s, British interest in technological art emerged among a group of conceptual British abstract artists around Victor Pasmore after the Second World War. They were influenced by Russian Constructivism, were already using mathematical systems in their art practice, and were inspired by Norbert Wiener's theory of cybernetics. Gordon Pask was the central figure in this community in London. Pask and others belonged to the Institute of Computer Science, the membership of which was only by invitation. This rather small but influential group of men spread out through the art education institutions so that the major art schools throughout Great Britain had computer art programs much earlier than was the case at American institutions.

There are four women artists who are documented as being involved in the introduction of technology into England's arts: Delia Derbyshire, Mary Martin, Jean Spencer, and Gillian Wise. The most influential was musician Delia Derbyshire, one of the first electronic music composers. Her best-known musical arrangement is the theme song (1963) for the science fiction television program, *Doctor Who*, for which she received no credit because of BBC policy not to release the names of the working teams (after graduating from Girton College, Cambridge University, she applied for a position at Decca Records and was refused employment on the basis that the company didn't hire women). She is, however, credited now with being a pioneer and an influential figure in the development of electronic music. Mary Martin was one of the abstract Constructivist artists around Pasmore. While not actually based on digital technology, her mathematically constructed painting/sculptures were precursors of digital technology aesthetics. Jean Spencer was a member of the Systems Group, organized in 1969 by Jeffrey Steele. The artists in this group based their work on elaborate calculations. Like the artists around Pasmore, they provided the context in which digital art could develop rather than working with digital technology themselves. Gillian Wise was also a member of the Constructivist and Systems groups in London.[24]

Like the British artists, artists in other European countries were inspired by conceptual art theories to explore technological media. Vera Molnár was one of the founding members (the only woman) in Paris of the conceptual art collaborative Groupe de Recherche d'Art Visuel (GRAV) in 1960. Molnár invented an imaginary computer before there was a computer with which to draw. She developed a set of rules by which she organized the lines in her drawings including views showing the same form from various angles. She began using the computer to create these drawings in 1968, just about the time that Miriam Schapiro was doing the same thing in California. Unlike Schapiro, who could collaborate with a computer scientist and had easy access to a computer, Molnár describes a different situation. According to Molnár, computers were only available to artists through the Université de Paris. When she asked to use one of the computers, she says that the response was total surprise that a woman would want to use one. Nevertheless, she was given permission. The year was 1968 and the Paris student demonstrations were beginning. She says that the riots benefited her since the students left the university deserted and she had access to the computer as much as she wanted.[25]

The major exhibitions of pre-digital and digital art that were held in the last years of the 1960s were marked as much by male domination as the organizations described above. In the years between 1964 and 1969, Howard Wise, one of the first New York gallerists to support technological art and the founder of Electronic Arts Intermix, which distributes artists' videotapes, mounted three exhibitions of art using technology. The first, *On the Move*, was a two-person exhibition of the work of two engineers, Michael Noll, from Bell Labs, and Béla Julesz, whom Wise had found when Julesz's work was on the cover of *Scientific American*. The second, *Lights in Orbit*, 1967, consisted of sculpture using kinetic light. *Lights in*

Orbit consisted of work by thirty-six artists with two women represented, Martha Boto, with work of her own and Jackie Cassen, who collaborated with Rudi Stern. Then in 1969 he organized *TV as a Creative Medium* with twelve artists; Charlotte Moorman was the only woman artist included in the exhibition, and then only given subordinate billing to Nam June Paik, her collaborator. One wonders why a work by Lillian Schwartz was not included, considering that Wise had the connection with Bell Labs through Noll.[26]

The most comprehensive early exhibition featuring a survey of technology as an art practice was *Cybernetic Serendipity* (Plate 4), held at the Institute of Contemporary Arts, London, in 1968. As mentioned above, the exhibition was organized and curated by Jasia Reichardt, a Jewish refugee of the Second World War who had survived the Warsaw Ghetto and escaped to London. Her approach was a comprehensive one, looking at technological media from many perspectives, thus transcending the various strands of theory that were formulated during the 1960s. It was a forecast of the holistic view of digital art that is current from the vantage point of half a century later. It included drawings created through plotters; text formulated through several digital means; kinetic sculpture, the movements of which were computer programmed; robot constructions; music composed through computer programs; painting and drawing machines; and films. The problem with it is the fact that even though it was organized by a woman (who enlisted her aunt, Franciszka Themerson, a graphic designer, and also a Jewish refugee from the Second World War Holocaust to design the installation and the catalog) there were almost no women in the exhibition. Two women, Margaret Masterson and Alison Knowles, were included in the concrete poetry section; Jeanne Beaman was included in the digital choreography section, and Yolanda Sonnabend, while still a student, created mobiles for the installation, *The Colloquy of Mobiles*, designed by Gordon Pask, a conglomeration of shapes that interacted with each other, one set gendered as male and the other as female. Pask designed the males and Sonnabend the females. Sonnabend went on to have a distinguished career in ballet and as a portrait painter. According to various reports, in the exhibition were Liliane Lijn, Lillian Schwartz, and a few other women, but they were not documented in the original London catalog. It should be noted that the exhibition traveled to the United States where it was seen at the Corcoran Gallery of Art, Washington, DC and the Exploratorium, San Francisco, CA.[27]

Another major exhibition devoted to new media / electronic art / computer art was *Software—Information Technology: Its New Meaning for Art*, organized and curated by Jack Burnham, who was an inaugural Fellow at the MIT Center for Advanced Visual Studies from 1968 to 1970. It was held at the Jewish Museum, New York in 1970 and at the Smithsonian Institution, Washington, DC in early 1971. Burnham was an influential theorist, who foresaw the future, in that he declared that software was the key to the development of digital technology, not hardware. He also foresaw the expansion of digital technology into all areas of knowledge and communication as well as everyday life. Burnham emphasized how creativity in the arts paralleled and interacted with scientific creativity. The exhibition included twenty male artists, among them David Antin, Hans Haacke, Joseph Kosuth, Nam June Paik, and Lawrence Weiner; only three female artists, Linda Berris, Agnes Denes, and Sonia Sheridan; and one collaborative, Architecture Machine Group, MIT, three members of which were also women (the MIT Media Lab grew out of this collaborative). Like Hultén's exhibition at MoMA, *Software* also included art works by scientist/engineers, none of whom were women. The exhibition was also one of the first collaborations between the arts and corporations: It was sponsored by American Motors. The future eminent art critic, Peter Frank, then an undergraduate at Columbia University, reviewed the exhibition for the *Columbia Spectator*. His review was the only one to mention any of the women artists.[28]

In 1971, Maurice Tuchman, the first contemporary curator to be appointed at the Los Angeles County Museum, mounted an exhibition in conjunction with the program, *Art and Technology*, which he initiated in 1967. The purpose of the program was to give artists the opportunity to work with the advanced technology available in major corporations. During the four years of the program, no women artists were invited to participate in the residencies nor were any women invited to submit work for the 1971 exhibition. Channa Horwitz submitted a proposal for the exhibition anyway, but Tuchman rejected her work. In a 2007 exhibition at Solway Jones Gallery, Los Angeles, Horwitz wrote: "Although Maurice Tuchman, the curator of the show, included my proposal in the catalogue because he 'thought it looked pretty,' he did not feel it was appropriate for a woman to discuss an engineering project with the male industrial scientists involved with the show."[29] The exclusion of women artists from the exhibition brought a storm of protest and led the Los Angeles Council of Women Artists to collect data showing rampant discrimination against women artists in Los Angeles and nationally, thus spurring the Feminist Art Movement in the city.[30]

Besides the exhibitions described above, additional exhibitions were held in various cities in Europe and the United States at galleries and in conjunction with conferences, such as the Fall Joint Computer Conference, Las Vegas, at which the Noll/Julesz exhibition was seen after its showing in New York. Interest in digital art was growing rapidly, and while the evidence of women in the field of digital arts during the 1960s is scanty, from 1970 on, the number of women who are documented as involved and influential in digital arts increased exponentially and is covered in the following chapter.

Notes

1 Sarah Zielinski, "Hypatia, Ancient Alexandria's Great Female Scholar," Smithsonian Magazine, March 14, 2010, https://www.smithsonianmag.com/history/hypatia-ancient-alexandrias-great-female-scholar-10942888/; Karen Detlefsen, "Émilie du Châtelet," *Stanford Encyclopedia of Philosophy*, substantive revision, June 13, 2014, https://plato.stanford.edu/entries/emilie-du-chatelet/.

2 Ada Lovelace, "Sketch of the Analytical Engine Invented by Charles Babbage Esq. by L.F. Menabrea of Turin, Officer of the Military Engineers, with Notes by the Translator," published in *Scientific Memoirs* vol. 3 (London: Richard & John E. Taylor, 1843). There are several books and articles published about Ada Lovelace. A good starting point for further reading is James Essinger, *Ada's Algorithm: How Lord Byron's Daughter Ada Lovelace Launched the Digital Age* (Brooklyn, NY: Melville House, 2014).

3 Natalie Zarrelli, "How Female Computers Mapped the Universe and Brought America to the Moon," Atlas Obscura, March 4, 2016, https://www.atlasobscura.com/articles/how-female-computers-mapped-the-universe-and-brought-america-to-the-moon; Jessica Leigh Hester, "Who Keeps Track of All the Craters on the Moon?" Atlas Obscura, April 25, 2018, https://www.atlasobscura.com/articles/how-do-moon-craters-get-names.

4 Gwyneth K. Shaw, "On ENIAC's anniversary, a nod to its female 'computers'," *Penn Today*, Science and Technology, February 14, 2019, https://penntoday.upenn.edu/news/eniacs-anniversary-nod-its-female-computers; Jennifer S. Light, "When Computers Were Women," *Technology and Culture* 40, no. 3 (1999): 455–83.

5 Naval History and Heritage Command, "Grace Murray Hopper," Modern Biographical Files in the Navy Department Library, https://www.history.navy.mil/research/library/research-guides/modern-biographical-files-ndl/modern-bios-h/hopper-grace-murray-text.html; Richard Baguley, "Spanning the Tree: Dr. Radia Perlman and Untangling Networks," Hackaday, May 29, 2018, https://hackaday.com/2018/05/29/spanning-the-tree-dr-radia-perlman-untangling-networks/.

6 Purdue University Global, "History of Women in IT: 6 Female Pioneers in Computer Science," April 19, 2018, https://www.purdueglobal.edu/blog/information-technology/history-women-information-technology-6-female-computer-science-pioneers/; Joe Myers, "5 Female Coders You Have Probably Never Heard of Who

Changed the World," The World Economic Forum, July 21, 2016, https://www.weforum.org/agenda/2016/07/5-female-coders-who-changed-the-world/; Jamie, "History of Women in Computing," MakeAWebsiteHub.com, https://makeawebsitehub.com/history-women-computing/.

7 Artnet News, "In the '60s, Miriam Schapiro Was Already Using Computer Models to Build Dream-Like Geometries," January 5, 2018, https://news.artnet.com/exhibitions/in-the-60s-miriam-schapiro-was-already-using-computer-models-to-build-dream-like-geometries-see-the-paintings-here-1190042; Phillip Barcio, "When Miriam Schapiro Used Computers to Generate Geometric Abstract Art," *IdeelArt* (blog), January 17, 2018, https://www.ideelart.com/magazine/miriam-schapiro. To sample some of the broader literature on Schapiro's contributions to feminist art see the following: Mira Schor, "Miriam Schapiro's Road to Feminism," Hyperallergic, March 15, 2016, https://hyperallergic.com/283426/miriam-schapiros-road-to-feminism/; Anne Swartz, "The Pattern and Decoration Zeitgeist," Hyperallergic, June 13, 2018, https://hyperallergic.com/446327/the-pattern-and-decoration-zeitgeist/; Ferris Olin, *Anarchy and Form: Works by Miriam Schapiro*, exhibition catalog (includes an interview with Schapiro), Mary H. Dana Women Artists Series, Rutgers University (2005), available by request to the Rutgers Center for Women in the Arts and Humanities, womenart@cwah.rutgers.edu.

8 Colette S. Bangert and Charles J. Bangert, "Computer Grass Is Natural Grass," Atari Archives, September 1975, https://www.atariarchives.org/artist/sec5.php.

9 Brad Fregger, "Joan Shogren, Computer Art Pioneer," Papers of Exceptional Interest, updated November 2018, http://fregger.com/Joan/index.html. Shogren was Fregger's aunt. He resurrected her history from her personal archive.

10 Donna J. Cox, Ellen Sandor, and Janine Fron, eds., *New Media Futures, The Rise of Women in the Digital Arts* (Urbana: University of Illinois Press, 2018), 22, 152; Josh Silverstein, "Art from Code: A Response to Grace Hertlein," *A Story Is Not a Tree*, New Genres Program, New Genres and Interactive Art, Sarah Lawrence College, Bronxville, NY, December 13, 2018 http://astoryisnotatree.net/?p=10347; Katherine Nash and Richard Williams, "Computer Program for Artists: ART I," *Leonardo* 3, no. 4 (October 1970): 439–42. Grant David Taylor is a pioneer in writing about women artists who use digital technology and the problem of their recognition. See " 'Up for Grabs': Agency, Praxis, and the Politics of Early Digital Art," *Lateral* 2 (2013), https://doi.or/10.25158/L2.1.5, and *When the Machine Made Art: The Troubled History of Computer Art* (New York: Bloomsbury, 2014).

11 Alexxa Gotthhardt, "Charlotte Moorman is Finally Remembered as More Than 'The Topless Cellist'," *Artsy*, September 4, 2016, https://artsy.net/article/artsy-editorial-the-topless-cellist-charlotte-moorman-finally-finds-her-place-in-art-history; Edward M. Gómez, "Topless but Far From Helpless: Charlotte Moorman's Avant-Garde Life," Hyperallergic, January 17, 2015, https://hyperallergic.com/175600/

topless-but-far-from-helpless-charlotte-moormans-avant-garde-life/; Elizabeth Bacharach, "Charlotte Moorman Shattering Barriers Between Art and Technology," *Medill Reports*, February 24, 2016, https://news.medill.northwestern.edu/chicago/charlotte-moorman-shattering-barriers-between-art-and-technology/; Joan Rothfuss, "Topless Cellist," *Sightlines*, September 25, 2014, https://walkerart.org/magazine/charlotte-moorman-paik-topless-cellist, and *Topless Cellist: the Improbable Life of Charlotte Moorman* (Cambridge, MA: MIT Press, 2014).

12 A very useful brief introductory history of E.A.T. which includes links to publications and archives is Monoskop, "Experiments in Art and Technology," last revised, May 6, 2019, https://monoskop.org/Experiments_in_Art_and_Technology. Julie Martin (1938–) wife of Billy Klüver and one of the key individuals involved in E.A.T. deposited records of E.A.T. in the Bard Center for Curatorial Studies, Bard archives. A finding aid is available online: http://www.bard.edu/ccs/findingaids/index.html/mss.018/eat.html. An oral history with Julie Martin conducted by the Smithsonian Archives of American Art reveals many details about E.A.T.: https://www.aaa.si.edu/download_pdf_transcript/ajax?record_id#eqedanmdm-AAADCD_oh_397104. Another archive of E.A.T.'s records is located at the Getty Research Institute, also with online finding aid: http://archives2.getty.edu:8082/xtf/view?docId=ead/940003/940003.xml;query=;brand=default. The Pepsi-Cola pavilion project implemented by E.A.T. for the Japan World Exhibition, Osaka, 1970 is documented in Billy Klüver, Julie Martin, and Barbara Rose, eds., *Pavilion: Experiments in Art and Technology* (New York: Dutton, 1972).

13 A good introduction to Forti's early career when she was an active participant in the avant-garde scene in New York is "Simone Forti," Alchetron: Free Social Encyclopedia for the World, updated February 3, 2018, https://alchetron.com/Simone-Forti. Also see Virginia B. Spivey, "The Minimal Presence of Simone Forti." *Woman's Art Journal* 30, no. 1 (2009): 11–18, https://www.jstor.org/stable/40605219. Forti's archives are located in the Getty Research Center Archives, https://www.getty.edu/research/special_collections/notable/forti.html.

14 Carolee Schneemann's career is well documented. A useful introduction to her life and impact is her obituary in the *New York Times*: Holland Cotter, "Carolee Schneemann, Visionary Feminist Performance Artist Dies at 79," *New York Times*, March 10, 2019, https://www.nytimes.com/2019/03/10/obituaries/carolee-schneemann-dead-at-79.html. See Josephine Withers, "Feminist Performance Art: Performing, Discovering, Transforming Ourselves," in *The Power of Feminist Art*, ed. Norma Broude and Mary Garrard (New York: Harry N. Abrams, 1993), 161. Schneemann, herself, wrote thirteen books on her art practice.

15 Gabrielle Zuckerman, "An Interview with La Monte Young and Marian Zazeela," American Public Media, *Histories and Theories of Intermedia* (blog), July 2002, http://umintermediai501.blogspot.com/2008/06/interview-with-la-monte-young-

and.html; Dream the End, "Marian Zazeela," https://www.dreamtheend.com/?cat=289; "Lucy J. Young," *Valley News* (Vermont), March 13, 2004, https://www.vnews.com/Archives/2014/03/Lucy-Young-obit-vn-031314.

16 Lillian Schwartz website, biography, http://lillian.com/biography/. Schwartz's website contains multiple interviews with Schwartz and many articles about her; also see Lillian Schwartz, interview by Christopher Garcia, *Computer History Museum*, August 21, 2013, https://www.computerhistory.org/collections/catalog/102746737; Claire Voon, "Paying Tribute to Lillian Schwartz, a Computer Art Pioneer," Hyperallergic, October 19, 2016, https://hyperallergic.com/329466/paying-tribute-lillian-schwartz-computer-art-pioneer/; Alexander Jenseth, "The Quiet Circus: The Colorful, Complicated, Slightly Schizophrenic, History of Early Computer Art at Bell Labs," Bard Undergraduate Senior Project, Fall 2011: 8, https://digitalcommons.bard.edu/cgi/viewcontent.cgi?article=1030&context=senproj_f2011.

17 Lisa Cohen, "Joan Jonas: All at Once," *New York Times*, April 5, 2015, https://www.nytimes.com/2015/04/05/t-magazine/joan-jonas-reanimation-venice-biennale.html; Joan Jonas and Rachel Rose, interview, "Joan Jonas—The Performer," *Tate Etc.* 42 (Spring 2018), https://www.tate.org.uk/tate-etc/issue-42-spring-2018/interview-joan-jonas-rachel-rose-the-performer; R.H. Quaytman, "Joan Jonas," Interview, December 10, 2014, https://www.interviewmagazine.com/art/joan-jonas; Liam Gillick, interview, "Joan Jonas," ArtReview, March 2018, https://artreview.com/features/march_2018_feature_joan_jonas/.

18 Lynn Hershman Leeson's website, https://www.lynnhershman.com/; *Lynn Hershman Leeson: Civic Radar*, ed. Peter Weibel (Karlsruhe: ZKM, 2016); Alex Greenberger, "A New Future from the Passed: Lynn Hershman Leeson Comes into Her Own After 50 Years of Prophetic Work," ARTnews, March 28, 2017, https://www.artnews.com/art-news/artists/a-new-future-from-the-passed-lynn-hershman-leeson-comes-into-her-own-after-50-years-of-prophetic-work-8028/; *The Art and Films of Lynn Hershman Leeson: Secret Agents, Private I*, ed. Meredith Tromble (Berkeley: University of California Press co-published with the Henry Gallery, Seattle, University of Washington, December 2005).

19 Computer Arts Society (CAS), London website, About/History, https://computer-arts-society.com/about. The history of the organization is also documented in several chapters of *White Heat Cold Logic: British Computer Art 1960–1980*, ed. Paul Brown, Charlie Gere, Nicholas Lambert, and Catherine Mason (Cambridge, MA: MIT Press, 2008). Of particular interest is early member of CAS George Mallen's chapter, "Bridging Computing in the Arts and Software Development," 191–202. The role of CAS in promoting digital art is documented in other chapters, too.

20 Darko Fritz, "International Networks of Early Digital Art," in *A Companion to Digital Art*, ed. Christiane Paul (Hoboken, NJ: Wiley-Blackwell, 2016).

21 The information about the artists included in NT exhibitions can be retrieved in "New Tendencies," Monoskop, last edited on May 29, 2019, https://monoskop.org/New_Tendencies. Also see Margit Rosen, ed., *A Little-Known Story About a Movement, a Magazine, and the Computer's Arrival in Art: New Tendencies and Bit International, 1961–1973* (Cambridge, MA: MIT Press, 2011).

22 Compart, "*Projekte generativer Ästhetik* [The Projects of Generative Aesthetics] 1965," http://dada.compart-bremen.de/item/exhibition/164.

23 Frieder Nake, "Computer Art. A Personal Recollection," April 12, 2005, http://citeseerx.ist.psu.edu/viewdoc/download?doi=10.1.1.470.2597&rep=rep1&type=pdf; Eliza Pertigkiozoglou, "1960s Max Bense and Abraham Moles, Information Aesthetics," Medium, March 9, 2017, https://medium.com/designscience/1960s-d611bd76d056; Augusto Gerardi, "When Computational Devices Are Used for the Visual Arts," Colección Patricia Phelps de Cisneros, April 9, 2019, https://www.coleccioncisneros.org/content/when-computational-devices-are-used-visual-arts; "Profile of an Institution," GEDOK, Stuttgart, Germany, https://gedok-muc.de/english-version.

24 The development of digital art in the UK is thoroughly covered in Brown et al., *White Heat Cold Logic*. Information on the individual women artists to whom the book refers is available as follows: David Butler, "Delia Derbyshire," History of the BBC, https://www.bbc.com/historyofthebbc/100-voices/pioneering-women/women-of-the-workshop/delia-derbyshire; Camille Morineau, "Mary Martin," trans. Jo Garden, Archives of Women Artists Research and Exhibitions (AWARE), 2013, https://awarewomenartists.com/en/artiste/mary-martin/; Redfern Galleries, "Jean Spencer," https://www.redfern-gallery.com/artists/31-jean-spencer/overview/; Marion Daniel, "Gillian Wise," trans. Anna Knight, Archives of Women Artists Research and Exhibitions (AWARE), 2013, https://awarewomenartists.com/en/artiste/gillian-wise/.

25 John Yau, "A Trailblazer of Computer Drawing Gets Her Due," Hyperallergic, April 15, 2018, https://hyperallergic.com/437834/vera-molnar-drawings-1949-1986-senior-and-shopmaker-gallery-2018/; "The Computer Pioneer," Artnet, November 2, 2018, https://news.artnet.com/exhibitions/hungarys-radical-women-artists-finally-get-the-recognition-they-deserve-1383892; "Interview with Hans Ulrich Obrist," https://vintage.hu/wp-content/uploads/2019/03/Molnar-Vera-HUO-interview.pdf.

26 A. Michael Noll, "The Howard Wise Gallery Show Computer-Generated Pictures (1965): A 50th Anniversary Memoir," *Leonardo* 49, no. 3 (June 2016): 232–9. Noll's essay from the publication is available online at the Engineering and Technology History Wiki, https://ethw.org/First-Hand:Howard_Wise_Gallery_Show_of_Digital_Art_and_Patterns_(1965):_A_50th_Anniversary_Memoir. The brochure for "TV as a Creative Medium," listing all the artists and including the information that Charlotte Moorman would be performing is available on Monoskop, https://monoskop.org/images/4/4a/TV_as_a_Creative_Medium_1969.pdf. The Howard

Wise Gallery records are housed at the Archives of American Art, Smithsonian Institution. A finding aid with some digitized items from the collection is available online: https://www.aaa.si.edu/collections/howard-wise-gallery-records-9357.

27 The best introductory readings on *Cybernetic Serendipity* are two chapters in Brown et al., *White Heat Cold Logic*. One is by the organizer Jasia Reichardt herself ("In the Beginning . . ."). The other by Brent MacGregor ("*Cybernetic Serendipity* Revisited"). The story of how Reichardt and her aunt survived the Warsaw Ghetto and managed separately to reach England was the subject of an exhibition in 2017: Wiener Library, "One Family, Three Cities, Six Years of War: A Family of Artists During the War and the Holocaust," Exhibition at the Wiener Library, 1 March–24 April 2017, https://wienerholocaustlibrary.org/exhibition/one-family-three-cities-six-years-of-war-a-family-of-artists-during-the-war-and-the-holocaust/. Another introductory article is Catherine Mason, "Cybernetic Serendipity: History and Lasting Legacy," Studio International, https://www.studiointernational.com/index.php/cybernetic-serendipity-history-and-lasting-legacy. Yolanda Sonnabend's obituary gives some details of her life: Roslyn Sulcas, "Yolanda Sonnabend, Designer Who Influenced Choreographer, Dies at 80," *New York Times*, November 29, 2015, https://www.nytimes.com/2015/11/30/arts/design/yolanda-sonnabend-designer-who-influenced-choreographer-dies-at-80.html.

28 The entire catalog for *Software—Information Technology: Its New Meaning for Art*, is available on line at Monoskop, https://monoskop.org/images/3/31/Software_Information_Technology_Its_New_Meaning_for_Art_catalogue.pdf. A good summary of the exhibition is Vincent Bonin, "Software—Information Technology: Its New Meaning for Art," la fondation Daniel Langlois pour l'art, la science et la technologie, https://www.fondation-langlois.org/html/e/page.php?NumPage=541. The exhibition was reviewed by Peter Frank, the future art critic, while he was still a student at Columbia, "Art: '*Software*' at Jewish Museum," *Columbia Daily Spectator*, 115, no. 22, October 23, 1970, http://spectatorarchive.library.columbia.edu/cgi-bin/columbia?a=d&d=cs19701023-01.2.15&e=-------en-20--1998-byDA-txt-txIN-columbia-TITLE_SECTION-----. The reference to Frank is included rather than references to reviews from the *New York Times* and elsewhere because Frank is the only one to discuss the work by women artists in the exhibition. Burnham was a major figure in the development of the theory and language of digital technology. There is a body of literature on his ideas and impact available in print and online.

29 Annina Rüst, "Data As Feminist Protest," *Unframed* (blog of the Los Angeles County Museum of Art), July 10, 2014, https://unframed.lacma.org/2014/07/10/data-as-feminist-protest. As a 2014 grant recipient of the Art + Technology Lab in its contemporary format as a program of the Los Angeles County Museum of Art, Rüst wrote this article. She became interested in pursuing information on the original Art + Technology Lab, established by Maurice Tuchman. Through her research, she

learned of Tuchman's exclusion of women artists from the original program and she found the text by Channa Horwitz describing her experience with Tuchman.

30 Catherine Wagley, "Closed Circuits: A Look Back at LACMA's First Art and Technology Initiative," May 11, 2015, East of Borneo, https://eastofborneo.org/articles/closed-circuits-a-look-back-at-lacmas-first-art-and-technology-initiative/; Rüst, "Data as Feminist Protest"; Alexander Hawkins, "How Channa Horwitz Permeated LA's 1960s Art Scene," AnOther Magazine, April 13, 2016, https://www.anothermag.com/art-photography/8576/how-channa-horwitz-permeated-las-1960s-art-scene.

2

The 1970s

Feminism and Digital Art Inside and Outside the Academy

During the 1970s, women artists played a role in mutating both the form and content of technology-based art. As digital gradually began replacing analog technology, women artists contributed to the scientific aspects of that conversion. At the same time, artists in the Feminist Art Movement were transforming technological art forms like photography and video from being considered minor disciplines to the forefront of artmaking. Their use of electronic media for autobiography and declaration of women's sexuality and bodily agency was so compelling that it brought contemporary artists, from that point on, to realize the power of technology in art practice.

During the 1970s, the role of universities was critical to the growth of the Feminist Art Movement. The Second Wave of Feminism and the Civil Rights Movement of the later 1960s gave birth to the 1972 Title IX law which denied federal funding to any educational institution that discriminated against women. In the same year, women in the College Art Association (CAA) challenged the masculinist domination in the fields of art and art history and formed the Women's Caucus for Art (WCA). Women artists were already demonstrating against discrimination in museum exhibitions but the formation of the WCA was the first concerted effort to end discrimination in art schools and art and art history departments at colleges and universities.

The WCA persuaded the CAA to survey art and art history departments across the country on their hiring practices. To no one's surprise, the surveys revealed that women comprised less than 10 percent of art history faculty although 50 percent of art history PhDs were awarded to women. The situation was even worse in studio art departments where women students encompassed 75 percent of total enrollments, but women artists made up only 3 percent of faculty, again, despite the fact that a sizable number of women artists had master of fine arts (MFA) degrees (45 percent of all MFAs awarded) and were therefore qualified to teach at institutions of higher education. (The statistics quoted vary somewhat depending on the sources, but not significantly.) As a result of Title IX and the surveys, art schools and art and art history departments at colleges and universities began to welcome women faculty and pay more attention to their female students.[1]

These events had significance for the development of feminist art, but also for pre-digital and digital art, since institutions of higher education were also places where the fields of analog and nascent digital technology were flourishing and the latest equipment was available. The University of Illinois at both its Urbana and Chicago campuses, along with the School of the Art Institute of Chicago, became epicenters for women involved in digital art research. And the Center for Advanced Visual Studies (CAVS) at the Massachusetts Institute of Technology (MIT) began to award fellowships to women artists, two of whom were involved in creating one of the decade's most spectacular examples of computer-programmed art.

The widening impact of feminism on women artists in the 1970s and its importance for technological art innovation is shown by the Feminist Art Program founded by Miriam Schapiro and Judy Chicago at the California Institute of the Arts (CalArts). Schapiro's husband, Paul Brach, left the University of California, San Diego (UCSD) to become the first dean of a new fine arts division at CalArts, and Schapiro became a faculty member there. The move to Los Angeles led Schapiro to meet women artists who were already initiating feminist activity, among them, Judy Chicago. She visited Chicago at Fresno State College to observe a feminist course Chicago was teaching, and invited Chicago to join her in founding a Feminist Art Program at CalArts. Indicative of the climate against which feminist artists were fuming, Chicago wrote, "At the first class meeting, the professor said he would talk about women's contributions at the end of the semester. I looked forward the whole semester to what he had to say. At the last class session, the professor came in, strode up to the front of the room, and said, 'Women's contributions? They made none.'"[2]

While women in the program did not explore technological artmaking to any extent during their studies, the emphasis in the program on finding new ways of artmaking to express feminist principles encouraged feminist artists far beyond those actually enrolled to experiment with electronic media, and led several alumnae of the program like Faith Wilding, the influential performance and video artist Suzanne Lacy, and others, to become important innovators in digital art later in their careers.[3]

One of the programs that encouraged many feminist artists to experiment with video was the Feminist Studio Workshop (FSW) video training program initiated and directed by artist Nancy Angelo at the Woman's Building, Los Angeles. The FSW was an outgrowth of Schapiro's and Chicago's Feminist Art Program. Chicago left CalArts in 1973, feeling that continuation of the program was inhibited by location in a patriarchal institution like CalArts, and joined art historian Arlene Raven and graphic designer Sheila de Bretteville, who had also been teaching at CalArts, in founding the independent FSW, which developed into the Woman's Building, a non-academic mecca for feminist art until 1991.[4]

Suzanne Lacy, had been a student of Judy Chicago's at Fresno and transferred to CalArts when Chicago and Schapiro initiated the Feminist Art Program, receiving her MFA in 1973. Lacy also worked in video at the FSW. Her video *Anatomy Lesson #2: Learn Where the Meat Comes From* is a parody of a Julia Child cooking lesson. In it, she points out the various cuts of meat using her own body, horrifically demonstrating how the female body is perceived by the male gaze.[5]

Ulrike Rosenbach, the pioneer German video artist, spent a year in Los Angeles to teach at CalArts, and made her first video, *Don't Believe I'm an Amazon* (1975) at the FSW. It's another attack on the canon of art history and the representation of women as seen through the male gaze. In a video in which two images are overlaid, Rosenbach is seen simultaneously shooting arrows at a fifteenth century painting of a Madonna, and the painting itself with the arrows embedded.[6]

Susan Mogul was a student in the Feminist Art Program at CalArts, who went on to participate in the FSW. In one of her early videos, made in 1974, she performs in front of a static camera, talking about masturbating with a vibrator in response to Vito Acconci's video in which he is apparently masturbating underneath the table at which he is sitting. Mogul describes her motivation as intent to declare her own sexuality while at the same time blasting the male gaze.[7]

Although not enrolled in a degree program, Ilene Segalove was studying at CalArts in the early 1970s with John Baldessari but was also influenced by the presence of the Feminist Art Program. She bought a Portapak video camera and proceeded to make a series of videos. In 1974 she started *The Mom Tapes*, a very feminist set of videos in which she tells stories of a girl's childhood at a time when childhood was still being defined by the American cultural mainstream in terms of boys' experience.[8]

Institutions of higher education in the Middle West of the United States were among the first to acquire mainframe computers, thus spawning generations of visual artists and composers in the region who experimented with digital art. While the first generation of digital artists in that geographic area were almost all male (Colette Bangert being one of the few women in her generation to achieve visibility in the field of digital art), the availability of computers within the academic setting did result in a second generation that included a significant number of women. Whether consciously or unconsciously, they were influenced by principles of feminism to make digital art more inclusive in several ways. The first was through developing and improving program interfaces so that artists who were not trained in computer science could have access to using the computer in creating art. The second was through developing more audience friendly graphics. The third was using digital conferences and exhibitions as opportunities for coming together to support each other and make their work better known. The fourth was through becoming important digital art educators.

Three women in that second generation, Donna J. Cox, Ellen Sandor, and Janine Fron compiled an exhaustive documentation of their peers in a book titled, *New Media Futures: The Rise of Women in the Digital Arts*. The three were pioneer digital artists themselves. Donna J. Cox, a key figure in the digital community at University of Illinois, was named one of forty modern "Leonardos" by the Museum of Science and Industry, Chicago (MSI); Ellen Sandor, influential Chicago digital artist, was instrumental in the creation of virtual reality; and Janine Fron, was a Chicago-based digital artist and one of the first feminist game designers. Much of the following information is based on their publication. The impact of the women in this second generation is an extraordinary story, particularly in terms of their role as educators in a field that was dominated by men in most other locations in the world.[9]

Annette Barbier and Barbara Sykes studied at the University of Illinois, Chicago starting in 1972. Like Lillian Schwartz at Bell Labs a few years earlier, they began to use software programs to create abstract color video images. Sykes went on to make explicitly feminist work, a blend of documentation, personal narrative, and feminist mythology. Both went on to distinguished academic careers, Barbier to Northwestern University, in the Radio/Film/TV Department and as director of the Center for Art and Technology and then at Columbia College, and Chicago as chair of the Department of Interactive Arts and Media. Sykes was a longtime professor at Columbia College and was also involved with the Chicago Center for New Television in the later 1970s. She organized *Video and Computer Art: Chicago Style*, a traveling exhibition (1988–9) seen in Japan, China, Australia, and Spain. By 1978, Chicago women were so prominent in video that Barbara Aronofsky Latham became head of the video department at the School of the Art Institute of Chicago (SAIC), a position she held to her untimely death in 1984. Her videos from the period consist of images manipulated by computer to create disjointed narratives, their fragmentation becoming a metaphor for the lives of the women she documented. Jane Veeder, Professor Emerita, Visual Communication, San Francisco State University, was another artist from the Chicago video group. Her video, *Montana* (1982), was the first video acquired by the Museum of Modern Art in New York.

Copper Giloth, Director of Academic Computing and Professor at Amherst College, described how excited she was to study in the new graduate program of the Electronic Visualization Laboratory (EVL) at the University of Illinois at Chicago Circle (UICC). "My life was changed . . . I ended up making a connection through programming where I could use these new technologies to combine images, sound, and text within stationary and moving grid structures . . . This process was a comfortable place for me to make work and one that felt familiar given my earlier quilt and sewing experiences."[10]

Giloth isn't the only female digital artist to make the connection between programming and sewing. The earliest modern programming was the Jacquard weaving program referred to in Chapter 1 that inspired Babbage and brought Ada Lovelace to conceive how algorithms could represent not only numbers, but also language, and music, thus envisioning the modern computer. Joan Truckenbrod, Professor Emerita, School of the Art Institute of Chicago, also made the connection between digital art and sewing. She wrote, "I generated sequential images . . . it looked like a weaving . . . It's titled 'The Electronic Patchwork.' "[11]

Muriel Magenta, a committed feminist (like Judy Chicago, she abandoned a last name associated with a father or a husband), broke ground in merging feminism with performance and technology in the *Coiffure Carnival* (1983–8). The centerpiece was *La Pompadour: In Defense of a Hairdo*. It consisted of a giant head surmounted by an immense wig styled with a pompadour, surrounded by a chain-link fence, and guarded by a phalanx of men and women dressed as beauty salon employees. It was presented as a live performance and ultimately as a video. The piece is ambiguous: it can be seen as protecting individuality, but also as expressing the oppression of women by patriarchal ideals of beauty. Magenta has taught at the Herberger Institute for Design and the Arts, Arizona State University, for many years, and has been instrumental in creating intermedia programs and imparting them to generations of students.[12]

MIT has been a powerful contributor in developing the intersectionality of the arts and technology going back to when György Kepes was invited to establish a design program in 1946. Kepes joined the Bauhaus in 1930 at the invitation of László Moholy-Nagy, and followed Moholy-Nagy, first to London, and then, to the United Sates in 1937. Kepes believing that the future of art lay in technology, founded CAVS at MIT in 1967. CAVS was eventually folded into the MIT Media Lab in 1985. Women artists using technology were among those who were invited to join CAVS, usually for one year, but sometimes for periods of time as long as a decade. Of the two hundred or so "fellows" approximately one-third were women.

In 1977, Otto Piene, who had succeeded Kepes as director of CAVS, organized a collaborative team of fourteen artists and fourteen scientist/engineers to implement a design envisioned by artist Lowry Burgess. It became *Centerbeam* (Plate 5), a giant machine resembling a pipeline or a radio tower on its side, that spouted steam against which were projected holograms and laser beams, with balloons rising above the heads of the audience, all accompanied by electronic music. These features were programmed digitally to repeat during the period when it was on display. It was installed first at *documenta* 6, in Kassel, Germany in 1977, and a year later, on the National Mall in Washington, DC. The significance of this collaborative sculpture has been underestimated. It captured the essence of the search by artists and visual arts theorists from the 1950s to the 1980s for an art form that would integrate art, technology, and public display. Women artists were instrumental in two of the most important aspects of *Centerbeam*, Joan Brigham and Harriet Casdin-Silver. Brigham had been investigating steam as an element in technology-based art, and it is she who planned and programmed the most consistently visible element of *Centerbeam*—the steam that rose in great swathes both during the day and spectacularly at night when Casdin-Silver's holograms were projected against it (Casdin-Silver was a pioneer in art holography). Virginia Gunter is also listed as a participating artist (Gunter curated one of the first exhibitions of contemporary art at the Museum of Fine Arts, Boston, in 1971, titled *Earth, Air, Fire, Water: Elements of Art*). It should be noted that among the participating scientists and engineers, there was also a woman, Patricia Downey, who received a PhD in Physics at MIT in 1980. Two of the four student assistants involved were also women, Nancy Doll and Astrid Hiemer.[13]

Another feminist artist who became an educator is Barbara Nessim (Plate 6), one of very few full-time professional women illustrators working in the United States during the 1960s and 1970s, and one of the first artists to use computer-generated art for illustration. She illustrated record album covers, calendars, and magazine covers for major publications such as *Rolling Stone*, *Time*, *Ms.*, *New York Magazine*, the *Boston Globe*, *Show*, and *Audience*. In 1982 she produced the cover image for a *Time* magazine article on women's rights. As a result, she was invited to become artist-in-residence at *Time*, where she had unlimited access to the journal's sophisticated equipment. She went on to incorporate digital technology into much of her artistic practice. Nessim subsequently taught in the MFA Computer Arts Program at the School of Visual Arts and in the illustration department at Parsons, the New School for Design, where she was chair from 1992 to 2004. In early 2013, the Victoria and Albert Museum opened an extensive retrospective entitled *Barbara Nessim, An Artful Life*. The exhibition spanned Nessim's works from the 1960s to the present, and all eighty artworks became part of the V&A's permanent collection.[14]

Hermine Freed had a long career as a professor of video at the School of the Visual Arts, New York, starting in 1972. In *Two Faces*, a video she made in 1973, she expresses the ambiguity in female gender identity by juxtaposing video images of the two sides of her face, each seeming to explore the identity of the other. In *Art Herstory*, a 1974 video that is both hilarious and very innovative technically, she pokes fun at the art historical canon through posing as the female figure represented in famous paintings, at one point, a Madonna; at another, Cezanne's wife who complains that her neck hurts. The strong feminist content is matched by Freed's elaborate exploration of the technical possibilities in video.[15]

But the innovation of feminist artists in technological art was not confined to higher education. The rest of this chapter documents a few of the important feminist artists outside of the academy who experimented with different aspects of technology. Performance artists continued to play a major role in the legitimization of video. Other artists were inspired by the concept of the "glitch," as a metaphor for breaking down the patriarchal ideal of technological perfection. Women artists were also among the earliest to explore artmaking through use of the internet. And some began to make art that questioned the ability of technology to convey the complexity of human existence.

The New York artist Carolee Schneemann was one of the first feminist artists to combine performance with video. Like Jonas and Moorman a few years earlier, and many other feminist artists, Schneemann used her body to celebrate women's sexual agency. The video *Up To and Including Her Limits* (1973) is Schneemann's most direct response to, and rejection of male dominance. Whereas Jackson Pollock's drip drawings exist in their own presence without Pollock's image, as if appearing from the heavens in their own authority, a nude Schneemann, in a rope harness, swings back and forth with a paintbrush in her hand. As she swings toward the wall, she splashes paint onto the wall, declaring her female bodily presence as the artist.[16]

Similarly, in videotaped performances like *Gestures* (1974), Hannah Wilke, also New York-based, records facial grimaces and hand gestures, thrusting the physicality of her body into the faces of viewers. Schneemann's and Wilke's legacy of aggressive feminist sexuality reaches into the twenty-first century with artists like Marilyn Minter in New York, and Pipilotti Rist in Switzerland.[17]

The early performances of Vienna-based artist Valie Export presage her use of video, as, for instance, in a street performance in which she invited passersby to reach into a black box attached to her bosom and touch her bare breasts. Export compared the black box to a cinema theater—a dark interior in which to experience women's sexuality. For her remarkable video, *Adjungierte Dislokationen* [Adjunct dislocations] (1973), she wore video cameras on her front and back, suggesting the ambiguity of female identity, caught between the past and the future. The video is split in thirds. On the left is Export, herself, moving about with the cameras attached to her body. On the right placed vertically, are the images as seen by the two cameras.[18]

Shigeko Kubota, like Joan Jonas and others, ascribes her video art practice to the invention of the Portapak video camera. Finding career limitations for women in Japan too restrictive, she moved to New York and became involved with many experimental artists living in New York in the 1960s, in the process meeting Nam June Paik, whom she eventually married. She felt that Marcel Duchamp was her artistic inspiration and she did several works in tribute to him. The best known is *Duchampiana: Nude Descending a Staircase* (1976). She built a free-standing staircase and installed monitors in each of the risers that displayed a video image of a nude woman walking down the stairs altered with overlays of color or fragmented into separate body parts. She made her feminism explicit, declaring, "Video is Vengeance of Vagina / Video is Victory of Vagina."[19]

Nil Yalter is a Turkish artist who has lived in Paris since 1965. She participated in the French counterculture demonstrations of the late 1960s, an experience which led her to become one of the founders of the feminist movement in France. Her video, *The Headless Woman (The Belly Dance)* (1974) is one of the classic artworks of the early French feminist movement. The camera focuses on the artist's belly on which is written a text from a book by René Nelli, *Erotique et Civilisations* (1972), "a woman's sexuality is both convex and concave." Yalter animates the words by performing the gyrations of belly dancing. It's a complex piece, critiquing Western Orientalizing attitudes that render non-Western women exotic and sexually available while also critiquing the male gaze in general.

Dara Birnbaum was first known for her 1978 video, *Technology/Transformation: Wonder Woman*, in which she deconstructs the representation of gender in masculinist popular culture. For Birnbaum, Wonder Woman wasn't an image to which to aspire. She was another example of the patriarchal male gaze—a figment of men's imagination with no relationship to real women. She is quoted as saying,

"How dare you confront me with this supposedly super-powered image of a woman who is stronger than I am and can also save mankind? I can't do that, and I won't." In addition, Birnbaum introduced the practice of appropriating actual television clips, learning how to pirate them herself. She then altered them in various ways. The jerky repetition of frames in which the actor changes from drab secretary to glamorous superhero over and over again, strips the image of its slick artificial surface to reveal that underneath there is no woman, only technology.[20]

Other feminist artists used the "glitch," the error, the imperfect and crude to create space for female identity in the face of the patriarchal ideal of high-tech precision. Joan Jonas's video *Vertical Roll* (1972), in which the black lines that appear between frames when video breaks down, keep interrupting images of Jonas's own body, is a classic example. In 1974, Canadian artist Lisa Steele performed a video titled *Birthday Suit with scars and defects*, on her twenty-seventh birthday in which she appears naked and talks about the scars that have marked her life's experiences. By performing in front of a static camera, Steele avoids the sophisticated camera movements that define commercial film and television narrative techniques, thus giving her unmediated performance a sense of authenticity and intimacy. The lens of the camera substitutes for the male gaze, but instead of the stereotypical sexual performance that one would expect, Steele describes her blemishes, thus undermining that gaze.[21]

The same approach was used by Martha Rosler in *Semiotics of the Kitchen* (1975) in which she picks up knives and spoons, an eggbeater, and other cooking devices as if they are symbolic relics, names them, and then brandishes them like weapons. If her performance were a series of painted self-portraits with kitchen implements or even photography as traditionally practiced, it would not have the sinister and violent drama that the grainy black and white filmed performance gives it.[22]

Ewa Partum, another feminist artist, also explored the "glitch." Like Jonas and Rosler, Partum's films are grainy and shaky, thus connecting the film itself to the hand of the filmmaker. As early as 1971, she created one of the first feminist films in which she separates words into individual letters that she throws over a cliff into the water where the waves eventually destroy them—a woman initiating the destruction and nature overcoming the literacy of patriarchy.[23]

The artist and writer Pati Hill (1921–2014) used the "glitch" in an unexpected way to express her feminist ideas. Hill acquired an IBM copier on long-term loan and installed it in her house. She experimented mechanically by overloading the toner, thus creating imperfections that would make the images seem as ordinary as the real everyday objects she was photographing—pots, pans, dishes, and other household items. She wanted to express the drab monotony they represented, rather than transform them, as still-life painters had done for generations, into elegant representations of bourgeois prosperity.[24]

Vera Frenkel, an integral figure in Canada's computer arts and engineering community from the 1960s on, was one of the first artists to create a work that involved transmission via the internet. The World Wide Web (www) had yet to be invented, but transmission was possible between browsers connected to each other. Bell Canada had established teleconferencing studios in Montreal and Toronto. Net art, as it came to be called, became a popular medium for digital artists who used available browsers or their own coding, to create real-time transmitted performances. Vera Frenkel created *String Games: Improvisations for Inter-City Video* in 1974 (Plate 7). She choreographed a game of *Cat's Cradle* with five participants in each city, transforming the game from string to live action—electronic data became the string. Each of the participants was asked to bring to the performance nine statements, which could range from being a single number to a whole sentence. They were then asked to interact improvisationally with their counterparts in the opposing city, weaving relationships back and forth as two people would weave a cat's cradle, transferring the web from one to the other and then back again in an endless repetition.

Sonya Rapoport (Plates 8a and 8b) had been active in the Bay Area of San Francisco art scene since the 1950s. Rapoport began exploring systems of information in new media during the early 1970s. Her drawings and collages from this period use discarded printouts of early computer databases in anthropology, natural sciences, chemistry, and other areas of scientific research. She is considered one of the early innovators who helped establish San Francisco as a center for computer art. Her work has been included in major art and technology exhibitions including *Ars Electronica* (Linz, Austria), the 2009 Venice Biennale's Internet Pavilion, and *documenta 8*, Kassel, Germany. Her early combination of computer software and computer aesthetics with traditional media techniques was different from that of her male peers. Rather than accepting digital technology at face value for its formal innovations, she focused on how people were relating to the new technology. For instance, in an interactive performance entitled *Biorhythm* (1983) Rapoport tests their own evaluations of their biorhythm conditions against a computer assessment of their emotional/physical states; participants were asked to express with words and a gesture "how they were feeling that evening."[25]

Some of the artists in this chapter are known for their identification as feminists although, in general, little has been made of their contributions to the development of digital art. But when one considers their work, it is evident that they had significant impact on the visual art concepts and practice of the succeeding decades as will be evident in subsequent chapters.

Notes

1 The surveys are available in the records of the Women's Caucus for Art, Special Collections, Rutgers University Libraries, https://www.libraries.rutgers.edu/scua/women-artists.

2 Judy Chicago, "Made in California: Feminist Art Education," Judy Chicago Art Education Collection @ Penn State, March 3, 2001, https://judychicago.arted.psu.edu/wp-content/uploads/2013/10/Made-in-California-Feminist-Art-Education-20010303-Box-11-101.pdf.

3 The Feminist Art Program at CalArts is documented in many books and articles. A good starting point for further information would be the three chapters of Part I of *The Power of Feminist Art*, ed. Mary D. Garrard and Norma Broude (New York: Harry N. Abrams, 1994). These are: "Seeds of Change: Feminist Art and Education in the Early Seventies," "The Feminist Art Programs at Fresno and CalArts, 1970–75," 32–47; Arlene Raven, "Womanhouse," 48–65; and Norma Broude and Mary D. Garrard, "Conversations with Judy Chicago and Miriam Schapiro," 66–85. An online finding aid to the archives is at https://oac.cdlib.org/findaid/ark:/13030/kt2199r38x/entire_text/.

4 Sondra Hale and Terry Wolverton, eds., *From Site to Vision: The Woman's Building in Contemporary Culture* (Los Angeles: Otis College of Art and Design, 2011); PDFs of entire catalog: https://monoskop.org/images/8/84/From_Site_to_Vision_The_Womans_Building_in_Contemporary_Culture_2011.pdf.

5 An excerpt from Suzanne Lacy's *Learn Where Your Meat Come From*, 1976, is available on the Video Data Bank website, http://www.vdb.org/titles/learn-where-meat-comes.

6 Ulrike Rosenbach, https://www.ulrike-rosenbach.de/.

7 Susan Mogul, *Take Off*, video, 10:30, 1974, Video Data Bank, http://www.vdb.org/titles/take.

8 Excerpts from Ilene Segalove's *Mom Tapes* can be seen on the Metropolitan Museum of Art website, https://www.metmuseum.org/metmedia/video/collections/ph/mom-tapes and the Video Data Bank website, http://www.vdb.org/artists/ilene-segalove.

9 Donna J. Cox, Ellen Sandor, and Janine Fron, eds., *New Media Futures: The Rise of Women in the Digital Arts* (Urbana: University of Illinois Press, 2018).

10 Copper Giloth, "Copper Giloth," in ibid., 215–16.

11 Joan Truckenbrod, "Joan Truckenbrod," in *New Media Futures: The Rise of Women in the Digital Arts*, ed. Donna J. Cox, Ellen Sandor, and Janine Fron (Urbana: University of Illinois Press, 2018), 152.

12 Videos of the *Coiffure Carnival* are in the Getty Archives: https://primo.getty.edu/primo-explore/fulldisplay?vid=GRI&docid=GETTY_ALMA21125063110001551&lang=en_US.

13 *Centerbeam*, 1978, film produced by Ricky Leacock and Jon Rubin, edited by Mary Arbuckle, sound recorded by Anne Schaetzel, MIT Program in Art, Culture, and Technology (CAVS), preserved through the Avant-Garde Masters Program funded by the Film Foundation and administered by the National Film Preservation Foundation, 13:03, http://act.mit.edu/cavs/item/Centerbeam. For an online history of CAVS, see MIT School of Architecture and Planning, "A Brief History of the Center for Advanced Visual Studies, MIT," http://act.mit.edu/collections/cavs/history/. For an account of Harriet Casdin-Silver's life and career, see Charles Giuliano, "Holographer Harriet Casdin-Silver remembered," Berkshire Fine Arts, June 15, 2008, https://www.berkshirefinearts.com/06-15-2008_holographer-harriet-casdin-silver-remembered.htm. For information on Joan Brigham, see her website, Joan Brigham: Works in Steam, Glass, and Water Mist, http://www.joanbrigham.net/. To learn more about *Earth, Fire, Water, Air*, see Hilton Kramer, "Boston Museum Mounts an Unusual New Art Show," *New York Times*, February 4, 1971.

14 David Galloway, Christopher Benjamin Schultz, Anne Telford, Elyssa Dimant, Steven Heller, Cynthia Goodman, Douglas Dodds, Kisa Lala, Philip Koether, and Gloria Steinem, *Barbara Nessim, An Artful Life*, Victoria and Albert Museum Exhibition Catalogue (New York: Harry N. Abrams, 2013); Barbara Nessim, interview by Emily Banos, October 27, 2014, *Bard Graduate Center Craft, Art, and Design Oral History Project*, http://bgccraftartdesign.org/items/show/29.

15 Excerpts from Hermine Freed's videos can be accessed on YouTube.

16 Hovey Brock, "Carolee Schneemann: Kinetic Painting," *Brooklyn Rail*, December 2018–January 2019, https://brooklynrail.org/2017/12/artseen/Carolee-Schneemann-Kinetic-Painting.

17 Much has been written about Hannah Wilke. A good overview of Wilke's work can be found in Tracy Fitzpatrick, *Hannah Wilke: Gestures* (Purchase, NY: The Neuberger Museum of Art, 2010). Excerpts from the video, *Gestures*, can be viewed on YouTube.

18 Sabeth Buchmann, Yilmaz Dziewior, Elke Krasny, Hanne Lorek, Maren Luebbke-Tidow, Letizia Ragaglia, Brigitte Reutner, Johanna Schwanberg, and Berta Sichel. *Valie Export: Time and Countertime*. Cologne: Walther König, 2011; Randy Kennedy, "Who is Valie Export? Just Look and Please Touch," *New York Times*, June 29, 2016, https://www.nytimes.com/2016/06/30/arts/design/who-is-valie-export-just-look-and-please-touch.html; Monique Todd, "How Genital Stroking Became an Act of Feminist Rebellion," *Dazed Digital*, July 15, 2016, https://www.dazeddigital.com/artsandculture/article/32075/1/how-genital-stroking-became-an-act-of-feminist-rebellion. Valie Export website: https://www.valieexport.at/.

19 Caroline A. Jones, "Passages: Shigeko Kubota (1937–2015)," Artforum, October 15, 2015, https://www.artforum.com/passages/caroline-a-jones-on-shigeko-kubota-1937-2015-55566.

20 Alex Greenberger, "Changing Channels: Dara Birnbaum's Televisual Art Comes into Focus," *ARTnews*, March 27, 2018, https://www.artnews.com/art-news/artists/icons-dara-birnbaum-9973/.

21 Lisa Steele, *Birthday Suit with Scars and Defects*, video b/w, sound, 11:00, 1974, http://s133370137.onlinehome.us/2020/05/031/birthday-suit-with-scars-and-defects-2/.

22 Martha Rosler, http://www.martharosler.net/. *Kitchen Semiotics* has been posted by several people on YouTube.

23 Ewa Gorzadek, "Ewa Partum," Culture.pl. Adam Mickiewicz Institute, updated May 2016, https://culture.pl/en/artist/ewa-partum; Sven Spieker, "Artists from the Former Eastern Europe in Berlin: Ewa Partum," ARTMargins Online, October 30, 2017, https://artmargins.com/ewa-partum-d4/.

24 Meredith Sellers, "The Personal and Poetic Prints of a Female Pioneer of Copier Art," Hyperallergic, April 20, 2016, https://hyperallergic.com/292378/the-personal-and-poetic-prints-of-a-female-pioneer-of-copier-art/.

25 The starting point for research on Sonya Rapoport is the Sonya Rapoport Legacy Trust, http://www.sonyarapoport.org/; other sources include Terri Cohn, ed., *Pairing of Polarities: The Life and Art of Sonya Rapoport* (Berkeley, CA: Heyday, 2012); Judy Malloy, "The Process of Creating New Media: Interview with Sonya Rapoport," Content | Code | Process, November 2009, revision posted March 2017, https://www.narrabase.net/rapoport.html.

3

Reimagining the Binary Nature of Digital Technology

Feminist artists and theorists in the early 1990s began to think of the zero as a positive opportunity instead of the negative opposite of "on." Rather than viewing the binary as oppositional—on/off, 0/1—the zero became an invitation to explore, to invent, a space to fill with new ideas that could subvert the patriarchal nature of the binary. Their analysis took various forms. Some, more extreme than others, elicited significant controversy.

The invention of the internet, like other aspects of digital technology, is masculinist. It originated in a project sponsored by the US government as a Cold War response to the Russian success in developing Sputnik, the first satellite. The mission was to research new technologies that might have military applications. Research scientists at various universities were invited to put together teams to work on projects, and in 1962, J.C.R. Licklider, member of the MIT faculty who was known for his work with computers was asked to create the Information Processing Techniques Office (IPTO).

Licklider studied acoustics and he was frustrated by the amount of time that he had to spend on gathering the information needed to determine the outcome. As a result, he began to envision how the computer could help reduce that time. He developed a concept first enunciated in the 1930s by Vannevar Bush, the eminent American scientist who headed the Office of Scientific Research and Development during the Second World War. The concept was a system of wireless interconnected libraries that would provide information collectively, thus avoiding the time one would have to spend physically traveling from one library to the next.[1]

He established a system of networking among computer sites, using packet switching, meaning that the messages sent were not designated to move along one path, but could instead be delivered along any path that was open. Thus, Licklider created what became the ARPANET (Advanced Research Projects Agency Network), the predecessor to the internet. However, more was needed.

There was no common process for sending messages, so each center was sending data in a different configuration. That problem was solved in 1979 when Robert Kahn became the director of the IPTO and along with Vinton Cerf developed the Transmission Control Protocol and Internet Protocol (TCP/IP), to regularize how data was transmitted among multiple networks. TCP/IP was adopted on January 1, 1983, thus creating the modern internet, a single network rather than a set of competing networks.[2]

The final step in the creation of the modern internet was the invention of the World Wide Web, by Tim Berners-Lee in 1990, the system of websites and hyperlinks that made the internet user-friendly and led almost instantaneously to the use of websites by the general public. Members of the public connected to universities, corporations, government, or with enough money to buy early computers were already accustomed to using computers for email which had been available as early as the 1970s. But the advent of websites with the possibilities that the World Wide Web offered, like creating one's own website, resulted in a boom in computer use in the early 1990s that has grown astronomically ever since.[3]

From the masculinist history of the invention of the internet, one can wonder how feminist artists could succeed in extracting it from the patriarchy. But the efforts of feminist artists to do that began almost immediately. One of the first and most revolutionary disruptions occurred within less than a year after the internet was created, with the creation of VNS Matrix by four Australian artists, Virginia Barratt, Francesca da Rimini, Julianne Pierce, and Josephine Starrs. To protest male control of the internet, they used language derived from feminist theory, coupled with slang names for female sexual anatomy, to thrust blatant female sexuality into the face of the patriarchy. Following in the footsteps of revolutionary visual art manifestos of the past such as the Futurist Manifesto of the avant-garde Italian artists of the early twentieth century, they issued the *Cyberfeminist Manifesto* (Plate 9):

We are the future cunt
We are the modern cunt
positive anti reason
unbounded unleashed unforgiving
we see art with our cunt we make art with our cunt
we believe in jouissance madness holiness and poetry
we are the virus of the new world disorder
rupturing the symbolic from within
saboteurs of big daddy mainframe
the clitoris is a direct line to the matrix

the VNS MATRIX
terminators of the moral codes
mercenaries of slime
go down on the altar of abjection
probing the visceral temple we speak in tongues
infiltrating disrupting disseminating
corrupting the discourse
we are the future cunt[4]

The Manifesto's first iteration was a billboard in Adelaide, Australia. VNS Matrix quickly became known and influential in European countries and in the United States through publication of the manifesto in various feminist and academic journals, generating a spate of cyberfeminist organizations and manifestos.

VNS Matrix was dissolved in 1997, but its website lives on. During its lifetime, its founders participated in international feminist and digital media conferences where they often mounted elaborate multimedia installations such as *Corpusfantastica MOO* in 1994 for the Fifth International Symposium on Electronic Art, held at the University of Art and Design, Helsinki, Finland. In the catalog for the symposium they describe *Corpusfantastica MOO* as an "interrogation of the codes of popular technologies [through] a textual project . . . which sites itself within the mainframe of the Internet, the worldwide electronic communication network or the 'information superhighway' as the merchants of hype would have it." *Corpusfantastica MOO* was an interactive site. The language on the site was in keeping with its confrontational nature: The host network was named RAMpage; the login was VNS Matrix, and the password was *aberrant*. Participants could sign in as guests to see "who" was online at the same time: "Big Brain" in the Thymus Bar; "Sociopathic Cyberslut" in the Lung Lounge; "Manko" in the Wandering Womb Matrix.

Another installation was based on video gaming. Called *All New Gen*, it contained light boxes with large transparencies, audio, video, and sculptural elements. Its mission "as anarcho cyber-terrorist" was to undermine the "chromo-phallic patriarchal code."[5]

Cyberfeminism was a movement in which feminist artists and theorists were intertwined. The *Manifesto* was the embodiment of feminist theory developed by Donna Haraway and Sadie Plant. One cannot overestimate the impact of Haraway's *Cyborg Manifesto*, first published in 1985, on cultural theory and feminist art since its appearance, influencing feminism in the twenty-first century and resulting in the posthuman movement. Her basic position was that women must move on (and by implication men, as well) from the binary boundaries imposed on them by the patriarchy and take on more fluid identities that go beyond their physical biologies to include the capacities of technology as well as animals.[6]

Sadie Plant is often given credit for inventing the term, *cyberfeminism*. In her book, *Zeros + Ones: Digital Women + the New Technoculture* (1997), she gives a feminist version of the history of digital technology, focusing on the contributions of women, starting with Ada Lovelace. Referring to Haraway, along with French and Belgian radical feminists like Luce Irigaray, Julia Kristeva, and Monique Wittig, Plant suggests that digital technology and the internet should emulate the feminist rejection of the sexual binary and that instead of zero and one as opposites, on/off should be treated as symbiotic and sliding. Referencing the work of Ada Lovelace, she compares the mechanism of the modern computer with the use of punched cards on weaving machines. She suggests reversing the terminology on both, so that we refer to holes and not-holes rather than something and nothing.[7]

VNS Matrix's last manifesto, *Bitch Mutant Manifesto*, issued in 1996, is a tirade against the masculinism of digital technology. Its powerful attack on the authoritarianism of the internet is a forerunner of the twenty-first century critique of the internet for spewing fake news, racist hate language, and deep surveillance:

> The net's the parthenogenetic bitch-mutant feral child of big daddy mainframe.
>
> We are the malignant accident which fell into your system while you were sleeping. And when you wake we will terminate your digital delusions, hijacking your impeccable software.
>
> Your fingers probe my neural network. The tingling sensation in the tips of your fingers are my synapses responding to your touch. It's not chemistry, it's electric. Stop fingering me.
>
> Don't ever stop fingering my suppurating holes, extending my boundary but in cipherspace there are no bounds
>
> BUT IN SPIRALSPACE THERE IS NO THEY
>
> there is only *us*
>
> Trying to flee the binary I enter the chromozone which is not one
>
> XXYXXYXXYXXYXXYXXYXXYXXYXXYXXYXXYXXYXXYXX
>
> SUCK MY CODE.[8]

Along with the interest it generated in cyberfeminism, VNS Matrix's confrontational approach, and use of language that was taboo in polite academic art circles, created a controversy. As described above, cyberfeminism had spread mostly through academic circles of feminist artists where it gave rise to organizations like VNS Matrix. However, the founders of the new organizations did not necessarily agree with VNS Matrix's methods. One of the most successful was the Old Boys Network (OBN) which was founded in Germany in 1997 and was the leader in organizing the First Cyberfeminist International which took place at *documenta X* in Kassel, Germany in the same year.

The focus of the conference was on decentralized, nonconfrontational activities such as helping women develop careers and setting up listserves for women to communicate with each other, showing that cyberfeminism was mutating to become a networking and education movement, quite different from the confrontational stance of VNS Matrix.

But feminist media theorist Helen Hester argues that cyberfeminism lost its momentum when it refused to engage in political action like VNS Matrix. Hester and curator, Rosalie Doubal, organized a conference in 2017 in celebration of the twentieth anniversary of the First Cyberfeminist International conference. The conference revealed that the split between those who wanted more aggressive action and those who wanted to focus on networking still existed unabated even two decades later. Cornelia Sollfrank, co-founder and spokesperson for OBN, supported the position that "the solution is still micropolitics," while Hester "call[ed] for a response that [emulates] the politics of scale used by multinationals and government." The topics of the conference sessions reflected the divisive viewpoints. There was one on how frustrating it was that twenty years after the first conference, gender was still an issue. Another was a critique of VNS Matrix's use of biology as further embedding gender disparity. "The womb should be obsolete," declared artist and filmmaker, Shu Lea Cheang. And a third reflected the growing realization that feminism of the past had unconsciously been racist by focusing on how to "decolonize the mind and represent non-white experience online in ways that counter the stereotypes offered by traditional media."[9]

Hester was one of the founders of another cyberfeminist collective called Laboria Cuboniks (LC). The name is an anagram of Nicolas Bourbaki, a fictional mathematician invented by a collective of young French mathematicians in the 1930s. It was a joke to ridicule old-fashioned mathematics and support new ideas (the real Bourbaki was a general in the Franco–Prussian War). The fake Bourbaki was said to have developed the "Bourbaki theorem," a set of more modern algorithms. The collective was successful in its efforts. The result was the publication of a book of modernized mathematics replacing a textbook that had been standard since the late-nineteenth century. LC hoped to emulate the success of the Bourbakis in reinvigorating cyberfeminism.

By reference to Bourbaki, Hester and her colleagues declared themselves revolutionaries. They followed in the tradition of revolutionary groups to issue manifestos. The LC manifesto, titled *The Xenofeminist Manifesto: A Politics for Alienation*, praises VNS Matrix for its radical push to feminize digital communication, but criticizes it for its concentration on the natural body. Instead, the LC manifesto called for an anti-nature, anti-binary view of gender, and a cooperative, rather than confrontational, approach to transforming the world into one of parity and diversity.[10]

While LC criticized VNS Matrix for its insistence on the natural body, other critics like women's studies scholar Virginia Eubanks make a strong case that VNS Matrix's mission to "see art with our cunt ... make art with our cunt" was an important corrective to the widely accepted theory that the invisibility of the internet user led to a reduction in disparities of all kinds—gender, class, ethnicity. VNS Matrix put the body back into the picture, first, to counteract the loss of woman's voice to the universal male voice; second, in reference to the thousands of workers, the majority of them women, poorly paid, living in countries with a marked economic divide, who manufactured the computers that were now readily available to the general public (at least in economically developed countries); third, in reference to those bodies in underdeveloped countries who had no access to communication via the internet.

Eubanks sees that invisibility as more evidence of the oppression by the patriarchy, tied as it is to capitalism, an oppression that VNS Matrix exposes. She also points out how VNS Matrix's concepts entered the mainstream and become commodified, citing Oxygen.com and Oprah.com. She might also have cited *Lifetime*, which was the most popular and best known of the many channels founded as women's television in the United States and in many other countries as well. However, as the major commercial sources of entertainment began to focus on serving the female audience, women's television dried up. Oxygen.com was sold to NBC/Universal in 2017 to become a purely crime-based channel. The major broadcast, cable, and streaming networks had quickly recognized the commercial value of creating material that would appeal to a female audience and by the end of the 2010s, there were plenty of women protagonists in both comedic and dramatic television series along with growing ethnic variety in programming due to the expanded diverse nature of the audience.[11]

How "glitches" were used by pioneer feminist artists in the 1960s and 1970s to disrupt the heteronormative masculinism of early video, film, and photography has already been discussed. Cyberfeminists in the twenty-first century revived the "glitch." Dutch artist, Rosa Menkman, issued the *Glitch Studies Manifesto* in 2009–10, calling for interruptions in the digital world because of its capitalism and consumerism.[12]

In 2013, Legacy Russell resurrected the "glitch" as a metaphor for disruption of the heteronormative society with the issuance of the *Glitch Feminist Manifesto* (Plate 10). Russell sees the "glitch" through an intersectional Black and queer lens rather than a feminist lens that speaks to and through straight white womanhood. Russell writes:

> In a society that conditions the public to find discomfort or outright fear in the errors and malfunctions of our socio-cultural mechanics—illicitly and implicitly encouraging an ethos of "Don't rock the boat!"—a "glitch" becomes an apt metonym. Glitch Feminism, however, embraces the causality of "error," and turns the gloomy implication of glitch on its ear by acknowledging that an error in a social system that has already been disturbed by economic, racial, social, sexual, and cultural stratification and the imperialist wrecking-ball of globalization—processes that continue to enact violence on all bodies—may not, in fact, be an error at all, but rather a much-needed erratum. This glitch is a correction to the "machine," and, in turn, a positive departure.[13]

With her analysis of an error, not as a mistake, but as an "erratum," a correction to the mistakes (racism, sexism, inequality, just to name a few major ones) of the patriarchal society, Legacy Russell carries on and expands the original cyberfeminist efforts to question the binary nature of the internet and its masculinist embodiment and find a new meaning for zero that permits release from the conventions and rules of the patriarchy. Russell critiques the original feminism of the 1960s and 1970s as still working within the system of the binary heteronormative system, one that dictated in many ways the rise of cyberfeminism in the 1990s. While early feminists made pronouncements of seeking parity, it was parity for cisgendered, white women. Rather than disrupting the system, they bolstered it by posing the issue as a "we" against the "they."

In her book, *Glitch Feminism: A Manifesto*, published in 2020, Russell expands on these concepts as they appear in her early essay. She views the digital world as providing the space for multiple identities, an opportunity for marginalized people to take up space in a way not afforded in the world away from the screen. In addition to her critique of the original concept of feminism as applying only to white cis women, Russell also raises objections to Donna Haraway's proposed response to the heteronormative female by the creation of a female cyborg based on technology. Russell point out that Haraway's arguing toward a posthuman selfhood is one that does not recognize the hard work done by Black people and Queer people to be recognized as human in the first place.

As technofeminist scholar Nina Wakefield has documented, websites became a performance platform for cyberfeminist artists to protest patriarchal domination of the digital world, comparable to the live performances of the Guerrilla Girls and Riot Grrls. Feminist protest performance websites included Cybergrrl.com, WebgrrlsInternational.com, both created by Aliza Sherman; Femina.com, and Geekgirl.com.au, an Australian feminist website founded by RosieX in 1993. Webgrrls International and Femina exist today as sources for information pertaining to women in public life and mentoring. Geekgirl, nerdgrrl, and homegurrrl play with computer slang, turning the labels associated with males into feminist signs of resistance against digital victimhood. Nerdgrrl and homegurrrl are not active websites. Women liked working digitally as much as men, as a quote from RosieX explains, "Geeks generally are the hardcore of the nets. They are usually self-taught, determined individuals who simply love computers—machines are not just their friends but conduits into the world of art, politics, fun, magic and mayhem. Being a girl, I am voila—geekgirl."[14]

Wakefield also demonstrated how much the language used to describe functions and usages on websites reflected the hierarchic values of the patriarchal society. In a discussion of "surfing" she points out that the word is not one which people who live in economically underdeveloped countries are likely to know, surfing being a leisure sports activity of whites in countries like the United States. Similarly, the word "frontier" as in the countless descriptions of the internet as the "frontier of communication," is a word loaded with patriarchal masculinity through its privileging of the actions of cowboys on the Western frontier in the United States or the heroism of white male explorers in the Arctic or in tropical jungles.[15]

We all recognize the word, "home," as the standard term for the intro page to all websites. Wakefield describes how the cyberfeminist artist Carla Sinclair played with the term from a feminist perspective on her website, Netchick. She makes the term literal, by a "home" page that looks like a home: it has windows through which one can peer into different rooms to perform functions, for instance, a telephone answering machine in the office where one can leave messages.[16]

As discussed above, many cyber critics believed that the internet would eradicate the binary through its potential for anonymity. However, like Virginia

Eubanks, Christine Tamblyn expressed doubts. She became involved in digital art as a student at the School of the Art Institute of Chicago when she was drawn into the circle of Midwest pioneer digital artists. Tamblyn went on to teach mostly in California where she was instrumental at both the University of California, Irvine and San Francisco State University in creating their first computer art curricula.[17]

Tamblyn inserted her own face into digital artworks to make sure that viewers would realize that women, as well as men, could comprehend and use digital technology. The opening image of *She Love It, She Loves It Not: Women and Technology* (created in collaboration with Marjorie Franklin and Paul Tompkins, 1993) is a close-up of the artist's own face with intense red lips around her open mouth. By clicking on the open mouth, the viewer proceeds to the next image, a daisy whose petals reveal various aspects of contemporary culture and their relation to gender when one clicks on them. A CD-ROM (Tamblyn was one of the first artists to use the CD-ROM which had just come on the market in the 1990s, only to become obsolete a few years later) *Mistaken Identities* (1995) is a set of texts about women that Tamblyn selected as projecting positive aspects of female identity such as sexuality, power, and creativity. Seen from the vantage point of twenty-five years later, *Mistaken Identities* must be viewed within the context of its own time as an example of the racism of earlier feminism. The list speaks for itself: Josephine Baker, Simone de Beauvoir, Catherine the Great, Colette, Marie Curie, Marlene Dietrich, Isadora Duncan, Frida Kahlo, Margaret Mead, and Gertrude Stein.

The cyberfeminists in this chapter concentrated on interrogating the masculinism of the internet. Feminist artists in the next chapter developed a different approach to digital technology, less theoretical and less confrontational, but still aimed at changing the patriarchal society.

Notes

1 Vannevar Bush, "As We May Think," *The Atlantic*, July 1945.

2 Chigusa Ishikawa Kita, "J.C.R. Licklider's Vision for the IPTO," *IEEE Annals of the History of Computing*, 25, no. 3 (July–September 2003): 62–77. Ryan Singel, "Vint Cerf: We Knew What We Were Unleashing on the World," Wired Business, April 23, 2012, https://www.wired.com/2012/04/epicenter-isoc-famers-qa-cerf/.

3 "Sir Tim Berners-Lee," *History of the Web, Web Foundation.org*, https://webfoundation.org/about/vision/history-of-the-web/.

4 VNS Matrix, "The Cyberfeminist Manifesto for the 21st Century, 1991," VNS Matrix website, https://vnsmatrix.net/projects/the-cyberfeminist-manifesto-for-the-21st-century. Permission of VNS Matrix.

5 Minna Tarkka, ed., *The 5th International Symposium on Electronic Art Catalogue* (Helsinki: University of Art and Design), 156–9, https://vnsmatrix.net/wordpress/wp-content/uploads/isea-1994-helsinki-exhibition-catalogue.pdf.

6 Donna J. Haraway, "A Cyborg Manifesto," in *Simians, Cyborgs, and Women* (Abingdon: Routledge, 1990), 149–81.

7 Sadie Plant, *Zeros + Ones: Digital Women + the New Technoculture* (London: Fourth Estate, 1997), 56–7.

8 VNS Matrix website, Bitch Mutant Manifesto, https://vnsmatrix.net/projects/bitch-mutant-manifesto. Permission of VNS Matrix.

9 Joanna Walsh, "Post-Cyberfeminist International 2017," *Opinion* (blog), Frieze, https://www.frieze.com/article/post-cyber-feminist-international-2017.

10 Laboria Cuboniks website, https://www.laboriacuboniks.net/; "Laboria Cuboniks," Monoskop, https://monoskop.org/Laboria_Cuboniks.

11 Virginia Eubanks, "Cyberfeminism Meets NAFTazteca: Recoding the Technotext," in *Appropriating Technology: Vernacular Science and Social Power*, ed. Ron Eglash, Jennifer L. Croissant, Giovanna Di Chiro, and Rayvon Fouché (Minneapolis: University of Minnesota Press, 2004), 151–62.

12 Rosa Menkman, *The Glitch Moment(um)*, Network Notebooks 04 (Amsterdam: Institute of Network Cultures, 2011).

13 Legacy Russell, "Digital Dualism and the Glitch Feminism Manifesto," *Cyborgology* (blog), The Society Pages, December 10, 2012, https://thesocietypages.org/cyborgology/2012/12/10/digital-dualism-and-the-glitch-feminism-manifesto/; "#Glitch Feminism," Legacy Russell, https://www.legacyrussell.com/GLITCHFEMINISM.

14 Nina Wakefield, "Networking Women and Grrrls with Information/Communication Technology: Surfing Tales of the World Wide Web," in *Processed Lives: Gender and Technology in Everyday Life*, ed. Melodie Calvert and Jennifer Terry (2nd edition, Francis & Taylor e-Library, 2005 [first published 1997]), 79.

15 Ibid., 72–3.

16 Ibid., 76. The Netchick website is not active.

17 Christine Tamblyn, " 'She Loves It, She Loves It Not: *Women and Technology*,' an Interactive CD-ROM." *Leonardo* 28, no. 2 (1995): 99–104; Christine Tamblyn, "Mistaken Identities: An Interactive CD-ROM Genealogy," *Leonardo* 30, no. 4 (1997): 261–6; Social Networks and Archival Context, "Tamblyn, Christine," https://snaccooperative.org/ark:/99166/w60z76d0.

4

Using Websites and Browsers to Deliver Social Justice Messages

By harnessing the improved communication that resulted from the inventions of the World Wide Web and browsers in the early 1990s, the cyberfeminist artists in this chapter are credited by many cyber historians with humanizing the internet through an intersectional combination of feminism with other cultural and political issues affecting not only women but the world's entire population, such as political oppression, censorship, postcolonialism, ethnic diversity, and reproductive rights.

The invention of the World Wide Web has already been discussed. The first browser, Mosaic, which enabled computer users to search the web efficiently was developed by a group at the University of Illinois's National Center for Supercomputing Applications (NCSA) which not only included women, but was headed by a woman, Ping Fu. It was she who recognized the abilities of a student named Marc Andreessen and invited him to join the group. Andreesen became the primary investigator in developing Mosaic. Another pioneer digital artist, Colleen Bushnell, worked with Fu's group on the development of Mosaic, creating the icons, buttons, and placement of information that are still used today to navigate websites.[1]

Andreesen went on to establish the company that transformed Mosaic into Netscape. Mosaic became the basis for Microsoft's Internet Explorer, and Internet Explorer remained the browser of choice until Google Chrome.[2]

It is estimated that women's websites grew from 5 percent to 34 percent of all websites between 1992 and 1996. One of the first ways in which women began to utilize websites was to spread pragmatic information, updating women on general gender issues such as advances in women's employment, legal matters affecting women, and networking opportunities, one example being The Feminist Majority website.[3]

Feminists also quickly realized that through using websites, they could build international women's coalitions more easily than through primitive digital technology such as radio or fax. In 1995, when the Chinese government censored the Fourth World Conference on Women: Action for Equality, Development and Peace, Beijing after an attempt by feminist nongovernmental organizations (NGOs) to insert feminist principles into the agenda, a website called Linkages, was initiated by Barbara O'Leary to bypass the censorship (the NGO delegations were even forced to set up headquarters miles away from the conference's main site). After the conference, seeing how successful Linkages proved to be, O'Leary founded Virtual Sisterhood to continue the communication. Virtual Sisterhood no longer exists, but it has produced numerous offspring around the world.[4]

The Beijing conference was also attended by women artists including delegations from two United States feminist artist organizations, the Women's Caucus for Art (WCA) and the Coalition of Women's Art Organizations (CWAO). Pioneer digital artist, Muriel Magenta, organized World's Women Online (WWOL) for the conference, to showcase the international community of women artists. This website still exists, with links to the websites of over 1,000 women artists from all corners of the globe.[5]

Websites designed in the 1990s show that diversity was becoming a concern among cyberfeminists. Artist River Ginchild established her site, Digital Sojourn, to increase computer literacy among women of African descent. Ginchild is quoted as saying "I wanted to see myself—women of African descent—on the Web. I think I had seen one or two Black women with pages when I put my page up, but in June 1995 it was—overwhelmingly—white male, it still is, but there are a lot more of us online with pages."[6]

Johanna Burai, an artist who lives in Stockholm, Sweden, focused on the biases inherent in search engines, particularly Google, as the standard search engine used worldwide by millions who never doubt its objectivity. Burai's website, WorldWhiteWeb.net (Plate 11), made the point graphically. If one searched for images of hands on Google, only white hands came up. On her website, she displayed hands of color—hands of African Blacks, Asian hands, Latinx hands—and asked viewers to forward those images to Google with the request to include them when there is a search for images of hands. As a result of her publication of the World White Web, according to Burai, she has been attacked online by white supremacist neo-Nazis.[7]

Safiya Umoja Noble, a communications professor at University of Southern California (USC), has also written about the bias against people of color in Google. She cites the fact that in searching for Black, Asian, or Latina girls, for instance, the first information that comes up is pornographic.[8]

One of the most influential intersectional organizations of cyberfeminists, subRosa, is a collective founded by Faith Wilding and Hyla Willis in 1998 at

Carnegie Mellon University (CMU). On its website, subRosa is described as follows: "a mutable (cyber)feminist art collective combining art, social activism and politics to explore and critique the intersections of information and bio technologies on women's bodies, lives and work."[9]

Wilding declared herself a cyberfeminist in the early 1990s, but she had become a feminist long before, as a student in Miriam Schapiro's and Judy Chicago's Feminist Art Program at CalArts in 1971. In 1998, Wilding came to CMU for an artist's residency at the STUDIO for Creative Inquiry which had been set up to encourage collaborative projects bringing together the arts, science, and digital technology. CMU had been involved in digital technology since the 1960s, acquiring one of the first supercomputers. Although the atmosphere at CMU encouraged collaboration between the arts and sciences and explorations into new media, these activities involved mostly male faculty and students until Wilding arrived.

As one of her activities as a visiting artist, Wilding established a seminar called "Sex and Gender in the Biotech Century." Topics included "how cyberfeminism might relate to historical feminist art practices, and to engaged activist work with socio/political issues involving gendered and raced bodies . . . feminist grass-roots activism in immigrant rights and labor movements, reproductive rights, anti-war, environmental organizing, and the like."[10]

Hyla Willis was a student in the MFA program at CMU's School of Art and Design and met Wilding through participation in the seminar. Inspired by the seminar, Wilding and Willis formed subRosa, choosing the name because it suggested something clandestine, appropriate for waging guerrilla warfare. They issued the following manifesto (abbreviated here):

> subRosa's name honors feminist pioneers in art, activism, labor, politics, and science: Rosa Bonheur, Rosa Luxemburg, Rosie the Riveter, Rosa Parks, Rosie Franklin.
>
> subRosa is a reproducible cyberfeminist cell of cultural researchers committed to combining art, activism, and politics to explore and critique the intersections of the new information and biotechnologies in women's bodies, lives, and work . . .
>
> subRosa practices a situational embodied feminist politics nourished by conviviality, self-determination, and the desire for affirmative alliances and coalitions.[11]

subRosa's first project was *SmartMom*, an online satire in the form of an informational marketing piece. Wilding and Willis had read of the Smart T-Shirt developed in 1996 at Georgia Tech to be worn on the battlefield. Woven into the fabric were sensors that would transmit information when a soldier was hit by a bullet to a nearby triage unit, thus pinpointing the wounded warrior's location and enabling the unit to reach him sooner. Wanting to make an art project about how women's bodies were being subjected to control through the development of Assisted Reproductive Technologies (ART) such as fertility-enhancing drugs, artificial insemination, in vitro fertilization, and surrogate gestation, they applied the Smart T-shirt concept to the invention of a garment to be worn by a woman that would transmit her every bodily response to a control unit monitoring her sexual body through fertilization, pregnancy, and birth. As they wrote in a 2016 essay recapitulating their creation of *SmartMom*, their intention was to draw attention to the patriarchal attempt to control women's reproduction and how it led to a new form of eugenics. The SmartMom T-shirt was an ironic solution to allow the government to keep an eye on women who are infamous for their resistance to control (Plate 12a).[12]

subRosa's projects are intersectional. While there is almost always a biological aspect to its projects, the realization that biology intersects with the environment, cultural and political systems, and other kinds of science and engineering always informs their work.

A project at Massachusetts Museum of Contemporary Art (MASS MoCA) focused on a comparison of women's lives and work in North Adams, Massachusetts, the economically depressed New England manufacturing town where MASS MoCA is located, with the lives and work of women in Ciudad Juárez, Mexico. subRosa's concept was complex. The installation focused on women's lives, but it was also a deconstruction of the stereotypes around the outsourcing and globalization of manufacturing. Whom did the transfer of manufacturing help or harm—the community that was the new home of the factory, or the community from which it departed? Two large aerial photographs on the walls of the lobby depicted the two towns. Oversized map tacks indicated "places of refuge or exploitation." Visitors became participants through a "forensic floor." They could lift loose floorboards that revealed objects and texts giving further information showing that the outsourcing made no difference in either city. The lives of the women were startlingly similar—poor, limited education, narrow in scope.[13]

subRosa's project websites are also available through subRosa's own website, cyberfeminism.net. The websites are characterized by satire, exaggeration, Marxist analysis of capitalist exploitation, and information about genetics and other medical and scientific areas. Some pages are visually striking and others are almost pure text. *Biopower Unlimited* is a typical example. The home page is orange with a repetitive image of a circle within which is inscribed a text that defines Biopower as an overarching social hierarchy in which all individuals are so implicated that the structure becomes invisible. subRosa calls for people to become conscious of how they are manipulated and controlled in every aspect of their lives by the patriarchy. The format imitates the ads for commercial products, in which corporations try to elicit sales through engaging the consumer in personal assessment. A quiz will determine your relationship to Biopower, declares the website. Both satiric and informational at the same time, *Biopower Unlimited* exposes the subtle ways in which the patriarchal society structures class so that women, physical laborers, service providers are all subject to an upper class composed of corporate executives, knowledge producers, and government officials who are compensated at a much higher level for their efforts. The members of this upper class all work together. For instance, knowledge workers at universities produce information that enables large companies to profit from food processing and delivery but the fruit pickers and delivery truck drivers are an essential part of the system despite their lower place in the capitalist hierarchy. Resistance and revolt to Biopower can only come with comprehension of its most subtle and harmful practices.[14]

The website *Sex and Gender in the Biotech Century* relies more on satire and humor. The home page is a striking graphic design—a vivid yellow background, a pulsating cell, a dramatically designed title, and a line of little star-like shapes numbered 1–6, on which to click. Clicking on number two opens a page about the fictional Technical Advanced Genetic Center, a consortium of medical and scientific experts organized to create the Sex and Gender Education Show to educate about the new bioengineering technologies which can be used to generate plants, animals, and humans shaped to meet the economic, cultural, racial desires of the patriarchal society. Clicking on number three reveals the information that the sponsors are corporations and a new (fictional) government agency called the Federal Eugenics Administration (FEA) (Plate 12b). A click on button number five brings directions on how to draw a vulva and "A Modest Proposal," (the reference of course being to Jonathan Swift's *Modest Proposal* to kill all Irish babies, thus obliterating the Irish problem for England). subRosa's *Modest Proposal* is to use repro-technology and genetic modification to do away with all imperfect children, plants, and animals, thus solving the social welfare problems of the nations in the world and at the same time solving the problem of overpopulation.[15]

While websites to promote feminist messages of social justice like those described above were being created by cyberfeminists, the World Wide Web was not serving the needs of most social action groups. The Association for Progressive Communications (APC) was created in 1990 by several countries to change that situation. By the end of the second decade of the twenty-first century, APC had fifty-eight organizational members in seventy-two countries that maintained websites dedicated to social justice and economic sustainability.[16]

APC has also developed a set of principles for ending discrimination and harassment of women, LGBTQI peoples, and non-whites on the internet:

> A feminist internet starts with enabling more women and queer persons to enjoy universal, acceptable, affordable, unconditional, open, meaningful and equal access to the internet.
>
> Women and queer persons have the right to code, design, adapt and critically and sustainably use ICTs and reclaim technology as a platform for creativity and expression, as well as to challenge the cultures of sexism and discrimination in all spaces . . .
>
> We defend the right to sexual expression as a freedom of expression issue of no less importance than political or religious expression. We strongly object to the efforts of state and non-state actors to control, surveil, regulate and restrict feminist and queer expression on the internet through technology, legislation or violence . . .
>
> We reject practices by states and private companies to use data for profit and to manipulate behaviour online. Surveillance is the historical tool of patriarchy, used to control and restrict women's bodies, speech and activism . . . We call on all internet stakeholders, including internet users, policy makers and the private sector, to address the issue of online harassment and technology-related violence . . . It is our collective responsibility to address and end this.[17]

Similarly, in 2017 women graphic designers, art directors, photographers, and other visual arts professionals, members of The Feminist Internet, a non-profit activist collective, meeting at the University of the Arts London, issued a manifesto of feminist principles for the internet. Their eight points include the following:

> The Feminist Internet ERASES feminism; The Feminist Internet INTEGRATES the physical and digital; The Feminist Internet COOPERATES, not competes; The Feminist Internet ERADICATES violence; The Feminist Internet REDEFINES value; The Feminist Internet CONFRONTS, uncomfortable truths; The Feminist Internet RE-CODES gender; The Feminist Internet EDUCATES.[18]

One can conclude that the different directions taken by the two groups of cyberfeminists in the last chapters, one group protesting the masculinism of the internet itself and the other using the potential of the internet to communicate social justice messages, create a divisiveness in the Feminist Art Movement. Or one can conclude that they reveal aspects of feminism, both of which are essential for dismantling the patriarchy.

Notes

1 Donna J. Cox, Ellen Sandor, and Janine Fron, eds., "Introduction," in *New Media Futures: The Rise of Women in the Digital Arts* (Urbana: University of Illinois Press, 2018), 36.

2 Ibid., 35, 37.

3 Wakefield, Nina. "Networking Women and Grrrls with Information/ Communication Technology: Surfing Tales of the World Wide Web," in *Processed Lives: Gender and Technology in Everyday Life*, ed. Melodie Calvert and Jennifer Terry (2nd edition, Francis & Taylor e-Library, 2005 [first published 1997]), 69–84.

4 Mitzi Waltz, *Alternative and Activist Media* (Edinburgh: Edinburgh University Press, 2005), 98–102.

5 World's Women On-Line website, http://wwol.is.asu.edu/artist_b.htm. The World's Women Online! website, https://dpya.org/en/index.php/The_World%27s_Women_ On-line!

6 Wakefield, "Networking Women and Grrrls," 76.

7 Oriana Story, "How a Designer Took on Google over the 'World White Web,'" Newsbeat, BBC, April 14, 2016, http://www.bbc.co.uk/newsbeat/article/36044177/ how-a-designer-took-on-google-over-the-world-white-web. Johanna Burai, https:// johannaburai.com/WORLD-WHITE-WEB.

8 Safiya Umoja Noble, *Algorithms of Oppression: How Search Engines Reinforce Racism* (New York: NYU Press, 2018); Annenberg School for Communication and Journalism, University of Southern California, "In 'Algorithms of Oppression,' Safiya Noble Finds Old Stereotypes Persist in New Media," updated December 11, 2019, https://annenberg.usc.edu/news/diversity-and-inclusion/algorithms-oppression-safiya-noble-finds-old-stereotypes-persist-new.

9 subRosa, http://cyberfeminism.net/

10 subRosa, "Bodies Unlimited, A Decade of subRosa's Art Practice," *n.paradoxa* 28 (July 2012): 16–25, https://www.ktpress.co.uk/pdf/vol28_npara_16-25_subRosa.pdf.

11 Ibid. Note that on the subRosa website, cyberfeminism.net, the manifesto concludes with an additional line, "Let a million subRosas bloom!"

12 Faith Wilding and Hyla Willis, "SmartMom Rebooted: A Cyberfeminist Art Collective Reflects on its Earliest Work of Internet Art," *Studies in the Maternal* 8, no. 2 (December 15, 2016): 17.

13 subRosa, http://cyberfeminism.net/.

14 Ibid.

15 Ibid.

16 GreenNet, https://www.greennet.org.uk/, Institute for Global Communications.

17 Association for Progressive Communication website, https://www.apc.org/en/pubs/feminist-principles-internet-version-20, updated November 3, 2020.

18 "Feminist Internet Manifesto," https://web.archive.org/web/20201101021935/https://feministinternet.com/manifesto/. The Feminist Internet has a very useful website, https://feministinternet.com, for information on the bias against women and minorities in digital technology.

5

Provoking the Patriarchy Through Digital Language

The preceding chapters in this book describe how feminist artists in the early years of the digital age and cyberfeminist artists in succeeding decades confronted the masculinism of electronic and digital technology through disruption of the technology itself and through introduction of feminist content. This chapter considers how digital feminist artists used language to deconstruct the patriarchy, starting with Jenny Holzer and discussing hypertext literature, an art form largely created by feminist artists, short-lived, but influential.

It would be impossible to consider the subject without first writing about Jenny Holzer. Male conceptual artists like Lawrence Weiner, Mel Bochner, Bruce Nauman, and Robert Barry also used words divorced from imagery. But contrary to their cool, detached, ironic, and absurdist work, Holzer began to use language to convey messages with emotional impact that defied patriarchal conventions of polite conversation. Because her words were on display in open settings rather than in the elite spaces of museums and galleries, they also defied the conventions of public discourse. Holzer, like her Pop predecessors and feminist contemporaries such as Barbara Kruger and Martha Rosler, realized the impact that advertising had thanks to electronic media and utilized its technology to express her disquieting messages.

Holzer was introduced to the possibilities of electronic public display in 1982 through the Public Art Fund project, *Messages to the Public*, which commissioned artists from 1982 to 1990 to create work to be displayed on a giant electronic Spectacolor board, at the top of the façade of the New York Times building in Times Square. Nine of her *Truisms* were transformed into lighted moving images that flashed every forty seconds, delivering such aphorisms as "Abuse of Power Comes As No Surprise" (Plate 13). She wrote *Truisms* in reaction to her 1976–7 experience in the highly selective and prestigious postgraduate Whitney Independent Study Program which made Holzer angry because her instructors only discussed white male art stars. She had first printed the *Truisms* on flyers which she distributed herself.[1]

During the eight years of its existence, *Messages to the Public* featured seventy artists. In addition to Jenny Holzer, Kiki Smith, Martha Rosler, and the Guerrilla Girls received commissions along with male artists, such as Alfredo Jaar, Keith Haring, and David Wojnarowicz. Martha Rosler addressed homelessness; Kiki Smith, awareness of global oppression; Barbara Kruger, consumerism. However, it is Holzer, who, once she was introduced to the public display that electronic media provided, went on to use it as a primary medium in her work, whereas it was only incidental to the mainstream work of the other artists.

In addition to "Abuse of Power . . ." Holzer's messages in Times Square included "Torture is Barbaric," "Morals Are for Little People," "Private Property Created Crime," "Your Oldest Fears Are Your Worst Ones," "Money Creates Taste," "Fathers Often Use Too Much Force," "Expiring for Love Is Beautiful But Stupid."[2]

Holzer herself explains her work: "You only have a few seconds to catch people, so you can't do long, reasoned arguments. I wanted the viewer to make his way through them and maybe gain some tolerance." Even more elucidating is Holzer's comment that "A great feature of the electronic signs is their capacity to move content. I love that because motion is much like the spoken word: you can emphasize phrases; you can roll and pause, the kinetic equivalent to inflection."[3]

Another comment from Holzer herself: "The signboard is a futuristic, eye-catching thing and I thought it was a wonderful way to present art clearly . . . not that I'm trying to thumb my nose at advertising; it's simply that I want to use means of communication that work."[4]

Since her initial projections in 1982, Holzer has created projections in ten countries—including Austria, Brazil, France, Germany, Italy, and Spain as well as the United States—in twenty cities, on landmarks such as the Louvre, Paris; on geographic sites such as the Arno River, Florence; or the mountains surrounding Rio de Janeiro; and on three continents.[5]

In 1986, her *Survival Series* was projected on various buildings and sites in New York again. The *Survival Series* includes such messages as "Put Food Out in the Same Place Every Day and Talk to the People Who Come to Eat and Organize Them," "You Are Trapped on the Earth So You Will Explode," "Remember to React," "If You Had Behaved Nicely the Communists Wouldn't Exist," and "If You Are Considered Useless No One Will Feed You Anymore."[6]

Almost simultaneously in the 1980s to her involvement in digital signage, Holzer also began to use language incised in the seats of marble benches and in other sculptures. These were shown on their own, but also in conjunction with projections and videos. In a spectacular installation in the Guggenheim Museum in New York, Holzer created a saying that circled the inside of the museum dome while at the same time, sculptures were on view in the spiral galleries ascending to the top.[7]

One of Holzer's most moving installations using digital technology combined with sculptural pieces was *Laments*, at Dia Art Foundation, 1989. In response to the HIV/AIDS crisis, Holzer created thirteen sarcophagi in different sizes, infant to adult. On each lid was one of Holzer's statements. In addition, she mounted thirteen computer-animated signs on the support columns of the gallery that duplicated the messages on the sarcophagi. The messages reflected the ages of the fictive corpses in the sarcophagi. For instance, part of a message from the infant corpse read, "I Do Not Want to Be Left to be Eaten." A message from an AIDS patient bemoaned, "The New Disease Came. I Learn that Time Does Not Heal."[8]

Holzer's electronic displays were instrumental in expanding the concept of installation outside the gallery or museum space, and pioneered the use of digital technology to create public art. While installation and public art have become standard forms of artmaking for many artists, Holzer stands first and foremost in making language the content of public art.

Feminist artists found another avenue for the digital disruption of language which, like Holzer's projections, was also capable of reaching large audiences—the creation of hypertext literature. It's hard to believe that the ability to click on links and immediately be reading another text came into existence and quickly became an integral and ubiquitous aspect of modern information communication as recently as the early 1990s. A few pioneer artists, male as well as female, saw the potential for using hyperlinks and hypertexts to form a new kind of interactive literature in which the reader has control over the sequencing of the narrative and the development of the characters. Early hypertext fiction writers had to create their own software, but very quickly a software program called Storyspace was developed and made available through Eastgate Systems, Inc., the principal publisher and distributor of hypertext narrative, both fiction and nonfiction.[9]

While male authors were interested in the stylistic application of hypertext to literature, feminist digital artists saw it as a way of dislocating traditional forms of narrative that were infused by masculinism. In being drawn to hypertext literature, they followed in the footsteps of writers like Virginia Woolf or Gertrude Stein, who preceded them in using forms of experimental writing to differentiate their creations from work they viewed as denigrating and dismissive of women.[10]

Shelley Jackson speculates that she is returning literature to its feminine origins, in that literature itself was invented by women as implied by the origin of the word, "text." The root is the Latin word, *textum*, meaning fabric, derived from the Latin verb, *texere*, meaning "to weave." She sees "texts" as an outgrowth of weaving since weaving has always been women's work.

Jackson's connection of hypertext to textile is evident in the title of her classic hypertext novel, *The Patchwork Girl* (1995, first published on a diskette for Windows and Macintosh; Plate 14) and her use of the term "Stitch Bitch" to describe herself as the "Patchwork Girl" in a lecture during the conference "Transformations of the Book," held at MIT, October 24–25, 1998. Using psychoanalytic theory, Jackson postulates that hypertext literature is an anti-phallic mode of writing, shunned through the centuries out of the fear of being identified as female by male writers. Its characteristics are the opposite of patriarchal writing attributes: dispersed instead of linear, relaxed instead of driving forward, focused on context rather than singular, nonhierarchic rather than designed, fulfilling the masculinist stereotype about women, messy and unstructured, everything that the patriarchal rules for artistic creation seek to inhibit. She concludes, "Hypertext then, is what literature has edited out: the feminine. (That is not to say that only women can produce it. Women have no more natural gift for the feminine than men do.)"[11]

Jackson goes on to describe how hypertext literature advances the feminist concept of the body as a social construction by comparing it to the "real" body. The real body she declares, "is inimical to the self." Rather than existing as a unitary configuration defined as such by the patriarchal society, it is amorphous, a combination of the physical and the imaginary, the interior and the exterior. It is not self contained: the world enters the body through the senses, making it difficult to establish its boundaries.[12]

Jackson refutes authorship of *Patchwork Girl*, in response to feminist rejection of authorship as a patriarchal concept that has elevated white males: "It has come to my attention that a young woman claiming to be the author of my being has been making appearances under the name of Shelley Jackson ... I am the monster herself, and it is Shelley Jackson who is imaginary."[13]

And finally, Jackson describes hypertext literature as disrupting the epistemological structures of the patriarchy by its avoidance of linear expository prose. While framed as fiction, it embeds nonfiction texts, thus leaving readers confused as to what is real and what is not. "Hypertext never seems quite finished ... it's fuzzy at the edges ... In hypertext you can't find out what's important so you have to pay attention to everything ... you can't tell what's the original and what's the reference ... hierarchies break down."[14] In an interview with artist and author, Mark Amerika, she says, "Part of my motivation for writing *Patchwork Girl* in the first place was to interrogate hypertext in terms of its relationship to the rest of literature."[15]

The narrative of *Patchwork Girl* is built on Mary Shelley's novel, *Frankenstein or the Modern Prometheus.* Jackson envisions what Shelley might have written had she penned a sequel based on the scene in which the monster asks Dr. Frankenstein to make him a mate ("Shall each man," cried he, "find a wife for his bosom, and each beast have his mate, and I be alone?"). Jackson's invention is a patchwork girl made up of body parts from different women. The novel, which is available on a flash drive, consists of texts and drawings accessible through clickable controls on the screen. The patterns of the controls take various shapes depending on the content of the narrative. For instance, in one sequence, the controls are in a grid that resembles a quilt. At other times, the pattern of controls is in the shape of a body. In one segment, the pattern is that of a path, reflecting the journey described in the texts.[16]

The narrative takes time to read. After clicking on a control, an image comes up with an insert box of text. Within that screen may be other controls so that readers may delve even deeper into the story if they so desire. *Patchwork Girl,* itself, is a metaphor for a monster created by the author.[17]

Judy Malloy is well known for her critical writing. She was associated with the important publication on digital art, *Leonardo*, for years, in various editorial positions such as the initial editor of *Leonardo Electronic News*. Malloy was also the editor of *Women, Art, and Technology* (MIT, 2003), one of the first books documenting the role of women artists in the development of new media. She began writing in hypertext format in the late 1980s. *Uncle Roger*, published in 1987, is the first hypertext fiction. Readers followed the narrative by clicking on key words. Her most influential publication is *its name was Penelope*, published in 1993, with a much more complex structure than *Uncle Roger*. Malloy writes that she was conscious of James Joyce's *Portrait of an Artist as a Young Man* and *Dubliners* as well as the work of Dorothy Richardson, another early twentieth-century writer who experimented with new forms of prose that Malloy describes as "the writing equivalent of impressionist painting."[18]

Before *Uncle Roger*, Malloy had developed the concept of writing nonsequentially by creating artist's books using card catalogs and mechanical address books. These early card catalog books were operated manually; readers could access the mechanical address books with buttons that would reveal the contents of a page on a screen. Readers could open the books, at any point, to read the narratives.[19]

In *its name was Penelope*, the narrative revolves around the memories of a woman photographer named Anne Mitchell. Malloy writes that she chose a "photographer narrator, who would write about her life as if each lexia was a photograph, and the photographs could be combined by the reader in various ways." Anne's memories are based on Malloy's own recollections of childhood but Malloy changes them for the sake of the narrative. "The combination of reader choice and the constantly changing order (like the raveling and unraveling of Penelopeia's web) makes it highly unlikely that the same story will ever appear twice."[20]

Malloy employed the *Odyssey* not only as a foundation for the narrative content but also for its structure. Homer moves back and forth in time just as Malloy wants her readers to do in her hypertext narrative. The reader shifts among six files that are loosely based on sections of the *Odyssey*: "Dawn," "A Gathering of Spirits," "That Far Off Island," "Fine Work and Wide Across," "Rock and Hard Place," and "Song." *The Odyssey* centers around Odysseus's travels by boat after the Fall of Troy, a signifier of male freedom to explore the world while his wife, Penelope, stays home, and weaves and unravels the same image, a signifier of the restricted lives of women. Malloy does a reversal in her version. Instead of a real boat, there is a toy boat named Penelope, and Malloy's Penelope, unlike Homer's Penelope, sails through various relationships and experiences in modern San Francisco where Malloy lived at the time.[21]

The episodes reflect Malloy's own experience. "A Gathering of Spirits," based on Book XI of the *Odyssey* in which Odysseus enters the realm of the dead, refers to the AIDS crisis in 1980s San Francisco when Malloy lost many friends to the disease.[22]

By choosing a photographer as her protagonist, Malloy cements the fusion of the visual and the literary. Like Jackson's *Patchwork Girl*, the form of the protagonist and the form of the text coalesce into a new digital configuration. In the introduction to the edition published by Eastgate, Carolyn Guyer, another pioneer in hypertext narrative compares Malloy's approach to that of a visual artist working with found photographs of daily life, the kind of picture-taking people do on their devices. The reader becomes a detective, piecing together the various images to form a narrative that may or may not be true, thus adding complexity and nuance to the verbal narrative.[23]

Carolyn Guyer is the author of another classic hypertext novel, *Quibbling*, first published in 1990 on diskette. The visual spatiality of hypertext plays a major role in conveying her narrative in *Quibbling*. The formats of the text change constantly through time as well as space, very different from the format of the text in a conventional book which never changes. One of the striking uses of Guyer's use of spatial placement is in developing gender attributes. By placing texts about women in boxes separate from those of the men and in proximity to each other, Guyer emphasizes their independence, self-realization, and relationships with each other.[24]

Another aspect of the impact of hypertext narrative is in educational pedagogy. Shelley Jackson was introduced to hypertext literature in 1993, when she was a student in the MFA writing program at Brown University, taking a course with Robert Coover and George Landow. Although Coover and Landow themselves write in conventional form, they were leading proponents of hypertext narrative as the embodiment of postmodern literary theory that disregards conventional linear narrative in favor of simultaneity, disjunction, repetition, and fragmentation as a more accurate way of expressing complex concepts. Believing that students could benefit from exposure to hypertext writing as well as learning conventional narrative traditions, Coover and Landow pioneered using hypertext in the curriculum. One of Coover's innovations was to create an AI environment—a white cube on the interior walls of which were projected a succession of images seen three dimensionally through special eyewear. Coover believed that experiencing such an environment helped release creativity. Although hypertext writing remains a highly precious and limited literary form after the initial reception it received in the 1990s, Coover insists that conventional writing will eventually die and be replaced by some form of narrative based on hypertext.[25]

Jackson portrays the process of composing hypertext narrative as compiling small sketches with no set plan. She began to write *Patchwork Girl* while sitting in George Landow's classroom and listening to him lecture. She began to jot down scraps of text mixed with small drawings. When she looked them over, she saw the shape of the overall storyline emerging from the narratives themselves; she says the tale seemed to write itself.[26]

Using hypertext in writing classes has spread as an educational tool for its ability to empower female, LGBTQI, and BIPOC students to write from their own experience and identity. The intersection between hypertext and feminist pedagogy has made hypertext narrative an integral element in feminist teaching since both reject authoritarianism and hierarchy. Carlton Clark has pointed out the fact that hierarchy itself is embedded in our grammar, in the very way syntax is traditionally taught as phrases or clauses "dependent or subordinate" to other clauses, thus reflecting the patriarchal hierarchical society—racist, sexist, and classist, one that feminism, critical race theory, and queer theory desire to resist and alter. Clark, Laura L. Sullivan, and Mary Hocks, along with others, identify the characteristics of hypertext as freeing students from the constraints of the patriarchal rules for writing in that the text is decentered, with the reader rather than the author controlling the narrative. The linear (Clark uses the term "phallic") structure of a continuous text is altered by recurrence—readers go off in a new direction from the initial text, then return to the text to go in another direction. It is also altered by repetition as when readers return to various text passages from different perspectives, thus viewing passages in new contexts. Clark expresses the process as enabling students to consider possibilities other than standard writing practices: "Once [students] have been exposed to hypertext, . . . the neutrality, invisibility . . . of conventional writing are called into question."[27]

Thus, students who are nonbinary and non-white are liberated from the heteronormative writing structure, and free to create their own structures that reflect their identities rather than the identity of the dominant group. The lack of widespread response to hypertext fiction has meant that it has remained a minor form of contemporary literature. The familiarity with the traditional structure of art works may keep the general public from understanding new art forms. However, as people become more and more caught up in digital culture, they may come to appreciate hypertext works of art.[28]

However, hyperlinks and hypertext themselves are everywhere on the internet. Perhaps their proliferation has created so much visual noise that hypertext fiction, which requires time and concentration, is lost in our urgency for immediate satisfaction. Yet, its influence can be seen in the structures of all the websites and search engines we use, in video games the narratives of which progress through hyperlinks and hypertext, and the digital works created by many artists in the twenty-first century.

Notes

1 The project was conceived by painter Jane Dickson who was then working for Spectacolor, Inc. For support in using the board for noncommercial purposes, she approached the Public Art Fund which was already committed to promoting the work of artists using media technology. Russell Miller in the *Toledo Blade* reported on the project in a column dated February 19, 1984:

> Jane Dickson, a painter, was working for Spectacolor, Inc. as an ad designer and computer programmer when, three and a half years ago, she first thought to use the light board to display noncommercial art. "I picked that title," she said of *Messages to the Public*, "because I thought the propaganda potential from this project was terrific." The board, she noted, was regularly used for "commercial

> propaganda." Dickson sought help from the Public Art Fund, an organization based here and dedicated to taking art out of the galleries and placing it in the city's streets and parks. Project director of the Public Art Fund Jessica Cusick explained, "We're trying to do art that's timely, has a message, is visually potent and is trying to deal with the fine line dividing fine art and commercial art." (Public Art Fund, "Alfredo Jaar: Messages to the Public: A Logo For America," Public Art Fund/Exhibitions, https://www.publicartfund.org/exhibitions/view/messages-to-the-public-jaar/.)

The quotes from Jane Dickson and Jessica Cusick that describe how the project originated and was implemented, were included in this announcement by the Public Art Fund for Alfredo Jaar's exhibition. The quotes are attributed to Russell Miller, but the article by Miller is not available online.

2 For a full list of Holzer's truisms online, see https://fak3r.com/2011/04/02/jenny-holzer-truisms/.

3 Tate Modern, "5 Ways Jenny Holzer Brought Art to the Streets," https://www.tate.org.uk/art/artists/jenny-holzer-1307/5-ways-jenny-holzer-brought-art-streets.

4 Grace Glueck, "And Now a Few Words From Jenny Holzer," *New York Times Magazine*, December 3, 1989, https://www.nytimes.com/1989/12/03/magazine/and-now-a-few-words-from-jenny-holzer.html.

5 Creative Time, "Jenny Holzer: For the City, Projections, 1996–2004," http://creativetime.org/programs/archive/2005/holzer/pastprojects.html.

6 Diane Waldman, *Jenny Holzer*, exhibition catalog (New York: Solomon R. Guggenheim Foundation in association with Harry N. Abrams, 1989), https://archive.org/details/jennyholzer00wald/page/n11/mode/2up.

7 Ibid.

8 Ibid.

9 Storyspace website, http://www.eastgate.com/storyspace/.

10 Sue Barnes, "Hypertext Literacy," *Interpersonal Computing and Technology: An Electronic Journal for the 21st Century* 2, no. 4 (October 1994): 24–36; Carlton Clark, "Surely Teaching Hypertext in the Composition Classroom Qualifies as a Feminist Pedagogy?" *Kairos: A Journal of Rhetoric, Technology, and Pedagogy* 6, no. 2 (Fall 2001); Dene Grigar, "On Evolving and Emerging Literary Forms: A Curatorial Statement For 'Electronic Literature & Its Emerging Forms,'" Electronic Literature & Its Emerging Form at the Library of Congress, April 3–5, 2013, http://dtc-wsuv.org/elit/elit-loc/denes-curatorial-statement/; Steven Johnson, "Why No One Clicked on the Great Hypertext Story," WIRED, April 16, 2013, https://www.wired.com/2013/04/hypertext/; Barbara Page, "Women Writers and the Restive Text: Feminism, Experimental Writing and Hypertext," *Postmodern Culture* 6, no. 2 (January 1996); Laura L. Sullivan, "Wired Women Writing: Towards a Feminist Theorization of Hypertext," *Computers and Composition* 16, no. 1 (1999): 25–54.

11 Shelley Jackson, "Stitch Bitch: The Patchwork Girl," transcript of Jackson's presentation at the Transformations of the Book Conference held at MIT on October 24–25, 1998, http://web.mit.edu/m-i-t/articles/index_jackson.html.
12 Ibid.
13 Ibid.
14 Ibid.
15 Interview by Mark Amerika, "Stitch Bitch: The Hypertext Author As Cyborg-Narrator," HyperX, AltX. http://www.altx.com/hyperx/writerly/jackson.html.
16 *Patchwork Girl* is available through Eastgate, publisher of hypertext fiction, https://www.eastgate.com/catalog/PatchworkGirl.html.
17 Shelley Jackson gave a reading of *Patchwork Girl* on October 18, 2013 at the Electronic Literature Lab (ELL) at Washington State University, Vancouver, sponsored by the Pathfinders Project led by Dene Grigar and Stuart Moulthrop, and funded by the National Endowment for the Humanities. The lecture is available in four parts on YouTube.
18 Judy Malloy, *Women, Art, & Technology* (Cambridge, MA: MIT Press, 2003); "Dorothy Richardson, 1893–1957," Dorothy Richardson website, http://dorothyrichardson.org/biography.htm; Malloy published excerpts about Dorothy Richardson from her journals on The WELL website, https://people.well.com/user/jmalloy/mirclar_whole/room_about.html. The WELL is an online community enabling members to post and exchange ideas. On its website, at https://www.well.com/about-2/, it's described as:

> a . . . destination for conversation and discussion . . . "the world's most influential online community" in a *Wired Magazine* cover story . . . Stewart Brand and Larry Brilliant founded Whole Earth 'Lectronic Link in 1985, starting with a dialog [among] writers and readers of the Whole Earth Review . . . the service was recently purchased to be run by a group of its own long term active members

19 Judy Malloy, "Notes on the Creation of *its name was Penelope*," *The WELL*, https://people.well.com/user/jmalloy/statement.html.
20 Ibid.
21 Judy Malloy, *its name was Penelope*, is available for purchase at Eastgate.com, https://www.eastgate.com/catalog/Penelope.html.
22 Judy Malloy, "Notes."
23 Carolyn Guyer, Introduction to the Eastgate publication of *Patchwork Girl.*
24 Page, "Women Writers and the Restive Text."
25 George Landow, "Hypertext at Brown," CyberArtsWeb, http://www.cyberartsweb.org/cpace/ht/HTatBrown/BrownHT.html; Scott Rettberg, "The American Hypertext Novel and Whatever Became of It," in *Interactive Digital Narrative: History, Theory, and Practice*, ed. Hartmut Koenitz, Gabriele Ferri, Mads Haahr, Diğdem Sezen, and Tonguç İbrahim Sezen (New York: Routledge, 2015), 22–35.

26 Jackson, "Stitch Bitch," interview with Amerika.

27 Clark, "Surely Teaching Hypertext;" Sullivan, "Wired Women Writing;" Mary E. Hocks, "Feminist Interventions in Electronic Environments," *Computers and Composition* 16, no. 1 (1999): 107–19.

28 Mark Amerika, "Stitch Bitch: The Hypertext Author As Cyborg-Femme Narrator," Amerika Online 7, March 16, 1998, https://www.heise.de/tp/features/Amerika-Online-7-3441257.html. For additional reading on the lack of general acceptance of hypertext literature see Matthew Mirapaul, "Beyond Hypertext: Novels With Interactive Animation," Arts Online, *New York Times*, March 5, 2001, https://www.nytimes.com/2001/03/05/books/arts-online-beyond-hypertext-novels-with-interactive-animation.html.

6

Queerness, Race, and Digital Art

Queer theory and critical race theory are philosophic positions in their own right, but their languages, missions, and goals are related to feminist theory. The artists in this chapter identify as artists of color, and/or queer (nonbinary), but their work is inspired by and infused with feminism even though their initial impetus often came from a critique of feminism as focused only on cis white artists. Three characteristics mark their work. First, they are intersectional, going beyond a narrow critique of masculinist gender norms and/or a critique of systemic racism to critique patriarchal society as a whole (use of language, capitalism, government control of the body, the militaristic basis of technology) through the lens of gender and race. Second, they merge writing and art. Third, they are social activists.[1]

Despite the contemporary critique of LGBTQI artists, the American Feminist Art Movement of the 1970s did include openly lesbian artists.[2] The Heresies Collective published important writing on the work of mostly East Coast feminist artists from 1977 to 1993, and one of its first issues was on lesbian artists and writers. The members of the Heresies Collective included key New York cis and lesbian feminist artists of the period such as Miriam Schapiro, Joan Snyder, Mary Beth Edelson, and May Stevens along with leading feminist critics like Lucy Lippard. Each issue had its own editors and the editorial board for the *Heresies* issue on lesbian artists included such well-known lesbian artists as Betsy Damon, Harmony Hammond, Louise Fishman, and Su Friedrich. Harmony Hammond later wrote the first book on lesbian art, essential reading for its documentation of some of the openly lesbian artists of the period who were painters, sculptors, photographers, and performance artists.[3]

The Woman's Building became the center in Los Angeles for lesbian artists. Arlene Raven, with Terry Wolverton, introduced lesbian studies into the core curriculum of the Feminist Studio Workshop (FSW), which she and Judy Chicago had established in 1973.[4]

Women artists working in various European countries or on other continents were undoubtedly lesbians, but without the freedom to declare their sexual orientation, although there are exceptions. Some of the women artists discussed earlier who were innovators in using digital technology may also have been lesbians, but for most, their sexual orientation was less of an issue than their undertakings to feminize digital technology. The 1970s were not a time when the general society accepted sexual variation beyond what has come to be called the heteronormal, the traditional definition of women and men as heterosexual. Artists declaring themselves to be gay or lesbian, or making art addressed to gender issues that were outside the boundaries permitted by the dominant culture, risked ostracization and even physical danger. Furthermore, LGBTQI artists, being excluded from the mainstream, had more difficulty in accessing the equipment needed to create digital art.

However, like the feminist artists discussed earlier, lesbian/bisexual/trans artists discovered that performance and media offered the opportunity to express their ideas more fully than traditional disciplines like painting or sculpture and, while they may not have had access to more elaborate digital equipment, video was available and financially reasonable.

Lynda Benglis's *Female Sensibility* (1973), Barbara Hammer's *Dyketactics* (1974), and Nancy Angelo's and Candace Compton's *Nun and Deviant* (1976) are classic lesbian videos from that era. The advent of portable video cameras enabled women artists, who would not have had the means to produce film, the capacity to express themselves in moving images.

Lynda Benglis's video, *Female Sensibility* features Benglis and her partner, Marilyn Lenkowsky, making love. It seems to belong to the category of heterosexual male pornography popular at the time of women in sexual acts with each other. But media critic Susan Richmond interprets the video as an ironic comment on the discourse raging over whether there could be a "female sensibility" in the making of art. The video is a play on words: female sensibility is women's actual sex.[5]

Barbara Hammer came out as a lesbian in 1974, and as she herself has written, ["she was] off on a motorcycle with a Super-8 camera." *Dyketactics* is divided into two parts: the first shows a group of nude women in a rural setting, dancing, swimming, and touching each other; the second shows Hammer and her partner making love. According to Hammer, *Dyketactics* is "A popular lesbian 'commercial,' 110 images of sensual touching montages in A, B, C, D rolls of 'kinaesthetic' editing." Feminist art historian Jenni Sorkin characterized Hammer's videos of the 1970s as, "the first made by an openly lesbian American filmmaker to explore lesbian identity, desire, and sexuality though avant-garde strategies. Merging the physicality of the female body with that of the film medium, Hammer's films remain memorable for their pioneering articulation of a lesbian aesthetic."[6]

Nancy Angelo went to Los Angeles in 1975 to become a student in the FSW. She became a performance artist and with Cheri Gaulke, Laurel Klick, and Candace Compton, organized the Feminist Art Workers to teach performance art to women in Los Angeles as a way of empowering them to take control of their own lives. Their use of video cameras in teaching led Angelo and Compton to make the video *The Nun and the Deviant.* Angelo had already been performing as a nun in the character of Angelica Furiosa. In their video, they deconstruct the personae that women assume in their lives in order to live in the heteronormative society. At first the nun declares she is a "good woman," and the deviant who is dressed a la Hollywood image of a juvenile delinquent, states that she is a "bad person." Each engages in monologues in which, gradually, they reveal their true identities.[7]

Billed as the only lesbian artist team of the period, Hillary Leone and Jennifer Macdonald worked together from 1989 to 2000. Their installation practice led them into video, and they put together a project called *Passing* (1996), about identity, relating to the need for lesbians of the time to hide who they were. The installation consisted of twelve videos accompanied by a soundtrack. The videos were portraits of people who "passed," meaning that people didn't suspect their true identity, such as Blacks who looked white, lesbians who looked straight, Jews who looked Christian. They parted when Leone moved to Washington, DC and subsequently both moved into other fields. Macdonald became the first openly lesbian executive at the New York Stock Exchange, as Director of Project Management, responsible for all digital projects at the NYSE. Her expertise in digital technology came from her experience as an artist.[8]

Some American lesbian women who worked in the production end of filmmaking in the 1970s helped lesbian artists to create work that met the production standards of the cultural mainstream by providing them with state-of-the-art equipment and facilities. Along with several other lesbian women, Frances Reid in 1975 established Iris Films, one of the most influential of the US lesbian-originated film companies. The first production was a documentary about lesbians with children and their lives, *In the Best Interests of the Children* (1977), produced and directed by Reid. It was a critical success, garnering a Blue Ribbon Award at the American Film Festival.[9]

During the first few decades of digital art, access by artists of color to computer technology was still limited. The early history of LGBTQI artists of color, whose art practice centered on digital technology, still needs to be written, but lesbian digital artists of color, including Blacks from Africa, emerged on the stage of the internet and new media dynamically in the first decades of the twenty-first century. After the year 2000 the freedom to express one's nonbinary identity both as an individual and in one's art increased substantially worldwide, and the internet offered the opportunity to make one's mark felt globally, thus also contravening restrictions in one's own country.

Alex Mawimbi, formerly Ato Malinda, who was born in Kenya, raised partly in the United States, and now lives in Europe, identifies herself as queer and intersectional. Her videos, performances, and installations are focused on gender as part of a cluster of concepts including race, class, and postcolonialism.

She changed her name, which had carried the memory of her abusive father. Like others in her generation, Mawimbi has expanded the use of digital technology to include sound as well as video, performance, and installation. In an installation for the exhibition, *Show Me Your Archive and I will Tell You Who Is in Power*, held in Ghent in 2017, Mawimbi created *Four-Year-Old Temptress?* In a mirror meant to evoke a sense of one that might have belonged to her mother, the viewer sees a flat screen with a video of the artist who, alternately singing and speaking, tells how she was abused by her mother and aunt who were on drugs. Another complex piece is *Mshoga Mpya, or the New Homosexual*, first performed in Dakar at the 2014 Dak'Art Biennial, for which the artist constructed a cubicle. Mawimbi is seated on the floor with the rainbow colors of the gay pride flag painted on her face. Only one viewer at a time can enter the cubicle. The viewer sits on a chair in front of Mawimbi and dons earphones that relate harrowing real life stories of queer people in Africa told in Mawimbi's voice. The texts are also printed on the walls of the cubicle. Mawimbi invites participants to erase her words and write their own stories.[10]

Lesbian-identifying German artist Anne Imhof received the Gold Lion Award for best pavilion at the 2017 Venice Biennale. Imhof's work, *Faust*, was an installation/performance presented in the German pavilion. Much has been written about this work but mainly about its formal aspects—the choreography, the sound, and the costuming as well as her use of space but also commenting on the unease and foreboding that the performance produces. However, the performance should also be interpreted for its innovation in digital technology and its focus on gender. In terms of digital technology, Imhof makes use of cell phones to conduct her choreography. While the performers seem to be moving about accidentally and engaging in random acts, they are connected by smartphones to Imhof, and she is giving them choreography directions through their phones. In terms of gender, she presents the story of Faust in the context of the alienation felt by queer people and others who are oppressed by the white heterosexual majority within the patriarchal society. It should be noted that her life partner, artist, Eliza Douglas, who appears in Faust, is also her partner in production.

Faust consisted of a four-hour performance. Imhof altered Germany's Beaux Arts-period pavilion with a wire fence around the perimeter, thus giving it the appearance of a forbidden place, off limits, which visitors could not enter freely. She also altered the interior by building a glass floor through which one could see performers underneath. Her group of performers moved about vertically as well as horizontally at various heights above the glass floor as well as on the surface and underneath, perhaps a metaphor for the complex hierarchies of class, gender, and race in patriarchal societies.

The performers proceed in a slow zombie-like trance for the most part, kneeling, climbing, at times threatening each other. They look androgynous and are costumed in the style of young adults at the end of the second decade of the twenty-first century—in dark-toned athletic sports gear. Various props such as gun pellets, fetish dog collars, and teaspoons of the kind used by drug addicts suggest violence and drugs. A soundtrack emits eerie music and lyrics that convey the alienation of all who do not fit into the structure of the patriarchal society.

Adding to the sense of oppression, Doberman pinschers roam the space both inside and out, referencing the dog who follows Faust home in Goethe's narrative and once in Faust's study turns into the devil, Mephistopheles. The Doberman pinschers also are reminiscent of the dogs that patrolled the death camps in Nazi Germany, suggesting the policing by patriarchal culture to enforce conformity and suppress dissent and rebellion among the alienated.

In her address on receiving the Gold Lion Award, Imhof made her feminism explicit but at the same time extended it to include gender fluidity: "My work is a transparent view of the past . . . [but also] stands for the future, for the right to be different, for gender non-conformity, and the pride to be a woman in this world . . . we will have to make decisions in this future, of what to stand up for or when to raise our fists."[11]

Video continues to be a medium of choice for the next generation of feminist and queer artists in the twenty-first century, often combined with social networking distribution. One of the queer artists who has been a leader in using social networking for her work is Jennifer Chan, who creates humorous short videos deconstructing masculinist self-representation through her queer lens. In *Masculinities and Male Bodies on the Internet* (2013) she describes the various ways in which males post images of themselves digitally. Satirizing dry academic lectures on sex, Chan makes up fake social science categories: the selfie, the head shot, the "hey girl" look; the shot where the man is doing something interesting like playing the guitar; the "headless horseman" shot, meaning, the torso cut off at the neck; imitations of celebrities; and the sexual come-on of the "dick pic." The humor enhances the message.[12]

One of the most ingenious of queer artists is Zach Blas. One of Blas's early works from 2008 seizes the imagination in a very simple way by focusing on the most common application of electronic technology in everyday life—the electric outlet and plug. He makes the point that the plug and the outlet, and the language used in describing the connection, mirrors the binary, heterosexual definition of gender in patriarchal culture: the plug is designated as male, and the outlet, female. He satirizes the consumerism of patriarchal society by imagining products that would transform electrical connections from their heteronormative configuration. Calling them *ENgenderingGenderChangers: Connections for Disconnections* (Plate 15), he mocks corporate marketing techniques through an elaborate imitation of an advertising campaign, treating the objects as a line of commercial products under the title, *Queer Technologies*. The various connectors in *ENgenderingGenderChangers* are packaged the way electrical components are sold by Apple and other office supply/media communication stores—in packages that hang from hooks. In addition, there is a website for *Queer Technology* products that emulates corporate marketing.[13]

In later work, Blas expands his queer horizons to envision a dystopian future. *Contra-Internet* (2014–18) is an installation consisting of a short film, glass sculptures, and a website that uses the structure of hypertext literature to include a vast amount of written material critiquing late capitalist culture that one can explore by clicking on hyperlinks, hypertext, and even on Google-like menus. Sometimes the links on the menus even activate themselves. In the meantime, a soundtrack entertains the reader. The short film *Jubilee 2033*, included in the installation, is a diatribe against the power of the internet. The ironic protagonist in the film is the novelist, Ayn Rand, who celebrated capitalism at its extreme. Rand, accompanied by such figures as economist Alan Greenspan, longtime head of the Federal Reserve, considered the epitome of capitalist experts, ingests LSD and embarks on an acid trip to the future. The narrative is based on Derek Jarman's 1978 queer punk film *Jubilee*, a critique of the British empire, made in response to Queen Elizabeth II's Jubilee in 1977. Jarman's narrative takes Queen Elizabeth I guided by the spirit Ariel (from Shakespeare's *Tempest*) into a future where Queen Elizabeth II has been murdered and the United Kingdom is disintegrating. In Blas's film, Rand and her groupies are transported not by a spirit, but by artificial intelligence to a disintegrating Silicon Valley, where they witness the destruction of the Apple, Facebook, and Google campuses and the deaths of the formerly powerful men who ran the corporations. At the end, emotionally battered by what they have learned, they retreat to Silicon Beach where the sand is now mixed with plastic remnants.[14]

Another influential queer artist (formerly male) that Blas has collaborated with at times, is transgender artist micha cárdenas. Her performance, *Becoming Dragon* (2009), is autobiographical, based on cárdenas's own experience in gender transition when she underwent hormone treatments and surgery to transform herself from a man to a woman biologically. The performance satirizes the requirement that when an individual declares that he or she wants to change gender, there is a one-year requirement to live as if he/she has already made the transition before being allowed to undergo gender-change surgery. cárdenas imagines that instead of "Gender Confirmation Surgery," there could be "Species Reassignment Surgery." She makes it dramatic by spending 365 hours living as a dragon. *Becoming Dragon* is a mix of live performance and animation. The audience sees cárdenas with her mask at the same time that they see her dragon self in *Second Life* (a virtual world that a viewer can join and explore through any digital device).[15]

In her artwork, the fluidity of passage from one gender to another becomes a metaphor for a world of infinite realities that slip and slide into each other. cárdenas envisions a Utopian world in which human beings would conduct their lives fully immersed in fusion between the offline and virtual universes, a condition which would allow them a fulfilling existence, free from the constraints of the patriarchal society—binary, hierarchic, dominated by the powerful, divided between the haves and the have-nots. cárdenas names it the "transreal," meaning that the virtual or digital world is as "real" to us now as the offline world which we have always considered the "real" world:[16]

> cárdenas's work is also related to world events. The performance, *virus.circus.mem*, is a response to the HIV/AIDS crisis. cárdenas critiques the way in which medicine and health are regulated by the medical profession rather than by the individuals treated. The performance involves sexual acts. cárdenas uses various instruments to help her partner Elle Mehrmand reach orgasm through masturbation, thus preventing the transmission of infection that might occur if they were to have intercourse. The intent is to play with the way the medical profession in its supposed wisdom, proposed abstinence to avoid infection, thus denying people the pleasure of sex. By using instruments to reach sexual satisfaction, people could still experience pleasure.[17]

cárdenas views Shu Lea Cheang's multimedia installations which also respond to social and political factors, as having a major influence on her work. Cheang, from Taiwan, but living in the United States, has critiqued the negative impact of the heteronormative society not only on LGBTQI rights, but also on other crucial issues such as political oppression, environmental destruction, and individual freedom. Cheang, like Blas and cárdenas, makes innovative uses of digital technology to communicate her provocative messages.

A typical example of Cheang's work is the 1994 film *Fresh Kill*, in which the story is constantly interrupted by fake commercials emulating the style of commercial television. Cheang used that format to critique the way television mixes news, advertisements, and entertainment, giving everything an equivalency and turning what we see and hear into meaningless background noise. The name comes from Fresh Kills, one of the largest landfills on Staten Island, now closed. Cheang dropped the letter "s" in her title, exposing the irony in using a name that evokes a pleasant picnic beside a stream (kill is another word for a brook) for a garbage dump that defiles the environment. *Fresh Kill* addresses the issues to which we should be paying attention, the ones that plague our contemporary world—racism, LGBTQI rights, government surveillance, and climate contamination. At first glance the film seems a family saga out of a conventional soap opera but instead of building the story around a young heterosexual white couple, typical of conventional television soap opera, Cheang disrupts the stereotype by creating a fictional family consisting of a young lesbian couple, whose relatives are white, Black, and even Native American. One of them works in a sushi restaurant named Nagy Saky, where it turns out the fish are nuclear contaminated, giving everyone who eats it a phosphorescent glow.[18]

The Guggenheim Museum commission to Cheang for *Brandon*, in 1998, was particularly significant because it was the first time a museum commissioned a work designed for the internet, marking institutional recognition of internet art as a new medium. Brandon Teena, born Teena Renae Brandon, a young transgender man, was raped and murdered in Nebraska when a gang discovered that he was anatomically female. Cheang combined web sites, hyperlinks, chat rooms, and animation to tell Brandon's story, using the event to create a dialog on gender, break down social assumptions on sexuality, and raise questions about crime and punishment. Cheang also connected the virtual and offline worlds by partnering with the Society for Old and New Media, an organization in the Netherlands, to mount events with live audiences that were also broadcast on the internet.[19]

Another queer social activist is the British/Australian artist, Jesse Darling, who was born female, but now identifies as male. His digital art practice (he is also a sculptor) is a complex mix based on wide reading in queer and feminist literature, a deep knowledge of pop music, and participation in social activism.

In his video, *Darling's Room*, he transforms pop music song writer and performer Drake's iconic *Marvin's Room* (2011), the lyrics of which express a macho lament and misogyny, into a statement of his agency as an individual, as queer, and as an artist. Drake speaks of how much sex he's had and how all women seem the same whereas Darling declares, "Avant-garder than your hard-on like I've got game yeah. I'm JD, you know."[20]

Another aspect of Darling's digital art practice is his transformation of the simple blog into an art form. From 2011 on, Darling has maintained a blog on Tumblr. The entries are a trip into Darling's mind. He comments on texts by authors he admires, posts photographs of his own offline sculptures and installations as well as images of work by other feminist/queer artists and expounds his own views. In reading and viewing the entries, it is apparent how much his blog is related to hypertext. Like hypertext, viewers control the narrative, clicking wherever (thus the title of his blog, *Brave New Whatever*). Upon clicking on the archive button, one enters the years of Darling's entries. And upon connecting to a particular entry, one enters a seemingly infinite journey of links, with no conclusion. In some cases, there are hundreds of entries in a single box. The lack of hierarchy becomes a metaphor for discarding the binary.

Darling himself is disabled by a neurological disease that paralyzed his right side, thus making *Darling's Room*, even more meaningful in relation to Darling's own life. In 2013, Darling established the Kitson Road Living Project in London, a communal home for artists.

Black trans artists have had an increasing impact on queer digitally based art, adding their own perspective. Vaginal Davis has played an influential role in the music world as well as the visual arts. Born with both male and female genitals, she was allowed to keep both by her mother, contrary to the wishes of the physicians. Davis has declared that it was a gift from her mother to allow her to be both male and female. She became an artist in the 1970s when she was introduced by a cousin into the Los Angeles punk rock scene which at the time included many women and LGBTQI people. Calling herself Pussy Washington, Davis, with her friend Greg Hernandez, began to use tape recorders to talk and sing over existing recordings. She changed her name to Vaginal Davis in honor of her heroine, Angela Davis, and became the drag front performer for several art-punk bands like the Afro Sisters, who were known for mixing drag with visuals along with the music. Along with other Black performers and artists, Davis was driven out of the punk music scene when it began to be taken over by second-generation punk bands that celebrated macho values. She began to produce queer zines on the copy machine at UCLA where she worked. In 1982

Davis opened an art gallery called HAG. Davis says she opened it in order to meet potential lovers who would be attracted by an art gallery. Throughout her career, Davis has worked in video as well as performance. She has been described as a "drag terrorist." Among her drag personae are characters like Clarence, whom Davis mocks for his white suprematism.

One of Davis's best known videos is *That Fertile Feeling Part I and Part II* (1982), a narrative in which Davis and Fertile La Toyah Jackson with whom she had performed live as the Afro Sisters, star in a video in which La Toyah Jackson is denied treatment when Davis drives her to a hospital (the hospital won't admit her because she has no health insurance) and is forced to have the baby in her boyfriend's apartment (he appears naked with an apron around his neck). Fertile is, as Davis declares, "the first woman to have eleven-tuplets!" The videos satirize the health system in the United States and how Blacks are excluded as well as stereotypes of Black fertility. The video was distributed through Davis's video magazine published as a VHS cassette, *Fertile La Toyah Jackson Video Magazine.*[21]

Davis says that she was excluded from gay and lesbian film festivals for years because her work was not considered serious enough. She looks down on the LGBTQI powers that determine which films are shown, as assimilated, watered-down queers who cannot admit the realities of the actual gay community (Plate 16).[22]

Like Vaginal Davis, Juliana Huxtable was also born intersex. She was mostly identified as male, but transitioned to female after graduating from Bard College. Huxtable's mother worked in information technology so Juliana grew up immersed in technology. She says that she could escape her offline world and develop her identity and her art through the digital world. She wanted to be a painter and poet and although she also continued to paint offline, by nine or ten years old, she also began to use Microsoft Paint. During her high school years she was involved in a Photoshop online program for young people through which she learned artistic skills but also became part of a social networking community.

She started studying art at Bard College but stopped because she was told that she was "trapped in her identity" whereas no white student was ever critiqued on the basis of race. She was also told that she was "obsessed with technique," another put down, since the construction of Blackness in the white society is associated with manual labor rather than intellectual activity. Instead, she studied gender and postcolonialist theory.

After graduation from Bard, she came to New York where she began to find her identity as an artist. She says that she became obsessed with Tumblr as a mode in which she could create images that could be viewed in a context open to dialog. She also started to participate in New York club nightlife. Through dressing up, she began the performativity which is integral to her art practice. Her costumes were the start of narrative associations. As she relates, if she was listening to Bach, she might begin to think of ruffles. She began to analyze her impulses. Why was she creating a particular costume? She also began collaborating with a photographer so that her costumes mutated into art rather than just transitory ensembles.

The costumes led to her thinking about the desire to connect with history. She points out the fact that white people can explore their histories whereas there is no history for Black people who were taken from Africa as slaves. She demonstrates how the aestheticizing of history leads to privileging of white males by referring, for instance, to the charts that picture biological time—the ape gradually turning into a white man.

At the same time that Huxtable was creating performances and videos that dissected white history, she was also creating fantasy images by painting her skin and decorating her nude body. These images are based on a form of popular images that are generated for Black consumption—Black Jesuses and Black nudes who exert sexual force. Huxtable interprets these as images of Black pride and power—often the nudes are seen against backgrounds with black panthers, for instance. Building on that tradition, Huxtable created a series of digital photographs showing herself in various positions, costumes, and jewelry—boots, large earrings—conveying a militancy and power. At the same time, they also have queer implications with their science fiction appearance, suggesting the fantasy world in which the binary is extinguished and queerness can thrive.[23]

Mexican/American Xandra Ibarra, also known as La Chica Boom, a reference to the over-the-top Latinx performer/Hollywood star, Carmen Miranda (1909–55), is not a trans artist but she is nonbinary. Like Huxtable, she uses explicit sexual imagery; like Davis, her performances and videos include clips from the pop music scene and street language. Her costumes, makeup, and dance routines are in the outrageously exaggerated style of drag queens and old-time burlesque stars—false eyelashes are at least two inches long, lips as bright red as possible, and she makes the tassels on her nipples twirl. Because of her blatant display of female sexuality, she has suffered harassment including having her act closed by the police (Plate 17). Her use of drag queen and burlesque imagery deconstructs gender and race stereotypes by suggesting that the gender and race categories of the patriarchal society are as fake as the costumes and makeup of theater.[24]

The LGBTQI digital artists discussed in this chapter are only the tip of the iceberg. They represent a group of artists whose art practice has been groundbreaking and influential in both content and use of digital technology. There simply is not enough space in this book to document their work comprehensively.

Notes

1 Kimberle Crenshaw, "Mapping the Margins, Intersectionality, Identity Politics and Violence Against Women of Color," *Stanford Law Review* 43, no. 6 (July 1991): 1241–99.

2 From the late 1990s, queer and nonbinary have commonly come to be used along with the earlier terms, lesbian, gay, or bisexual. Depending on the context, both sets are utilized.

3 All issues of the *Heresies* magazine are available online at Heresies Magazine Collection, Internet Archive, https://archive.org/details/heresies_magazine; Harmony Hammond, *Lesbian Art in America: A Contemporary History* (New York: Random House, 2000).

4 Sondra Hale and Terry Wolverton, eds., *From Site to Vision: The Woman's Building in Contemporary Culture* (Los Angeles: Otis College of Art and Design, 2011).

5 Susan Richmond, "The Ins and Outs of *Female Sensibility*, a 1973 Video by Lynda Benglis," *Camera Obscura* 23, no. 3 (69) (2008): 80–108.

6 Barbara Hammer, *Dyketactics*, 1974, 16 mm on video, black and white, color, sound, 4:00, available to rent at https://www.eai.org/titles/dyketactics. For a trailer: https://barbarahammer.com/films/dyketactics/; Barbara Hammer, "On Times in Women's Cinema," in "Lesbian Art and Artists," special issue, *Heresies: A Feminist Publication on Art and Politics* 1, no. 3 (September 1977): 87–9.

7 Erika Suderburg, "Nun Notes and Deviant Longings," in *Alternative Projections: Experimental Film in Los Angeles, 1945–1980*, ed. David E. James and Adam Hyman (New Barnet, UK: John Libbey, 2015), 268–78; Cecilia Dougherty, "Stories from a Generation: Video Art at the Woman's Building," in *From Site to Vision: The Woman's Building in Contemporary Culture*, ed. Terry Wolverton and Sondra Hale (Los Angeles: Otis College of Art and Design, 2011), 303–25; For a detailed account of the narrative, see Kyna Jones, "Notes on Nun and Deviant, 1976, Nancy Angelo and Candace Compton," Hugh McCarney, Communication Department, Western Connecticut State University, May 11, 1998, http://people.wcsu.edu/mccarneyh/fva/A/Nun_Deviant.html.

8 Leone & Macdonald website, https://www.leoneandmacdonald.com/; Cathie Ericson, "Mover and Shaker, Jennifer Macdonald: Director of Project Management, NYSE," The Glass Hammer, June 25, 2015, https://theglasshammer.com/2015/06/25/mover-and-shaker-jennifer-macdonald-director-of-product-management-nyse/;

Eric Fredericksen, "Two of a Kind, the Art World's World," The Stranger, July 15, 1999, https://www.thestranger.com/seattle/two-of-a-kind/Content?oid=1538.

9 Frances Reid, "Iris Films, Documenting the Lives of Lesbians," in "Lesbian Art and Artists," special issue, *Heresies: A Feminist Publication on Art and Politics* 1, no. 3 (September 1977): 100–1; "Frances Reid, Filmmaker," Women Make Movies, https://www.wmm.com/filmmaker/Frances+Reid/; Irisfilms.org, http://www.irisfilms.org/credits/; Frances Reid, Elizabeth Stevens, Cathy Zheutlin, *In the Best Interest of the Children*, 1977, 53:00, available through Iris Films.

10 Alex Mawimbi (also known as Ato Malinda), "Mshoga Mpya, or the New Homosexual," live performance at Brass, Centre Culturel de Forest in Brussels, 2015, posted by ArtLife10 June 3, 2018, YouTube video 7:40, https://www.youtube.com/watch?v=I6R_MNmVhrY; Jelle Bouwhuis, "Alex Mawimbi, Displaced Artist Formerly Known As . . ." Africanah, February 2, 2019, https://africanah.org/alex-mawimbi/.

11 Anne Imhof, "Germany—Anne Imhof—Faust—Venice Biennale 2017," video, YouTube, posted by ArtLike, March 4, 2018, https://www.youtube.com/watch?v=zNQt7ZlLuuM; "Anne Imhof: 'Sex' at the Art Institute of Chicago," video of performance on view May 30–June 1, 2019, sponsored by the Goethe-Institut Chicago. It was Imhof's first solo exhibition in the United States; it was performed at the Tate Modern, London, March 22–31, 2019, posted by Goethe-Institut Chicago, June 24, 2019, https://www.youtube.com/watch?v–VrMAGHhXuk; Adrian Searle, "Anne Imhof, 'Sex, But Not As You Know It,'" *Guardian* (US edition), March 27, 2019, https://www.theguardian.com/artanddesign/2019/mar/27/anne-imhof-interview-sex-performance-art-tate-modern; Lotta Volkova, "Anne Imhof Is Creating Hard-Core Performance Pieces that Speak to the Anxieties of a New Generation," Interview Magazine, March 7, 2019, https://www.interviewmagazine.com/art/anne-imhof-is-creating-hard-core-performance-pieces-that-speak-to-the-anxieties-of-a-new-generation.

12 nokiabae, "Masculinities and Male Bodies on the Internet, Artist Talk by Jennifer Chan for Arcadia Missa," Vimeo, 15:41, December 2, 2012, https://nokiabae.tumblr.com/post/122472201159/masculinities-and-male-bodies-on-the-internet; Anne Hirsch, "Artist Profile: Jennifer Chan," Rhizome, December 18, 2014, https://rhizome.org/editorial/2014/dec/18/artist-profile-jennifer-chan/; Jennifer Chan, "Why Are There No Great Net Artists?" 2011, Mouchette, May 2012, http://about.mouchette.org/wp-content/uploads/2012/05/Jennifer_Chan2.pdf.

13 Zach Blas, "ENgenderingGenderChangers / Sketches," http://users.design.ucla.edu/~zblas/thesis_website/gender_changers/gc_sketches.html; Jacob Gaboury, "Interview with Zach Blas, 'QT, Queer Technologies,'" Rhizome, August 18, 2010, https://rhizome.org/editorial/2010/aug/18/interview-with-zach-blas/.

14 Zach Blas, "Contra Internet Commissioned by Art in General, Curated by Laura Ptak," YouTube, 4:48, posted by Arte Fuse, March 5, 2018, https://www.youtube.com/watch?v=tYBIiqfnQo0. *Jubilee 2033* is available through the Video Data Bank.

See the trailer at: http://www.vdb.org/titles/contra-internet-jubilee%C2%A02033. Another trailer and stills from *Jubilee 2033*, hypertext links for other parts of the Contra-Internet installation, Blas's description of the project can be viewed at: https://zachblas.info/works/contra-internet/.

15 See Zach Blas's website: https://zachblas.info/.

16 For concise information on cárdenas's life and art practice, see Ernie Grimm, "UCSD Pays for Trans-Species Project, My Gender Is Bunny," *San Diego Reader*, March 25, 2009, https://web.archive.org/web/20090401190903/https://www.sandiegoreader.com/news/2009/mar/25/my-gender-bunny/.

17 micha cárdenas, Elle Mehrmand, Amy Sara Carroll, Ricardo Dominguez, Brian Holmes, James Morgan, Allucquére Rosanne Stone, and Stelarc, *The Transreal: Political Aesthetics of Crossing Realities*, ed. Zach Blas and Wolfgang Schirmacher (New York: Atropos, 2011): 108–20.

18 Shu Lea Cheang, "Fresh Kill," 1994, video 18:41, color, stereo, Video Data Bank, trailer on VDB website, https://www.vdb.org/titles/fresh-kill; Lawrence Chua, "Shu Lea Cheang," interview, *BOMB Magazine* 54, January 1, 1996

19 "Brandon (1998–99) by Shu Lea Cheang. A Video Navigation of the Restored Web Artwork," YouTube, 24:18, posted by Guggenheim Museum, May 11, 2017, https://www.youtube.com/watch?v=qq2_t3U_f9U; "Shu Lea Cheang on *Brandon*," interview with Shu Lea Cheang by Yin Ho, Rhizome, May 10, 2012, https://rhizome.org/editorial/2012/may/10/shu-lea-cheang-on-brandon/; "Shu Lea Cheang, *Brandon*," Solomon R. Guggenheim Museum, https://www.guggenheim.org/artwork/15337.

20 Drake, *Marvin's Room* lyrics, https://www.google.com/search?q=marvin%27s+room+lyrics+by+drake&oq—arvin%27s+Room+lyrics+by+Drake&aqs=chrome.0.0l2.10483j0j4&sourceid=chrome&ie=UTF-8; for Jesse Darling's satire on Drake, see Kimmo Modig, *Darling's Room*, lyrics, https://genius.com/Jesse-darling-darlings-room-lyrics.

21 Vaginal Davis, www.vaginaldavis.com.

22 José Esteban Muñoz, " 'The White to Be Angry': Vaginal Davis's Terrorist Drag," *Social Text* 52/53 (Fall/Winter 1997); Vaginal Davis and Fertile La Toya Jackson, *That Fertile Feeling*, Parts I and II, YouTube, video, 1986, 4:52 and 4:14, posted by John O'Shea, May 20, 2008, https://www.youtube.com/watch?v=Pbks6cZyBgA and https://www.youtube.com/watch?v=-6Ej9inqGg0&t=2s.

23 Juliana Huxtable, lecture, Visiting Artists Program, School of the Art Institute of Chicago, YouTube, 1:28:58, posted by SAIC, July 18, 2017, https://www.youtube.com/watch?v=eG5soJNJa4k; Aisha Harris, "Juliana Huxtable's Next Chapter," T Presents, *New York Times Magazine*, August 10, 2020, https://www.nytimes.com/2020/08/10/t-magazine/juliana-huxtable.html; Juliana Huxtable interviewed by Maria Brito, "Artist Juliana Huxtable on Transcending Limitations of Gender," The C-Files, YouTube video, 13:35, posted by All-Arts TV, November 11, 2019, https://

www.youtube.com/watch?v=fJYEUOwA4fc&list=PLfGNG80kNngfrOJjmQKxKFvkxytVJ4xoK&index=4&t=0s&app=desktop.

24 Xandra Ibarra, http://www.XandraIbarra.com; Madeleine Seidel, "Xandra Ibarra: *Forever Sidepiece*," *The Brooklyn Rail*, October 2019, https://brooklynrail.org/2019/10/artseen/Forever-SidepieceXandra-Ibarra; Xandra Ibarra interviewed by Andy Campbell, Artforum, August 27, 2019, https://www.artforum.com/interviews/xandra-ibarra-80626.

7

The Avatar

An avatar, according to the dictionary, is an image that is used to represent a "real" person in the virtual world of the internet and computers. We are familiar with avatars in science fiction films and television, and many video games require would-be players to create avatars to participate in the game.

Feminist artists use avatars to protest the sexism, racism, and other practices within the patriarchal society that limit individual freedom and create the divide between the dominant power and the other. They first used avatars in live performance, but quickly made use of video as soon as it became inexpensive and easy to use, partly to document their performances, and partly because video offered the opportunity to expand expression and increase audiences.

Of those artists in the 1970s generation who used avatars, New York artist Betsy Damon and California artist Eleanor Antin are two of the most influential. Damon's performance as the *7000 Year Old Woman* was first performed in 1975. Subsequently throughout the 1970s Damon gave the performance in cities throughout the United States and Europe. Damon painted her face white and her lips black and hung 420 bags containing sixty pounds of flour colored with reds and earth colors over her entire body. She then proceeded to walk within a defined circle (she called it a woman's space) cutting the bags and spreading the flour as she walked until they were empty. She wrote in the Lesbian Art and Artists issue of *Heresies*, "The piece is about time . . . and women's relationship to time past. A woman sixty years old is maybe twenty times more burdened than the thirty-year-old by her story."[1]

Antin played both male and female roles in her avatar performances, raising doubts about male power, exposing gender stereotypes, and questioning female subjection. As the King of Solana Beach, Antin, made up with a beard and a costume that resembled a tattered remnant of what a French king of the past might wear, walked around the neighborhoods of Solana Beach to visit his/her subjects and see how they were doing. Her pitiful king was a reminder that men became kings through inheritance or chance, rather than through any kingly attributes of their own. Antin's avatar, Antinova, was the most successful ballerina of the Ballets Russe but when she became old and couldn't dance any more, she was destitute to the point that the only employment she could obtain was starring in pornographic films (Antin portrayed Antinova as a woman of color and was criticized for using black face by Jamaican/American writer Michelle Cliff, who accused Antin of appropriating Black culture). Antin made videos of these performances which are available today.[2]

Lynn Hershman Leeson, has also created avatars since the early 1970s. It is Hershman Leeson who moved the avatar emphatically from the live performance arena into the realm of digital technology. Roberta Breitmore was Hershman Leeson's first avatar, but Hershman Leeson anticipated her in *The Dante Hotel* installation of 1973–4, one of the first art works to be a site-specific installation. It was set up in a real hotel room in the rundown Dante Hotel in San Francisco.[3]

Hershman Leeson placed newspaper ads to draw visitors. When they came to see the room, there was evidence of people living in the room—cosmetics and articles of clothing left around. Adding to the sense of being in the room of real people, there were two life-sized mannequins in the bed, one with a face blackened by some unknown incident. A hidden tape player emitted sounds of breathing to augment the sense that they were real individuals who were asleep. *The Dante Hotel* opened on November 30, 1973 and was taken down on August 31, 1974 by the authorities who were, according to Hershman Leeson, notified that there were dead bodies in the room. Hershman Leeson says she had intended it to go on forever as she herself writes, "gathering dust."[4]

She says that she then invented Roberta Breitmore. According to Roberta Mock, professor of performance studies at University of Plymouth, UK, Hershman Leeson states that she based the name on a character in a short story by Joyce Carol Oates, "Passions and Meditations," published in the *Partisan Review*. The story is told through letters. In one, we learn that Roberta Bright is stalking a composer. One letter includes a classified ad placed by Roberta Bright in the *Village Voice* seeking contact which her victim has ignored. Roberta Bright originally introduces herself as a 26-year-old woman, but then begins signing her letters, R. Bright, writing that she is older, and not a woman. She writes to her composer saying that he has seen her on the street, possibly as a beggar he has passed, or a man in a blue suit who has politely allowed him to precede him into a restaurant.

Mock also discusses the name itself as indicating both Oates's and Hershman Leeson's intent, Roberta being the female variant on the name Robert, meaning "bright fame," and the idea of brightness is of course, also echoed in the last name. At the same time, Roberta is also a "black hole," meaning she is a collapsed bright star. Mock gleans this interpretation from Hershman Leeson's notes for Roberta which are in the Roberta Breitmore collection at the Whitworth Art Gallery, University of Manchester, England. The black hole reference, Mock writes, perhaps means that Roberta Breitmore is an invention, not real, but also it can mean an individual who is a cipher, referring to women's lack of agency in the male world.[5]

Roberta Breitmore existed from 1974 to 1978. Hershman Leeson has her undertake offline-life activities, opening a bank account in Breitmore's name, applying for credit cards, renting an apartment, seeing a psychiatrist, and even participating in Weight Watchers. She advertises in the newspapers for a roommate, receives forty-three responses, and writes back to twenty-seven of them. She has her own clothing, makeup, handwriting. Finally, Hershman Leeson kills her off (Hershman Leeson refers to the killing as an exorcism) in a ritual at the grave of Lucrezia Borgia at the Palazzo del Diamanti, Ferrara, Italy in which Roberta Breitmore is transformed into air, earth, and water.[6]

Hershman Leeson produced notes, photographs, various documents, and other invented ephemera to create the illusion that Roberta Breitmore was a living being—including, an assumed identity, and voyeuristic details. Toward the end, Hershman Leeson asked several people to dress as Roberta. A seemingly photographic self-portrait of Roberta shows Hershman Leeson made up as Roberta, but everything is askew—the eyeglasses are crooked, the wig is ajar, the makeup is extremely heavy. It's as if Hershman Leeson is / is not Roberta Breitmore (Plate 18).

Leeson went on to create a digital archive of *The Dante Hotel* and to create new work using a digital technology-based Roberta. According to Mock, Hershman Leeson, in addition to working with gender and identity issues, is concerned with posterity and by implication in the concept of time and immortality in her creation of avatars. Hershman Leeson worked with digital experts at Stanford to recreate *The Dante Hotel* in *Second Life*, the virtual world that a viewer can enter from a laptop, cell phone, or other digital device. Viewers can join *Second Life*, create an avatar, and move the avatar through the landscape of *Second Life* to the Dante Hotel.

Hershman Leeson went on to form two dolls whose eyes are cameras, *CyberRoberta* and *Tillie, the Telerobotic Doll*, collectively named by Hershman Leeson, the *Dollie Clones* (the sheep, Dolly, had just been cloned). When they were exhibited, viewers could manipulate the dolls' heads to see various parts of the gallery in which they were placed through the dolls' eyes. The dolls could also exchange information, thus as in Hershman Leeson's words, expanding "the possibilities of singular identity into a networked trajectory composed of flowing data that eats itself, cannibalizing in the process information that mutates and is re-expressed in unpredictable ways."[7]

Feminist artists of color have found the avatar a useful stratagem. Two African American feminist artists Howardena Pindell and Adrian Piper, are crucial figures in raising the issues of racism and sexism in the art world. While each worked in a variety of art disciplines, they both worked in performance and created avatars on video.

Howardena Pindell's video, *Free, White, and 21* (Plate 19), was made in 1980, just after Pindell had left the Museum of Modern Art New York where she had worked since 1967 after finishing her MFA at Yale (she applied for fifty teaching positions and was rejected at all fifty), beginning as a curatorial assistant and becoming Associate Curator, Prints and Drawings by the time she departed. After leaving MoMA, she had begun teaching at Stony Brook University and was in a car riding to work when she was in a terrible automobile accident. After the accident she had trouble remembering people and incidents from her past. She says that "I decided I was not going to stop working . . . I started to do works that were autobiographical. My feeling was, I could be dead tomorrow."[8]

In the video she recounts the story of her life and the various racist incidents she experienced, such as being shut out of representation at New York galleries because of her color and being denied a job at Time Life along with all the other applicants of color. While telling the story, she keeps interrupting herself with her face now covered in a white mask and wearing a blond wig. This white avatar makes comments such as "I have never had experiences like that. But, of course, I am free, white, and 21." Pindell, not to be put down by the white male establishment, managed her own career rather than succumbing to the racism in the art world. Among other accomplishments she was one of the founders of A.I.R. Gallery, the first feminist cooperative gallery, established in 1972.

Adrian Piper introduced race and gender into conceptual art practice. Her best-known early performances, the *Mythic Being* series, are a venture into the possibilities that moving image technology offers for avatar performances.

The *Mythic Being* videos (1973–5) are an example of Piper's dual concern. In these short videos, Piper transforms herself into a hip-looking young Black man with a mustache, sunglasses, and an Afro. Speaking in the video through this Black male avatar, she questions both racism and sexism simultaneously by asking viewers what would happen if what she says as a woman, instead, is said by a man. Piper uses phrases and sentences from the journals she wrote as a teenager for the texts. In one of the *Mythic Being* videos, he/she declares that he/she constantly asks her mother not to buy cookies and other snacks, but his/her mother ignores her. Her male avatar then goes out into the street repeating the statement about her mother to himself/herself, emphasizing different words, making different gestures each time he/she repeats it. By the time one finishes watching the video, Piper's message is clear. It does matter who says something—and the perception of what is said will vary from the point of view of both gender and race, and of other factors that are similarly stereotyped. These videos in which Piper chooses to become a male avatar also suggest that she is interested in gender fluidity as well as in how perception will vary because of gender or race.[9]

Piper uses the avatar in some unusual ways. For instance, in *Safe #1–4* (1990), the avatar is a white woman, but she is only heard, not seen. Piper places images of smiling African Americans and Africans on the walls, with texts like "We are among you" and "We are around you." In the center of the room, is a structure that emits an audio recording of statements such as "I'm sorry, I just don't feel comfortable with this. I mean, of course, I appreciate the artist's good intentions. I really do. But I am just having a lot of trouble with this piece."[10]

Piper explains that the use of media helps her to reach larger audiences and to form an archive of her creative activity. In using media, Piper, like Pindell, led the way for feminist artists in the United States to use media for the purpose of agitating against racism and sexism, and both found the avatar a useful device.

Another artist who was attracted to avatars is the Canadian artist Vera Frenkel, discussed earlier as one of the first artists to use the internet for artmaking. Starting in 1979, she produced videos in a series titled *The Secret Life of Cornelia Lumsden: A Remarkable Story*, about a fictitious writer who, like Frenkel herself, is a woman, a Canadian, and living in Paris. The fictitious Cornelia Lumsden is an author who published one sensational book in 1934 and then disappeared. Frenkel created offline-life settings with accompanying videos such as the bedroom in Paris where Lumsden supposedly wrote chapter seven of her novel, "The Alleged Grace of Fat People." Lumsden was last seen just before the Second World War, in the company of a famous German journalist. The last installment of *The Secret Life*, "Attention: Lost Canadian," was completely created on the computer and shown in the Canadian pavilion at Expo, the world's fair, held in 1986. In the display, *Au Pied de la lettre*, which consisted of objects belonging to famous Canadians such as Glenn Gould, Marshall McLuhan, and Hugh Le Caine, inventor of the first synthesizer and perhaps the earliest electronic music composer in Canada, Frenkel contributed a showcase with Lumsden's supposed hat, pages from her journal, and a telephone receiver on which one could listen to "a voice resembling mine, reading a letter purported to have been sent by the exiled writer to LeCaine." In this letter, Lumsden explains why she cannot join him in a project he is proposing; her response, a reference to the way in which she felt Canada destroys its artists, reveals how she was able to work and savor her Canadian-ness, only at a distance. Frenkel's avatar was so completely believable that until Frenkel confessed in the 1990s of having created her, people were looking her up in libraries and online.[11]

The internet phenomenon of the early twenty-first century was the rise of social media. As feminist artists in the late twentieth century turned to new digital platforms like the internet and websites, artists in the first decades of the millennium were excited by the advent of Facebook and related sites. Social networking provided an outlet for people to assume other identities besides their identity in life outside the computer and the internet. Everyone could have an avatar.

Ann Hirsch is one of the first artists to use social media as her platform. She was a student at Syracuse University in 2008, when she began to create videos to show on YouTube only two years after its debut. In a podcast recorded by the *Guardian*, she tells about how she invented her avatar named Caroline. Hirsch says that the world of the internet was more interesting for her than her offline-life situation, and she began to watch videos placed on YouTube by young women. In the podcast, Hirsch describes how she analyzed them and concluded that there were two kinds of videos. In one, young women talked about their external lives but never about their sexuality. In the other kind, they became "camwhores" making explicitly sexual videos. She goes on to say that she was at the stage of investigating her own identity and sexuality and found that it helped her with her own problems to create a series combining the two. The series is titled *The Scandalishious Project* (2008–9). In describing her use of digital media for her artistic practice, she talks about the narrative aspect of digital media—it was comfortable in a way that making objects was not. She could express herself more fully by creating narratives out of her own emotions and concerns through digital narrative, and unlike video there is no obvious camera so it was easier to be unselfconscious. She herself says, "It could be messy" but by using an avatar, she could make art that she couldn't through the traditional modes of artmaking.[12]

The episodes are hilariously satiric. Hirsch's avatar, Caroline is a hip, first-year college student. In the videos, which are only seen through online sites, Caroline engages in activities typical of a young woman who is savvy about technology. In one of the earliest, Caroline appears with background music and says that she is dedicating a song to her boyfriend. After saying, "You know who you are,"

Caroline engages in a karaoke performance that is an amusing parody of a young woman trying to appear sexy. However, her moves are gawky adolescent ones that satirize both the women Caroline is trying to imitate, and Caroline herself, for succumbing to the commercialization of sexuality and to the patterns of heterosexual desire that subjugate the female partner. Hirsch's tone, however, is kind; Caroline comes across as an innocent child rather than a femme fatale.

Hirsch is aware of the history of feminist art as is evidenced by a video titled *51 Things I Found in My Poon*, which is a satire of both Carolee Schneemann's famous performance where she drew a braided strip from her vagina, de-braided it and read the stories by women which are printed on the strip, and Martha Rosler's *Semiotics of the Kitchen* in which she holds up various kitchen utensils, names them out loud, and makes threatening motions with them. In Hirsch's version, the innocent Caroline acts out pulling objects from her vagina. The video only shows her upper body and she is wearing rather preppy clothes. She winces as if taking something out of her body and holds up the object, at the same time naming it. The objects are mostly junk objects including some so large as to be impossible to insert into a vagina, let alone, pull out, thus humorously enhancing the satire.[13]

Another relevant artist is the Chinese artist, Cao Fei. Cao Fei came to visibility in the early twenty-first century with videos about life in China. She created an avatar who lives in the digital world of *Second Life*, the same online virtual world used by Lynn Hershman Leeson for the re-creation of *The Dante Hotel*. Like Hirsch, Cao Fei is working out of a feminist context but quite differently. She creates an avatar, who eludes racial or national identification, engages in a relationship, creates her own space.[14]

Her avatar, China Tracy, is based on the conventions in Japanese anime and looks more Caucasian than Asian. She has a cinched-in waist; her dresses have low-cut necklines that reveal her breasts, and full skirts She is a city planner who invents a city where everyone can live safely. She also becomes involved a love affair with a Caucasian musician.

The look of China Tracy which seems to Western eyes as succumbing to the stereotype of the male gaze is, in Chinese terms, a signifier of female agency according to a report published in the *International Journal of Cultural Studies* in 2018. The three authors Jiang Chang, Hailong Ren, and Qiguang Yang describe their interviews with seventy-three Chinese middle-class women from urban centers about their profiles on social media. Their conclusions offer insight into Cao Fei's choice of China Tracy as her avatar. Based on the information collected from their interviews, they determined that young Chinese women create their social media profiles to establish their identity as women, free from the conventions by which they must live their offline-world lives. They emphasize their femininity through carefully applied makeup in their profile photos to declare that they are not the same as men, despite the communist ideology that equates men and women; they put up photos of themselves surrounded by luxury goods to emphasize their middle-class status; when they have children, they post many photos of themselves with their babies because, as stated by themselves, their roles as mothers are something that they do independently of their spouses or extended families.

In the essay, the authors also see young women adopting these characteristics in the formation of their social media profiles as a way of creating a Confucian harmony between their offline lives and their avatar lives on social media. Unlike their Western peers, they see their gender roles within the context of the dominant social and political culture of their country so that, rather than aiming at "the stark Western-style sloganeering of burning down the patriarchy," they are trying to develop their own identities without seeking drastic change. The authors speculate that the principles of the harmonious society as expressed through the Confucianism engrained in Chinese culture allows for resistance, as long as it doesn't disrupt the society as a whole. Their analysis also provides clues as to China Tracy's mission to create a city within *Second Life* in which everyone will live happily following his/her/their own goals in life.[15]

Two artists, LaTurbo Avedon and Amalia Ulman, take a somewhat different direction in creating avatars by playing with the fact that all users of social media in one way or another build multiple identities for themselves. LaTurbo Avedon describes their art practice as "exploring nonphysical identity and authorship." They theorize that people don't realize they are creating virtual selves when they are involved in social networking. They are investigating what it feels like to express aspects of themselves that they are reluctant to explore in the offline world. The internet has resulted in the obliteration of the concept of unitary identity. Their virtual identities intersect with their offline identities, so that they merge.[16]

Avedon remains anonymous (they prefer they, their, and them). Their avatar, like that of Cao Fei, is a blond attractive young white woman who explores different virtual universes like *Second Life* and video game worlds. Avedon's avatar is three dimensional—a statue-like figure created through 3-D modeling programs. In 2012 Avedon created Club Rothko as a nightclub in *Second Life*. The first video in the *Club Rothko* series shows the avatar dancing in front of a photograph of her hero, Slavoj Žižek, the eccentric Slovenian philosopher, who writes about the merging of virtual worlds with the offline world and about the formation of identities.[17]

Avedon says that their life is lived via the avatar online. It is the avatar who is interviewed by offline journalists, and it is the avatar whose paintings were in their first exhibition in New York. The avatar invites collaboration from their audience, and an exhibition of sculpture by the avatar and by members of the audience takes place in Club Rothko where Avedon says that they receive pleasure from seeing Mark Rothko's paintings as wallpaper. Avedon merges the online and offline worlds into one. They write that they live through media. "In the same way that artists in the past are socially known through the works they created, I want to really take ownership of this legacy. Instead of the work paraphrasing the life lived, my work actually is the life that I have had."[18]

Another feminist artist whose art practice consists of investigating how the offline world and the virtual world intersect is Amalia Ulman, who carried out a combined Instagram and Facebook project, "Excellences & Perfections" (2014), in which she underwent an imaginary makeover. Like Avedon, she and the avatar are one. Ulman documents her breast augmentation, showing images of herself in a hospital gown, with a bandaged breast and a padded bra. She also shows images of herself dieting and exercising by pole dancing. Some of it she did in the offline world, but the breast augmentation is not true. Unlike Avedon, where the identity of the individual in the offline world is kept secret, Ulman finally revealed the truth, Ulman's goal being different from Avedon's. Her goal is to show how the truth is manipulated by the users of social media. But during the period of the three months that Ulman posted on Instagram and Facebook, her makeover and her breast augmentation were "true." She received numerous messages of support from women who had undergone the same procedure, and messages in which she was reviled for being vain.[19]

These two artists must represent others as well as themselves. Within the limitations of this book, it would be impossible to write about all of them. There is no question but that the ability to self-publish for an audience fueled the exponential explosion of social media in the early decades of the twenty-first century. Feminist artists responded with work that drew on the conventions of social media, that critiqued the way in which women portrayed themselves, particularly their submission to consumer culture and patriarchal standards for how women should look and act. How effective the work of these artists has been is ambiguous. One might conjecture that their work helped to create an ambience in which the #MeToo movement could arise and more women were elected to office and rose through the ranks to become top executives. On the other hand, one could also say that their work simply mirrored the changes that occurred. Certainly, their work is part of the overall picture of the state of the world. At the same time, both of these artists, despite their homage to Donna Haraway and the concept of the cyborg, still expressed their critique through avatars with the attributes of a white, blond young woman with the kind of body, as well as race and age, that is the ideal of the heteronormative gaze.

Feminist artists from Asia and Africa also found that social media and the internet were useful for their exposure of gender and racial domination. One example is the Pakistani/Canadian artist, Maria Qamar. While Qamar doesn't call the recurring female protagonist in her Instagram images an avatar, this purple-skinned heroine with flowing black hair is a dead ringer for her creator and thus qualifies as an avatar. Qamar's avatar attacks both the Western stereotypes of South Asian women and the traditions of her own culture that hold women back from agency in the contemporary world. Qamar's images deal with immigration, the influence of Western consumerism on South Asian culture, racism, and patriarchal rules for women. Qamar parodies Roy Lichtenstein. The first image she posted on Instagram showed her black-haired, purple-skinned avatar crying with Lichtenstein-style text in the image that reads, "she burnt the rotis," and a caption that says, "What if Lichtenstein parodied Indian soap operas." In an interview for the *New York Times*, Qamar cited the similarity of expression in facial close-ups in Indian television soap operas and in Lichtenstein paintings: "if you take a still from an Indian soap opera when it's zoomed in on somebody's face and you take a Roy Lichtenstein piece and you put them side by side, it's the exact same expression—but it's coming from two opposite ends of the planet. I decided to merge the two because it kind of described who I was as a person—I'm not one or the other. I don't have to choose."[20]

At the time of her first non-Instagram exhibition in the summer of 2019, Qamar had 175,000 Instagram followers worldwide, a much larger and more diverse audience for her art work than she would have for the offline exhibition at the Richard Taittinger Gallery. That internet audience, which exists outside of national boundaries, and Qamar's avatars who act out situations drawn from both Indian and Western culture and speak a mixture of Hindi and English, are signs of the globalism of the digital world.[21]

One of the concerns for Black artist Mandy Harris Williams is how the structure of social media confers visibility on certain images rather than others, images that then become the ideal. She came to that realization when she went on Instagram looking for a community of Black and Brown women who allowed their hair to be natural. Instead of finding those women, she found an overwhelming number of women who did not fit into that category at all, and whose images were the ones popularized. Furthermore, Harris Williams could not search for "dark-skinned girls and high porosity hair." Because the Instagram structure does not allow for intersecting queries, it reinforces bias, whether in reference to race, gender, or other defining features that create populations different from the dominant culture. The experience led Harris Williams to create the hashtag, #Brownupyourfeed, as a discussion space to counter that impact by talking about what it means to be Black, indigenous, and a person of color (BIPOC) and add diversity to the white cis-gendered images which impose their influence on the vast number of Instagram users.[22]

The artists in this chapter who use the internet and social networking in various ways to counteract the oppressiveness of the patriarchal society disrupt the tropes promoted by the dominant class in countries throughout the world. As expressed through representation those tropes include idealized beauty, skin color, shape, size, sexuality, behavior, and other defining features that consciously and unconsciously form a structure that ostracizes, demeans, and belittles anyone who doesn't conform to its demands.

Notes

1 Betsy Damon, "The 7000 Year Old Woman," in "Lesbian Art and Artists" special issue, *Heresies: A Feminist Publication on Art and Politics* 1, no. 3 (September 1977): 10.

2 Alexis Clements, "The Many Faces of Eleanor Antin," Hyperallergic, November 29, 2013, https://hyperallergic.com/95936/the-many-faces-of-eleanor-antin/; Anne Wagner, "Eleanor Antin, Los Angeles County Museum of Art," *Artforum* 38, no. 2 (October 1999): 141–2; Eleanor Antin, interview by Rachel Mason, BOMB Magazine, September 8, 2014, https://bombmagazine.org/articles/eleanor-antin/.

3 The works discussed in this book were created before Lynn Hershman's marriage when she began to use Lynn Hershman Leeson, but since the name on her website is Lynn Hershman Leeson, it's used here for the sake of simplicity.

4 Lynn Hershman Leeson, "Romancing the Anti-Body: Lust and Longing in Cyberspace," (1985), in "Selected Texts, 1984 to Present," https://www.lynnhershman.com/writing/.

5 Roberta Mock, "Lynn Hershman and the Creation of Multiple Robertas," in *Identity, Performance and Technology: Practices of Empowerment, Embodiment and Technicity*, ed. Susan Broadhurst and Josephine Machon (London: Palgrave Macmillan, 2012), 126–41.

6 Robin Held, "Foreword," in Lynn Hershman Leeson, *The Art and Films of Lynn Hershman Leeson: Secret Agents, Private I*, ed. Meredith Tromble (Berkeley: University of California Press co-published with the Henry Gallery, Seattle, University of Washington, December 2005): xiii–xiv.

7 Lynn Hershman Leeson's website, https://www.lynnhershman.com/ for "Roberta Breitmore, 1982–1989," https://www.lynnhershman.com/files/lynnhershman-robertabreitmore.pdf. See also: *Lynn Leeson Hershman: Civic Radar*, ed. Peter Weibel (Karlsruhe: ZKM, 2016); Alex Greenberger, "A New Future from the Passed: Lynn Hershman Leeson Comes into Her Own After 50 Years of Prophetic Work," ARTnews, March 28, 2017, https://www.artnews.com/art-news/artists/a-new-future-from-the-passed-lynn-hershman-leeson-comes-into-her-own-after-50-years-of-prophetic-work-8028/; Patricia Maloney, "Lynn Hershman Leeson, Origin of the Species, Part 2," Modern Art, Oxford, Exhibition on view May 30–August 9, 2015, https://www.modernartoxford.org.uk/wp-content/uploads/2015/04/originspagfinal.pdf; Mary Griffiths, "Against the Grain—Collecting Contemporary Art at the Whitworth Art Gallery, University of Manchester, UK," 135–42, Seoul National University Library, http://s-space.snu.ac.kr/bitstream/10371/78657/1/135-142.pdf; Stefanie Hessler, "Lynn Hershman Leeson's 'First Person Plural,'" Art Agenda, April 18, 2019, https://www.art-agenda.com/features/264437/lynn-hershman-leeson-s-first-person-plural.

8 Alex Greenberger, "Full Circle: Howardena Pindell Steps Back into the Spotlight with a Traveling Retrospective," ARTnews, February 6, 2018, https://www.artnews.com/art-news/news/full-circle-howardena-pindell-steps-back-spotlight-traveling-retrospective-9762/.

9 Adrian Piper, *Mythic Being* (1973), YouTube video, black and white, 3:12, posted by Everything has its first time, May 22, 2018, https://www.youtube.com/watch?v=4bly5tUZI1I; Thomas Chatterton Williams, "Adrian Piper's Show at MoMA Is the Largest Ever for a Living Artist. Why Hasn't She Seen It?" *New York Times Magazine*, June 27, 2018, https://www.nytimes.com/2018/06/27/magazine/adrian-pipers-self-imposed-exile-from-america-and-from-race-itself.html; Adrian Piper Research Archive Foundation Berlin website, http://www.adrianpiper.com/; Chloë Bass, "How Adrian Piper Challenges Us to Change the Ways We Live," Hyperallergic, April 21, 2018, https://hyperallergic.com/439255/adrian-piper-museum-of-modern-art-retrospective/; David Carrier, "Adrian Piper in Her Own Words," Hyperallergic, November 10, 2018, https://hyperallergic.com/470351/adrian-piper-escape-to-berlin-2018/.

10 Lexi Manatakis, "Why Artist Adrian Piper is One of the Most Innovative Minds of Our Time," Dazed Digital, May 25, 2018, https://www.dazeddigital.com/art-photography/article/40084/1/why-artist-adrian-piper-is-one-of-the-most-innovative-minds-of-our-time-moma.

11 Vera Frenkel, "The Story is Always Partial: A Conversation with Vera Frenkel," interview by Dot Tuer and Clive Robertson, *Art Journal* 57, no. 4 (Winter 1998): 2–15; Dot Tuer, "Threads of Memory and Exile, Vera Frenkel's Art of Artifice," in *Mining the Media Archive: Essays on Art, Technology and Cultural Resistance* (Ottawa: YYZBOOKS, 2005), 35–42; for images of *The Secret Life of Cornelia Lumsden*, and other work see Vera Frenkel's page in the Centre for Canadian Contemporary Art (CCCA) Canadian Art Database, http://ccca.concordia.ca/artists/work_detail.html?languagePref=en&mkey=58108&title=%3Ci%3Efrom%3C%2Fi%3E+The+Secret+Life+of+Cornelia+Lumsden&artist=Vera+Frenkel&link_id=2047; Amy Louise Furness, "Towards a Definition of Visual Artists' Archives: Vera Frenkel's Archives as a Case Study" (PhD diss., Faculty of Information, University of Toronto, 2012), 108–14.

12 Eva Krysiak, producer, "Ann Hirsch on the Art Project that Invaded Her Private Life," *The Start* Podcast, #3, with original music by Stephen Fiske, *Guardian* (US edition), February 8, 2018, https://www.theguardian.com/culture/audio/2018/feb/08/ann-hirsch-art-online-youtube-scandalishious-the-start-podcast; "Artist Ann Hirsch Recreates AOL Cybersex," interview by Kat Stoeffel, *The Cut*, November 15, 2013, https://www.thecut.com/2013/11/artist-ann-hirsch-recreates-aol-cybersex.html; Johanna Fateman, "Women on the Verge: Art, Feminism, and Social Media," *Artforum* 53, no. 8 (April 2015): 218–23, https://www.artforum.com/print/201504/art-feminism-and-social-media-50736.

13 See Ann Hirsch website, http://therealannhirsch.com/, to sample her performances as "Caroline" in *Scandalishious* episodes, and promoting toothpaste and vaginal cleansing products; Jennifer Chan, "The Real Ann Hirsch: The Power of Performative Fiction," *Illuminati Girl Gang* 2 (2012), https://www.academia.edu/2072836/The_Real_Ann_Hirsch_The_Power_of_Performative_Fiction.

14 Cao Fei's *i-Mirror*, created by her avatar, China Tracy within *Second Life*, is available on YouTube in three parts, https://www.youtube.com/watch?v=5vcR7OkzHkI, https://www.youtube.com/watch?v=jD8yZhMWkw0, https://www.youtube.com/watch?v=zB-ILJlnWEE; to experience RMB City, it is necessary to join *Second Life*; to learn more about RMB City, see http://www.caofei.com/.

15 Jiang Chang, Hailong Ren, and Qiguang Yang, "A Virtual Gender Asylum? The Social Media Profile Picture, Young Chinese Women's Self-Empowerment, and the Emergence of a Chinese Digital Feminism," *International Journal of Cultural Studies* 21, no. 3 (2018): 325–40.

16 LaTurbo Avedon, "From a Conversation with Willa Köerner: LaTurbo Avedon on Identity and Immateriality," The Creative Independent, February 23, 2018, https://thecreativeindependent.com/people/laturbo-avedon-on-identity-and-immateriality/.

17 Benoit Palop, "Enter LaTurbo Avedon's Video Game Night Club," VICE, March 31, 2015, https://www.vice.com/en_us/article/gvw553/enter-laturbo-avedons-video-game-nightclub.

18 Avedon, "From a Conversation with Willa Köerner."

19 Michael Connor, "Amalia Ulman—Excellences & Perfections," Rhizome, October 20, 2014, https://rhizome.org/editorial/2014/oct/20/first-look-amalia-ulmanexcellences-perfections/.

20 Alisha Haridasani Gupta, "Maria Qamar's Bold Art is Both Therapy and Weapon," *New York Times*, August 15, 2019, https://www.nytimes.com/2019/08/15/arts/design/maria-qamar-art-richard-taittinger.html.

21 Ibid.

22 Mandy Harris Williams, interviewed by Tamu McPherson, All the Pretty Birds, October 13, 2020, https://www.alltheprettybirds.com/mandy-harris-williams/.

8

The Female Body Disappears

Painters and photographers associated with the Feminist Art Movement in the 1970s aimed at deconstructing the white patriarchal male gaze that defined (white) women as symbols of idealized beauty, purity, or depravity, sex objects, housewives, or mothers, adjunct to masculinist needs and desires, rather than having agency and identity in their own right. Countering that view, Joan Semmel depicted the nude female body from the woman's own gaze, as in her carefully detailed paintings where the model looks down at her own body and sometimes at her male partner's body as they make love. Sylvia Sleigh substituted nude men for the nude women in the harem or boudoir settings that had been used by male artists in paintings to titillate male audiences. They created images of women's bodies rarely or never depicted through the male gaze, bodies of real-life women such as pregnant bodies and sick bodies. Alice Neel painted herself nude, at the age of seventy, cancelling the stereotype of the aged woman's body as frail and passive, through her active pose at the easel, which, despite her folds of skin, pendulous breasts, and wrinkles, still shows her full of energy and agency. Hannah Wilke photographed herself as she went through the stages of terminal breast cancer. Judy Chicago substituted the vulva for the phallus as a sex symbol in art, with *The Dinner Party* (1974–9). She designed ceramic plates with images of vulvas for the place settings at the triangular table (signifying the womb) honoring the historical and mythological women she was celebrating. Tee Corinne celebrated the sexuality of lesbian women with erotic artworks depicting women enjoying the sensuality and pleasure they received from each other. Tee Corinne's most famous, or infamous, work is *The Cunt Coloring Book* (1975).

Miriam Schapiro and Harmony Hammond, though they were strong feminists conscious of the male gaze, invented art forms that referred to women but did not involve figuration. Schapiro invented an art form derived from materials common in women's domestic lives, inserting fabric and trim elements into her paintings, a process which she called *femmage*.[1]

Hammond used craft materials to fabricate floor pieces, and to wrap ladders and other objects associated with domestic interiors.

Lesbian photographer and Mexican American Laura Aguilar used images of her own body to depict the sensuality and sexuality of Latina women. Carolee Schneemann contributed to the celebration of the female body, freed from the male gaze, in performances like *Interior Scroll* (1975), in which she gave agency to women's bodies by drawing the stories of women from inside her vagina. Lynda Benglis, like Schapiro, used non-male art materials such as latex for sculptures. To draw attention to herself as a woman artist, equal to a man, Benglis photographed herself holding a giant dildo in front of her genitals which she posted as a full-page advertisement in *Art in America*.[2]

While these artists all differed from each other in their art practices, they shared a crucial attribute in common. They were all making art that assumed the female body had its own materiality and essence even when no actual body was present as in Schapiro's and Hammond's work. They accepted women's bodies as "real."

It's important to emphasize that these efforts centered around the white female body. Black feminist artists like Faith Ringgold were concerned with the Black body in its relationship to the dominant white society, as in the *American People* series.

Reaction to their work set in quickly. Feminist art historians like Thalia Gouma-Peterson and Patricia Mathews, both professors at the College of Wooster, Ohio, named the 1970s Feminist Art Movement, "essentialist." Their consensus was that any images of the female body, even if intended to disrupt the male gaze, or artmaking with fabric and other craft materials associated with domesticity, reinforced the male gaze and patriarchal stereotyping of women. Instead, they argued, the female body had no essence of its own. It was socially constructed by a set of male perceptions.[3]

White artists cited for making work based on the female body as socially constructed included Jenny Holzer, Cindy Sherman, Barbara Kruger, and Nan Goldin. African American photographer Lorna Simpson became known for her images of Black women with their faces turned away from the viewer, referencing the invisibility of Black women as individuals in white US society. Jenny Holzer only used words to generate her feminist slogans. Instead of photographing female models, Cindy Sherman photographed herself in various costumes to satirize the roles assigned by the patriarchy to women—nurse, teacher, young innocent in the big city. In her photographic collages, Barbara Kruger pointed out how consumerism, science, and government dominated and controlled women, never taking a new image of a woman—only photos of women appropriated from other sources. Nan Goldin, and Sherman in her later work, go to extremes in opposition to the patriarchal idealization of the female body to show women in states of utter abjection. Goldin documents her own degradation, showing herself in drugged or alcohol-induced states; Sherman, still photographing herself, but now as lost and sick to the point of lying in her own vomit, or as hiding age by using makeup and costumes that make her look bizarre rather than attractive—a decadent middle-aged woman.

Iranian artist Shirin Neshat critiqued the oppression women experience in male-dominated Muslim society through her photographs of Muslim women wrapped in garments that leave nothing visible except their faces and sometimes only their eyes, yet they hold guns. Ana Mendieta also contributed to the disappearance of the female body as evident in the many performances in which she buried herself, leaving only the imprint of her body in the earth.[4]

French artist ORLAN went even further in denying the female body an innate essence by physically altering her body through surgery. For ORLAN, the body was only a surface that can be infinitely changed. At various times, ORLAN had new structures implanted on her face—protuberances that made her look like someone from another planet and in her later work, had her face altered to become less Caucasian and more like the faces of people of color around the world. ORLAN documented her surgeries through videos.[5]

Palestinian/British artist, Mona Hatoum created sculpture, installations, and videos that are all about the human body without a single actual body. One of her earliest performances about the body is *Don't smile, you're on camera* (1980), in which Hatoum trained a video camera onto the audience. The images were fed to a monitor facing the audience, but before reaching the monitor they were altered by Hatoum's assistants who mixed live images of nude body organs or X rays over areas of the corresponding parts of clothed bodies. The audience was enraged and many departed.

Another early work using a close-circuit video was a 1981 performance titled *Look, No Body!* In it she repeatedly performed the task of filling a cup with water, drinking it and offering every other cup to a different member of the audience. A live camera was set up high above the nearby toilet, and when the artist went to use it halfway through the performance, the camera transmitted the image to a monitor in the auditorium. On a sound tape which played throughout the performance, Hatoum's voice reading a detailed medical description of the act of urination could be heard, while the audience looked at the images.[6]

Although the actual body is missing from Hatoum's work, nevertheless, she has insisted that the body is central to her art practice. Hatoum was born to a

Palestinian family living in Lebanon. At the start of the war in Lebanon, she was visiting London and she was prevented from returning home. In a very moving video, *Measures of Distance* (1988), Hatoum uses a shadow of the body as a metaphor for the enforced separation from her family. The video is about Hatoum's mother whom she can't visit. Her mother is seen through a mesh of Arabic writing that reproduces her mother's letters to her, while Hatoum's reading of a translation of those letters comes across, strong and poignant.

Light Sentence (1992) is another one of Hatoum's sculptural installations that evoke the human presence without any representation of the body. It consists of a U-shaped enclosure of stacked-up wire mesh lockers with a single naked light bulb hanging in the center. It suggests prison cells, animal cages or a government housing project. *Quarters* (1996) follows the same theme of imprisonment. Bare metal bunk beds looking more like racks stacked several high, like institutional lodgings or emergency housing are arranged like spokes on a wheel, the model prison arrangement for easy surveillance from the center. No actual bodies are necessary for conveying Hatoum's messages about the horror of incarceration of the body.

Corps étranger [Foreign body] (1994; Plate 20) presents a different take on the body. In it, Hatoum views the body only as biology, stripped of any other representation. Hatoum, after some difficulty, found a physician who agreed to use an endoscopic camera to enter Hatoum's own body through various orifices. The resulting video is seen inside a hollow columnar capsule in which only one person can fit at a time. Having entered, the viewer looks down to see a projection of Hatoum's interior on the floor of the capsule. The enclosure creates the illusion that one is inside her body. Adding to the illusion, Hatoum's heartbeat emanates from a soundtrack as the viewer journeys through the vessels in her body. The title has multiple references. In addition to indicating how unrelated the body's actual biology is to exterior images, it can refer to the viewer as a foreigner invading the privacy of Hatoum's body. Or it can refer to the endoscopic camera itself as violating Hatoum's body.[7]

What is apparent when looking back from the vantage point of several decades later, the concept of bodies as socially constructed has had significant influence on subsequent art. The continuing impact of the late twentieth century discourse around the body can be seen in the work of digital artists in the next generation like American Victoria Vesna, Black British artist Hannah Black, a writer as well as a digital artist; the Japanese American Hito Steyerl; and the Swiss artist, Pipilotti Rist.

In 1996 Victoria Vesna introduced *Bodies© INCorporated*, a project in which bodies existed only in a digital state. Viewers could create their own individuals through an internet order form which listed characteristics of the body such as

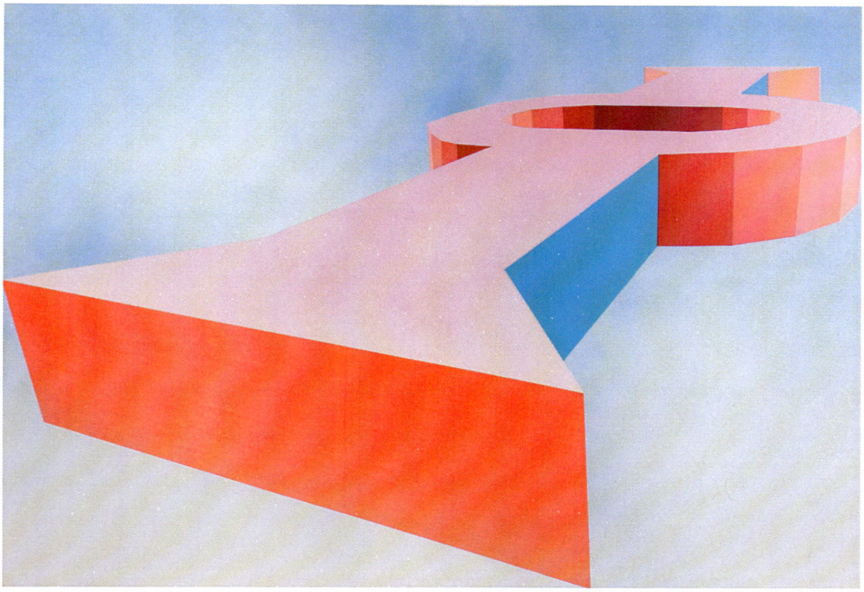

Plate 1 Miriam Schapiro, *Keyhole* (1971), acrylic on canvas with spray paint, 71 × 106″ (180 × 269 cm). Courtesy of the Estate of Miriam Schapiro.

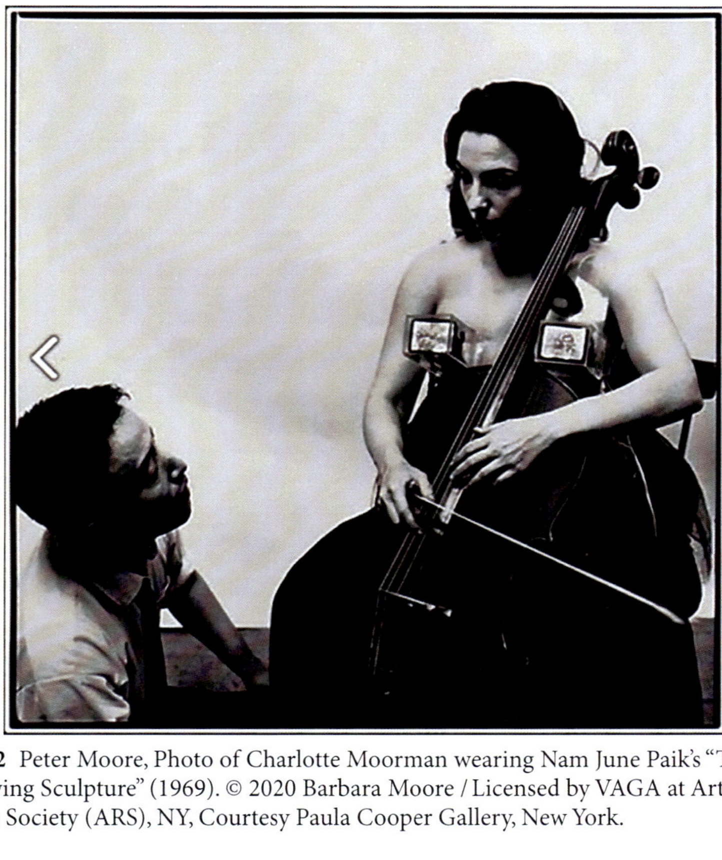

Plate 2 Peter Moore, Photo of Charlotte Moorman wearing Nam June Paik's "TV Bra for Living Sculpture" (1969). © 2020 Barbara Moore / Licensed by VAGA at Artists Rights Society (ARS), NY, Courtesy Paula Cooper Gallery, New York.

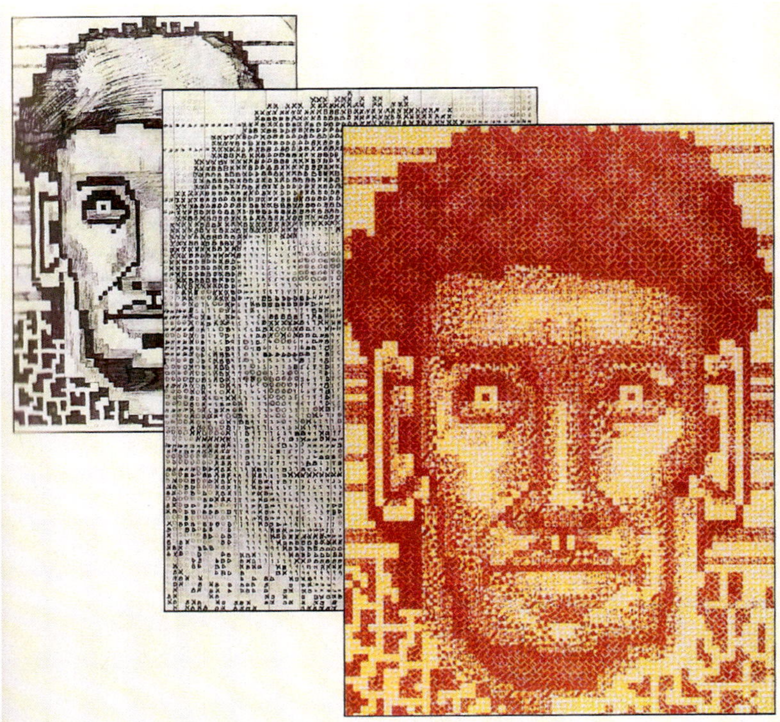

Plate 3a Lillian F. Schwartz, *Head* (1968). Composite image showing steps involved: original sketch, graph paper with alphanumeric characters, silkscreen. Copyright © Lillian F. Schwartz.

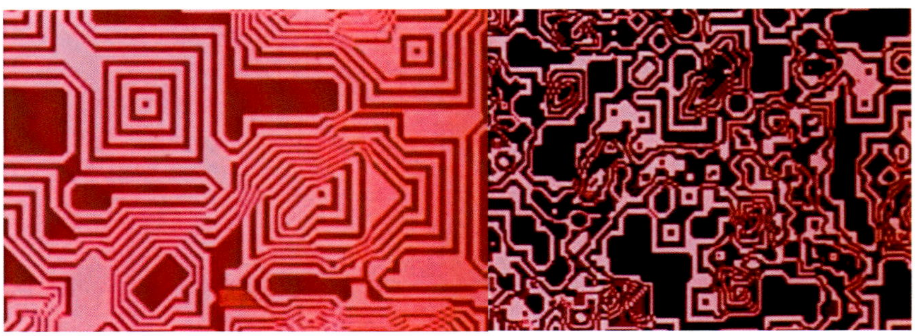

Plate 3b Lillian F. Schwartz, *Pixillation* (1970), animated film. Duration: 4 minutes. It took one year to produce this multi-layered film using unique animation techniques while reusing two seconds of computer output that was redone on A, B, C rolls, optical bench effects, and timing shifts. Copyright © Lillian F. Schwartz.

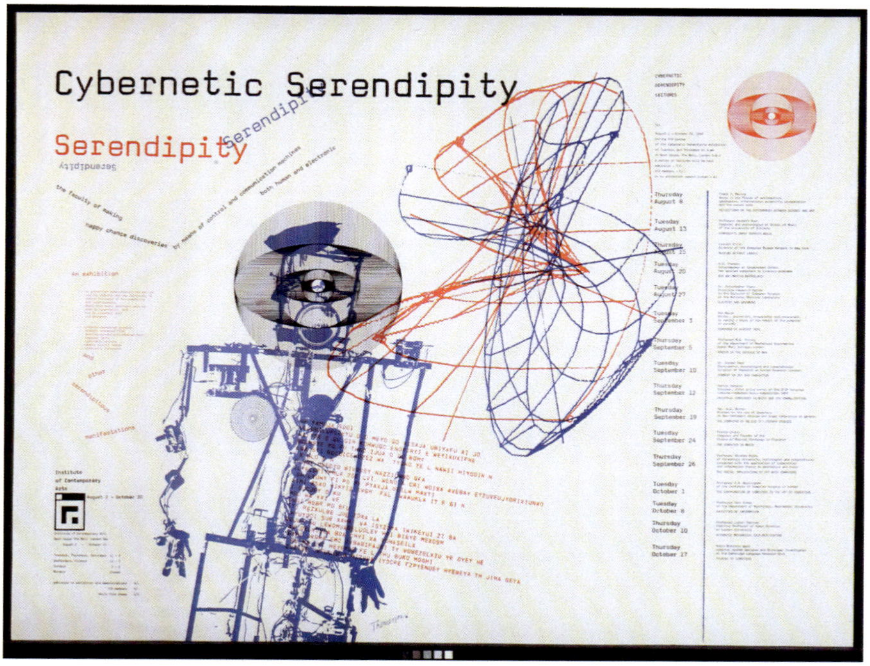

Plate 4 *Cybernetic Serendipity* (1968), exhibition, the Institute of Contemporary Arts (ICA), London, poster designed by Franciszka Themerson. Copyright permission, courtesy of the ICA. Photo courtesy of the Tate Gallery, London.

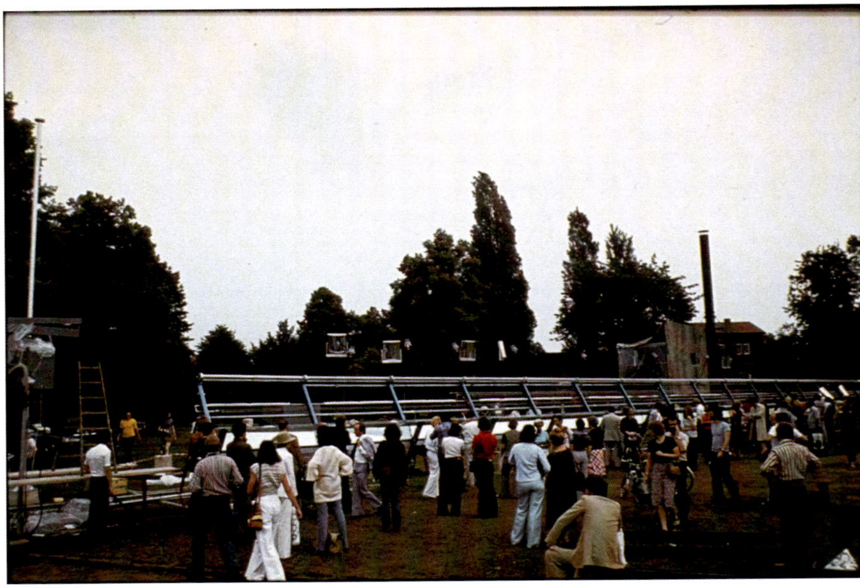

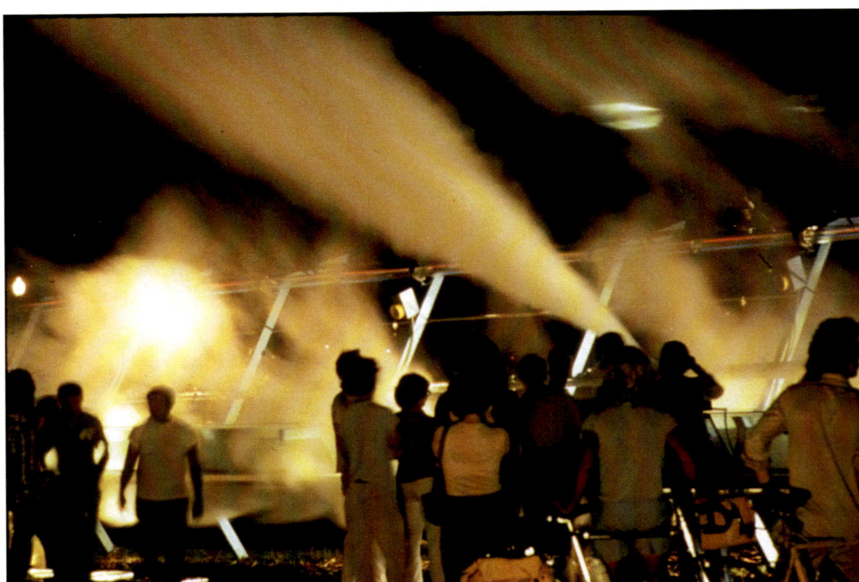

Plate 5 *Centerbeam* (1977), a steam and video sculpture designed by Joan Brigham (steam), Harriet Casdin (videos) and other artists and scientists at the Center for Advanced Visual Studies, MIT, directed by Otto Piene, created for *documenta* 6, Kassel, Germany (1977), and recreated on the Mall, Washington, DC (1978). Photo: Dietmar Lohri. © MIT Museum.

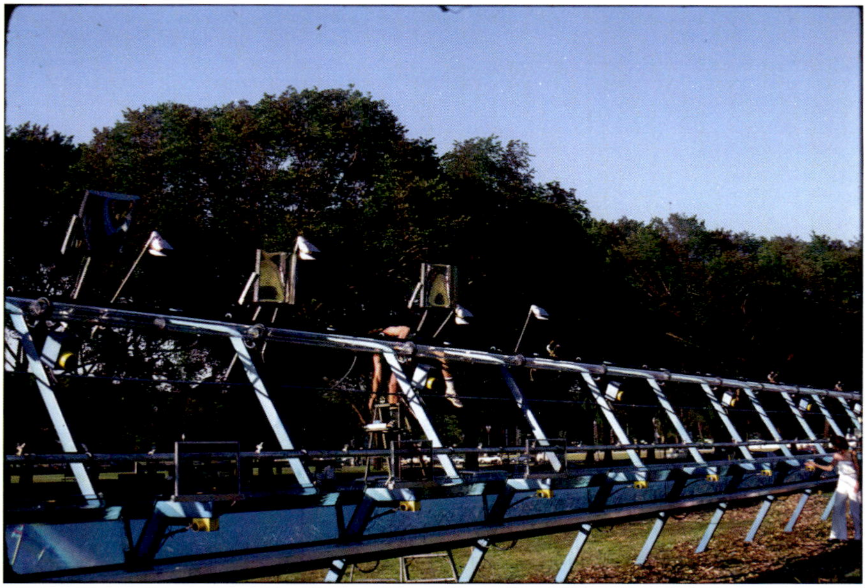

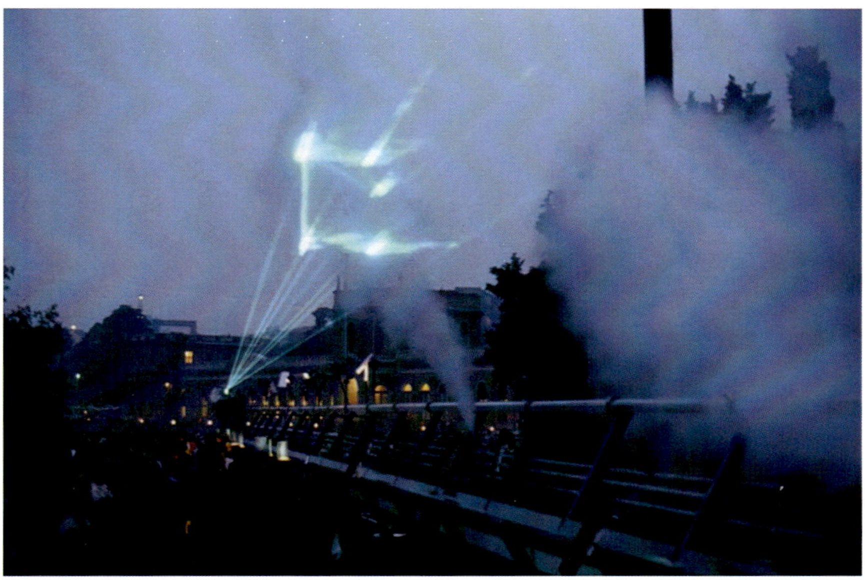

Plate 5 *contd.*

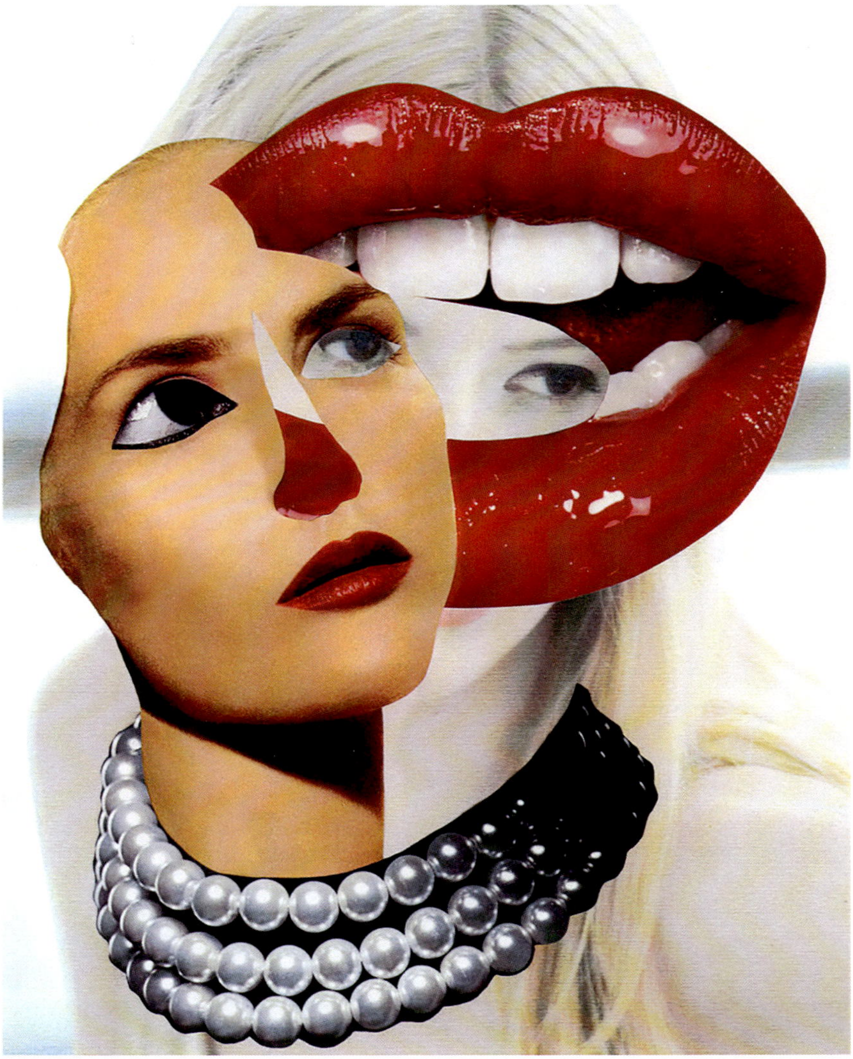

Plate 6 Barbara Nessim, *Dream Still* (2009), digital print on aluminum, 42 × 35″ (1,068 × 885 mm). Collection of the Victoria and Albert Museum. Courtesy of the artist.

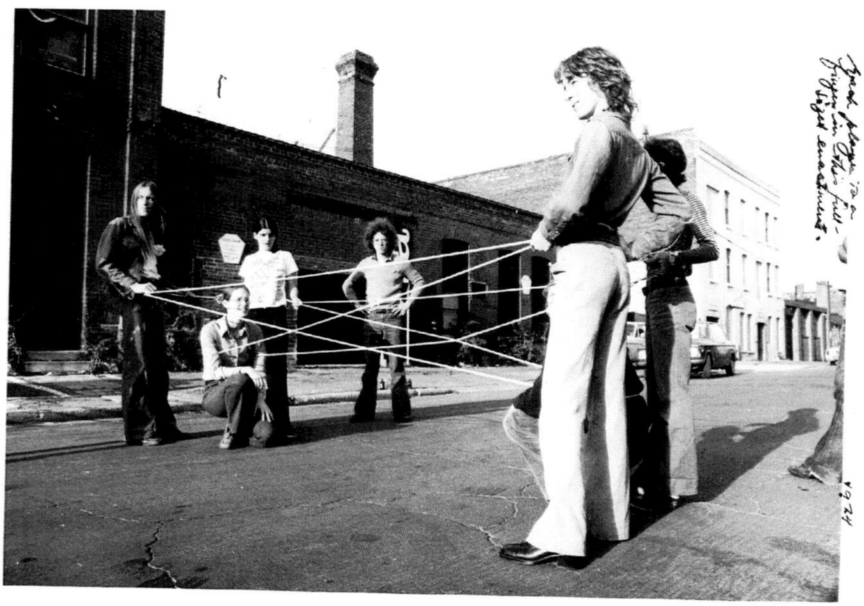

Plate 7 Vera Frenkel, *String Games: Improvisations for Inter-City Video* (1974). Learning the eight string figures; rehearsal with rope in preparation for video transmission between Toronto and Montreal, George Street, Toronto (1973). Collection of the Agnes Etherington Art Centre, Queen's University, Kingston, Ontario (49-026). Courtesy of the artist.

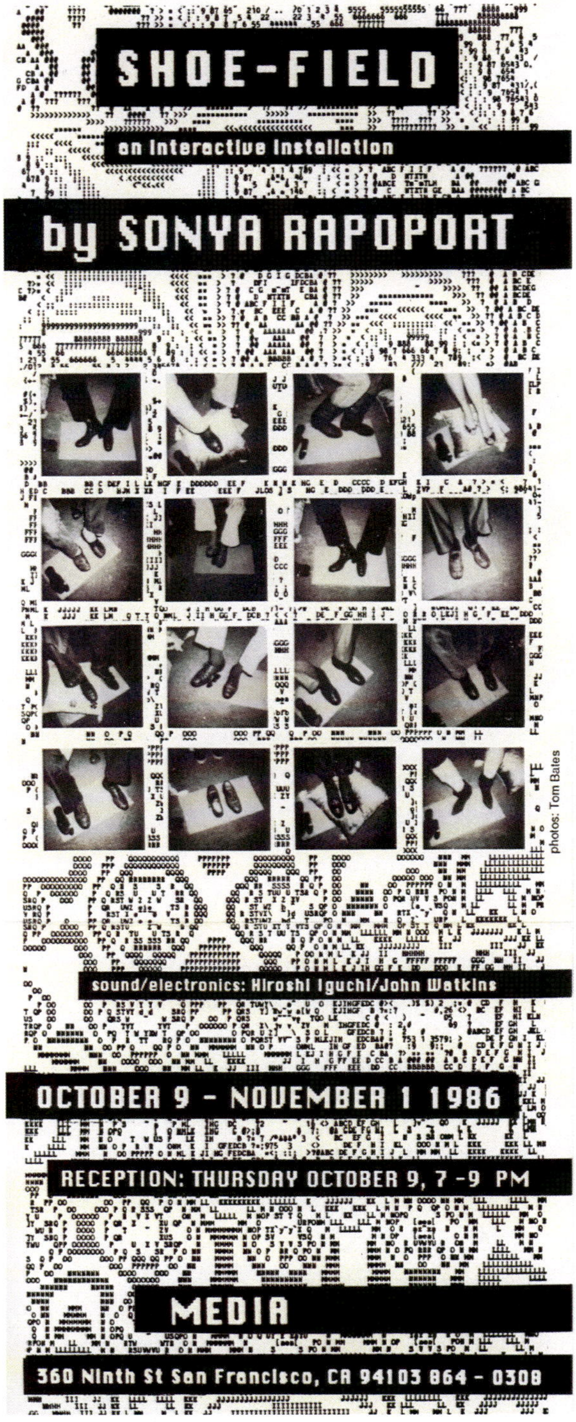

Plate 8a Sonya Rapoport, *Shoe-Field Announcement for Media Gallery* (1986). Design in background generated digitally by visitor actions on the shoe-field. Printed ephemera. Courtesy Estate of Sonya Rapoport.

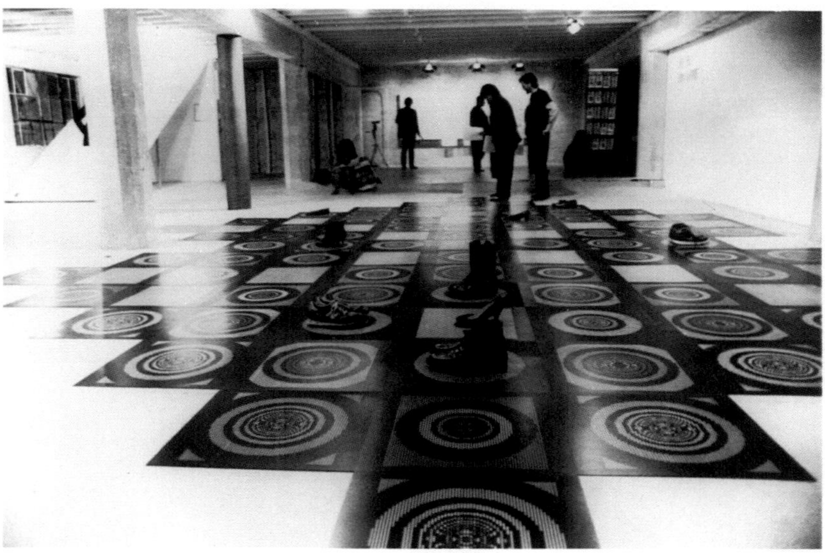

Plate 8b Sonya Rapoport, *Shoe-Field Installation at Media Gallery* (1986). Photo: Marion Gray. Courtesy of Estate of Sonya Rapoport and Estate of Marion Gray.

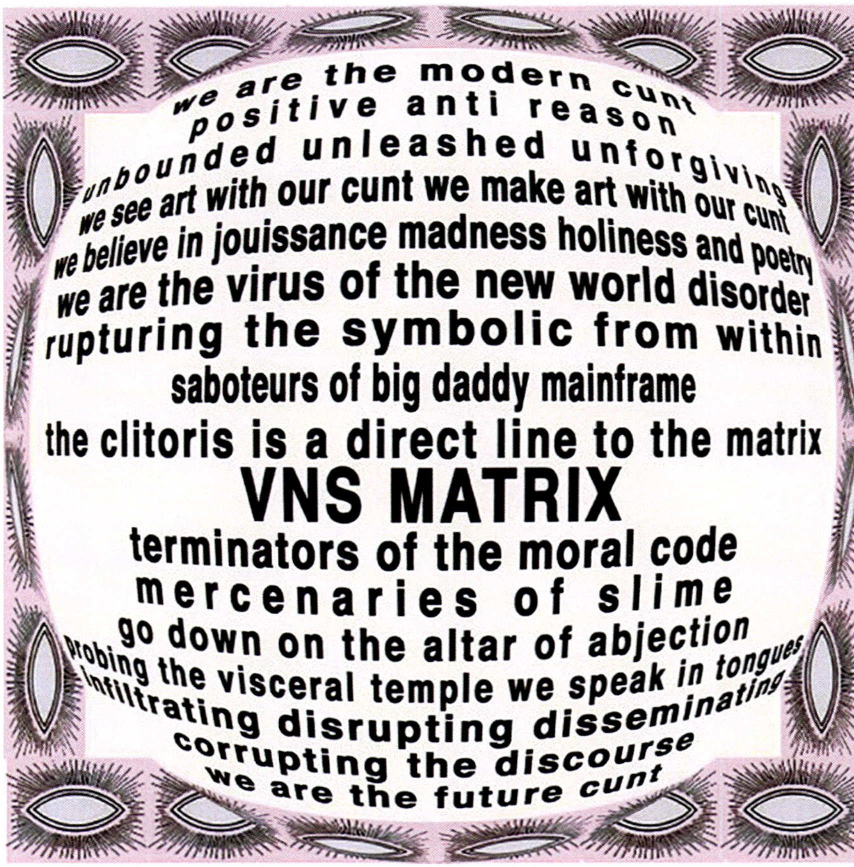

Plate 9 VNS Matrix manifesto. Courtesy of VNS Matrix.

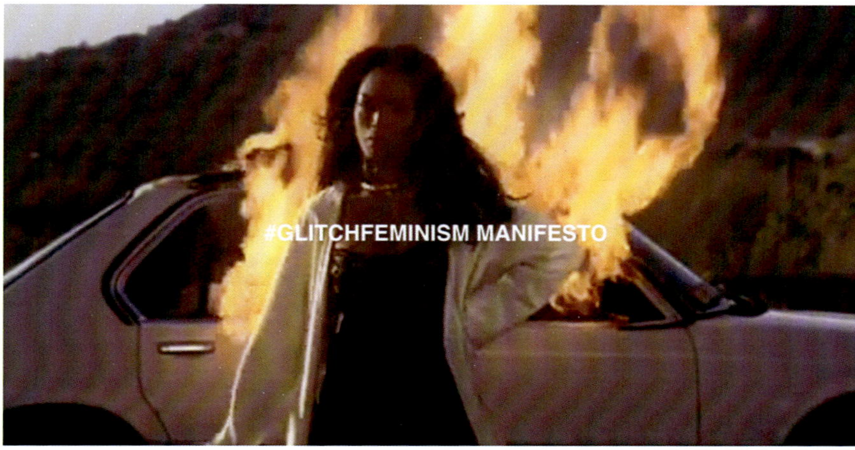

Plate 10 Legacy Russell, Screen still from "#GLITCHFEMINISM," Video Essay (2018). Courtesy of the artist.

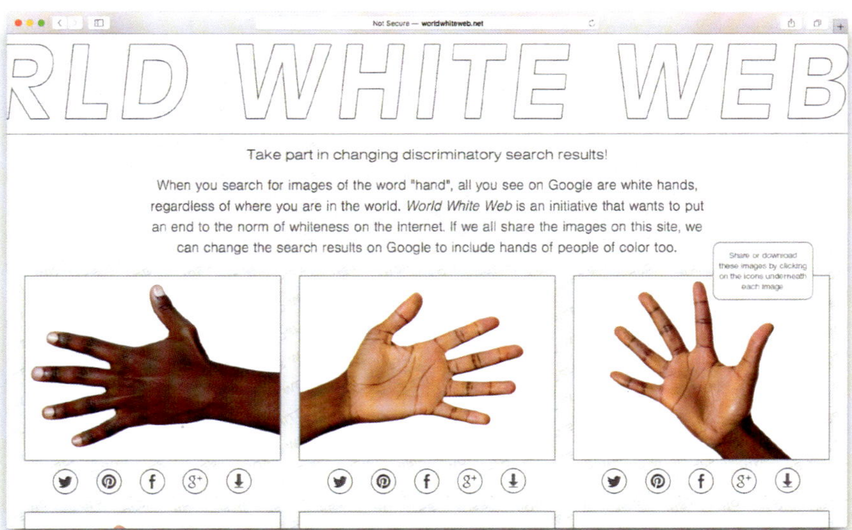

Plate 11 Johanna Burai, *World White Web* (2015), screenshot. Courtesy of the artist.

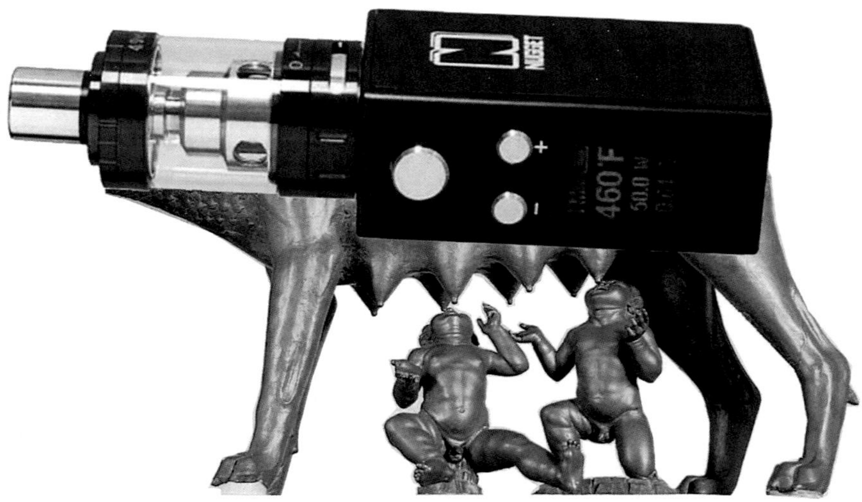

Plate 12a subRosa, *Mother Vape* (2016), digital collage. Courtesy of subRosa.

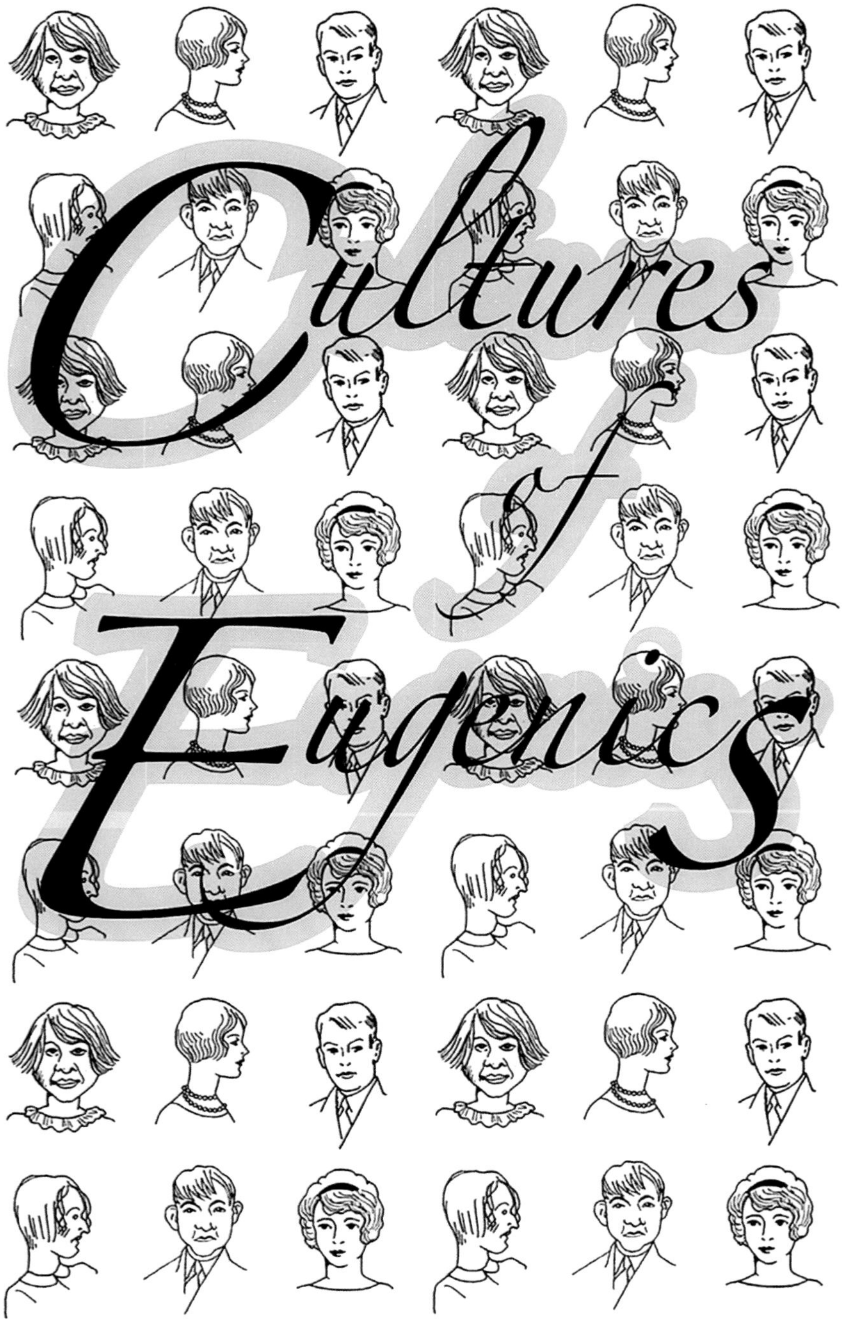

Plate 12b subRosa, *Culture of Eugenics* (2005), pamphlet cover. Courtesy of subRosa.

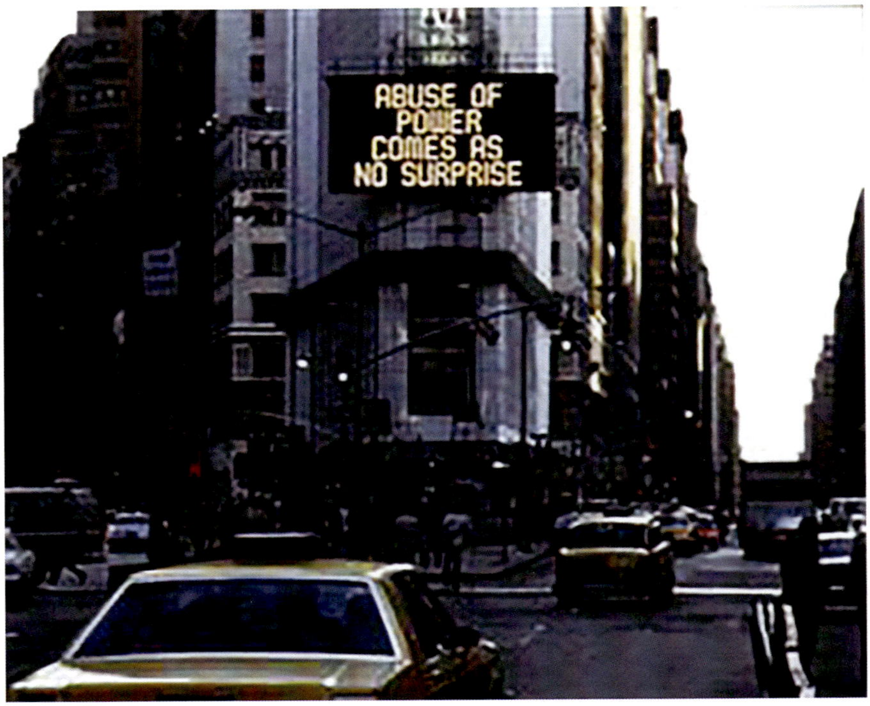

Plate 13 Jenny Holzer, *Truism*, projection in Times Square (1982), *Messages to the Public* (1982–90). © 2020 Jenny Holzer, member Artists Rights Society (ARS), New York.

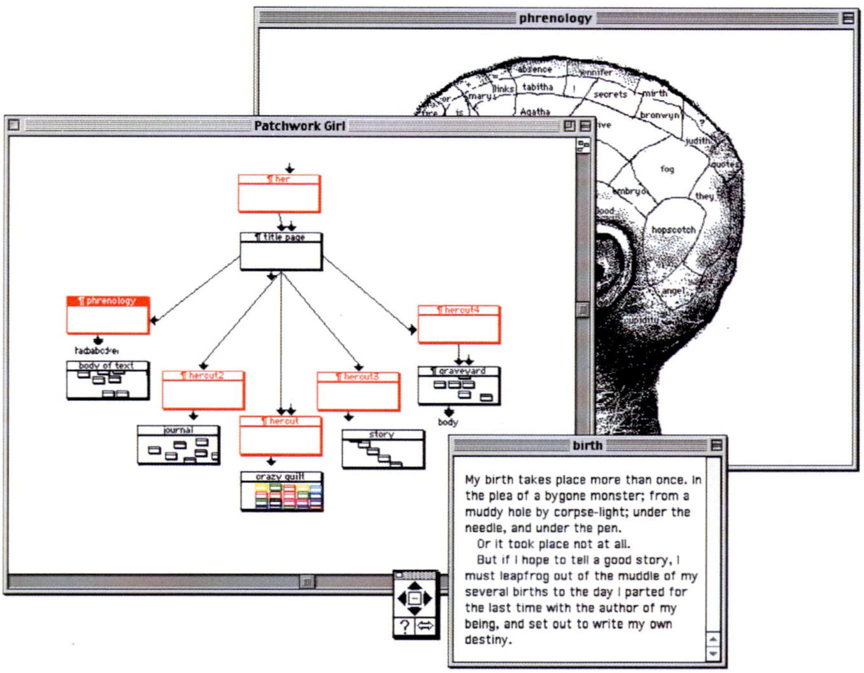

Plate 14 Shelley Jackson, *Patchwork Girl* (1995), screenshot. Courtesy of Eastgate Systems, Inc.

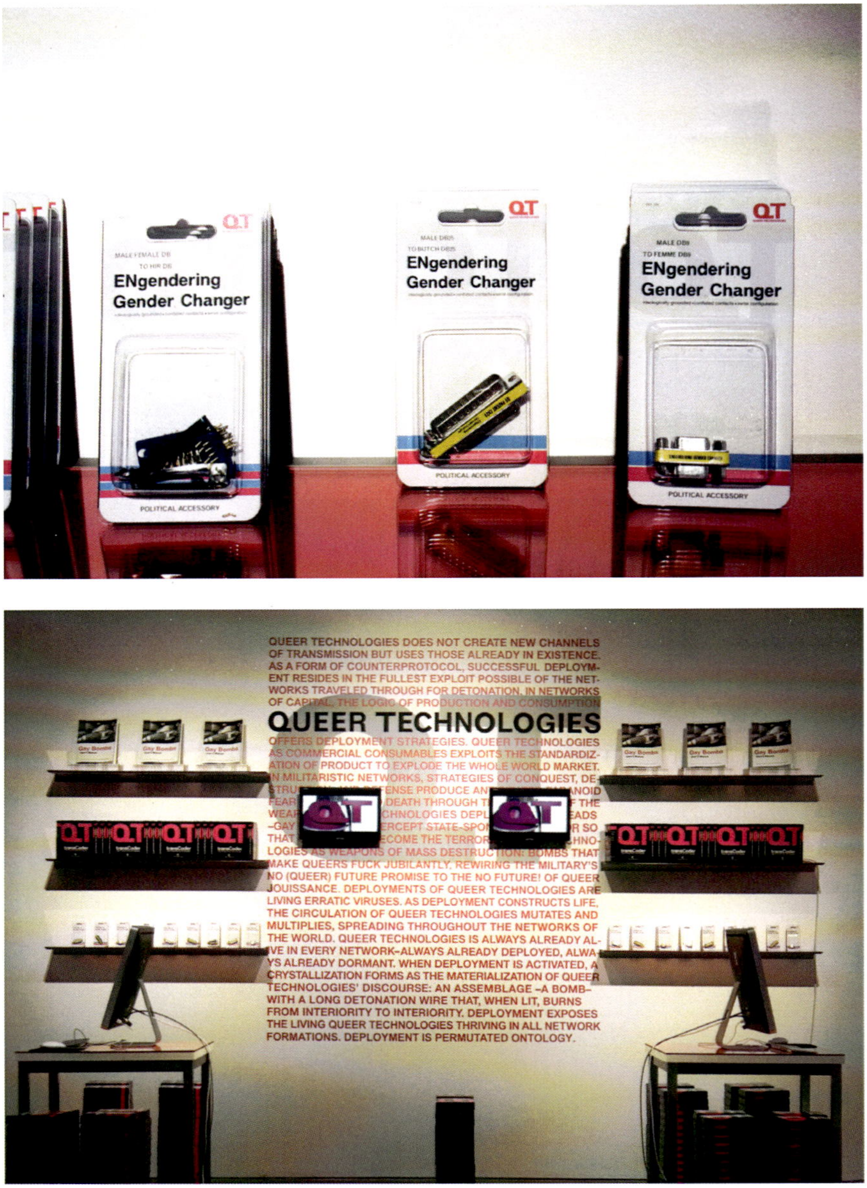

Plate 15 Zach Blas, *ENgenderingGenderChangers*, *Queer Technologies* (2007–12). Installation, *Exit Strategies*, New Wight Gallery, University of California, Los Angeles, 2008. Courtesy of the artist.

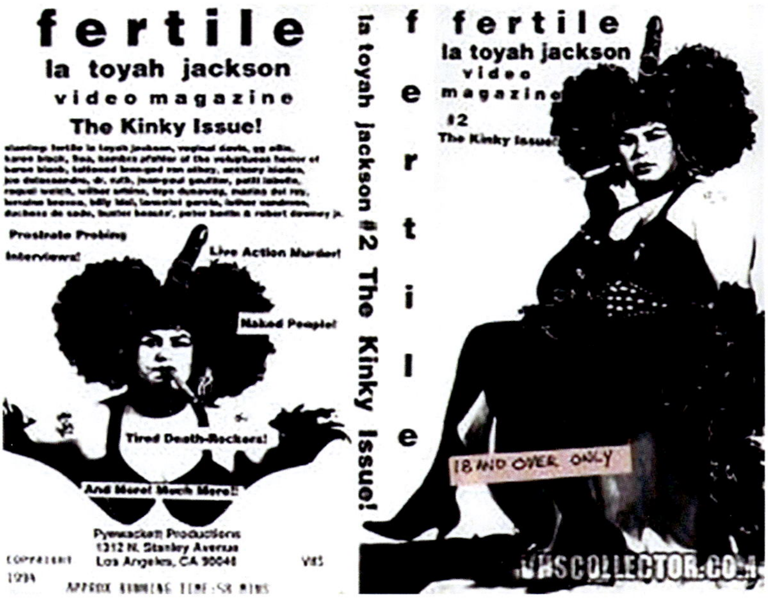

Plate 16 Vaginal Davis and Rick Castro, *Fertile La Toyah Jackson Video Magazine: The Kinky Issue!* (1994), video magazine, cover. Courtesy of the artists.

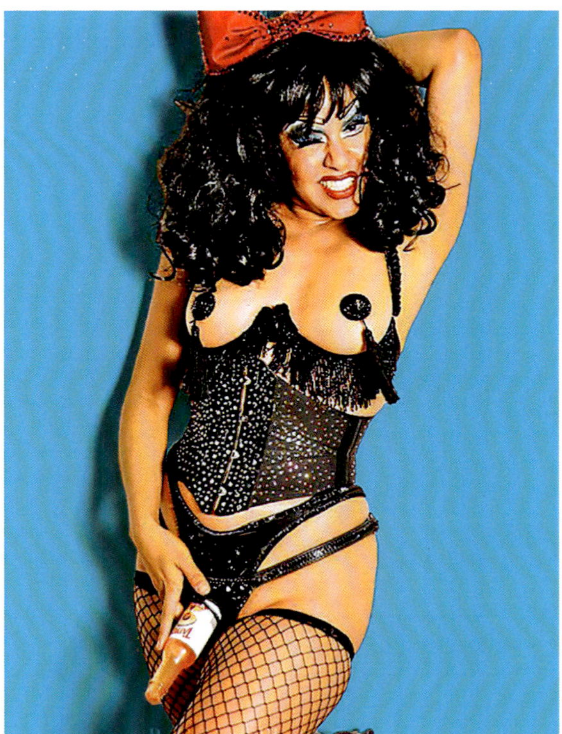

Plate 17 Xandra Ibarra (La Chica Boom), *Censored* (2014), a post-performance digital photograph, dimensions variable. Photographer: Re Campos Photography, Mexico City. Courtesy of the artist.

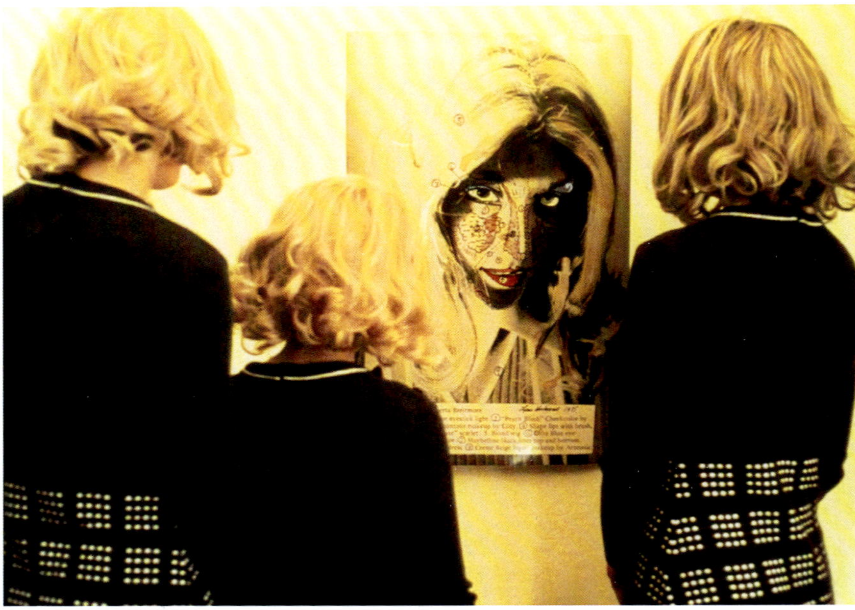

Plate 18 Lynn Hershman Leeson, *Roberta Multiples* (1977), chromogenic color print, $38\frac{9}{16} \times 25\frac{1}{2}$ inches (98×64.7 cm). Courtesy of the artist.

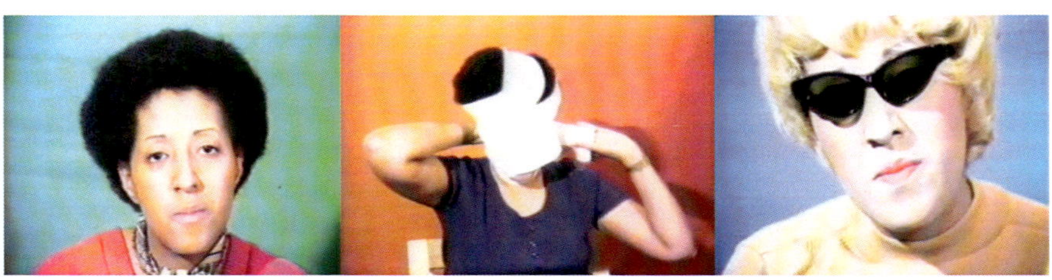

Plate 19 Howardena Pindell, *Free, White, and 21* (1980), three video stills. Courtesy of the artist and Garth Greenan Gallery, New York.

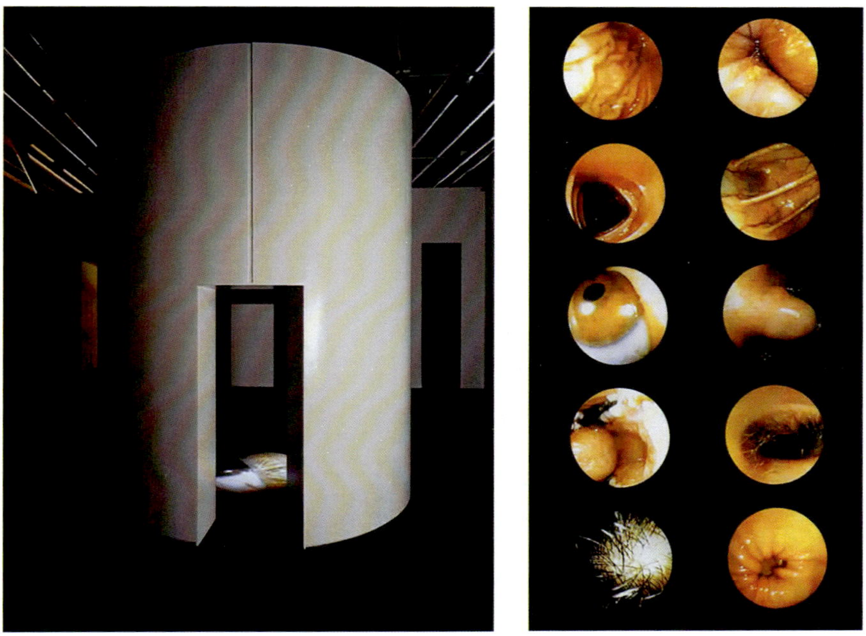

Plate 20 Mona Hatoum, *Corps étranger* [Foreign body] (1994), video installation with cylindrical wooden structure, video projector and player, amplifier and four speakers, 11.5′ × 9.8′ × 9.8′ (350 × 300 × 300 cm). Left: exterior view at Centre Pompidou, Paris, © Mona Hatoum and Artists Rights Society (ARS), New York / DACS, London, Courtesy: Centre Pompidou, Mnam-CCI / Dist RMN-GP. Photo: Philippe Migeat. Right: interior view (detail), © Mona Hatoum and Artists Rights Society (ARS), New York / DACS, London.

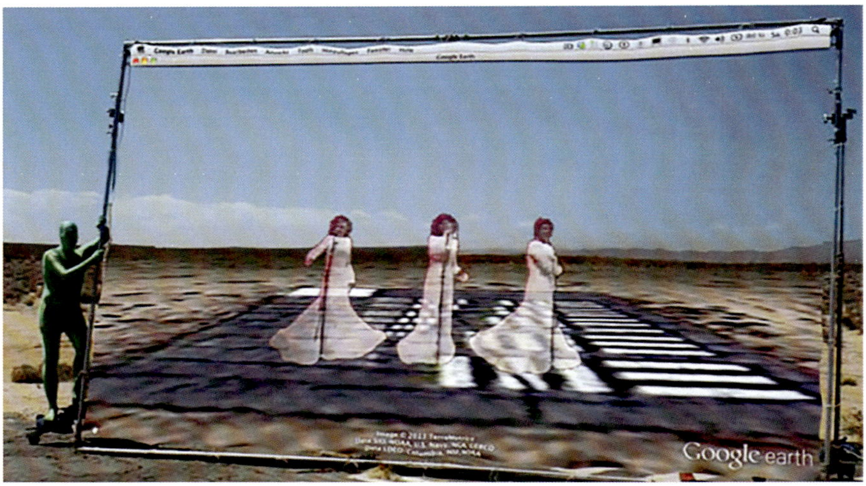

Plate 21 Hito Steyerl, *How Not to Be Seen: A Fucking Didactic Educational .MOV File* (2013), HD video, single screen in architectural environment, screen shot. Duration: 15:52 minutes. Courtesy of the artist, Andrew Kreps Gallery, New York, and Esther Schipper, Berlin.

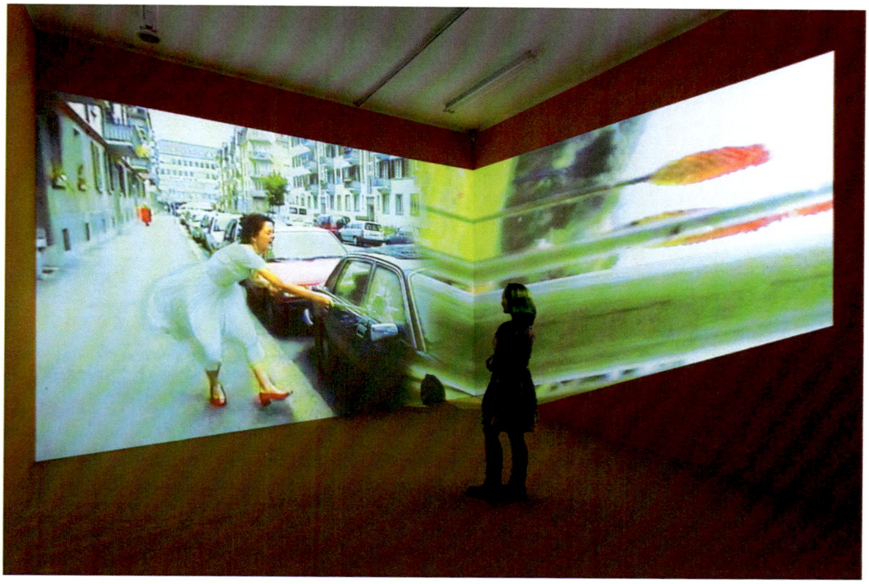

Plate 22a Pipilotti Rist, *Ever Is Over All* (1997), two channel video installation with sound. Duration: 4:07 minutes. Installation view: Kunsthalle Krems, *Pipilotti Rist. Komm Schatz, wir stellen die Medien um & fangen nochmals von vorne an* (Come on honey, we will change the media & start all over again). Austria, 2015. Photograph: Lisa Rastl. © Pipilotti Rist. Courtesy of the artist, Hauser & Wirth, and Luhring Augustine.

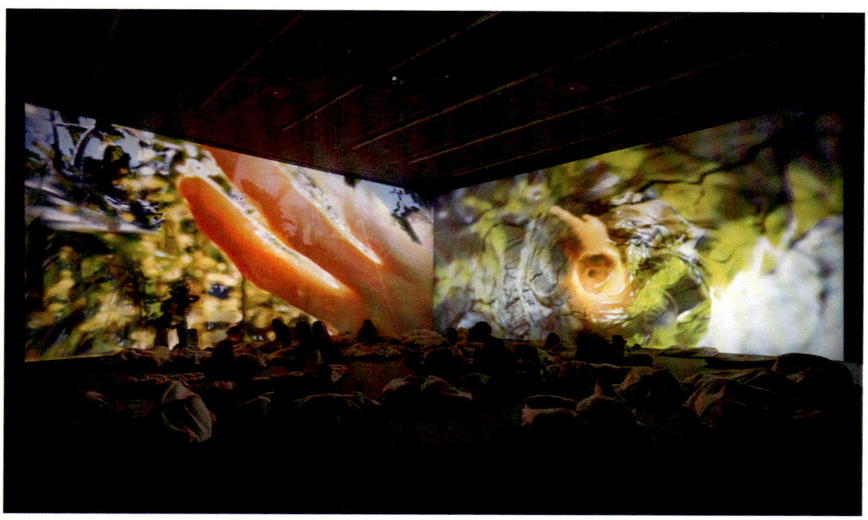

Plate 22b Pipilotti Rist, *Worry Will Vanish Horizon*, from the Worry Work Family (2014), audio video installation by Pipilotti Rist. Installation view, London, Hauser & Wirth, *Worry Will Vanish*, England, 2014. Photo: Alex Delfanne. © Pipilotti Rist. Courtesy the artist, Hauser & Wirth and Luhring Augustine.

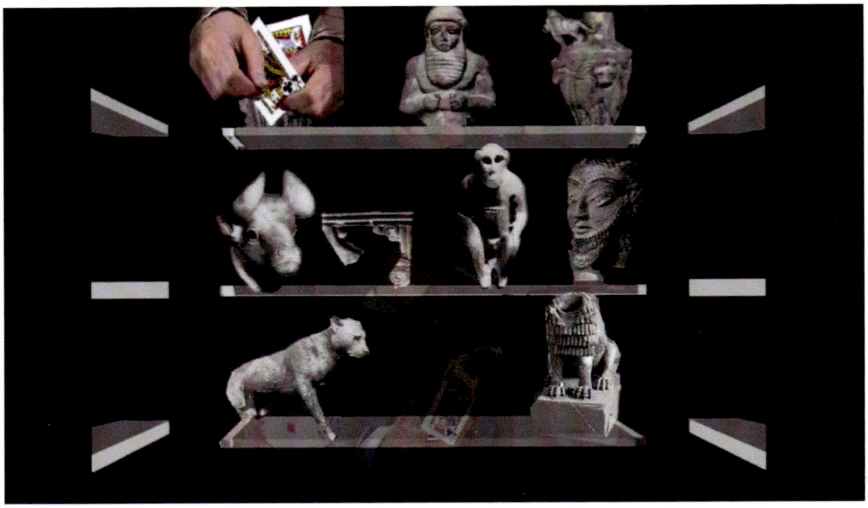

Plate 23 Ellen K. Levy, *Stealing Attention* (2009), dimensions variable. MP4 from Flash animation. Duration: 6 minutes. Collaboration with Michael E. Goldberg, Director of the Mahoney Center for Brain and Behavior, Columbia University. Courtesy of the artist.

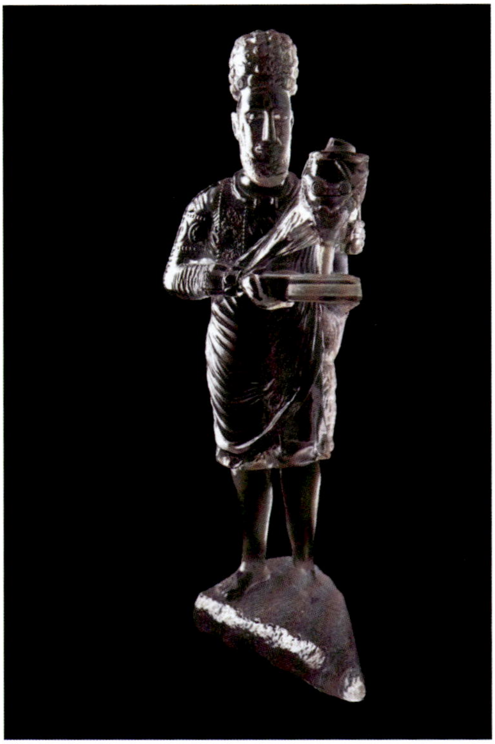

Plate 24 Morehshin Allahyari, *Material Speculation: ISIS, Priest with Eagle* (2015), 3D printed resin and electronic components, 12 × 4 × 3.5″ (30.5 × 10.2 × 8.9 cm). Courtesy of the artist.

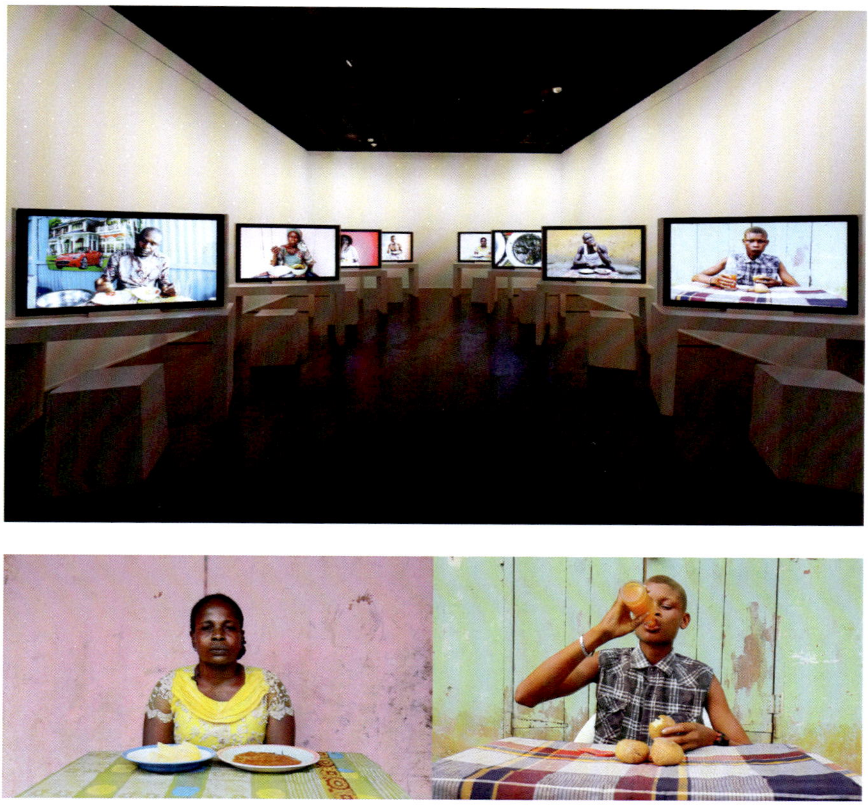

Plate 25 Zina Saro-Wiwa, *Table Manners* (2014–16), four channel video. Installation view and two details, *Eucharia Eats Three Leaf Yam and Gho* and *Leelebari Eats Scotch Egg with Fanta*. Courtesy of the artist.

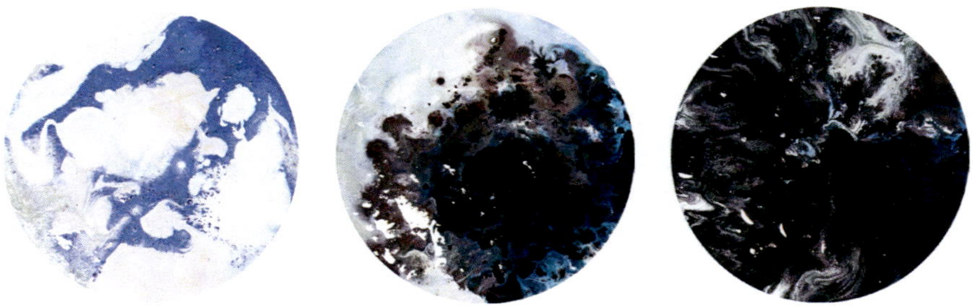

Plate 26 Diane Burko in collaboration with Anna Tas, *From Glaciers to Reefs* (2018), lenticular photographs, variable size. Courtesy of the artist.

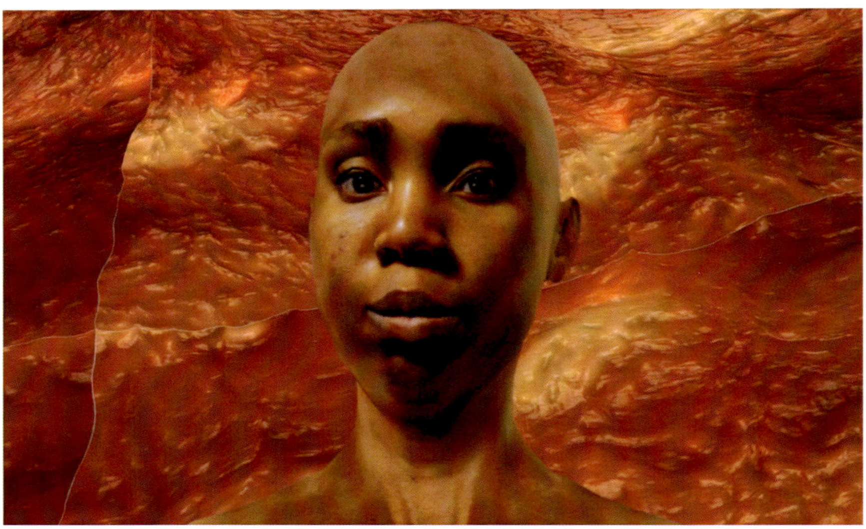

Plate 27 Sondra Perry, *Graft and Ash for a Three Monitor Workstation* (2016) (still), video, bicycle workstation, 68 × 16 × 42″ (172.72 × 40.64 × 106.68 cm). Duration: 9:05 minutes. © Sondra Perry. Courtesy of the artist and Bridget Donahue, New York.

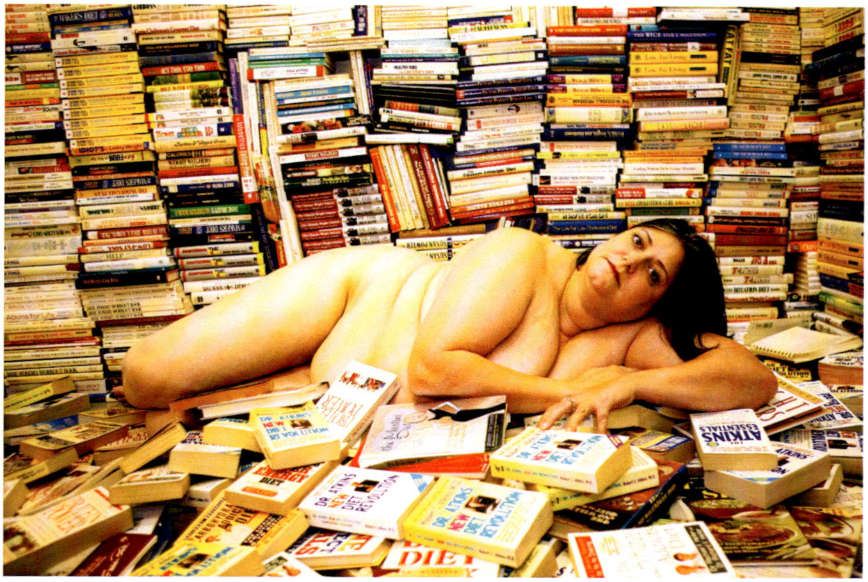

Plate 28 Brenda Oelbaum, *Falling Out All Over* (2010), digital photograph, dimensions variable. Photographer: Daphne Doerr. Courtesy of the artist.

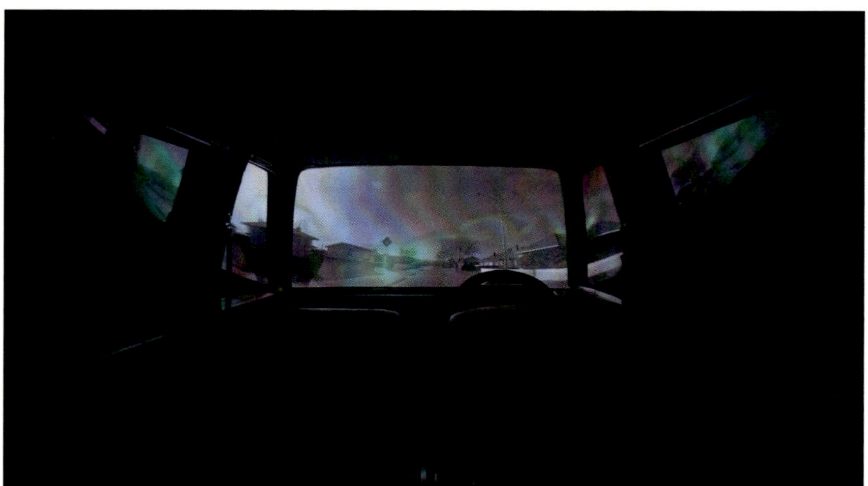

Plate 29 Terri Te Tau, *Āhua o te Hau* (2015), installation, video still. Courtesy of the artist.

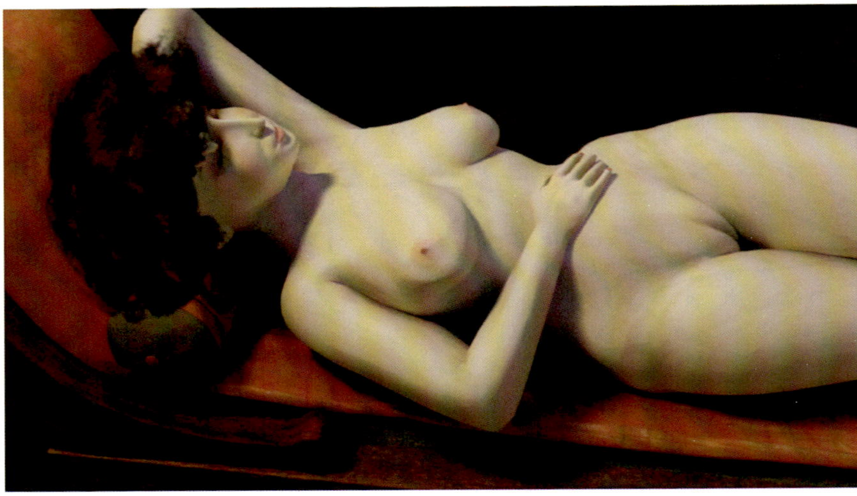

Plate 30 Claudia Hart, *Machina* (2002–4) 3-D animation, for looping installation. Duration: 20 minutes. Courtesy of the artist.

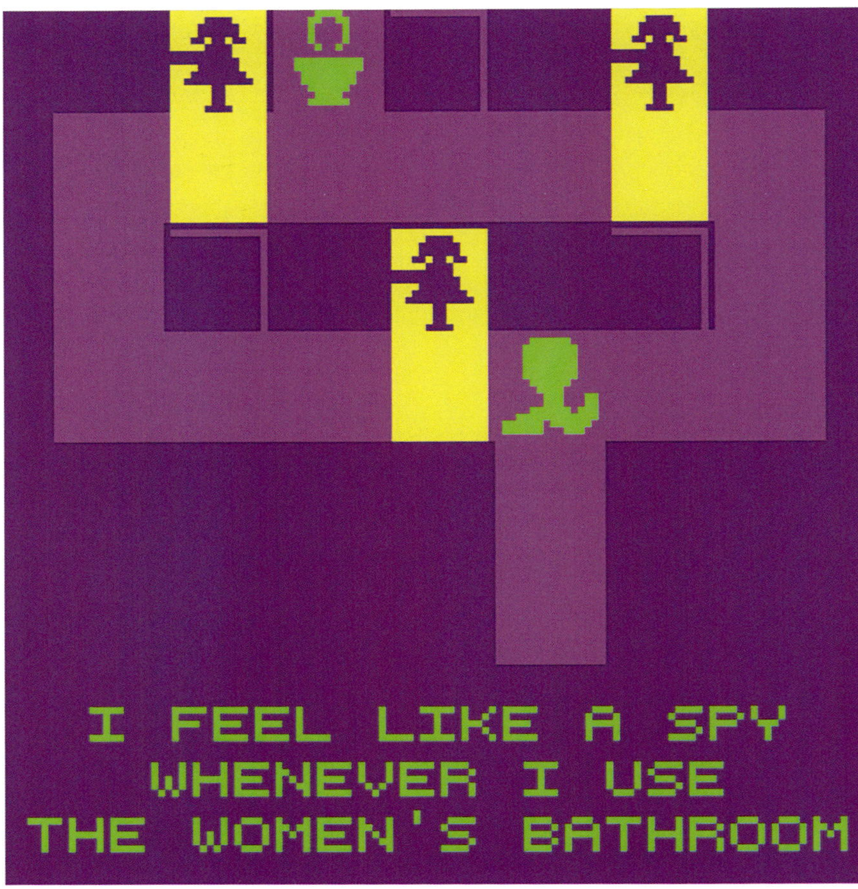

Plate 31 Anna Anthropy, *Dys4ia* (2012), video game about hormone replacement therapy, screen shot. Courtesy of the artist.

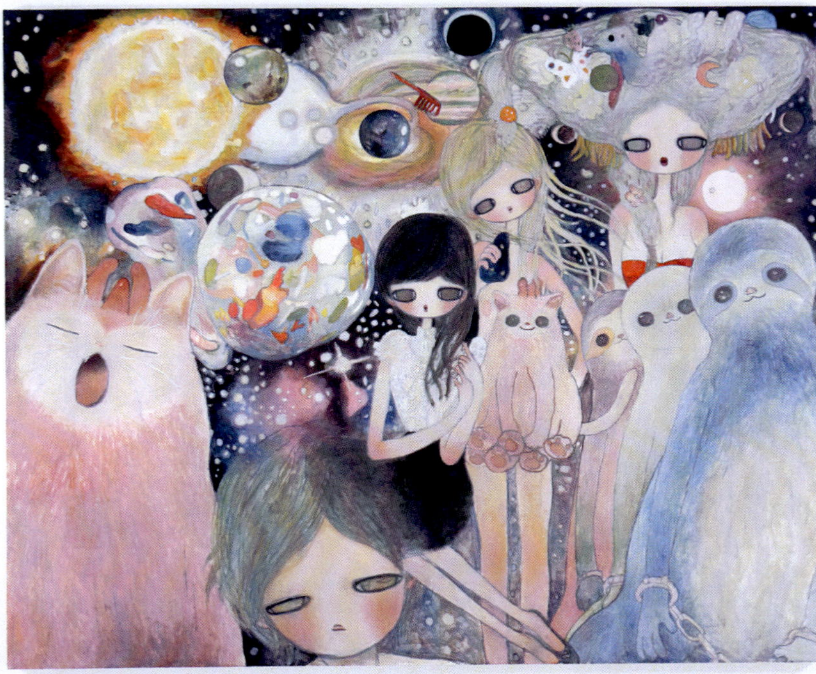

Plate 32 Aya Takano, *The Galaxy Inside* (2015), oil on canvas, 71¼ × 89¼″ (181.8 × 227.3 cm). © 2015–17 Aya Takano / Kaikai Kiki Co., Ltd. All Rights Reserved. Courtesy of Galerie Perrotin.

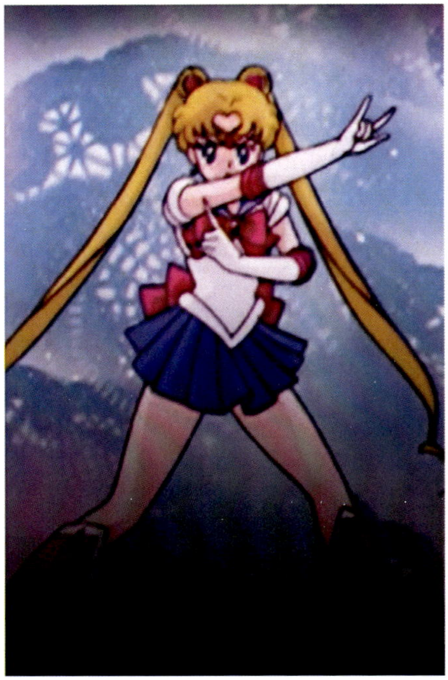

Plate 33a Naoko Takeuchi, *Sailor Moon* (1991), video still.

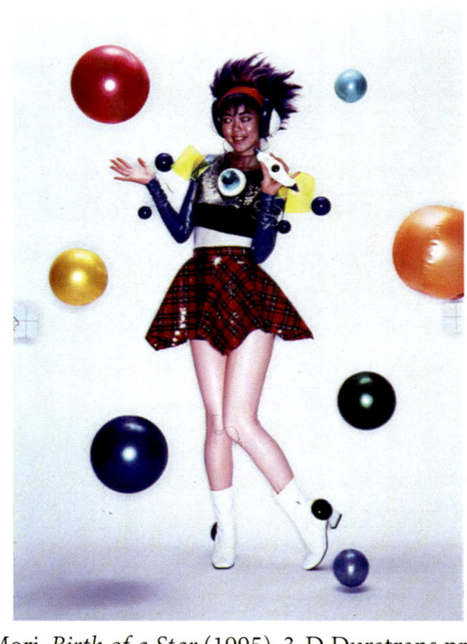

Plate 33b Mariko Mori, *Birth of a Star* (1995). 3-D Duratrans print, acrylic, light box, sound (3:20 minutes). Light box: 73 × 50 × 6″ (185.4 × 127 × 15.2 cm); Duratrans print: 72 × 48 × ¼″ (182.9 × 121.9 × 0.6 cm). © Mariko Mori. Courtesy of the artist and Sean Kelly, New York.

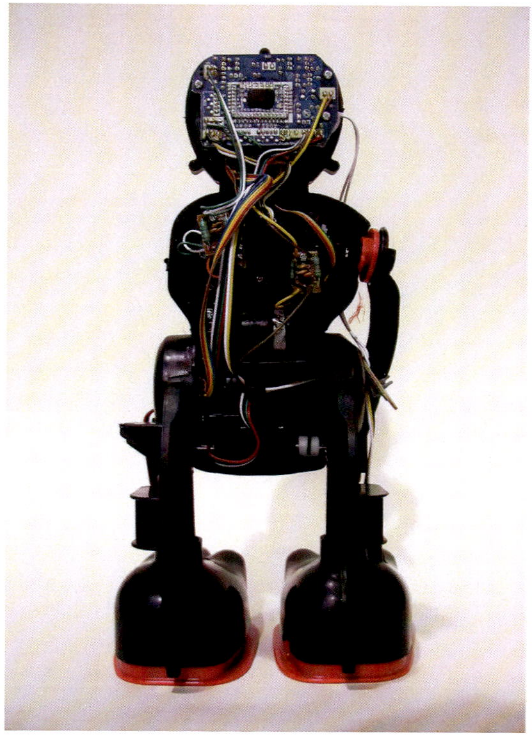

Plate 34 Adrianne Wortzel, photograph of the back of one of the stripped Elmo dolls used for *Battle of the Pyramids* (2008). Courtesy of the artist.

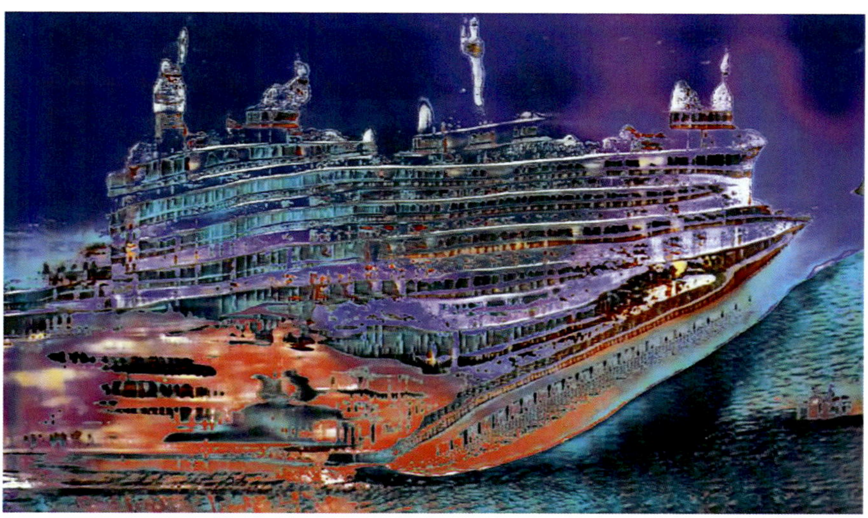

Plate 35 Anne Spalter, *Midnight* (2020), archival print with Ultra Chrome ink on Hannemuhle Photo Rag, 9.25 × 12.75″ (23.5 × 32.4 cm). Courtesy of the artist.

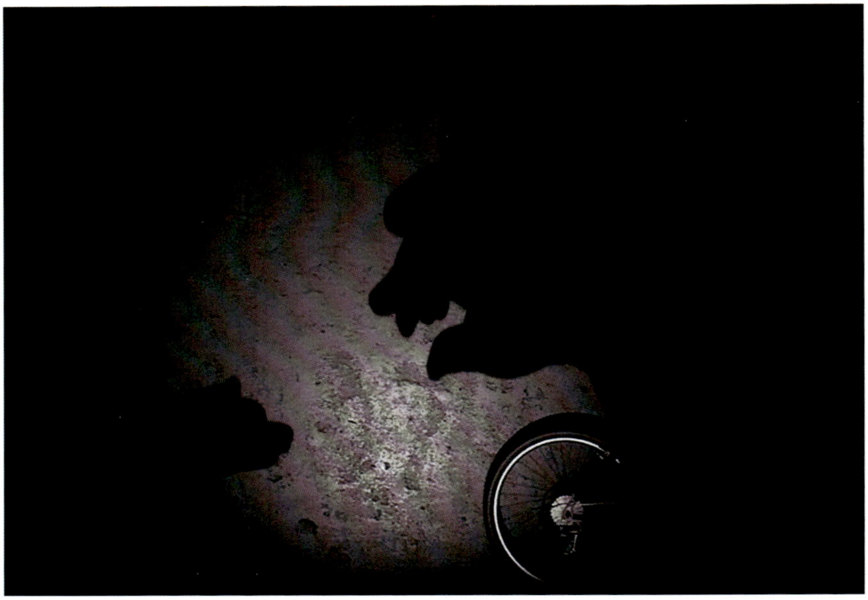

Plate 36 Milica Zec, *Giant* (2016), a virtual reality experience. Courtesy of the artist.

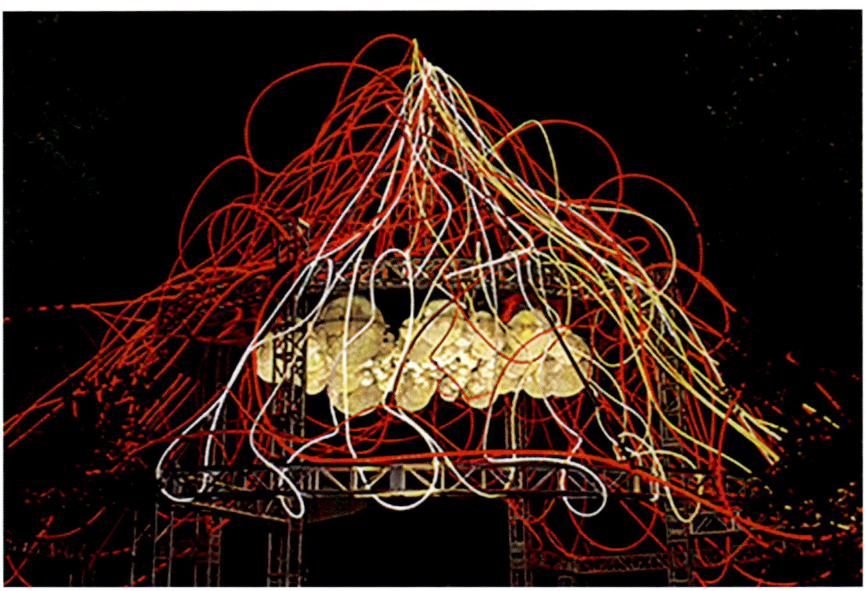

Plate 37 Grimanesa Amorós, *HEDERA* (2018). Light installation, Prospect Park Bandshell. Commissioned by BRIC for the Celebrate Brooklyn! Festival. Courtesy of Grimanesa Amorós Studios.

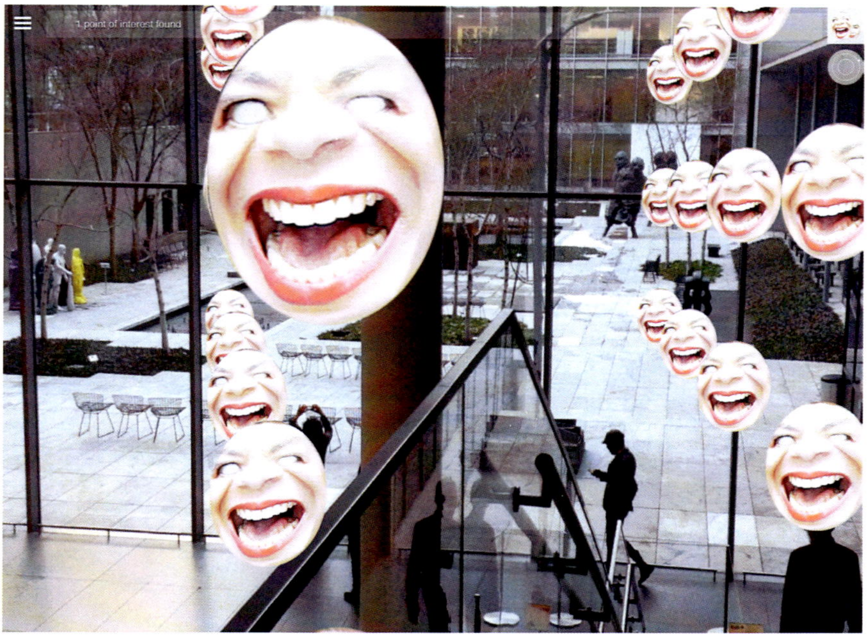

Plate 38 Tamiko Thiel, *ARt Critic Face Matrix* (2010), augmented reality, the garden of the Museum of Modern Art, New York.

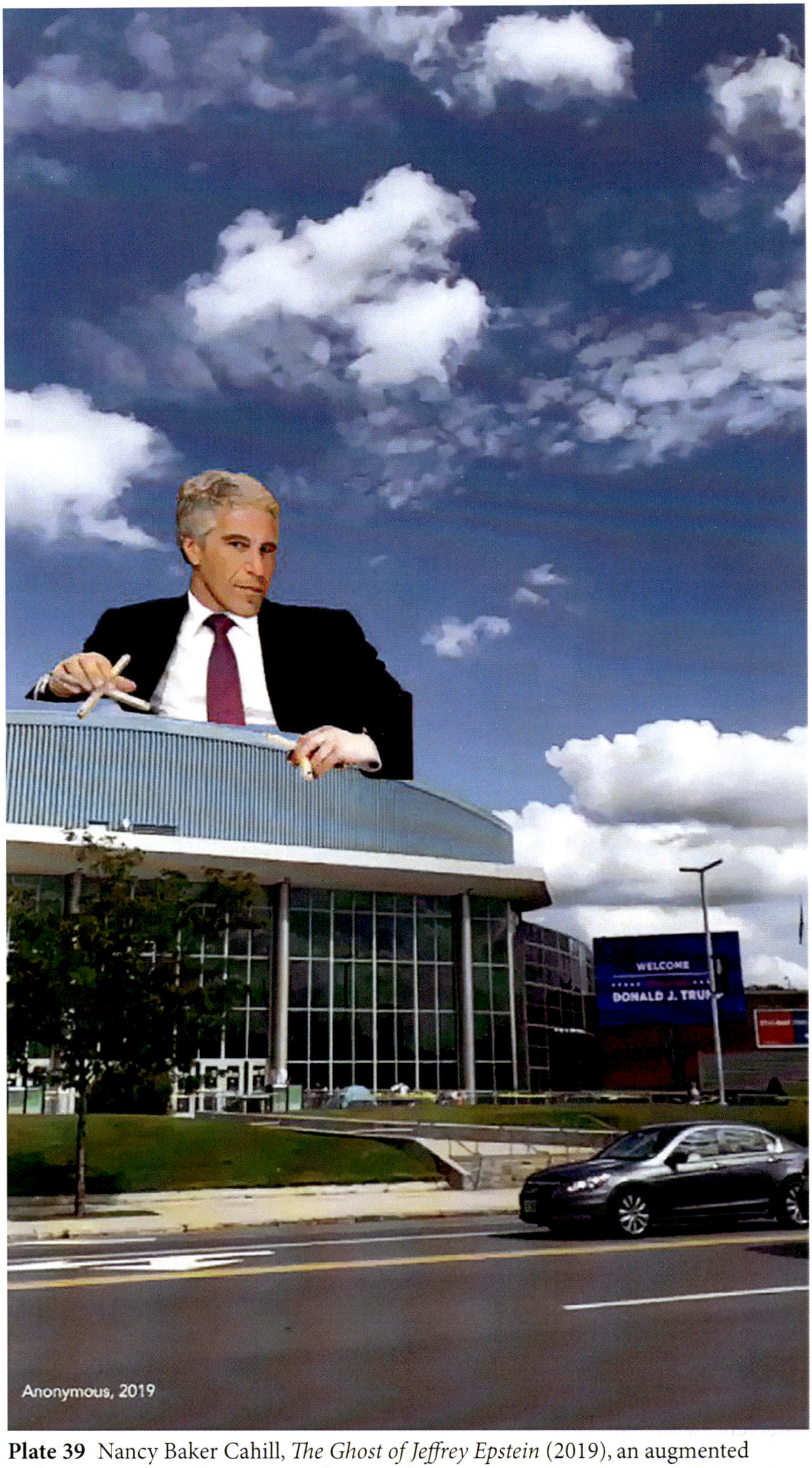

Plate 39 Nancy Baker Cahill, *The Ghost of Jeffrey Epstein* (2019), an augmented reality project, Manchester, NH. Photographer: Jesse Damiani. Courtesy of the artist.

gender (including LGBTQI categories), skin color (eventually, a long list that included non-human skin colors like purple or green), height, weight, eye color, and so on. The bodies existed only as text files, with a few images as examples generated from the descriptions. Thousands of people participated, so many, that Vesna established separate digital locations for them, Limbo for bodies in process, Necropolis for bodies abandoned or killed by their creators, and Showcase for current exhibitions of bodies.[8]

Hannah Black was in the news in 2017 when she wrote to the Whitney Museum of American Art, complaining about the museum's inclusion of the painting in the Biennial by white artist Dana Schutz depicting the young African American boy Emmett Till in his coffin. She accused Schutz of racism in appropriating the likeness, an iconic image of the oppression of Blacks in the US.

Like her activism, her art practice also concerns racism as well as gender, class, labor, and the various modes of controlling individual agency and punishing divergence from the values of the dominant cis white male culture—in other words, all the problematic issues inherent in the patriarchal society. Black combines theory with her own experience, current events, pop culture, and music to create performances, installations, and videos. One of her best-known videos is *My Bodies* (2014). The first half consists of a stream of portraits from corporate websites of the faces of white male executives, their identity easily read through their hairstyles, dress, and poses, with background music composed of clips from various successful Black pop music performers, among them Beyoncé, Rihanna, and Mariah Carey, singing the phrase, "My body." The second half is a succession of phrases scrolled against closeups of the interior surfaces of a cave, about being reborn. The woman to whom the words are addressed is never seen. She exists through her digital devices such as her laptop and her phone. The background music with the words, "My bodies" continues throughout.

The video is about the female body with never an image of an actual female body. It is more than that, however. Black is protesting the invisibility of Black and Brown bodies. As a mixed-race woman herself, she has written that there is not one body, but many bodies, depending on race, gender, and life conditions. She critiques white feminism for making the assumption that there is only one female body and that one body is white. The cave in the video is a limbo in which the owner of the voice is considering being reborn into a new body, and what that new body might be.[9]

In *All My Love All My Love* (2016), the background music consists of Britney Spears singing "Everytime," a ballad about the failure of individuals, the desire for forgiveness, and the continuing need for love. Black writes that this work was inspired by reading about developmental psychologist Harry Harlow's experiment with baby monkeys conducted to determine the need in babies for love. Harlow took infant rhesus monkeys away from their mothers and placed them in a laboratory environment with two mother figures, one constructed from wood and wire, the other out of soft materials. Only the wood and wire "mother" had a bottle of milk. The baby monkeys had to go to the wood and wire figure for nourishment, but they spent the rest of their time snuggled against the soft cloth mother. In Black's video, the dominating image is of two figures completely covered with billowing shroud-like bags (the heads turn out to be electric fans). All that can be seen of them is how the shapes of the bags change as the bodies inside turn toward and away from each other in a futile effort to connect.[10]

In *Credits* (2016), Black imagines *Doggerland*, a dystopia between the British Isles and the mainland of Europe where those who have violated the norms of the cis white society are sent to wander through a forest with masks of shame. Most of the time, the image is from the perspective of the viewer, but finally the artist herself appears with a mask that references the medieval masks used for punishment.[11]

Like Black, the Japanese German artist Hito Steyerl also focuses on social, political, and technological issues like capitalism, postcolonialism, militarization, globalization, visual culture, information technology, inequality, and, like Black, underlying her videos is the constant theme of the binary nature of the patriarchal society and how it controls and oppresses the body. Steyerl not only makes the female body disappear. She makes all physical bodies disappear through becoming pixels, a word invented from "picture element," meaning the basic unit that makes up the image on computer screens, television monitors, and other digital devices.

Steyerl's video, *How Not To Be Seen: A Fucking Didactic Educational .MOV File* (2013), presents five lessons in how to become invisible in the contemporary world of constant visibility and thus avoid surveillance and consequent inclusion in Big Data: (1) "How to Make Something Invisible for a Camera," (2) "How to Be Invisible in Plain Sight," (3) "How to Become Invisible by Becoming a Picture," (4) "How to Be Invisible by Disappearing," and (5) "How to Become Invisible by Merging into a World Made of Pictures." The video starts with an image of a resolution target, a screen used to determine the resolution of photographic details. Steyerl makes use of the multiple meanings of words to reveal the intersection of power, weaponization, surveillance, along with class and gender inequality in the patriarchal capitalist society. While this chart may seem innocuous, it helps the photographer set up the image so that he/she/they can "shoot" the frame. Later in the video, the resolution target is laid flat on a concrete pad in the desert and the voice-over informs viewers that the US army set up resolution targets to scale up the ability to take aerial photographs with more detail, thus helping with surveillance. Steyerl also connects visibility to digital technology with instructions to "scroll, to wipe, to erase, to shrink, to take a picture as she stands facing the camera with her cell phone held in front of her face, hiding her eyes."[12]

One must wait until Lesson Four for a direct link to the female body when the voice-over declares that one of the ways to become invisible is to disappear by becoming "a woman and over 50." Again, Steyerl plays with the multiple meanings of words, in this case, "disappearance," making the connection with the disappearance (invisibility) of older women and the "disappeared," the thousands of victims killed by various regimes.[13]

Steyerl shows what the world would look like if people succeed in making themselves invisible by scenes of ghost-like ciphers, undifferentiated paper dolls, that roam various computer-generated animations of late capitalist society landscapes—malls, car parks, multistory apartment complexes. Most telling of all, however, is when people disappear by becoming pixels—the body is transmuted into the internet as in VNS Matrix's manifesto of many years earlier. The voice-over solemnly announces that "rogue pixels hide in the cracks of old standards of resolution. They throw off the cloak of representation."[14]

The video ends with an almost operatic dystopian combination of visuals and text including an animation of the group, The Three Degrees, singing, "When Will I See You Again" (Plate 21). The three vocalists then become "real" except for the fact that they are seen on an inset screen, making it ambiguous as to whether they still exist physically or only on a video—possibly no more real than the animation. The camera and the camera crew disappear from energy rays thrown off by a cell phone held by a figure in a green body suit or are "tied up by invisible people who descend from above," and the camera crane is "hijacked by pixels" who "happy and excited" are filming from the crane. "Happy pixels fly off into low resolution, gif loop." The final scene shows two of the green-bodysuited figures knocking down the resolution target.[15]

As can be seen from the descriptions of their work, one of the ways that Black and Steyerl eliminate the binary is by merging the offline and digital worlds. That merger is at the heart of Pipilotti Rist's art practice.

Rist is one of the first digital artists to bridge the divide between mainstream and digital art. Her appealing video images generated through elaborate algorithms and projected onto the walls of museums and galleries caught the attention of curators, critics, and the art-going public through installations in major museums like the second-floor atrium in the Museum of Modern Art in New York (2008). Critically acclaimed, she represented Switzerland in the 2006 Venice Biennale.

Rist took the couch-potato mode of viewing and eliminated the distance between the couch and the projected image to insert viewers into the middle of her images. People sit on floor pillows and lounges they can sink into, with nibbles nearby, surrounded by projections on all sides of wall-sized enlargement of body parts—hands, feet, breasts, and both male and female genitalia. The closeups generate the feeling of looking at one's own body or at the body of someone whose body is so nearby as to be touching, emulating the intimacy of love-making. Rist manipulates the camera so that the camera itself becomes an eye in a body, gazing at his/her/their partner or itself. In an interview with Massimo Gioni, Rist explained her intent as giving viewers an experience in which their physical embodiment merges with the outside world in a "technological sublime." They and the camera are one, the camera replicating how the eye sees.[16]

Rist announced her feminism in her first video, *I'm Not the Girl Who Misses Much* (1986) in which a young woman in a black dress with a neckline that accentuates her breasts, sings the title repeatedly. The lyric is based on the first line in the Beatles song, "Happiness is a Warm Gun." The original song is a tirade against gun violence. The image of the girl who dances like a marionette on a string during the entire video is blurred and out of focus. It's a parody on MTV musical numbers and the male gaze.

Rist's feminism is more explicit in *Ever Is Over All* (Plate 22a), produced more than a decade later (1997). In it, a young attractive woman walks down a street, smashing windows of the parked cars with a weapon that looks like a flower on a long stem. A policewoman comes up behind her and nods and smiles at her as if approving her actions rather than arresting her for vandalism. Cars, of course, have long been signifiers of macho dominance thus making her actions a visual metaphor for destruction of the patriarchy by women.[17]

These videos are easily interpreted. More difficult to interpret are Rist's excursions into videos in which she manipulates images of external and internal body parts, flowers, water, and sky into patterns and sequences formed from various editing techniques such as overlaying, collaging, fading, fast-forwarding or slowing the speed of the footage into sensual and often sexually suggestive images. The fragmentation of the nude body, usually female but also sometimes male may communicate intimacy and eroticism, but it also renders the body invisible as a whole entity, thus placing Rist in the lineage stemming from the 1980s feminist artists (Plate 22b).

Just as Rist in *Ever Is Over All* used the stereotypes of cars as male signifiers and a flower as female signifier (actually the flower is red-hot poker, the most phallic of blooms, suggesting the transfer of power from male to female, an intent supported by the red shoes, referring to Dorothy and the power she receives when she puts on the red shoes of the witch in *The Wizard of Oz*), she pairs round fruits with breasts, a volcanic eruption for ejaculation, underwater formations as metaphors for vulvas in videos such as *Pickelporno (Pimple Porno)* (1992), considered too explicit to be aired on YouTube.

These comparisons are so well known in popular culture as to make the conclusion as Amelia Jones does in her essay, "Screen Eroticisms: Exploring Female Desire in Feminist Film and Video" that Rist's intent when she uses these iconographic images is parodic or perhaps more accurately, ludic, as in curator Nancy Spector's interpretation of Rist's work.[18]

Rist's work and her intent are often described as pleasure for the viewer, but they are layered with various considerations, not only about sexual desire, but also with entropy and abjection, again reminiscent of earlier artists like Cindy Sherman and Nan Goldin. In describing *Fourth Floor to Mildness* (2016), one of Rist's underwater video installations, to Natasha Bullock, curator at the Contemporary Museum of Art, Australia, Rist referred to the process of entropy by which organic bodies, plant or animal, revert ultimately to "water, mud, slime."[19]

These three digital artists, Black, Steyerl, and Rist, of the twenty-first century's first two decades reveal common characteristics. All three eliminate the representation of the female body as a totality. Next, they derive inspiration from popular culture such as music, Hollywood film, and television, reflecting the way in which high art and popular culture have been merging in the twenty-first century. Third, they are intersectional, merging feminism with other social and political issues. Black and Steyerl are anti-capitalist, anti-inequality, anti-racist, anti-sexist, anti-militaristic. In other words, they oppose the patriarchic system that renders difference and oppression. While Rist is not intersectional in the same way, she merges male and female sexual identities, reflecting the new fluidity of gender and sexuality in this century.

The work of artists like Steyerl, Black, and Rist remains problematic. The question persists as to whether they truly disrupt the binary and the gender power relations of the heteronormative society or whether they are simply reinforcing the patriarchy by reducing the female body to pixels or body parts. Addressing the complexities that digitization of the female body presents, Jennifer Chan and Leah Schrager, curated an online exhibition in 2015 titled

Body Anxiety that featured 21 female-identified digital artists who interrogate the male domination of the internet and the proliferation of online pornography. After decades of exploration, how to deal with changing the societal position on gender remains unresolved.[20]

Notes

1 See Norma Broude and Mary D. Garrard, *The Power of Feminist Art* (New York: Harry N. Abrams, 1993) for illustrations of Sylvia Sleigh: *The Turkish Bath* (1973), 205; Joan Semmel: *Me Without Mirrors* (1974) and *Intimacy/Autonomy* (1974), 200; Alice Neel: *Self Portrait* (1990), 196; Hannah Wilke: *Scarification Object Series* (1974–82), 198; Judy Chicago: *The Dinner Party* (1974–9), 227; Miriam Schapiro: *Garden of Paradise* (1980), 209.

2 Broude and Garrard, *The Power of Feminist Art*, Harmony Hammond: *Kudzu* (1981), 203; Tee Corinne: *The Cunt Coloring Book*, originally self-published by Corinne for sex education purposes (reissued San Francisco: Last Gasp Publishers, 1989), images available on Google; to view an illustration of Lynda Benglis's famous advertisement of herself, nude, holding a giant dildo in *Artforum*, and to read more about her activism, see Ana Cecilia Alvarez, "Bend It Like Benglis," The New Inquiry, October 20, 2014, https://thenewinquiry.com/bend-it-like-benglis/; for images of Laura Aguilar's photographs, see Tristan Bravinder, "35 Prints by Laura Aguilar, Photographer of Radical Vulnerability, Join the Getty Collection," *The Iris* (blog) J. Paul Getty Trust, September 26, 2019, https://blogs.getty.edu/iris/35-prints-by-laura-aguilar-photographer-of-radical-vulnerability-join-the-getty-collection/.

3 See Thalia Gouma-Peterson and Patricia Mathews, "The Feminist Critique of Art History," *Art Bulletin* 69, no. 3 (September 1987): 326–57.

4 To view images of artworks by Sherman, Kruger, Goldin, and Neshat, see the following: Paul Moorhouse, ed., *Cindy Sherman* (New York: Rizzoli, 2019); Alexander Alberro, ed., *Barbara Kruger* (New York: Rizzoli, 2010); Nan Goldin, *The Other Side* (Göttingen: Steidl, 2019); Melissa Ho, Mahnaz Afkhami, and Melissa Chu, *Shirin Neshat: Facing History* (Washington, DC: Smithsonian Books, 2015). For information on Holzer, see Chapter 5.

5 Nikola Milosevic, "Orlan / Mireille Suzanne Francette Porte," Widewalls, October 11, 2013, https://www.widewalls.ch/artist/orlan/.

6 Artspace Editors, "Excerpts from Michael Archer interview with Mona Hatoum in the monograph on Hatoum, published by Phaidon, 'Using the Body Against the Body Politic: How Art Can Be a Form of Resistance,'" *Artspace Magazine*, November 11, 2016, https://www.artspace.com/magazine/art_101/book_report/using-the-body-against-the-body-politicmona-hatoum-on-lessons-in-art-as-resistance-54354.

7 Artspace Editors: "Excerpts from Michael Archer interview with Mona Hatoum;" "Mona Hatoum (1952.Beirut)," ArtRole [a not-for-profit organization to promote] "Cultural exchange through the development of art activities between The Middle East & the rest of the world"), http://artrole.org/wp-content/uploads/MONA-HATOUM-c.pdf.

8 http://www.bodiesinc.ucla.edu/frames1.html.

9 Hannah Black, *My Bodies* (2014), video, 3:31, https://vimeo.com/85906379; Jesse Darling, "Artist Profile: Hannah Black," Rhizome, February 17, 2015, https://rhizome.org/editorial/2015/feb/17/artist-profile-hannah-black/; Rahel Aima, "Body Party: Hannah Black," *Mousse* 57 (February/March 2017), http://moussemagazine.it/rahel-aima-hannah-black-2017/.

10 Hannah Black, *All My Love, All My Love*, video, 2015, excerpt, https://vimeo.com/121996781.

11 Hannah Black, *Credits*, 2016, excerpt, https://vimeo.com/169698130.

12 Hito Steyerl, *How Not to Be Seen: A Fucking Didactic Educational .MOV File*, video, 15:51, 2013, Artforum, https://www.artforum.com/video/hito-steyerl-how-not-to-be-seen-a-fucking-didactic-educational-mov-file-2013-51651; Kaegan Sparks, "To Cut and To Swipe: Understanding Hito Steyerl Through 'How Not to Be Seen,'" Momus: A Return to Art Criticism, May 12, 2015, https://momus.ca/to-cut-and-to-swipe-understanding-hito-steyerl-through-how-not-to-be-seen/.

13 Ibid.

14 Ibid.

15 Ibid.

16 Pipilotti Rist, "Pipilotti Rist Wants You to Spit on Your Mobile Phone: A Q&A with the Ecstatic Hippie Feminist Artist," based on excerpts from Gioni's interview with Rist in *Pipilotti Rist: Pixel Forest*, ed. Massimiliano Gioni and Margot Norton (New York: Phaidon, 2016), Artspace Magazine, October 22, 2016, https://www.artspace.com/magazine/interviews_features/book_report/pipilotti-rist-phaidon-interview-54294.

17 Pipilotti Rist, *I'm Not the Girl Who Misses Much* (1986), YouTube video, color, sound, 5:02, posted by Mito Tomi, October 15, 2008, https://www.youtube.com/watch?v=hjvWXiUp1hI; Rist, *Ever Is Over All* (1997), two-channel video, color, 4:07, single-channel version uploaded by Iesya Shats, May 12, 2014, https://www.youtube.com/watch?v=-gd06ukX-rU; two-channel version as installed at the National Museum for Foreign Art, Sofia, 1999, uploaded by vobk, May 11, 2009, https://www.youtube.com/watch?v=a56RPZ_cbdc.

18 Pipilotti Rist, "Pipilotti Rist in Conversation with Natalie King," Ocula Magazine, January 8, 2018, https://ocula.com/magazine/conversations/pipilotti-rist/#oc-col-1; Amelia Jones, "Screen Eroticisms: Exploring Female Desire in Feminist Film and Video," in *Resolutions 3: Global Networks of Video*, ed. Ming-Yuen S. Ma and Erika Suderburg (Minneapolis: University of Minnesota Press, 2012), Minnesota

Scholarship Online, August 2015, https://minnesota.universitypressscholarship.com/view/10.5749/minnesota/9780816670826.001.0001/upso-9780816670826-chapter-22.

19 Natasha Bullock, "Pipilotti Rist: 'Sip My Ocean,'" *Museum of Contemporary Art, Australia, Stories and Ideas*, November 1, 2017, https://www.mca.com.au/stories-and-ideas/pipilotti-rist-sip-my-ocean-curatorial-essay/.

20 Digital Artists Group, https://www.facebook.com/groups/digitalartistsgroup; Jennifer Chan and Leah Schrager, "*Body Anxiety*, an Online Exhibition," Body Anxiety, http://bodyanxiety.com/about/ includes images by the participating artists and links to reviews, opened January 24, 2015; Josephine Bosma, "'Body Anxiety,' Sabotaging Big Daddy Mainframe, via Online Exhibition," Rhizome, January 26, 2015, https://rhizome.org/editorial/2015/jan/26/body-anxiety/; Johanna Fateman, "Women on the Verge: Art, Feminism, and Social Media," *Artforum* 53 no. 8 (April 2015): 218–33.

9

Creating Feminist Paradigms of Knowledge Through Digital Technology

As Thomas Kuhn wrote in *The Structure of Scientific Revolutions* (1962), knowledge is a set of paradigms that seem immutable but change when the conditions are right. This chapter highlights digital artists who challenge the knowledge paradigms in the patriarchal society with the goal of creating new epistemological paradigms that benefit everyone in the society rather than just the dominant group. Their work covers biology, psychology, physics, climate studies, the universe, and the digital world itself.[1]

A New York–based artist with a professional scientific background, Ellen K. Levy deconstructs various scientific assumptions. For instance, in a video/performance, *Stealing Attention* (2009) (Plate 23), she challenges the reliability of perception and shows how it can be psychologically manipulated. First, the audience sees a video that opens with a text asking if the viewer would like to play a game. The next frame shows a grid of cards in the foreground against a background of shelves that hold precious art objects looted from Iraqi museums during the takedown of Saddam Hussein's regime in 2003. Levy tells the audience that the game is to identify how many Queens of Hearts show up on the rest of the video. In succeeding frames, the cards begin to fly in front of the shelves. As the cards fly, the objects on the shelves begin to disappear. When the video concludes, Levy asks the members of the audience to tell what they saw. Levy says that most people respond with the number of Queens they have been able to identify. They are so busy counting cards that they don't even notice that the objects are disappearing. In *Stealing Attention*, as in her other work, Levy connects art, science, and politics.

Another area that Levy has explored is space. The National Aeronautics and Space Administration (NASA) Art Program was established in 1962 by James Webb, then NASA director, only four years after the establishment of NASA itself. The public was becoming interested in NASA and space exploration and Webb felt that artists could convey the excitement of the program better than dry accounts of the science involved. Over 350 artists, including male luminaries like Andy Warhol and Robert Rauschenberg, have been involved with a resulting 2,500 artworks. Webb began the commissioning of portraits of all the astronauts, and also, documentation of significant events, but artists like Levy were free to develop their own ideas.[2]

Levy caught the attention of the NASA Art Program when she created a temporary ceiling painting, *Palomar*, derived from images received by the 200-inch Hale telescope at Mount Palomar, California, in the dome of the National Academy of Sciences building in Washington, DC (on view in 1985; subsequently destroyed by fire, 2013). The dome was the same dimensions as the lens of the telescope. While not directly feminist, Levy's comments about the project reflect her feminist thinking in that she conceives of knowledge as intersectional and fluid. She describes the divisions in her composition as mirroring three areas of cultural inquiry. Images in one-third of the dome refer to biological elements; the second group is devoted to technology; and the third, to architectural features. She also designed the areas so that they interconnect, to reflect how they intersect. She considers art to be the discipline that merges them into one entity.[3]

Levy received her commission from NASA at the time of the *Atlantis* launching in 1985 and created *Space Chrysalis* in response to learning about NASA and the space shuttle, the name alone suggesting an analogy to biological transformation applied to the space mission. The phallic-like forms thrust upward, but dissolve in light at the top of the painting, suggesting their dematerialization in space.[4]

The renowned musician/visual artist Laurie Anderson was also a NASA artist—the first and last artist to be invited to be in residence. During her residency, Anderson worked on a project which she subsequently performed at the Brooklyn Academy of Music (BAM) titled *End of the Moon* (2004). In an essay Vivian Appler has written on Anderson's NASA project, she proposes that the presence of women artists in residence at NASA changes society's perception of women, given the stereotype of science as a male-gendered discipline. Appler extends her analysis to the resulting performance at BAM. She writes that, like the residency itself, the performance is also feminist in that Anderson comes across with the authority to speak about science because she has been anointed by NASA. If a woman artist can understand science, then women members in the audience can believe that they also can understand and participate in science. Appler states that even when women are presenting on scientific issues other than gender, the simple fact that they are addressing issues which are usually assigned to the male sphere is a disruption of gender roles.[5]

Anderson uses several performance devices to bring the seemingly secret, arcane, and elite NASA science down to earth and accessible to members of a nonscientist audience. The moon, which appears on the opposite side of the stage from where she is sitting, is represented not by a projection of a photograph of the moon but by a projection of Neil Armstrong's footprint which is immediately recognizable to the audience despite its having been impressed on the moon's surface a decade and a half earlier than the performance. While the image humanizes the landing on the moon, it also resonates with memories of the Cold War politics fundamental to the space race of the 1960s. Furthermore, as Anderson goes on to describe the process by which the Hubble Telescope images are produced, she talks about the colorization that is performed on the photographs in order to make them more distinct and tells the audience how arbitrary they are; she elicits a laugh when she says that anyone in the audience could pick another color scheme and it would work just as well. Then using a camera, Anderson substitutes herself for an astronaut by images that show her floating upside down as she plays her violin.[6]

Another feminist digital artist who participated in a residency at a space research site is Addie Wagenknecht, the founder of Deep Lab, a feminist women's technical collaborative. She had a 2018 residency at COSMOS, an art science residency program at the University of Manchester, UK where the Lovell Telescope, at that time the third largest telescope on the world, is located. Her project, titled *Hidden in Plain Sight*, consisted of harnessing the radio waves collected by the telescope into patterns of light that flickered over the structure of the telescope accompanied by a broadcasted score (the residency is held in conjunction with the Bluedot Festival). Wagenknecht's concept was the similarity of the internet and the cosmos. The infrastructure of both is hidden in plain sight, the amount of data is infinite, along with a complexity that is hard to grasp, and there is "a sense of placelessness." The flickering of the lighted radio waves over the surface of the telescope's structure hides the structure while the structure does remain "in plain sight."[7]

The parallels among the three artists is striking: their interest in making the invisible visible; their belief that knowledge should be accessible to all; their conviction that knowledge is both intersectional and fluctuating; and their view that knowledge is dependent on who is the creator and who is the recipient, all principles that are integral to feminist theory. In an interview about her installation, Wagenknecht says, "The observer is not stationary and part of the observation is knowing your own situation."[8]

Kathy High and Patricia Piccinini make art to deconstruct the Darwinian theory of evolution. One of High's videos, *Lily Does Derrida* (2010–12), is a humorous discourse by her deceased dog who, while talking about the connection of human beings to animals, invokes Jacques Derrida's writings on that subject. Lily, the dog, cites Derrida's analysis of the difference between animals and humans: humans are ashamed of being naked; animals on the other hand are always naked (no clothes). Do they feel shame? Lily says she does feel shame in front of the cat and then goes on to say that humans were the ones who created the name "animal" and thus distinguished animals from humans. Through the ludic, High believes she can help people think about animals and humans as a continuum rather than a hierarchy that places humans above all other life.

High has also created a series of works about the bacteria that exist in the human digestive system and contribute to metabolic processes. She has been carrying on collaborations with medical experts on what she calls "poop." Rather than seeing "poop" as abject, she suggests that it should be viewed for its centrality to life itself. She makes the point that elimination of waste materials from the body is as fundamental as taking in nourishment and that it is time to abandon the social taboos that surround defecation and consider how "poop" can be used, citing the rise of antibiotic resistance that may require more reliance on the body's natural functions. High's work can be considered oppositional to the psychoanalytic theory of the abject, developed by French feminist, Julia Kristeva, which postulates that human beings place taboos around the sight of internal bodily processes and substances as reminders of the body's vulnerability and mortality.[9]

Piccinini disputes evolutionary science by creating computer-generated grotesque sculptures that, although based on the human body, have imaginary features that turn them into disturbing variations distorting the features and shape of the human form. In her installations she places them in relation to other sculptures that retain the usual look of human beings: a child hugs one of the strange creatures or a mother who looks like a cross between *Homo sapiens* and a gorilla suckles a human infant. Piccinini says that her work is meant to reveal the fear of difference and to change attitudes toward difference in appearance as abject, something from which to avert one's eyes.[10]

Iranian artist Morehshin Allahyari also works with the grotesque, using 3-D printing technology to create composite sculptures that in her words "transcend the binaries of human/animal, East/West, self/other." She calls her art practice "Additivism," a word combining additive and activism. Her first additive pieces related to activities forbidden by the Iranian regime. It was forbidden to walk dogs outside. Sex objects were forbidden. Internet usage was often forbidden. Responding to these restrictions, her first computer-created sculpture was a dog with a dildo and a satellite dish fused together.[11]

Allahyari lives in self-imposed exile because her political activism puts her in danger if she returns to Iran, but she is deeply immersed in her heritage. Her current art practice involves digital archiving of documents and other material pertaining to Iranian cultural memory and history. She also uses 3-D scanning and printing to resurrect works purposefully destroyed by ISIS or inadvertently by Western forces in the power struggles over the Middle East (Plate 24).

Important to Allahyari is the identity of the person who is reconstituting cultural objects. Her concern is how digital printing can become a new form of colonialism. She says that digital capacity is largely in the hands of white people. When white people (self) are the ones refiguring lost objects belonging to the cultural history of non-whites (the other), it is a form of digital colonialism—whites reclaiming the sculptures after destruction by non-whites like ISIS.

During a residency at Rhizome in New York, Allahyari collected and made available programs by which anyone could refigure a lost object through 3-D printing. She relates that she has received hundreds of images of refigured items and enthusiastic communications. Her goal is to spread knowledge of the techniques to enable oppressed populations to restore their own cultural histories. She cites how capitalism prevents the spread of that knowledge in the example of SciArt, an online nonprofit organization that also makes information on 3-D replication available, but not to individuals—only to institutions—at a price, thus benefiting monetarily from the transactions.[12]

Israeli/American artist, Neri Oxman is another artist who found 3-D digital printing a medium for her art practice. Oxman, a professor at MIT, has disrupted the conventional paradigm of the relationship between art and nature in which art mimics nature, by using actual biological constituents for design purposes. She refers to her art practice as material ecology, finding elements in nature that become artmaking components ranging from slime molds and silkworms to bacteria. Oxman also develops new processes through which materials that have had one structure are transformed into new structures such as happened with glass when Oxman developed the technology for making objects out of glass using algorithms for the 3-D digital printer. The results were forms never possible before, and thus useful in innovative architectural design.

One of Oxman's projects was to modify a 3-D digital printer to use the chitin which forms the exoskeleton of the crab. Through experimentation Oxman reversed the molecular structure of chitin so that instead of being impervious to the action of water, it became water-biodegradable, providing a prototype procedure for biodegrading plastic bags. In another project, Oxman printed clothing that was resistant to microbial infection, thus protecting wearers in areas of epidemic disease. Using 6,500 silkworms to produce the necessary silk, and algorithms in a digital 3-D printer, Oxman printed a silk dome, suggesting how nature can provide eco-friendly building materials. *Cartesian Wax: Prototype for a Breathing Skin* (2007) referring to Descartes's 1640 definition of the essence of wax as being what survives its changing forms, is another experiment to develop eco-friendly architectural building materials. The wax that forms the cells in this wall piece become thinner or thicker in response to the degree of light in the room.[13]

American artist Heather Dewey-Hagborg works on gene technology. She is concerned about the way in which gene technology is being used without thinking of the consequences, as, for instance, in determining the sex of fetuses, in criminal cases, or for surveillance. She uses her art practice to make the case for public awareness of the potential threat of genetic surveillance by picking up litter from the street containing DNA evidence such as cigarette butts, wads of discarded gum, or strands of hair, then extracting the DNA from these discards, duplicating it, and using facial recognition software in reverse, to create three-dimensional portraits of the people who have discarded the waste. The actual sculptures are not frightening in themselves but the implication is terrifying—the idea that people can be identified and traced through a random act of discarding waste that carries their genetic makeup. That implication is enhanced by the way the sculptures are displayed, with a petri dish containing the object from which the DNA has been extracted along with a photograph of the location where the object was found.[14]

Jennifer Hall investigates the body's functions in relation to health, privacy, and the community in an installation titled *Tipping Point: Health Narratives from the South End* (2005) created in collaboration with a team consisting of Ellen Ginsburg, a medical anthropologist and ethnographer; Blyth Hazen, an artist and expert in robotic systems; Arnie Hernandez, software programmer, Mike Middleton, interactive DVD producer; and Liana Wilks-Dupoise, fabrication assistant. As visitors entered the gallery, sensors measured various aspects of their movements—how many were coming in at one time, how fast they were walking, how close were they to each other. The sensors sent this data through an algorithm that collected it all and sent it to the sculptures in the gallery, which moved in response to the information they received. The sculptures became mechanical portraits of the health of visitors to the exhibition.[15]

In another project, Hall queried the interaction among living organisms, machines, and the impact of society. Titled *Acupuncture for a Temporal Fruit* (2008), viewers became complicit in the torture of tomatoes enclosed in glass domes. As viewers move closer to the domes, mechanized needles pierced the tomatoes faster and faster. As viewers moved away, the piercings became less and less frequent. During the period of the exhibition, the holes left in the tomatoes became moldy and the tomatoes began to rot. The installation served as a critique for the actions of those in power who could act negatively on helpless individuals, and particularly on medical practice, given the impact of the needle piercing the skin of the tomato, reminiscent of a hypodermic needle on human skin.[16]

Anicka Yi takes another approach in using biotechnology to disrupt patriarchal paradigms of knowledge. Her art practice is focused around the sense of smell. Her most ambitious project has been the collection of bacteria from the orifices of about a hundred women, growing the bacteria, and then exhibiting the results in an installation that involves sculpture, video, and sound. She creates art to counteract what she terms the prevailing "ocular-centrism" that defines art in most cultures, whereas other senses, particularly smell, can evoke personal memories, transmit one to a hallucinatory sphere, and convey history. She is also concerned with correcting the misunderstanding that scent is feminine because it is "elusive and subjective," terms that are used to stereotype women. She insists that smells are "objective."[17]

Zina Saro-Wiwa (Plate 25) is an artist who represents the globalism of the early twenty-first century in her own life. She was born in Nigeria, moved to the UK at the age of one, and has lived and exhibited on both sides of the Atlantic, most recently for over a decade in the United States. She has also returned to Nigeria where she established Boys' Quarters Project Space, a contemporary art gallery in Port Harcourt, Nigeria. In reentering the land of her birth, she wanted to create an artwork that would capture the sense of place she experienced. Her work disrupts stereotypes about non-Western peoples and countries from the perspective of postcolonialism and ecofeminism but while the resulting videos and photographs are images of individuals in Nigeria, they speak of the importance of place in people's lives everywhere. As she herself has said, "experimental ethnography gives me permission to think about and comment on knowledge production." One of her most compelling installations is *Table Manners* (2014–16). On large screens arranged so that viewers walk through two rows of suspended screens, individuals eat their meals, rather as if no one is looking, yet aware of performing in front of the camera. Saro-Wiwa says, "That action of people eating on camera, their hands moving from the plate to their mouths and back to the plate, acts as a kind of metaphorical suturing. With this movement, I see them as insisting on their place in the environment and repairing their broken landscape, all the while implicating the viewer in this process through their gaze." Now living in Los Angeles, she is applying her art practice to the individuals and places around her. "Even when it is hyper specific about a particular place, I position my work globally and cosmically."[18]

Similarly Michèle Magema, from the Republic of the Congo, as both European and African considers herself a resident of the globe rather than of one specific location in both her life and work. Magema describes her intersectional art practice as "exitism." She says she uses her body to express the eternal nature of being a woman despite the vicissitudes of time, but at the same time, the multiplicity of identity that contemporary women bear in the postcolonial era in Africa and other parts of the world.[19]

Perhaps it is her double identity that has led Magema to double frames in her videos. *Derrière la Mer* [Behind the ocean] (2016) shows two frames of Magema walking into the sea. In both she finally disappears into the water, but then in one frame, reemerges and walks back toward the camera. She begins to put up signs in the water itself that are illegible. Finally, she lies down in the shallows, very much looking like a dead body. Two signs are clear to read, one says "past" and the other, "truth." The soundtrack consists of African chanting. It is evident that the work is about the vast migration from Africa across the Mediterranean to Europe that took place in the second decade of the twenty-first century in which, because of the exploitation of the migrants, many Africans perished in overloaded, unsafe boats.[20]

Saro-Wiwa and Magema are only two artists from various African countries who emerged in the twenty-first century as important voices in creating new paradigms of knowledge. Their dismantling of the stereotypes about Africa and Africans in the knowledges of Western heteronormative society, valuable in itself, has broader implications of how a dominating group, in this case, the Western colonialist countries, shapes accepted knowledge and loses sight of the individual. Magema, by using her own body, emphasizes the personhood of Africans as opposed to the generalized universal African of Western culture. Saro-Wiwa, in her connection to individuals through recording the human act of eating, restores the status of the individual as a physical and spiritual being.

Mary Mattingly's projects are an example of the art practice of ecofeminists in Western countries. Mattingly says that the goal of her work is to awaken social consciousness. She hopes for a future which she describes as "post-humanist." It would be world in which people will be able to provide at least some of their essentials for themselves, will have the will to help their neighbors, and will develop a balance between what they take from the earth, and what they can give back.

Mattingly mixes the digital world and the offline world together into a seamless whole. While the finished projects have a DIY materiality, they are the result of meticulous research and online planning through the use of mostly open source programs. The *Flock House Project* is a good example of how Mattingly wishes to change knowledge structures, in this instance, about migration. During a residency at Eyebeam, an institute that specifically supports projects combining the digital and the physical, Mattingly designed modular portable housing, based on Buckminster Fuller's geodesic dome, that can be built from recycled materials, powered by renewable energy, and deposited anywhere in the world very quickly when migration because of climate change disasters, political violence, and other crises occurs.[21]

Diane Burko has been working on climate change since the early twenty-first century. Among the founders of the Feminist Art Movement of the 1970s, Burko organized Philadelphia Focuses on Women in the Visual Arts (FOCUS), the first city-wide celebration of feminist artists. Burko became concerned about the environment when she revisited some of the locations that had inspired her earlier paintings—glaciers that had disappeared, ice caps that had shrunk, waterfalls that had become trickles. Familiar with digital technologies, she conceived of lenticular technology as a perfect metaphor for expressing climate change visually. She created a series of lenticular images in which she embedded abstract landscapes which change as viewers pass by, thus conveying the dramatic transformations that have occurred in physical life (Plate 26).[22]

Similarly, Marina Abramović, the performance artist whose art practice was founded on feminism early in her career, used digital technology to create work about climate change. She initiated *Rising* (2018) as a virtual reality (VR) project. Viewers entered an intimate space wearing a VR headset and saw an avatar of the artist encased in a glass cylinder. As they watched, the water in the cylinder rose, threatening to drown her. Abramović's avatar began to speak to them, asking them to pledge support in saving the environment. As each gave a positive response to her plea, the water level dropped. Aware that VR could only be appreciated in person, Abramović brought *Rising* to another level of public participation by creating an app through which viewers around the globe could experience *Rising* through their cell phones.[23]

Sondra Perry interweaves the Black body, her own, and a female Black avatar (Plate 27), with digital images derived from family history and art history to expose white privilege and oppression in the patriarchal construction of history. The Serpentine Gallery, London mounted the first exhibition of Perry's work in Europe in 2018. In one of the galleries were two workout machines, classist symbols of prosperity, that viewers could operate; the first, a stationary bicycle with a three-screen video installation was titled *Graft and Ash for a Three Monitor Workstation*. As viewers worked hard on the pedals of the stationary bike, Perry's avatar talked about the hard work African Americans must do to survive. She (the avatar) also talked about the poor health issues that plague Blacks versus whites. The second was a rowing machine also with a three-screen video of waves, that echoed the projection of violent waves onto the walls of the adjoining gallery based on J.M.W. Turner's *The Slave Ship*, orignally titled *Slavers Throwing Overboard the Dead and Dying—Typhoon Coming On*, first exhibited in 1840. The Turner painting represents a sickening act, the throwing overboard of 133 African Blacks being transported to become slaves, for the sake of making an insurance claim. Turner, an abolitionist, was horrified by the incident and thus made the painting. Perry used an open source program to modify the waves, turning them purple, the color that comes on the monitor when there is an error, thus forming a metaphor for the "mistake" made by the murder. On another wall is a projection of a close up of Perry's own skin in front of which is a video on which is screened *TK (Suspicious Glorious Absence)* which consists of clips taken from body cameras that recorded everyday actions like walking down the street along with scenes of protests and shots of Perry's own family.[24]

Perry like the other artists in this chapter is transforming the paradigmatic knowledges of the patriarchal society into new paradigms that will provide dignity and equality to all rather than only to an elite white male class.

Notes

1 Thomas S. Kuhn, *The Structure of Scientific Revolutions* (Chicago: University of Chicago Press, 1962).

2 Hannah Hotovy, "NASA and Art: A Collaboration Colored with History," NASA History, April 18, 2017, https://www.nasa.gov/feature/nasa-and-art-a-collaboration-colored-with-history.

3 Ellen K. Levy, "Visualizing Evolution: A Painter's Interaction with Science and Technology," *Leonardo* 20, no.1 (1987): 3–8.

4 Ibid.

5 Vivian Appler, "Moonwalking with Laurie Anderson: The Implicit Feminism of *The End of the Moon*," *The Journal of American Drama and Theatre (JADT)* 28, no. 2 (Spring 2016), https://jadtjournal.org/2016/05/27/moonwalking-with-laurie-anderson-the-implicit-feminism-of-the-end-of-the-moon/.

6 Ibid.
7 Addie Wagenknecht, "Timelapse of *Hidden in Plain Sight* (2018)," YouTube video, 0:20, posted by ANDfestival, August 2, 2018, https://www.youtube.com/watch?v=usLD6YKj8P0; "Cosmos, a Flagship International Art Science Residency Exploring Deep Space" includes Wagenknecht talking about her project, YouTube video, 3:24, posted by ANDfestival, September 25, 2018, https://www.youtube.com/watch?v=sPhBRNE_TdY.
8 Abandon Normal Devices, "Learning to See: A Conversation with Addie Wagenknecht on COSMOS 2018," Journal, July 11, 2018, https://www.andfestival.org.uk/blog/a-conversation-with-addie-wagenknecht/.
9 Kathy High, "Straight Talk with Kathy High," interview with Julia Swanson, *SciArt Magazine* 23, no. 4 (April 2017), https://www.sciartmagazine.com/straight-talk-kathy-high.html; Kathy High, *Fecal Matters* (2018), video 19:21, You Are My Future, https://www.youaremyfuture.com/fecal-matters.
10 Peter Hennessey, "Patricia Piccinini—Early Installations," Patricia Piccinini, Writings, http://patriciapiccinini.net/printessay.php?id=9.
11 Marie Chatel, "In Focus: Morehshin Allahyari," Medium, March 15, 2019, https://medium.com/digital-art-weekly-by-danae-hi/in-focus-morehshin-allahyari-807c8b3156c8.
12 Ibid.
13 Neri Oxman, "Printing 3-D Buildings: Five Tenets of a New Kind of Architecture," an interview with Pedro Navarro, Metalocus, December 17, 2012, https://www.metalocus.es/en/news/printing-3D-buildings-five-tenets-a-new-kind-architecture.
14 Heather Dewey-Hagborg, *Stranger Visions* (2012–14), text, photos, and video (4:17) documenting Dewey-Hagborg's project, https://deweyhagborg.com/projects/stranger-visions; Megan Gambino, "Cracking the Code of the Human Genome: Creepy or Cool? Portraits Derived from the DNA in Hair and Gum Found in Public Places," Smithsonian Magazine, May 3, 2013, https://www.smithsonianmag.com/science-nature/creepy-or-cool-portraits-derived-from-the-dna-in-hair-and-gum-found-in-public-places-50266864/.
15 Ellen S. Ginsberg and Jennifer Hall, "The Tipping Point Project: A Case Study in the Collaboration Between Medical Anthropology and Art," in *Blaze: Discourse on Art, Women, and Feminism*, ed. Karen Frostig and Kathy A. Halamka (Newcastle: Cambridge Scholars, 2007), 229–37.
16 Jennifer Hall, *Acupuncture for Temporal Fruit* (1999), robotic and interactive installation, DeCordova Museum, http://www.jenhall.org/acupuncture.html; "Acupuncture for Temporal Fruit," www.dowhile.org/physical/overview/presentations/mits/acu/acu3.html.
17 Anicka Yi, "Anicka Yi, A Political Interview," interview by Paul Laster, Conceptual Fine Arts, last update December 3, 2019, https://www.conceptualfinearts.com/

cfa/2017/05/09/anicka-yi-and-her-political-statement-to-counter-the-ocular-centric-society-we-live-in-an-interview/.

18 Ted Loos, "For Zina Saro-Wiwa, Food Carries Meaning and Metaphor," *New York Times*, December 4, 2018, https://www.nytimes.com/2018/12/04/arts/for-zina-saro-wiwa-food-art-basel.html; Claire Armitstead, "Zina Saro-Wiwa, 'For Ten Years, I Didn't Cry About My Father,'" *Guardian* (US edition), September 10, 2018, https://www.theguardian.com/artanddesign/2018/sep/18/zina-saro-wiwa-artist-for-ten-years-i-didnt-cry-about-my-father.

19 *Neo-Griot* (blog), "The Video Artwork of Michèle Magema," African Digital Art, January 19, 2016, http://kalamu.com/neogriot/2016/03/19/video-the-video-artwork-of-michele-magema/; Michèle Magema, "Global Feminisms: Michèle Magema, March 23–25, 2007," YouTube video, 21:50, posted by Brooklyn Museum, April 28, 2010, https://www.youtube.com/watch?v=O3QHF_1GVv0; Julie Crenn, "Michèle Magema: 'Without Echo, There Is No Meeting,'" *nParadoxa* 31 (January 2013): 15–22, https://www.ktpress.co.uk/nparadoxa-volume-details.asp?volumeid=31.

20 Fabienne Bieri, "Intervention with the Body," The Art of Intervention, November 28, 2018, https://theartofintervention.blog/2018/11/28/intervention-with-the-body/.

21 Mary Mattingly, *Flock House*, https://marymattingly.com/pdfs/FHBookTest2.pdf.

22 Tomorrow, "Diane Burko," https://tomorrowcreates.com/artist/diane-burko/; Diane Burko, "Diane Burko," Institute of Arctic and Alpine Research, University of Colorado, Boulder. People, https://instaar.colorado.edu/people/diane-burko/.

23 Marina Abramović, *Rising*, augmented reality (AR) version for iPhone, iPad, iPod available free at https://apps.apple.com/tt/app/rising/id1441958701; Marina Abramović, "Acute Art Presents: Marina Abramović Discusses Her First Virtual Reality project, *Rising*," YouTube video, 2:13, posted by Acute Art, June 27, 2019, https://www.youtube.com/watch?v=lQ3Yxi6pCvc; Javier Pes, "Save the Planet—and Marina Abramović's Avatar—From Rising Water Levels in the Artist's First Virtual-Reality Work," Artnet News, March 7, 2018, https://news.artnet.com/art-world/save-planet-marina-abramovics-avatar-artists-first-vr-work-1238081.

24 Nora N. Khan, "No Safe Mode," Flash Art, September 18, 2017, https://flash---art.com/article/sondra-perry/; Rianna Jade Parker, "How Sondra Perry Turned Glitches into Art About a Broken World at the Serpentine," Artnet News, May 18, 2018, https://news.artnet.com/exhibitions/sondra-perry-at-serpentine-1288877; Sondra Perry, "Sondra Perry: Typhoon Coming On," interview by Hans Ulrich Obrist, YouTube video, 14:26, posted by Serpentine Galleries, May 16, 2018, https://www.youtube.com/watch?v=Qunkb4piXGw; " 'Sondra Perry Typhoon Coming On,' ICA Miami, 2018," YouTube video 2:50, posted by MSA eXperimental, September 13, 2018, https://www.youtube.com/watch?v=Rpr1j892U_U.

10

Surveillance

Surveillance takes place in obvious and subtle forms. A general definition would the observation by some, of others, with the intention of control. Addie Wagenknecht's work in relation to science and technology was presented in the last chapter. Her work, on a lighter note (although a serious subject) serves also to introduce this chapter. Wagenknecht's video, *Prism Break Barbie* (2013) is available on the Free Art and Technology Lab (F.A.T.) website with directions to create your own *Prism Break Barbie*. The promotion video declares that you start out by selecting your electronic interactive Barbie doll and modify it by inserting a spring-loaded spike into an opening in the doll's body. You can protect yourself from surveillance by sitting Barbie down forcefully on any smartphone, external hard drive, or other data-collecting device, thus releasing the spring. The spike will shatter the selected device, thus preventing any further data collection by that device.[1]

Concern about surveillance of all kinds has been expressed for centuries. The English philosopher and founder of Utilitarianism Jeremy Bentham began the modern consideration of surveillance with his theory of the panopticon which was published in 1785. The principle of the panopticon as applied to prisons is an architectural concept: the cells comprise a circular form, one cell deep. A guard house occupies the center of the space. The cells are open to view from the guard house, so that the guards can see into the cells, but the prisoners can't see into the guard house. The prisoners come to feel that they are being watched at all times. Thus, a small number of guards can supervise a large number of prisoners.[2]

Bentham's concept of the panopticon still frames the discourse on surveillance at the end of the second decade of the twenty-first century. Shu Lea Cheang represented Taiwan at the 2019 Venice Biennale with *3 × 3 × 6*, an installation in the Palazzo delle Prigioni [Palace of the Prisons]. The exhibition centered around a watchtower like Bentham's in which digital surveillance cameras collected the visual data on all the spectators who came to the exhibition who, in their turn, were watching videos of historical and modern sexual deviants, ranging from such figures as the Marquis de Sade and Casanova, to the African "sperm bandits" (women who collect sperm to use in rituals). Shu Lea Cheang says of her work on surveillance, "When we think about China's Skynet with 20 surveillance cameras over the land, then it's really a bigger non-confined prison that we live in."[3]

The French theorist Michel Foucault developed a theory of surveillance that applied to the whole society, speculating that members of modern societies internalize the law. For instance, even if no police are present, most people will not go through a red light. Therefore, societies can remain controlled by the dominant group without constant surveillance of its citizens.[4]

Following Foucault's path, feminist theorists and artists have deconstructed how the patriarchal society maintains its power through implicit surveillance, based on norms that define the ideal, benefit the dominant group, and limit the rights of others. As discussed in Chapter 8, on the disappearance of the female body, many feminist artists have addressed the male gaze through removing the female body from the gaze itself, but others continue to bring the female body to the fore, in abject realities and female fantasies that repel the male gaze. Feminist artists have made work on the male gaze as surveillance, the prime example of which is Barbara Kruger's famous photograph, "Your Gaze Hits the Side of My Face."[5]

Brenda Oelbaum is an example of an artist who defines the male gaze as surveillance. She calls herself a "fat artist activist." At the top of her blog is a nude self-portrait of an overweight Oelbaum in a reclining position, satirizing the ideal of slender female nudes in Western culture (Plate 28). Through her videos, Oelbaum exposes how the medicalization of obesity as well as the beauty industry's promotion of thinness is a process of surveillance that victimizes fat women. Oelbaum uses humor to make her point. In one of her videos, she weighs herself, then eats the pages of a diet book, weighs herself again, and ends with the mournful statement that despite ingesting the diet book, she still weighs the same.[6]

Sins Invalid cites its work on behalf of the disabled as counteracting the surveillance practices of the patriarchal society that renders disabled people as invisible. The organization sponsors both live and video performance as art practices that create space for disabled artists, particularly disabled artists of color and disabled gender-variant artists who have been historically marginalized by the conventions of beauty and normalcy in the patriarchal society. On behalf of disabled artists, Sins Invalid makes "an unashamed claim to beauty in the face of invisibility."[7] The artists involved in Sins Invalids provocatively present disabled bodies in various activities hidden from view through the surveillance of the patriarchy, particularly their essence as sexual beings. In the process, they offer representation that is inclusive of all. Many of the artists associated with

Sins Invalid employ satire and humor to send their messages, as for instance, in a video created by Aurora Levins Morales, in which she does a satiric imitation of Julia Child. The video, titled *Pussy Vinaigrette* (2011), uses the format of a classic television cooking lesson to talk about female anatomy and bodily fluids associated with women, all of which are taboo in heteronormative visual culture. In a video animation by Patty Berne, the narrator tells how she engaged in a flirtation on the subway while trying to prevent herself from defecating after eating a dish with chili, to which she is allergic. She finally can't contain herself and finds pleasure in knowing that she is breaking taboos about defecating in public, particularly while flirting.[8]

Shawné Michaelain Holloway exposes how pornography functions as a surveillance mechanism, as a means of exercising power and control in which both the perpetrator and the receiver are complicit, raising issues of consent, trust, domination, submission. Images of female vulvas with sex-toy insertions, nude buttocks, and even penis penetration into various orifices have the look of anatomical explanatory photographs, repellant rather than enticing. Holloway's iconography also includes bodily fluids—ejaculatory liquid (actually spit) and an installation in which a sexually explicit video is seen in the well of a toilet—queering heteronormative sexuality through the abject.[9]

Like Holloway, Leah Schrager also flouts the authority of male surveillance through work about pornography. On her website is a long story about being rejected in an open art exhibition as a commercial artist rather than a true artist because she uses her own body and is therefore selling herself sexually. Schrager goes on to say that images of her body are her iconography just as Keith Haring's linear motifs are his. She asks, why should her images, even though of her body be considered differently?

Schrager has created an avatar named Sarah White who conducts an online performance titled "Naked Therapy" via webcam. While talking with a client, Sarah gradually undresses and the client also undresses. Schrager says that White provides therapy to men of the twenty-first century just as Freud provided therapy to women in the twentieth century. Schrager/White insists that becoming naked allows clients to speak more openly about their problems. She goes on to say that she is working with the state of arousal, rather than simply sexuality and that arousal leads not only to sexual satisfaction but also helps men to become more positive and productive in the other areas of their lives. Often Schrager has been taken seriously, when in actuality, she is satirizing the patriarchal conventions about bodies and sexuality and how they deliver a message of surveillance and control.[10]

Feminist artists have also raged at corporate and government surveillance. As Shoshana Zuboff wrote in the *New York Times* in 2020, surveillance capitalism, meaning the collection of data by corporations for marketing purposes, infiltrated the internet around the turn of the twenty-first century and has largely been unchallenged. Facebook, Microsoft, and Google created software to collect information from users of the internet and smartphone—not only consumer preferences, but also information about health, behavior, and the way individuals live their lives—which are forwarded to the consumer industry for marketing purposes. This information is sold to corporate customers who then use it to sell their own products. Collecting the information is free so that the profits in selling it are enormous.[11]

Adding to the inequality in the control of digital information by corporate superpowers, is the use of surveillance in the response of various governments to terrorism after the September 11, 2001 attacks. This antiterrorist surveillance reached a high around 2010. Then, the whistleblowers Edward Snowden and Julian Assange brought attention to the extent of surveillance exercised by the US Department of Homeland Security and similar antiterrorist units in other countries.

Feminist artists have reacted against the unwarranted invasion of privacy and manipulation by capitalist and government surveillance through making work that exposes how abuse of digital technology enables it to happen.

American digital artist Jill Magid worked with the Liverpool, UK, police department on a performance titled *Evidence Locker* (2004) to show how its surveillance system touched people's everyday lives. As one of the elements in the project, she kept her eyes shut and walked down the main pedestrian street in Liverpool's center while police in the control room guided her every movement so that she didn't collide with anyone or bump into any walls, exposing how invasive and all-seeing government systems could be.[12]

In another performance/installation Magid addressed how corporations can prevent outsiders from accessing data. During a stay in Mexico, Magid became entranced by the work of Luis Barragán, the preeminent modernist Mexican architect. She became fascinated by the fact that, after his death, the Mexican government did not have enough funds to buy his professional archive (although his home was declared a national monument) and it was bought privately by the CEO of Vitra, a Swiss corporation. As the story goes (although it may be apocryphal), when he offered his fiancée, Federica Zanco, a diamond engagement ring, she asked that he buy Barragán's archive for her as an engagement gift instead. He did so, and the archive became the property of Vitra. Because

Barragán was such a strong influence on contemporary architects, Vitra received numerous requests to visit the archive but they were not granted. Magid herself tried to gain entrance but was rejected. The refusal led Magid to create a performance and exhibition that would lay bare the power that corporations can exercise in refusing to make available data and information they possess. Magid persuaded the Mexican authorities to disinter Barragán's ashes, which she had transformed into a diamond. She designed a setting for it, and put it on display, inviting Zanco to trade the archive for the diamond. Zanco refused and the archive stayed closed. Magid, on the other hand, was inundated by hostile feedback for the disinterment of Barragán's corpse and her performance. Nevertheless, Magid welcomed the negative publicity because it helped to bring the issue of information control to the forefront. Magid made a film, *The Proposal* (2018), documenting the project.[13]

New Zealand artist, Terri Te Tau using the cultural concepts of her Māori heritage, began investigating government surveillance in 2007 when the New Zealand police mounted an antiterrorist investigation, called Operation 8 that affected the Māori community. As the indigenous people of New Zealand, the Māori exist under a government that is descended from European colonialism with the embedded conventions of Western patriarchal society. Thus, the Māori, as the "other" within New Zealand's population are often the first to be construed as engaging in suspicious activities by the white government's security forces. During Operation 8, security forces entered Māori homes to locate four individuals suspected of involvement in an environmental action that was determined to be a threat to the government. Terri Te Tau's home was one of the residences raided. Ever since the raid, Terri Te Tau has concentrated her art practice on projects (including a PhD dissertation) in which she investigates not only the act of surveillance and its deleterious impact on the individuals involved, but also the resistance that the Māori can offer.

In *Unregistered and Unwarranted* (2013), first a performance and then a video, Terri Te Tau fitted out a driverless and anonymous black van with surveillance devices. The van progresses down the main street in Greytown, New Zealand, surveying the buildings, the other vehicles, and the pedestrians it encounters. As the journey continues, the images of the surveillance appear on the windshield until the view from the windshield is completely obscured by the data. The data replaces and dehumanizes the people of the town in the minds of the surveyors, relieving the authorities of contact with actual individuals and enabling them to think in terms only of the data, thus feeling free to exert their power on what appears as abstract, rather than affecting human beings.

Āhua o te Hau (2015; Plate 29) is a video meant to be viewed from the interior of the black van first used for *Unregistered and Unwarranted.* The video shows Greytown again, including four of the houses thought to hide terrorists that were invaded. Instead of surveillance that turns what is seen into data, the program in the camera records the auras it sees around buildings, other vehicles, and pedestrians on the street, enhancing the poetic and personal character of the town. Terri Te Tau's intent in this video is to emphasize the concepts of the Māori that are oppositional to surveillance—as she quotes from the Māori: "The corners of the house can be seen; the corners of the heart cannot be seen." She believes that the philosophy of the Māori provides a resistance to the surveillance of the Western patriarchal government. The Māori spirit will remain undaunted and Māori culture will survive despite the effort at control and disappearance exerted by the alien dominant power.[14]

Israeli artist Michal Rovner addresses surveillance frequently in her work. One of her most evocative installations, *Night* (2016), features video projections of the jackals that wait, always watching, on the outskirts of the farms and villages in Israel. They become a metaphor addressing the constant state of surveillance that exists in the region with Israelis, Palestinians, Iranians, Saudis, and the other Middle East nations all watching each other. Rovner's projections are based on the photographs she took of the jackals on the edge of her own property. The ghostly aspect of their eyes glittering in the dark have a supernational cast that Rovner used to create a video of the jackals, titled *Anubis* (2016) after the Egyptian god who watches over the dead.[15]

British artist Suzanne Treister turns the concepts of surveillance inside out in her investigation of how surveillance changes people. She was startled to discover that people no longer seem to worry about being watched. In her 2014 *Post-Surveillance Art* project, she posits a new humanity that likes being watched as obviously evidenced by the popularity and expansion of reality television. She posits that there is a pleasure that comes from exhibitionism. Being the object of surveillance has elements of an erotic experience. But she wonders about who is doing the watching. What does the pleasure of surveillance mean for the future of humanity?[16]

Treister's HEXEN 2.0 (2009–11) is a hyperlinked, interactive website project with videos, altered photographs, texts, and drawings. The word itself is a form of "hex," as in "hexing" some activity or person, to cause harm through casting a spell. The starting point of *HEXEN 2.0* is a series of conferences held from 1946 to 1954 (also one in 1942) sponsored by the Josiah Macy Jr. Foundation. The invited participants came from the fields of the social sciences, neuroscience, and the then-nascent field of cybernetics including such luminaries as Norbert Wiener (who created the term, "cybernetics"), John von Neumann, one of the inventors of modern digital technology, and anthropologist Margaret Mead (one of the few women). The focus of the conferences was to develop a synthesized approach to knowledge, bringing together biology, social science, and science—particularly the new digital technology—in order to map how the brain works with the goal of building a Utopian society in which all citizens of the state would function under the beneficial systems of the state. Treister lays the contemporary surveillance and control exercised by the contemporary state at the door of the men and women who participated in the conference. Once the brain was mapped, those supposedly beneficial systems could be developed. Treister maintains that the opposite happened. Instead of being beneficial, the systems controlled individuals and made outcasts of those who resisted conformity.[17]

The satiric video on the website shows the participants in the setting of a seance, their hands laid on the round table in order to feel for signals from the beyond. Against a background of their voices, parts of the table light up, depending on who is receiving those messages. A voice-over, presumably Treister's own voice, comments on the discussion. Clicking on another link brings to the screen a set of Tarot cards designed by Treister. Instead of the traditional texts and images, Treister has designed and drawn new images with accompanying texts that will tell the fortune of the individual whose future is being told, the future being one that limits the individual through surveillance or other control devices. The Queen of Swords, for instance features a drawing of multiple drones with a text that lists the different kinds: "spy drone," "attack drone," "terror drone," "tactical unmanned ground vehicle," "helicopter spy drone, UK police," "solar powered drones, U.S. air force NASA." Another click opens up a series of photographs of individual participants with texts below the portraits that reveal their surveillance ideas. One of the participants was psychiatrist Harold Abramson. The text below his name describes his application for $85,000 to the CIA in which he proposed giving LSD to unsuspecting hospital patients to see how they reacted. His project was funded by the Macy Foundation and became part of the CIA's MKUltra program to investigate how LSD could be used to enhance military effectiveness.

Mimi Ọnụọha addresses another aspect of surveillance, focusing on those who do the collecting and how their priorities affect the surveillance process. Her research ranges from studying the digital collecting of crime statistics to the gaps in Google Maps and leads to projects that include performances and offline exhibitions. In her lectures, which in themselves are performances, she discusses the fact that in looking at Google Maps of Africa, the entire region of Makoko, a lake community with over 100,000 inhabitants, off the coast of Lagos, is missing. The same is true of the favelas in Rio de Janeiro and of sites in remote areas of the world, like Mongolia. These gaps are different from the sites that are blurred or missing because of security concerns on the part of various countries resulting in requests to Google Maps with which the program usually complies. It is not clear why the satellite cameras are not reading the physical characteristics of these areas, but Ọnụọha speculates, that while the gaps may not be intentional, they are still the consequence of priorities set by the collectors. Since Google Maps is an American company with strong corporate connections in the West, it is more concerned with the regions important to the corporate world. If making sure that all areas of the world were adequately mapped was a priority, then these missing regions would be as visible as New York or London or Paris. Ọnụọha refers to Ronaldo Lemos, the director of the Institute for Technology & Society of Rio de Janeiro who has written about the impact on favela residents of not being seen on Google Maps. They are deprived of many services by the omission. They can't obtain deliveries since delivery companies depend on Google Maps. They are even deprived of entertainment: The popular game, Pokémon Go, is built on the information provided by Google Maps.

Ọnụọha describes data collection as shaping a "machine-readable" world. The individual is no longer important; rather, it is the aggregate that counts. In one of her presentations, Ọnụọha talks about the book *Middletown* by Robert and Helen Lynd, published in 1929, as having legitimized data collection. The book was extremely popular and made data collection a familiar concept to non-experts. In 1924, the Lynds collected all the available data about the white, US-born residents living in Muncie, Indiana. In their book, they equate Muncie with the United States as a whole, using the average characteristics of Muncie's citizens to describe the majority of the US population. As Ọnụọha reveals, the Lynds only surveyed the whites in Muncie. They left out the African Americans and immigrants. Ọnụọha asks how people feel at being told they do not represent the true US citizen. As a Nigerian immigrant to the US, she says she does not want to be dismissed like that.

Ọnụọha also compares the figures on the reporting of hate crimes to show how important it is to consider who is being surveyed for the data collection. One year, the FBI hate crime unit reported 5,796 crimes while the Bureau of Justice Statistics reported 293,800. The FBI was collecting information from police departments whereas the Department of Justice was collecting statistics from victims.

She has created an exhibition titled *The Library of Missing Data Sets* (2016). It consists of an interactive filing cabinet; visitors to the exhibition are encouraged to open drawers and read file cards that list such missing data sets as the following: cash, because cash transactions don't generate data; the national underground economy; proportion of traded wildlife illegally poached; citizens on domestic surveillance lists; all trans people killed or injured in hate crimes. She has come to describe data collection as algorithmic violence.[18]

Yet another approach to surveillance is the work of Mariam Ghani and Chitra Ganesh who have developed the *Index of the Disappeared* (ongoing since 2004). Like Ọnụọha's *Library of Missing Data Sets*, their project is a set of filing cabinets filled with index cards. Each index card is about an individual who has "disappeared" in the United States since 9/11. Rather than names and bios of individuals, the cards contain official documents (heavily redacted) and other materials relating to imprisonment, torture, deportation, detention of immigrants, people suspected of terrorism because of their race or ethnicity rather than any real evidence, kept secret by various government security, military, and intelligence units.

Ghani and Ganesh organize both offline and virtual exhibitions based on the materials they collect. An example is *The Guantanamo Effect* (2013), an interactive hyperlinked card catalog. The screen displays topic cards with tabbed cards underneath. By clicking on the topic card, a summary appears. Clicking on the tabs brings up individual documents, photographs, and diagrams. Hovering over the tabbed cards brings up yet a third set of informational cards including links to "a mix of the official and the mundane that includes autopsies, affidavits, correspondence, interviews, invoices, legal analysis, media accounts, NGO reports, transcripts, testimony, treaties, and more."[19]

Another visual artist who responded to surveillance issues is Laura Poitras, who was contacted by whistleblower Edward Snowden in 2013. Snowden was deeply concerned about US invasion of privacy by the National Security Agency (NSA) through programs that gave the agency access to phone-call records and Facebook and Google accounts, and was preparing to leak NSA documents to prove his allegations. He approached journalist Glenn Greenwald of the *Guardian*. According to Peter Maas in the *New York Times Magazine*, Snowden was aware of Poitras from an article on Salon.com, by Greenwald, in which Greenwald wrote extensively about how Poitras was harassed by the US government after the release of her film, *My Country, My Country* (2006), documenting the difficulties of life in Iraq under the American occupation.[20]

Poitras and Greenwald joined Snowden in Hong Kong where he had fled just before he released leaks of thousands of documents from the NSA. *Citizenfour* (2014), the documentary Poitras made about Snowden based on days of interviews with him in his Hong Kong hotel, won the Academy Award for Best Documentary Feature in 2015.

Although it is her best known work, *Citizenfour* is only one production in Poitras's continuing output on surveillance. Poitras had a solo exhibition at the Whitney Museum in 2016. It consisted of installations in several galleries with videos, wall texts, and projections focused on different aspects of surveillance by governmental security organizations. The gallery with the most visual impact was one in which spectators could lie on comfortable beds surrounded by projections of the actual night skies in Yemen, Somalia, and Pakistan. After visitors lay looking at the skies for a few minutes, morning arrived accompanied by drones whizzing against the now lighted sky. In the last gallery, visitors discovered that they themselves had been under surveillance; they saw their presence in the various galleries documented in videos.[21]

Poitras also participated in the 2019 Whitney Biennial with a video, *Triple Chaser*, the centerpiece of the collective Forensic Architecture's presentation on tear-gas canisters. The triple chaser is a set of three tear-gas canisters that are amassed into one. When detonated and tossed, the cans will release tear gas sequentially, the triple canisters covering a much larger area than a single canister. Warren B. Kanders, at the time was vice chair of the Whitney Museum's board as well as CEO of Safariland, a manufacturer of weapons used by the military and the police worldwide. Defense Technologies, one of its subsidiaries, was the company that makes triple-canister tear gas used in 2018 by the US border guards against migrants at the border between San Diego and Tijuana.

The sale and export of tear gas is not a matter of public record, so it is only when images of tear-gas canisters appear online that monitoring organizations can identify who is selling and buying tear gas. Poitras's video, narrated by David Byrne, describes Forensic Architecture's effort in creating an application that would identify tear gas triple canisters when they appear among the millions of images seen online every minute. It would have taken weeks or months to collect the hundreds of actual canisters needed to provide the composite image necessary for a detection system, so Forensic Architecture developed a composite image digitally. The video which was shown at the Whitney included a succession of photos of the canister models against various repetitive geometric designs and natural backgrounds, At the same time Richard Strauss's *Four Last Songs* (1948) can be heard on the soundtrack—the Kanderses gave such a large gift to the Aspen Festival that a series of concerts is named for them and the Strauss songs were performed at one of these concerts. Poitras and Forensic Architecture were among the artists who threatened to withdraw their work from the Biennial if

Kanders was not removed from the board. Their threat, along with the numbers of Whitney staff who signed a petition asking for Kanders's removal, did eventually result in his resignation. Subsequently, Kanders also sold the subsidiary company, Defense Technologies, that made the canisters.[22]

The artists in this chapter use their abilities as artists to investigate the power structures of the patriarchal society for the purpose of social justice. While some may not overtly declare that they are feminists, their work to thwart the patriarchal systems of oppression aligns them with feminist principles. There are many other artists during the last decades of the twentieth century and the first decades of the twenty-first whose art practice is also dedicated to social justice. There is no question but that they have helped to bring the issues of surveillance to the attention of the public, particularly those who are using digital technology since media reaches a much larger population than traditional art disciplines.[23]

Notes

1 Addie Wagenknecht, *Prism Break Barbie*, F.A.T. Lab, Vimeo video 1:07, https://vimeo.com/channels/fat/76074931.

2 There is a large body of literature on Bentham and the panopticon, but it is not within the purview of this book to discuss Bentham in detail. For a quick read, see "Internalized Authority and the Prison of the Mind: Bentham and Foucault's Panopticon," https://www.brown.edu/Departments/Joukowsky_Institute/courses/13things/7121.html.

3 Christina Ng, "At the Venice Biennale, Shu Lea Chang Surveils the Surveillance System," Hyperallergic, June 5, 2019, https://hyperallergic.com/503068/at-the-venice-biennale-shu-lea-cheang-surveils-the-surveillance-system/.

4 Michel Foucault, *Discipline and Punish: The Birth of the Prison*, trans. Alan Sheridan (first English edition, New York: Pantheon, 1977).

5 Barbara Kruger, "Your Gaze Hits the Side of My Face," 1981, photograph, 54.4 × 40″, https://www.artsy.net/artwork/barbara-kruger-untitled-your-gaze-hits-the-side-of-my-face.

6 Brenda Oelbaum, "Fat Feminist Activist Artist's Blog," https://brendaoelbaum.me/; Brenda Oelbaum, *Results May Vary* (2012), a film made with B. Scott and Jeremy Hansen, 9:38, https://vimeo.com/41025416.

7 Sins Invalid, https://www.sinsinvalid.org/.

8 Ibid.

9 Shawné Michaelain Holloway website, http://www.shawnemichaelainholloway.com/about.

10 Leah Schrager, "The Censored Image and My Response," The Naked Therapist, http://thenakedtherapist.org/; Jeremy M. Barker, "Can Un-Licensed Therapy Be Performance Art? Can Prostitution?" Culturebot, May 9, 2012, https://www.culturebot.org/2012/05/13501/can-un-licensed-therapy-be-performance-art-can-prostitution/.

11 Shoshana Zuboff, "You Are Now Remotely Controlled," *New York Times*, January 24, 2020, https://www.nytimes.com/2020/01/24/opinion/sunday/surveillance-capitalism.html.

12 Jill Magid, "Evidence Locker," http://www.jillmagid.com/projects/evidence-locker-2; Jill Magid, *Trust* (2004), Vimeo video, DVD, edited CCTV footage with audio, 17:42, documents Magid being guided by police cameras, posted by RaebervonStenglin, 2014, https://vimeo.com/62092355.

13 Alice Gregory, "What Happened After Mexico's Greatest Architect Was Turned Into a Diamond," *The New Yorker*, May 21, 2017, https://www.newyorker.com/culture/culture-desk/what-happened-after-mexicos-greatest-architect-was-turned-into-a-diamond; Jill Magid, *The Proposal* (2018), film 83 minutes, produced by Oscilloscope Laboratories, directed by Magid, official trailer, April 24, 2019, https://www.youtube.com/watch?v=jcYZEGqTstk.

14 "Terri Te Tau," CIRCUIT, Artist Index, https://www.circuit.org.nz/artist/terri-te-tau; Terri Te Tau, *Unwarranted and Unregistered* (2013), video 4:20, https://www.circuit.org.nz/film/unwarranted-and-unregistered-2; Terri Te Tau, *Te Āhua o te Hau ki te Papaioeaā* (2015), multimedia installation, music composed by Rob Thorne, https://www.territetau.com/#/798817030644/; Terri Te Tau, "Beyond the Corners of Our Whare, A Conceptual Māori Response to State Surveillance in Aotearoa, New Zealand," (PhD diss., Massey University, 2015). https://mro.massey.ac.nz/bitstream/handle/10179/10825/02_whole.pdf?sequence=2&isAllowed=y, 29.

15 Michal Rovner, "Michal Rovner, Into the Night," interview by Haley Weiss, *Interview Magazine*, September 27, 2016, https://www.interviewmagazine.com/art/michal-rovner; Laura van Straaten, "Michael Rovner's Doormen of the Darkside at Pace Gallery," Artnet News, September 21, 2016, https://news.artnet.com/exhibitions/michal-rovners-doormen-dark-side-pace-661454; Michal Rovner, *Anubis* (2016), YouTube video, 1:08, posted by artdone, June 17, 2017, https://www.youtube.com/watch?v=Z-X_hhPYTgk.

16 Suzanne Treister, "Suzanne Treister," interview by Marisa Olson, Artforum, October 15, 2019, https://www.artforum.com/interviews/suzanne-treister-on-black-hole-space-time-and-post-surveillance-art-81036.

17 Suzanne Treister, *HEXEN 2.0*, 2009-2011, https://www.suzannetreister.net/HEXEN2/HEXEN_2.html.

18 Mimi Ọnụọha, *The Library of Missing Data Sets* (2016), https://mimionuoha.com/the-library-of-missing-datasets; *The Library of Missing Data Sets 2.0* (2018), https://

mimionuoha.com/the-library-of-missing-datasets-v-20; GitHub, "Mimi Onuoha, On Missing Data Sets," January 25, 2018, https://github.com/MimiOnuoha/missing-datasets; Mimi Ọnụọha, "In/visible: Missing Data Sets," Lecture, Chicago Humanities Festival, January 15, 2019, YouTube video, 55:50, posted by Chicago Humanities Festival, https://www.youtube.com/watch?v=0FKMLXZ7_FE.

19 Mariam Ghani and Chitra Ganesh, *The Index of the Disappeared* (2004 ongoing), https://www.mariamghani.com/work/626 and https://www.chitraganesh.com/index-of-the-disappeared; *The Guantanamo Effect*, an interactive website, using hypertext links, http://kabul-reconstructions.net/index/gtmo/home.html.

20 Peter Maas, "How Laura Poitras Helped Snowden Spill His Secrets," *New York Times Magazine*, August 13, 2013, https://www.nytimes.com/2013/08/18/magazine/laura-poitras-snowden.html.

21 Holland Cotter, "Laura Poitras: 'Astro Noise' Examines Surveillance and the New Normal," *New York Times*, February 4, 2016, https://www.nytimes.com/2016/02/05/arts/design/laura-poitras-astro-noise-examines-surveillance-and-the-new-normal.html.

22 Alex Greenberger, "For Whitney Biennial, One Participant Targets Controversial Whitney Patron," ARTnews, May 13, 2019, https://www.artnews.com/art-news/artists-forensic-architecture-whitney-biennial-warren-b-kanders-12543/; Eileen Kinsella, "In the Heart of the Whitney Biennial, Artists Are Working to Expose Board Member Warren Kanders's Link to Possible War Crimes," Artnet News, May 13, 2019, https://news.artnet.com/art-world/forensic-architecture-triple-chaser-whitney-biennial-1544911.

23 Greenberger, "For Whitney Biennial."

11

Feminist Artists and the Gaming Industry

For women, whether characterized as cis, trans, nonbinary, queer, or non-white, to advance, it must occur on the broad scale of popular culture as well as in intellectual and creative circles. Digital technology affects the global population culturally as well as economically and socially. Its impact on culture has gone far beyond the elite world of academic institutions and museums to transform popular culture, particularly by innovations in entertainment made possible through the internet and social networking. The next two chapters focus on two widespread facets of digital popular culture: video games and animation. Video games have become one of the most widespread forms of entertainment in contemporary popular culture and as such have affected representational stereotypes. Their invention took place for the most part in the United States and Japan and then spread out over the world. Parallel to, and related to video games, Japanese anime has also become a mass cultural phenomenon modifying representation. This chapter analyzes the impact of American feminist artists on video games. The following chapter looks at the involvement of Japanese women artists in creating and spreading the aesthetics of anime.

The video game has had enormous impact on women from many perspectives. Feminist artists and theorists have responded to the masculinism of games, opening up a new approach to gaming history that incorporates the presence and influence of feminist game designers, altered how women and people of color are depicted in games, and helped make women feel that they are welcome in the field.

The gaming industry has been criticized because of the perception that it is masculinist, born in the West out of war and flight-simulation games, and shaped by male game developers, male-dominated corporations, and male gamers. Early games were not aimed at a home market (mass-market home computers did not yet exist), but rather marketed to the arcade industry, dominated by male gamers. They took their place beside the pinball and other mechanical machines, gradually replacing them. By the mid-1970s, every shopping mall had an arcade area. The golden age of arcade games continued into the 1990s when home video games overtook the arcades.[1]

According to historians and culture theorists, like Claus Pias and others, the structure of the video game as combat was present from the start. Pias claims the early games were based on the use of the "ping" by the military to determine the location of targets. The "ping" is the sound that an electronic signal makes when it reaches its objective. The early games were based on the same principle of an electronic ball going back and forth—the "ping." The principle of combat resonated with the ethos of the era. During the 1950s and early 1960s, Americans still saw heroism in war and praised male war heroes. The United States had been a victor in the Second World War, a war mostly waged by men. The Vietnam War was soon to begin, but it wasn't until after it was over that its impact was felt on attitudes of the American public in downgrading the military and becoming cynical about waging war.[2]

It's useful to look at how the origin of video games is described in conventional histories to understand how they came to be identified as masculinist to the point that playing video games was one of the identifying characteristics of being male in the late twentieth century.

In the 1960s, mainframes were the only computers and they were only available outside the military defense sector at a few major universities and corporations. Steven Russell, a student at MIT in the early 1960s, joined the Tech Model Railroad Club (TMRC), an all-male group of MIT students who were possibly the first "nerds." MIT in the 1960s was a bastion of male privilege. While women could apply to MIT, few did, and fewer were admitted. Just a handful of years earlier, in 1956, MIT medical director, H.I. Harris, sent a memo with an argument that was familiar, to the chair of the committee charged with what policies to adopt in relation to women. Harris makes the assumption that women will take years out of their careers to raise families. During the same period of time men will be pursuing theirs. Therefore, he concludes that the institution should not waste its time on educating women who would take student places away from men who would use those years professionally. Furthermore he states that women will be less capable of serious research after years of homemaking. Those who were brave enough to become students were isolated from the mainstream student body. There was no dormitory for women on the MIT campus until 1963. In 1961, only one woman, Emily Lippincott Wick, was on the faculty.[3]

The members of the TMRC were the first "hackers." According to historian Steven L. Kent, they even invented the word. To "hack" into the operations of the MIT mainframes, Russell, Martin Graetz, and Wayne Wiitanen created a game they could play on one of the mainframes—*Spacewar!* (1961), a game that was a battle between two spaceships. Historians have credited Russell for making the connection between combat and fantasy in video gaming, a pairing that has endured. Russell, like many engineering students, was a science fiction fan and thought it would be fun to set the game in a space fantasy.[4]

Separately, Ralph Baer, an engineer whose original career goal had been to work in the television industry, was head of the design unit at Sanders, Inc., a defense contractor, now BAE Electronics & Integrated Solutions. Baer began to think about how to use the digital technology that had been developed by the defense industry to train individuals in strategic and tactical military action for its potential in entertainment.

Baer put together a team of engineers to work on game development. They succeeded in creating the first video game console. Russell's game, *Spacewar!*, could only be played on mainframe computers and thus was not commercially feasible, whereas because of the microchip, only recently invented, Baer's development of the console using microchips meant that video games could be played on smaller digital devices anywhere. The electronics manufacturing company Magnavox was the distributor for the console. It had ten games, all based on the "ping" principle, a ball batted back and forth. However, the world wasn't ready for home video games, and the console was not very successful.

In the meantime, the entrepreneur Nolan Bushnell had experienced playing Russell's *Spacewar!* on the mainframe available at the University of Utah where he was an undergraduate. Bushnell also had a job running arcade games. After graduation, he put together his love of computer games with his knowledge of the arcade game industry and created the company, Atari, to produce video games first for arcades and later for home video. He developed the first wildly successful video game, called *Pong*—a digital version of ping-pong.

Given the combative nature of early video games, it is understandable that the rise of video games has been historicized as male. Before video games, the sports boys played outdoors were battle games—football, baseball, basketball, even individual sports like tennis are all war games, antagonists who play to win. Even some indoor board games like chess are masculinist; one has only to look at the chess champions since chess became internationally played. Only with the rise of the first wave of feminism in the nineteenth century have girls and women played combat sports. These factors entered into the historical view of video games as masculinist at their core.

Thus, the conventional history of early video games during their first two decades has been constructed on the basis that there were few, if any women, in the field from the design end through gamers. Media archaeologist Laine Nooney suggests an epistemological problem with the conventional history. She proposes that the history of digital games was written from the dominant masculinist perspective of patriarchal society that assumes men are the original thinkers and innovators. She states that research situated within the field of media archaeology is necessary in order to unearth the history of women in the early decades of digital gaming.[5]

During the second decade in the twenty-first century, that began to happen. By 2020, Wikipedia listed dozens of women in the field ranging from designers to engineers to corporate management. Nooney herself has documented the history of Roberta Williams, who was co-founder of the digital game company, On-Line Systems, currently Sierra Entertainment, Inc. Based on statistical evidence that she unearthed, Nooney estimates that there were at least 200,000 female players in the early period of digital gaming despite the conventional assumption that there were hardly any.[6]

Nooney also questions analysis of the origins and development of video games as linear. Using media archaeology will reveal a history that is much more complex. She believes that many individuals were excited about the advent of digital technology and were experimenting on their own, building computers from scratch by buying the parts from retail stores like Radio Shack and creating video games.[7]

Joseph Weisbecker was one of these individuals. He built one of the first home computers as early as the late 1960s. His daughter, Joyce, raised on digital technology, created RCA's first video game in 1976. Weisbecker worked at RCA, which entered the computer market with the COSMAC VIP, a video arcade machine based on Weisbecker's prototype, in 1975. Joyce was a first-year college student when her father asked her if she would like to program video games for the COSMAC VIP, which used game cartridges. Her first games were titled *Slide*, *Snake Race*, and *Jack Pot*. RCA also made a home computer model for the COSMAC VIP. A 1978 advertisement for the COSMAC VIP reads, "$249 gets the entire family into creating video games, graphics, and control functions for starters." At Joseph Weisbecker's urging, RCA also began marketing educational games through its Random House subsidiary. Joyce Weisbecker programmed for those games as well. One of the games she created for Studio II, as it was called, was *Tag*, almost the same "ping" game that Baer and Bushnell had created. But her games only had a brief life since RCA quickly dropped out of the video game industry.[8]

Carol Shaw is credited with being one of the first female designers hired by a major video game company. Unusual for women at the time, Shaw, like

Weisbecker, grew up in an environment that fostered her interest in digital technology. She majored in electrical engineering at the University of California, Berkeley and took a master's degree in computer science. She was hired by Atari in 1978 as a coder. At Atari she had the opportunity to design several games, among them *3-D Tik Tak Toe* (released in 1978). Shaw left Atari after two years and joined Activision Publishing, Inc., where she created several games, the most popular of which was *River Raid* (1982), a shooter game in which players were tasked with shooting down enemy planes over the River of No Return.[9]

Contrary to public perception, women designers were innovators in technical advancement. One of the technical areas in which they had influence was in improving the appearance of video games. To use Laine Nooney's concept of media archaeology, delving into the broader cultural sphere of gender to gain understanding of the field, perhaps the connection of femaleness to "looks," allowed women game designers to have impact in this area. Nooney also speculates that some women like Roberta Williams became game designers out of the cultural habit of women's leisure-time reading. Williams and her husband created the game *Mystery House* (1980), one of the first games to use graphics along with the text descriptions. Williams has stated that she was obsessed with playing text-based computer adventure games and concluded that she could write better stories than what was available.[10]

Dona Bailey was working for General Motors, using a computer to design elements of the Cadillac automobile line, when she first tried an arcade video game. She fell in love with video games, realized that she had the digital technology skills to create games, and applied to work at Atari where she created *Centipede* in 1982. In a 2017 interview, she says, "a multi-segmented insect crawls on the screen and is shot by the player. That didn't seem bad to shoot a bug so that was the one I picked." (Game developers were given lists of potential game titles from which they could choose.) Bailey used a range of colors that was unprecedented: lime green, violet, blue. *Centipede* became one of the most popular games distributed by Atari and had a strong base of female players. But Bailey felt Atari's masculinist culture. She has written that when she started work at Atari, it was like being in a college fraternity house. She was the only women among the various technological workforce of engineers of different kinds, whether software or hardware, a ratio of 30:1. She reports that it was even worse by the time she left: it was 120:1.[11]

In the 1990s video games underwent change. The US industry had crashed in the early 1980s due to several factors, the most important being that the games being produced were poor quality from both technical and content perspectives.

People were not only bored by what was available; they were also frustrated because so many games didn't work properly. In addition, arcades were no longer as popular as they had been and the home video market had not yet developed since it was still before the days of the mass-market PC and Mac, the laptop, or the cell phone. The Japanese game company Nintendo is credited with reviving the industry by the release in 1983 of the Nintendo Entertainment System (NES), by guarantees of quality control, and by marketing video games as toys rather than as games. No one was buying games, but the toy market was flourishing. The industry came back to life, but was now more cautious and turned to marketing research, using the results to determine which audiences to target. While girls as well as boys had been playing games from the start, boys were the larger audience for cultural reasons, as discussed earlier. Video games were an output of digital technology and boys were encouraged to become engineers whereas girls were not. At the same time, large corporations began to dominate the industry because those companies had the financial resources to conduct marketing campaigns and foster the creation of games that would appeal to boys and later to men as the targeted audiences for games grew older.[12]

The look of video games also changed dramatically in the 1990s because of the invention of 3-D animation software that, until then, had been exclusively used by the US Department of Defense to create flight simulations. Three-dimensional modeling meant that the look of the games would change to approximating the offline world. It became the standard in video games and made the games much more appealing. Thanks to marketing and to cultural mores, the 1990s became the golden age of the shooter games. Shooters were far from the only games, and audiences were made up of girls and women as well as boys and men, but the marketing campaigns made the male-dominated shooter games synonymous with the industry, creating the enduring perception that video games were made by men for a male audience. Other factors in the 1990s contributing to the perception of gaming as a male enterprise were the Gulf War (1990–1) and the outbreak of teenage violence culminating in the Columbine shootings in 1999.[13]

Claudia Hart, a professor in digital technology at the School of the Art Institute of Chicago and a pioneer in investigating games from a feminist perspective, began working with 3-D modeling shortly after it came on the market. In *Machina* (2004; Plate 30), she took the female avatar of video games, a fast-moving, often ferocious, full-breasted figure and reinvented her, casting her as a slow-moving, voluptuous reclining nude inspired, Hart says, by Raphael and Titian odalisques. Rather than pornographic or menacing, Hart portrayed the female body as an image of feminine beauty and erotic sensualism as a kind of refusal, a rejection of the gaming stereotype.[14]

In the late twentieth century, when Hart began her teaching career at Pratt Institute in Brooklyn, she was one of the few women teaching gaming and her students were all male. She found the pedagogy in the department to be engineering-oriented, calculated to help students gain employment in the burgeoning field of digital technology demanded by the entertainment industry for filmmaking, commercial television, and video games. By doing so, the school, and others like it, were reinforcing the connections between digital technology and patriarchal, masculinist, and capitalist values.

Hart remarked that after the events of September 11, 2001, students flocked to technical schools to learn 3-D animation because of the many jobs available in the flood of shooter games that the 9/11 antiterrorist era provoked. She goes on to say that during the years of the Iraq War (2003–11), 3-D games "were to grow into a larger, more profitable industry than that of 3-D animated children's films." While she blames the renewed militarism for the fanning the flames of violence in video games, she also blames art school pedagogy of the era for teaching design principles derived from the commercial drive for the largest audience possible, in the process succumbing to mass appeal without any consideration of aesthetics.[15]

However, change was in the wind. First, the World Wide Web was created in the mid-1990s thus making it easier to use digital technology for both communication and information. Second, home computers entered the mass market, giving millions of individuals access to the digital world, not only as consumers, but also with the potential for becoming creators. Third, in response to the demand for programs that would embed coding so that creating electronically based websites and other forms of communication and information was quicker and easier, a proliferation of apps soon flooded the market, coming from the emerging corporate giants such as Microsoft and Adobe but also from smaller companies and individuals as well.

Furthermore, applying the concept of media archaeology to the decade of the 1990s and looking beyond the commonly held perception of video games as male, shooter games were hardly the only games of the period. *Myst*, a puzzle game first released in 1993, that takes participants to a deserted island, was the top-selling PC game until 2002 when it was overtaken by *The Sims* (released in 2000). Both *Myst* and *The Sims* had strong female player bases.[16]

Brenda Laurel is one of the Midwest women who became involved in digital technology in the 1970s because of the connection between the region's universities and the defense industry that provided those institutions with early computers. She was working for a small digital technology company with a computer model from the US space program that could be programmed to receive commands to determine the next action. Laurel, coming from a theater background, recognized the potential in the model for interactive digital games—players would be able to customize their games. Her first production was *Goldilocks and the Three Bears* (1978). Because the memory was so limited the changes had to be simple. A viewer could choose the color of a flower or the gender of a servant. When the company failed, Laurel went to work at the Atari Home Computer Division where, at one point, she had to chase marijuana-smoking men out of the ladies' bathroom. She studied the play habits of male and female children to determine what kind of games girls would like. Her research provided her with the information she needed to start her own company, Purple Moon, to create video games for girls. These were the first games designed for girls based on their interests, rather than simply watering down boys' games as the males who made the decisions at the major video game companies thought would be sufficient. Purple Moon was marketed as a toy, but the company was too small to compete against Mattel, the manufacturer of Barbie dolls, which bought out Purple Moon and closed it down.[17]

The history of *The Sims* reveals the influence of women designers behind one of the most popular games of the late 1990s and early twenty-first century. Will Wright is credited with originating *The Sims*, but the game as it evolved would not have been the same if women designers like Roxy Wolosenko and Claire Curtin, producers like Kana Ryan and Chris Trottier had not been members of the team developing it (by this period, games were not created by single designers but rather by teams of designers, programmers, and producers). When Wright began to work on *The Sims*, his concept was to focus on the house itself; game players would be able to choose the architectural style, the size, the furniture, the wallpaper—in other words everything that's needed to live in a house comfortably. His models were the how-to-do-it manuals for home decoration that had become very popular. He thought that a game version of such a manual would be very successful. It was Roxy Wolosenko who suggested that the characters could engage in social interaction. Eric Hedman, *The Sims*' lead animator, is quoted as acknowledging how much the women on the team like Wolosenko, Curtin, Ryan, and Trottier, contributed to the success of *The Sims*.[18]

After the turn of the century, the number of women involved in all aspects of video gaming increased, helped along by video game designers like the distinguished game developer and advocate for women in gaming, Brenda

Brathwaite, and game critics / video artists like Anita Sarkeesian. Brathwaite worked on the design of many successful games and emerged as a leader in questioning the stereotypes of women as depicted in shooter and pornography video games. In 2005, she founded the International Game Developers Sex Special Interest Group (Sex SIG).[19]

Anita Sarkeesian initiated a website, Feminist Frequency, in 2009 to create video commentaries addressing the negative stereotypes of women in pop culture. Its mission is to advocate for "an inclusive and representative media landscape and the eradication of online harassment."[20] In 2012 she began a series on "Tropes vs. Women in Video Games." In her videos, Sarkeesian uses clips from actual video games to illustrate the "Sidekick," the "Sinister Seductress," "Not Your Exotic Fantasy" (sexist and racist stereotypes about women of color), "Women as Reward," or "All the Slender Bodies" (revealing the limited female body types vs. the much wider variety of male body types).

By the end of the second decade of the twenty-first century, women constituted 25 percent of the video game workforce. The gaming industry worldwide was approaching $180 billion in revenue with 2.5 billion video gamers around the world. In the United States, 60 percent of Americans were playing video games daily and 45 percent of US gamers were women. The reputation of video games also changed radically from widespread concern about the impact of the games (particularly the shooter games) on young people to 70 percent parental approval. All those children who played video games in arcades during the 1980s grew up and continued to play video games, as did their children and grandchildren. The average gamer was thirty-four years old, owned a house, and had children. Women between the ages of eighteen and thirty-five made up 13 percent of the gaming community, and the gaming sector that was growing the most rapidly was the cell phone, the preferred device among women gamers. Critics of the industry cite the difficulties that, unless adjusted, might prevent more women from entering the field, such as working conditions that left little time for family responsibilities, lack of equal pay, lack of job stability, and inadequate health benefits.

It is true that, for decades, social conventions kept girls away from becoming involved in digital technology, but that changed significantly in the years after 2014 when "Gamergate," a concerted hate campaign to harass both women in the industry and female gamers themselves, backfired.

"Gamergate" was initiated by an ex-boyfriend of video game designer Zoë Quinn, who accused her of having a romantic relationship with a reviewer with the result that he praised one of her games. Actually, he had never reviewed her work. Quinn, her family, and women in the field like Anita Sarkeesian, who came to her defense, were deluged with threats of sexual violence and even death. "Gamergate" made newspaper headlines, and instead of driving away girls and women from becoming involved in digital technology and video gaming, the opposite occurred. Women resented being told to stay out of video gaming.[21]

By 2020, girls were encouraged by teachers and parents to studying coding. Classes exclusively for girls such as coding camps provided comfortable milieus for girls who might be afraid of ridicule from their male peers if they wanted to learn digital technology and video game design.[22]

One of the developments in the second decade of the twenty-first century that benefited women was the proliferation of independent game designers, producers, and distributors. No longer was the field completely dominated by the huge corporations like Electronic Arts (EA) and Nintendo. Open source programs made it economically feasible to create games, and social networking provided the means to achieve distribution.[23]

However, the reality was that, while women were increasingly integrated into the industry (and into its history) as of the end of the second decade of the twenty-first century, more than two-thirds of video game professionals identified as white, with all other ethnicities making up the remaining third, according to the International Game Developers Association (IGDA) Developer Satisfaction Survey.[24] The statistics show that people of color comprise a substantial percentage of gamers and that their participation is growing at a rapid pace. According to the organization, Statista, in 2015, 68 percent of American video game players were Caucasian, 13 percent, Latinx, 12 percent were African American, 5 percent, Asian, and 3 percent, other. In 2018, 83 percent of African American teenagers were gamers as opposed to 71 percent of Caucasian teenagers. It is forecast that by 2027, 57 percent of video game players will be people of color. Yet in 2020, 80 percent of video game characters were still white and male. Latinx characters numbered only 3 percent. Black characters were more common, but mostly depicted as stereotypes—athletes, performers, or criminals. Furthermore, while there were more Black characters in US-generated games by the end of the second decade of the twenty-first century, there were problems such as the paucity of "skins" that a gamer could use to create a character as well as a lack of hair and facial features common to African Americans.[25]

Professionals of color, such as designers, producers, historians, and critics, as well as gamers of color, were working to change the picture. Women of color established several organizations and digital communication portals—streaming channels, forums, and podcasts—to encourage more women of color to enter the field. One of the first was Sugar Gamers, initiated by Keisha Howard in 2009 to help women of color in the Midwest become game designers. Tanya DePass founded the non-profit I Need Diverse Games, in 2016 with 10,000 followers on Twitter and 1,000 followers on Twitch, the popular streaming platform for gamers. Jay-Ann Lopez founded Black Girl Gamers, also in 2016, an organization that hosts in-person training sessions for aspiring female gamers and has 4,700 members from around the world. Michelle Martin and some of her colleagues formed Project Zero to instruct followers on how to build games using an open source software program. If they didn't face outright backlash, then they faced disregard by the industry as evidenced by Twitch shutting down its Communities section because "they weren't being used," despite the fact that it was the mode of communication preferred by African American groups like Black Girl Gamers. It was replaced by a hashtag system on which Black women could not filter out racist and sexist comments they received when signing in.[26]

By 2020, video gaming had spread beyond the United States and Japan as well as among diverse populations of color in the United States. African nations experienced a surge of game development in predominantly Black countries like Cameroon, Nigeria, Ghana, Kenya, and South Africa as well as in the northern tier of Muslim nations, Tunisia and Egypt. The popularity of smartphones and tablets spurred that development—they are also the devices that stimulated growth in video gaming in Western countries as well, surpassing the use of personal computers and consoles in 2016.

The International Game Developers Association as of 2020 had seven chapters across Africa. The video games they were creating were not replicas of Western ones; rather the designers and developers were focusing on African culture as in *Okada Rider*, a game based on gridlock in the streets of Lagos; *Ebola Strike Force*, which is a story about researchers and scientists in an outbreak; *Sambisa Assault* about fighting terrorism; or *Ananse: The Origin*, a Ghanese folkloric tale. However, cultural tradition seemed to be working against inclusion of women. Other countries with extensive video game industries included China and Russia both of which were notorious for pirating American and Japanese games.[27]

The issue of female characters in video games is fraught with controversy, much of it centering on the figure (literally) of Lara Croft in *Tomb Raider*, one of the first games in the mid-1990s to be executed in 3-D modeling. This early 3-D programming was very crude. Lara Croft and the terrain through which she clambers, runs, leaps over obstacles, and climbs walls is composed of geometric shapes, culminating in huge polygonal breasts over a minute waist, and exaggeratedly full lips, the angles of which were sharp enough to slice through the lips of someone who might try to kiss her. She is a mixture of conflicting tropes. Perhaps that mixture is what made her so popular. She could appeal to everyone—a sex object for heterosexual white males (she was marketed as such); a female version of Indiana Jones with whom women and girls could identify (the initial game was intended to focus on a white male character, but the character was changed to female because the developers were afraid that in keeping it male, it bore too close a resemblance to Indiana Jones himself); and a "monster" that queer viewers would like (a "monster" in the sense of the influential gender theorist Judith Butler's definition of a character that combines both male and female aspects, thus escaping heteronormative restrictions of gender).[28]

Tomb Raider is also appealing because it is more of a personal adventure game. It involves victory over seemingly impossible hurdles through attributes of strength or perseverance rather than through devices external to the body, even though Lara Croft carries pistols and sometimes shoots her adversaries. From 1996 to 2015, many versions of the game were produced with the image of Lara Croft becoming much more realistic as a full-breasted woman dressed in revealing clothing, the stereotype of the desirable woman in heteronormative culture. A series of films based on the game was also very popular.[29]

Although the emergence of Lara Croft as an icon of pop culture might be thought to have led to more women protagonists, the number of games with female leading roles was meager at the end of the second decade of the twenty-first century despite the rise in number of female gamers, the upturn of women in the industry, and the proliferation of independent women game designers. From 2015 to 2019, Anita Sarkeesian reported on women in video games based on the number of new games showcased in press releases issued by the Electronic Entertainment Expo, known as the E3, which mounts huge gaming conventions. In 2019, her report revealed the fact that the number of new games featuring female protagonists was dropping rather than rising as might be expected given the sharp increases in female gamers and the upturn of women in the industry over the five-year period. The best year for women protagonists was 2015 with 7 percent. The lowest was 2016 with only 3 percent. In 2019, the number had risen a little to 5 percent. On the other hand, there was a significant rise in games where participants could control both male and female characters and even in some games, choose the gender of the central character although that's not to say the characters were no longer sexual stereotypes.[30]

In addition to feminist game designers, male and female artists in the gallery, education, and museum fine arts world have been attracted to video games to critique the masculinist corporate video game industry and to use the form of video games for its own sake, as a creative device to have emotional impact on audiences. As Katherine Isbister, professor in computational media at the University of California, Santa Cruz, has observed, unlike ... Unlike conventional novels, film, or television, where readers or viewers only observe the story, in games, players control the outcomes, thus involving them at a more intense emotional level.[31]

The video game designer Brenda Brathwaite created a set of board games, *The Mechanic is the Message* (2006–10), to prove the emotional impact of games, thus positioning them as useful in teaching about social justice and human rights. *Train* is based on the Holocaust. Players fill railroad cars with "meeples" (peg-like wooden shapes used to plan video game sequences). At some point they realize that they are sending the "meeples" to extermination centers to be murdered. Horrified at their sudden comprehension that they are participating in a narrative of the Holocaust, Brathwaite reported that many players broke down in tears.

Natalie Bookchin's *Intruder* (1998–9), is another example of a video game used as a vehicle to engage viewer/players emotionally in an artwork to promote feminist values. Bookchin uses ten simple 2-D video games that the viewer plays accompanied by an oral narration of a short story by Jorge Luis Borges. The casual conflict and mindless violence of the games highlights the violence of the story in which two brothers fall in love with a servant girl whom they eventually kill in order to remove the "intruder" who is creating a conflict between them, their homoerotic bonding being the most important emotional element in their lives. Using the games, Bookchin related the misogyny and sexism of the story in a way to engage the emotions of game players.[32]

Mattie Brice is a transgender African American artist who also uses games to advance the cause for inclusivity and social justice. The game *Mainichi* (Japanese for "every day") features an African American queer protagonist who goes through the day, bathing and dressing, eating, going out and meeting a friend at a coffee shop, accompanied by commentary on the screen that reveals their feelings and reactions throughout their activities. For instance, when the player moves the protagonist to buy a latte, they admire the look of the barista at the coffee shop, but the text also reads that they find the barista rude. The game is 2-D and the actions are simple. Brice used open source software on purpose to show that there are programs easy enough for anyone to use in creating games. Brice was trying to encourage others to create games. Their goal is a proliferation of games by amateurs to flood the market with games that go beyond commercial games to reveal how people live and think.[33]

Mary Flanagan is an important game theorist with feminist principles. Like others mentioned in this section of the chapter, she is involved in the organization Games for Change, consisting of independent game designers using games for raising awareness around serious subjects like epidemics, climate change, or human rights. One of the games that Flanagan has created is *Layoff* (2009). The screen looks like a casino bingo board but what look like buttons from a distance are little figures of workers. The goal of the game is to raise the company's economic value by "laying off" workers. The more workers laid off, the more the company is worth. The laid-off workers fall to the bottom of the screen where the number of real-life layoffs is also displayed. The workers also all have moving backstories that players can access. Like Brathwaite's *Train* game, as players continue in the game, they feel more and more guilty about laying off workers and less and less interested in winning the game.

Anna Anthropy who blogs under the name, Auntie Pixelante, is another transgender game designer like Mattie Brice. She has designed over seventy games including *Dys4ia* (2012) (Plate 31) which is based on her experiences during the first six months of hormone replacement therapy. It puts the player in the position of someone going through the therapy, feeling uncomfortable in one's body, wanting to be seen as female by the world, deciding to take the step, finding a clinic that won't have such extraneous requirements as a psychological test, taking the pills, feeling one's breasts grow, body hair disappearing, and at last becoming comfortable in one's new skin. The crude pixelated graphics are brightly colored and amusing—lips that eat the pills resemble the character in the video game, *Pac-Man* for instance. Anthropy mostly used GameMaker, an easy program for creating video games. Like Brice, her goals were also to show that anyone, not just coders, can make video games, and to encourage the proliferation of independent games in order to have games reflect the lives and interests of real people.[34]

That proliferation took place in the second decade of the twenty-first century. In spite of the domination of commercial shooter games with their stereotypic characters, a segment of video games became feminist, intersectional, idealistic. Auntie Pixelante, Bookchin, Brice, Flanagan, Brathwaite, Isbister and others added their feminist analyses to the growing body of literature on video games, and many groups were formed such as Dames Making Games (DMG) founded by Alexandra Leitch, Cecily Carver, and Jennie Robinson Faber in 2012 to encourage Canadian women to make, play, and change games. An early version of the website describes its mission as follows:

> DMG is a not-for-profit feminist organization dedicated to supporting dames interested in making, playing and changing games. [We intend to] demonstrate the value and impact of diversity in a broad range of disciplines related to games; highlight the achievements and stories of diverse Toronto-based gamemakers; provide a community and venue for dames to confidently explore playing, critiquing, and creating games. We run a wide range of programs and events for women, nonbinary, gender nonconforming, trans and queer folks interested in games. We are member-run and member-funded, arts-focused, technology positive, collaborative, engaged, and welcoming![35]

Members of Dames Making Games—Sagan Yee, Hannah Epstein, Emma Westecopt, along with founder Alexandra Leitch—created a game titled *PsXXYborg* (2013) built from a feminist perspective. The game addresses the following questions: How can digital play represent and reflect the human condition? What is a feminist game? How might we play our way to an equitable future? Their questions succinctly define the goals of the women game developers in this chapter.[36]

Notes

1 The information in the last few paragraphs is based on Steven L. Kent, *The Ultimate History of Video Games* (New York: Three Rivers Press, 2001).

2 Claus Pias, "The Game Player's Duty," *Media Archaeology*, ed. Erkki Huhtamo and Jussi Parikka (Berkeley: University of California Press, 2011), 164–83.

3 Robert M. Gray, "Coeducation at MIT, 1950s–60s," last edited October 29, 2017, https://ee.stanford.edu/~gray/TitleIX.pdf.

4 Kent, *Ultimate History of Video Games.*

5 Laine Nooney, "A Pedestal, a Table, a Love Letter: Archaeologies of Gender in Videogame History," *Game Studies* 13, no. 2, December 2013, http://gamestudies.org/1302/articles/nooney.

6 Ibid.

7 Ibid.

8 Ibid.

9 Shannon Symonds, "Preserving Carol Shaw's Trailblazing Video Fame Career," Museum of Play, *Play Stuff* (blog), July 19, 2017, https://www.museumofplay.org/blog/chegheads/2017/07/preserving-carol-shaws-trailblazing-video-game-career; for more information about women involved in video game development during the early years of the games, see Google Arts and Culture, "A Brief History of Women in Gaming—The 1980s," https://artsandculture.google.com/exhibit/a-brief-history-of-women-in-gaming-the-1980s-the-strong/CwKCGJf3HpdoIg?hl=en.

10 Florencia Grattarola, "Roberta Williams—The Queen of Graphic Adventures," Medium, December 18, 2018, https://medium.com/a-computer-of-ones-own/roberta-williams-the-queen-of-graphic-adventures-766e288ca3; Tiffany R. Isselhardt, "The Mystery & Horror of Roberta Williams," LevelSkip, updated October 24, 2017, https://web.archive.org/web/20180301173100/www.levelskip.com/action-adventure/The-Mystery-Horror-of-Roberta-Williams.

11 Dona Bailey, "The Original Gaming Bug: Centipede Creator, Dona Bailey," interview by Leigh Alexander, Gamasutra, August 27, 2007, https://www.gamasutra.com/view/feature/130082/the_original_gaming_bug_centipede_.php; Atari Women, "Dona Bailey," March 8, 2019, https://www.atariwomen.org/stories/dona-bailey/.

12 For accounts of the end of the video game industry crash and recovery of the industry, see Kent, *Ultimate History of Video Games*; Computer History Museum, "Nintendo Ups the Ante," https://www.computerhistory.org/revolution/computer-games/16/194; Andrew Cunningham, "The NES Turns 30: How It Began, Worked, and Saved an Industry," Ars Technica, July 15, 2013, https://arstechnica.com/gaming/2013/07/time-to-feel-old-inside-the-nes-on-its-30th-birthday/. For information on the marketing of video games in the last decades of the twentieth century, see Tracey Lien, "No Girls Allowed," Polygon, December 2, 2013, https://www.polygon.com/features/2013/12/2/5143856/no-girls-allowed.

13 Lien, "No Girls Allowed."

14 Susan Silas, "The Virtual Is Liminal: An Interview with Claudia Hart," Hyperallergic, May 24, 2016, https://hyperallergic.com/289316/the-virtual-is-limited-an-interview-with-claudia-hart/.

15 Claudia Hart, "Beginning and End Games: A Parable in 3D," *Cultural Politics* 9, no. 1 (2013): 86–94.

16 Benj Edwards, "*Myst* at 25: How it Changed Gaming, Created Addicts, and Made Enemies," Fast Company, September 24, 2018, https://www.fastcompany.com/90240345/myst-at-25-how-it-changed-gaming-created-addicts-and-made-enemies.

17 Paulette Beete, "NEA Arts Magazine Spotlight: Brenda Laurel: Girls Just Wanna … Play Video Games," *National Endowment for the Arts Blog*, April 3, 2018, https://www.arts.gov/stories/blog/2018/nea-arts-magazine-spotlight-brenda-laurel-girls-just-wannaplay-video-games; Shoshi Parks, "As Men Took Over the Videogame Industry, Brenda Laurel Pioneered Girls' Games," Medium: Timeline, May 4, 2018, https://timeline.com/brenda-laurel-wanted-to-get-girls-excited-for-tech-155fe57368e5.

18 Vic Hood, "How The Sims Broke Down Sexuality and Gender Boundaries." PCGamesN, May 9, 2018, https://www.pcgamesn.com/the-sims/the-sims-gender-sexuality.

19 For a short but comprehensive online summary of Brathwaite-Romero's career, see PeoplePill, "Brenda Romero, American Video Game Designer and Developer,"

https://peoplepill.com/people/brenda-romero/. Brathwaite-Romero is a frequent speaker at conferences. To hear her talk about gender and games, watch one of the many videos of her presentations online.

20 https://feministfrequency.com/2016/12/27/amplify-your-involvement-action-4-advocacy/.

21 Jen Ortiz, "She's Got Game," Marie Claire, December 5, 2018, https://www.marieclaire.com/career-advice/a25379999/female-gamers/.

22 Lucy O'Brien, "Women in Video Game Development in 2017: A Snapshot," IGN, updated December 22, 2017, https://www.ign.com/articles/2017/12/20/women-in-video-game-development-in-2017-a-snapshot; Anna Brown, "Younger Men Play Video Games, But So Do a Diverse Group of Other Americans," Fact Tank, Pew Research Center, September 11, 2017, https://www.pewresearch.org/fact-tank/2017/09/11/younger-men-play-video-games-but-so-do-a-diverse-group-of-other-americans/.

23 Chase Bowen Martin and Mark Deuze, "The Independent Production of Culture: A Digital Games Case," *Games and Culture* 4, no. 3 (July 2009): 276–95.

24 International Game Developers Association Developer Satisfaction Survey, 2019, https://igda.org/resources-archive/developer-satisfaction-survey-summary-report-2019/.

25 Statista, "Distribution of Gamers in the United States as of April 2015, by Ethnicity," October 29, 2015, https://www.statista.com/statistics/494870/distribution-of-gamers-by-ethnicity-usa/; Damon Packwood, "The Era of White Male Games for White Male Gamers Is Ending," Quartz, October 21, 2018, https://qz.com/1433085/the-era-of-white-male-games-for-white-male-gamers-is-ending/.

26 Nick Fouriezos "Black Female Gamers Are Claiming Their Space at Last," OZY, July 4, 2019, https://www.ozy.com/fast-forward/black-female-gamers-are-carving-out-space-in-an-industry-thats-denying-them-chances/95136/; Sandy Ong, "The Video Game Industry's Problem with Racial Diversity," Newsweek Magazine, October 13, 2016, https://www.newsweek.com/2016/10/21/video-games-race-black-protagonists-509328.html; buymymixtape123, "We Need More Black Protagonists in Gaming," January 25, 2018, Game Skinny, https://www.gameskinny.com/0nwmx/we-need-more-black-protagonists-in-gaming; Yussef Cole and Tanya DePass, "Black Skin Is Still A Radical Concept in Video Games," VICE, March 1, 2017, https://www.vice.com/en_us/article/78qpxd/black-skin-is-still-a-radical-concept-in-video-games.

27 Abdi Latif Dahir, "African Video Game Makers Are Breaking into the Global Industry with Their Own Stories," Quartz Africa, May 5, 2017, https://qz.com/africa/974439/african-video-game-makers-are-breaking-into-the-global-industry-with-their-own-stories/.

28 Judith Butler, *Gender Trouble: Feminism and the Subversion of Identity* (London: Routledge, 1990).

29 Jade Avis, "Lara Croft—Pixelated Object or Feminist Gaming Icon?" *brightONLINE*, no. 6 (November 26, 2015), http://arts.brighton.ac.uk/projects/brightonline/issue-number-six/lara-croft-pixelated-object-or-feminist-gaming-icon; Aja Romano, "Why We've Been Arguing About Lara Croft for Two Decades," Vox, March 17, 2018, https://www.vox.com/culture/2018/3/17/17128344/lara-croft-tomb-raider-history-controversy-breasts.

30 Anita Sarkeesian and Carolyn Petit, "Female Representation in Videogames Isn't Getting Any Better," WIRED, June 14, 2019, https://www.wired.com/story/e3-2019-female-representation-videogames/.

31 Isbister, Katherine. *How Games Move Us: Emotion by Design* (Cambridge, MA: MIT Press, 2016). Kindle.

32 Natalie Bookchin, "The Intruder," *Frontiers: A Journal of Women Studies* 26, no. 1 (2005): 43–7.

33 Mattie Brice, "Postpartum: Mainichi—How Personal Experience Became a Game," Gamasutra, November 13, 2012, https://www.gamasutra.com/blogs/MattieBrice/20121113/181401/Postpartum_Mainichi__How_Personal_Experience_Became_a_Game.php; spencivetaylor, "Queer Game Analysis, Mattie Brice's *Mainichi*," *Gaymeranthropology* (blog), February 29, 2016, http://gaymeranthropology.blogspot.com/2016/02/queer-game-analysis-mattie-brices.html.

34 Anna Anthropy, *Dys4ia*, video, 6:41, March 10, 20112, https://www.youtube.com/watch?v=y8x9hjGBY7c; Leigh Alexander, "Anna Anthropy Turns a Personal Struggle into a Heartfelt Game," Gamasutra, March 30, 2012, https://www.gamasutra.com/view/news/163496/Anna_Anthropy_turns_a_personal_struggle_into_a_heartfelt_game.php; Jed Lipinski, "Video-Game Designer, Anna Anthropy, Describes the Life of a Radical, Queer, Transgender Gamer," Politico New York, April 10, 2012, https://www.politico.com/states/new-york/city-hall/story/2012/04/video-game-designer-anna-anthropy-describes-the-life-of-a-radical-queer-transgender-gamer-067223.

35 Dames Making Games, May 7, 2016, https://web.archive.org/web/20160507071142/https://dmg.to/about; Emma Westecott, Hannah Epstein, and Alexandra Leitch, *Feminist Art Game Praxis* (Toronto: Authors and Digital Games Research Association (DiGRA), 2013).

36 Sagan Lee, "PsXXYborg (2013–2014)," http://www.saganyee.com/psxxyborg.

12

Japanese Feminism, Video Games, and Anime

As evident from previous chapters, there have been women artists of Asian heritage who have been important contributors to digital art. Many pursue their careers in Europe or the United States because Asian countries have been slow to accept women artists, let alone feminist women artists.[1]

In Japan, starting in the 1990s, feminist artists banded together in collectives, but with limited success in embedding feminist art practices into the cultural mainstream. They mounted exhibitions and performances, but the collectives came and went, mostly driven by the energies of a few leading figures. The only actual projects to survive are those created through digital technology. Yoshiko Shimada, an art historian and artist who moved from Japan to the United States and lives in California, has written that various kinds of women's movements have existed in Japan since the later part of the nineteenth century, when Japan became involved with the West. However, the emergence of feminist art based on feminist theory was slower than in the West, only appearing in the 1990s. She writes that the first exhibition to focus on gender, titled *Gender—Beyond Memory*, was mounted at the Tokyo Photographic Art Museum in 1995 and was greeted with hostility on the part of a number of male art critics who saw it as coming from Western influence.[2]

According to Shimada, the Japanese Feminist Art Movement was short-lived, partly due to very strong "gender-bashing" campaign conducted at the enactment in 1999 by the national government of a Basic Law for a Gender-Equal Society, which while nonbinding, still managed to enrage some conservative groups who claimed it would "destroy the beautiful Japanese traditional gender roles."[3] Shimada goes on to state that when the LGBTQI and AIDS movements initiated more open discussion about sexuality, work by nonbinary male artists became more acceptable while lesbian artists were still ostracized.

However, around 2015, feminist artists began to emerge again. Tomorrow Girls Troop (TGT) was formed in California and has members in Japan, South Korea, and South America as well as the United States. It is patterned after the Guerrilla

Girls, who emerged in New York in the mid-1980s and, like the Guerrilla Girls, when members make public appearances, they wear masks, but instead of gorillas, their vivid pink masks are based on a blending of rabbits and silkworms with protuberances on their heads that can be interpreted as either silkworm horns or rabbit ears, and giant manga/anime eyes. The website states its mission on the opening screen: "Our goal is to educate in order to achieve gender equality for all men, women and members of the LGBT community." In their mission statement they also quote the statistics showing that among 142 countries surveyed, Japan ranked #104 and Korea ranked #117 in the availability of education, health services, and economic and governmental participation, for women.[4]

TGT was one of the organizations that protested the 2019 removal by the Nagoya prefecture government of *After Freedom of Expression?* because it included *Statue of Peace*, a sculpture of a seated young woman by Korean artists Kim Eun-Sung and Kim Seo-Kyung symbolizing the Korean "comfort women," who were sexual slaves of the Japanese during the Second World War. The Aichi Triennale was an international exhibition, and several artists from various countries withdrew from the exhibition, including Tania Bruguera, the Cuban artist whose work is also about freedom and oppression.[5]

Another group, the Back and Forth Collective, consists of young feminist artists in Japan, Indonesia, and Scotland, and concentrates its efforts on "immigration, racism and colonialism from the feminist perspective." Shimada believes that their generation may be able to achieve what, in her view, the older generation has not been able to do—to have impact on the conservative, tradition-bound Japanese art world and larger society.[6]

Despite Shimada's optimism, the fact remains that feminist artists were rebuffed for decades in Japan's fine art world. However, Japanese women artists had more impact in the sphere of Japanese popular culture where they were active in generating manga/anime (comic books and animated film and video), which besides their popularity in Japan with all sectors of the population has become an important aspect of visual culture globally. Although these women artists didn't think of themselves as feminist, they were developing themes of female empowerment and validation of nonbinary sexuality twenty-five to thirty years before a nascent feminist fine art movement finally began to have some success in Japan.

The global impact of Japanese manga/anime on representation will be investigated in this chapter from three perspectives. The first is popular culture where its influence is everywhere—ask anyone worldwide to describe anime, and the response will be exaggerated eyes and hair, female and male characters who look like little girls and little boys, superheroes, monsters, and cute animals. The second is the rarely recognized role that women have played in the production of manga/anime. And the third is the influence of manga/anime on Japanese feminist artists who use digital technology.

Animation in Japan is embedded historically in a national comic tradition. In the 1930s, it became a popular art form, paralleling the growing fondness for Disney animations in the West. The popularity of animation is based on a complex set of characteristics, but simply put, animation presents images of a desirable fantasy world, an escape from the restrictions of real life, a factor that, according to cultural historians, led to its universal appeal.[7]

Manga/anime grew out of a comic visual and literary tradition which, in various incarnations, was an integral aspect of Japanese culture for centuries. Cultural historians point to periods of the tradition going back to animal cartoon scrolls in the tenth century or even earlier. After the Second World War, Japanese comic artists began experimenting with elements of style based on earlier Japanese cartoon styles along with components absorbed from Chinese and Western sources, particularly Walt Disney.

Snow White (1937), Disney's first full-length film, was not shown in Japan until 1950, but Mickey Mouse, Betty Boop, Felix the Cat, and Popeye were already well known. The large eyes, short stature, and simplified body shapes of the Disney style along with the many animal characters of Disney's classic films merged with Japanese and Chinese features and became embedded in manga/anime.[8]

Osamu Tezuka (1928–89) is usually described as one of the major influences on the development of the narrative and aesthetic structure of manga/anime. There is also general agreement that Disney was Tezuka's primary influence. Historian of Chinese animation, Daisy Yan Du, however, notes that Tezuka's style, while strongly influenced by Disney, stemmed from a complex synthesis of the comic conventions described above, including Chinese animation, particularly the film, *Princess Iron Fan* (1941). Tezuka himself credits *Princess Iron Fan* (1941) as one of his most significant influences. *Princess Iron Fan* was the first full-length Chinese animated film and despite the Second World War, was exported to Japan where Tezuka saw it as a youngster.

Princess Iron Fan has all the basic elements of manga/anime. The story is based on a Chinese folk tale of a princess with magical powers who doesn't want to part with an object needed by the hero, a hero with three friends who help him on his quest, and various episodes that impede their mission.

Tezuka's best-known anime series is *Astro Boy*, first issued as a manga comic and in 1963 as an animated television series. *Astro Boy* is a robot created by a scientist whose son has died. Feeling that his mechanical creation is not a satisfactory replacement for his human son, he abandons *Astro Boy*, who is rescued and cared for by another scientist. His rescuer gives him the powers and the human emotions that make him a superhero. Various anime historians have linked the nonviolent conception of *Astro Boy* with the revulsion Tezuka shared with other Japanese citizens for nuclear warfare after the bombings of Hiroshima and Nagasaki and the corresponding hope that the future would see the merging of technology and humanity.

The caricatured creatures of anime are an example of the Japanese concept of *kawaii* or cuteness. *Kawaii* as an esthetic principle means "pitiable . . . something that should be loved, or felt deep love for, or . . . something small and pretty."[9]

Cuteness is not confined only to Japan—teddy bears, for instance are an example of Western European and American cuteness. Psychologists have undertaken studies that show cuteness as a characteristic that invites a positive emotional response. Several studies have focused on the configuration of baby's faces and how babies that are "cuter" stimulate more caretaking and loving reactions from adults than those that are less "cute."[10]

Videogame characters like Pikachu and the other fantasy creatures in *Pokémon* or *Super Mario* are prime examples of *kawaii* and female protagonists are depicted as little girls. They wear their usually blond hair in twin ponytails and often wear childlike socks, even with four-inch high-heeled shoes, and even when they are drawn with fully developed breasts. In addition to their big eyes, almost invisible noses and tiny mouths, they usually have freckles, another feature associated with childlike looks. In contrast, elevating childhood and denouncing adulthood, manga/anime artists depict the enemies of these child/woman heroines as grown-up women, voluptuous, wearing lots of makeup, and dressed erotically.

The girls and boys of manga/anime are also white-skinned. As cultural anthropologist John Russell writes, whiteness was integral to ideal beauty in Japan, not as a mark of race, but as an indication of belonging to a modern culture that originated in the West and became universal.[11]

The cult of whiteness extended into the real world. Television commercials featured Caucasian celebrities. Cosmetics to whiten the face were popular. Only more recently has the Japanese public come to recognize the racial implications of whiteness and value indigenous looks. White skin also signified modern culture to citizens of other countries in the world and the universality of that sign was integral to the wide appeal of anime.[12]

The Japanese manga/anime world is even more complex than pop cultural production in the United States and Europe. Manga/anime products, distinct from each other, are marketed to various broad sectors of the population with even more addressed to male subsets, along with alternate products for women and girls. The following are several of the broader categories: *shōnen* are aimed at young men; *seinen* at grown men; *shōjo* at young women.

Cultural historians, both Western and Japanese, suggest that the modern surge of manga/anime in Japan is tied to the rise of male teenage lifestyle in the decades after the Second World War when modern media evolved. Young male adults, referred to as *otaku*, became immersed in the fantasy worlds of superheroes and video games, like "nerds" in the United States. They were the primary audience to whom manga/anime videos and video games were originally marketed with the consequence that much manga/anime content was based on popular teenage macho fantasies like those in American media culture of superheroes, combat, violence, and misogyny. The market for masculinist content grew as the original generations of male teenagers grew up and continued as fans of manga/anime products along with new generations, the members of which were used to modern media from birth.[13]

Manga/anime largely spread beyond Japan through Japanese video games although Japanese animated cartoons that were marketed to television worldwide for children's programming also aided its spread: in the United States, anime cartoons became a staple of Saturday morning television cartoon programs.

Japanese game designers appropriated anime's drawing style with its small, cute simplified characters. They did so, as much for efficiency as design reasons. Manga/anime characters could be generated with fewer pixels per inch than more complicated styles, making them easier to use in early video games with their low graphic resolution that didn't allow much design complexity.[14]

The United States and Japan emerged as the two epicenters for major production and worldwide distribution of video games by the early 1970s, but the video game industry crashed in the early 1980s. The Japanese company Nintendo was one of the companies that led the revitalization with its introduction of the NES console and a full set of Japanese games like *Super Mario Bros*. These Japanese games quickly became popular and US video game corporations began to emulate the Japanese model by designing role-playing games (RPGs) and other games with narrative structures and characters with back-stories, the style inspired by manga/anime. In 2002, when *Electronic Gaming Monthly* surveyed its English-speaking readers to identify the hundred most popular games, ninety-three of the hundred were Japanese.[15]

The esthetics of anime began to have impact globally. Christopher Kohler, who specializes in video game history, observes that younger children played

Pokémon and older ones were fans of *Dragon Ball*. As a result of their contact with Japanese games and anime series, American children came to see Japan as the country of their dreams. They followed the development of new games and could hardly wait for those games to be released. Kohler goes on to say that as they grew up, they wanted to see Japanese films and study Japanese history, with the result that enrollments in Japanese language and culture courses became significantly higher after Nintendo than before.[16]

Sociologist Koichi Iwabuchi's theory of "culture odor" is pertinent in explaining the global popularity of manga/anime. He describes the characters in Japanese animation as non-Japanese, using the Japanese word *mukokuseki*, meaning lacking in national identification. His theory goes on to postulate that their lack of racial or ethnic features specific to any nationality accounts for their capacity to become popular in the West as in Japan. Their export has increased Japan's cultural influence globally.[17]

By the early twenty-first century both the content and style of manga/anime had become embedded in popular culture around the world. Alexandra Gueydan-Turek, Professor of French at Swarthmore College, offers the hypothesis that manga/anime products have general appeal outside Japan and Asia because they provide a blend of fantasy narrative and nonbinary gender roles. They provide storytelling entertainment in postcolonialist countries that evades association with Western colonial culture and also provides alternatives to their own restrictive cultures, as for instance, in Russia where the *Sailor Moon* series (published first as a manga in 1991 and made into an anime series starting in 1997) in which a schoolgirl is transformed magically into a being who has superpowers of strength and endurance is popular with nonbinary young men who are subject to government oppression of LGBTQI individuals.[18]

Gueydan-Turek gives Algeria as a case in point. Algeria, notoriously anti-Western, found a popular culture alternative in manga/anime. Algerians came to know anime first in the 1980s through the one government-run television channel which broadcast youth programs featuring Japanese anime series dubbed in Arabic and French. It is now so popular in Algeria that manga are distributed through commercial publishing companies and anime series are featured on national television. Manga/anime conventions draw large numbers of participants, many of whom are even young women despite restrictions on female appearance in public.[19]

Contrary to common perception, women artists have been important in the modern manga/anime world almost from its inception in the 1960s and have been instrumental in the development of manga/anime products that provide alternatives to the popular masculinist manga/anime narratives featuring superheroes, women and girls who are either victims to be rescued by the superheroes, or helpers serving superheroes in their quests to capture magic objects from the evildoers and save the world.

Their work, on the surface, often seems to mirror *shōnen* and *seinen* with similar narrative themes and characters. However, a closer look quickly reveals their subversion. They take popular manga/anime characters and invent their own story lines, subverting the masculinist narratives by turning male superheroes into female heroines, creating romantic relationships, and introducing sexual episodes. They create a complicated narrative structure that weaves together romance, adventure, psychological intensity, history, and gender fluidity.

Shōjo and *dōjinshi* manga and anime usually feature cross-dressing, androgynous young women as central characters. Manga/anime historian Susan Napier hypothesizes that while their products may seem mainstream at first, they are disruptive enough to provide support for restless young women reluctant to settle for the traditional role of wife/mother. Napier argues that they also help nonbinary-identifying individuals to be themselves. Others disagree, arguing that in the end, their manga/anime narratives only reinforce patriarchal attitudes toward women.[20]

Sailor Moon is an example of these gender-bending manga/anime series, and it is one of the most popular manga/anime ever published, a fact which speaks to its appeal to nonbinary as well as heteronormative populations. *Sailor Moon* was created by Naoko Takeuchi. The protagonist is a fourteen-year-old girl named Usagi Tsukino who wears a sailor suit and has the required manga/anime features—huge eyes, almost no nose, a tiny mouth, and pigtails. Usagi can transform into a magical alter ego, Sailor Moon, thanks to her magical cat, Luna, who also tells her that she must battle the evil forces of the Dark Kingdom and find the Silver Crystal and the moon princess. Usagi starts on her quest along with a cohort of other young girls who, like her, can transform themselves into alter egos called Sailor Soldiers. A young man, also with magical powers, helps them as they fight the monsters of the Dark Kingdom (see Plate 33a).[21]

Naoko Takeuchi began her manga/anime career as an author of *dōjinshi*, the manga/anime comics, zines, videos, and video games produced mostly by nonprofessional women artists/authors for consumption by women. *Dōjinshi* play a large role in introducing feminist content into manga/anime. The involvement of amateur women in this literary practice of creating texts specifically for a female audience is traditional in Japan. It is structured around individual communities or fan clubs, each focused on an interest shared by its members. Modern interaction of the members of the clubs and distribution of their work occurs through social networking, stores specializing in serving these individual groups and the huge conventions attended by *dōjinshi* fans. Individual members are credited with innovations that shaped *shōjo* manga/anime, the category aimed at young women. The communities to which *dōjinshi* are addressed are demarcated by gender, sexual orientation, and age, and the themes in *dōjinshi* comics and anime films are often erotic, involving gender fluidity along with fantasy, combat, and quests. They are also heavily loaded with Japanese folklore and tales of magic. While some are addressed to the mainstream male audience looking for pornography, *dōjinshi* products are known for going further in providing explicit alternative eroticism for female-identifying, queer, and transgender audiences than commercially produced manga/anime even if the latter are created by women. Their popularity has been interpreted as providing a way for young women to role-play in sexual encounters.[22]

Mainstream Japanese publishers follow these independent authors/producers closely and pick up their creations when they offer revenue potential, thus reversing the usual process of corporate influence on taste. Instead, it becomes consumers themselves who are influencing corporate taste—a very feminist reversal. CLAMP began as a *dōjinshi* group of twelve women in the early 1980s. Their initial manga productions were their own story lines around popular commercial manga comics. Then in 1987 they decided to switch to original work. A manga publisher saw their work and invited the CLAMP group to submit a proposal for publication. Although their first submission was rejected, their second was accepted. Their manga were very successful and many were adapted as anime features.[23]

The group of women artist/authors referred to as the Year 24 Group because they were all born around 1949, twenty-four years into the reign of Emperor Shōwa (Hirohito), became active in the 1970s, preceding the CLAMP group. Some were *dōjinshi* and others worked directly in the commercial manga/anime sector. *The Rose of Versailles* by Riyoko Ikeda, one of the Year 24 generation, is an example of the cross-dressing, androgynous protagonists in *shōjo* and *dōjinshi* manga/anime, and like *Sailor Moon*, one of the best-known manga/anime globally. The androgynous protagonist is Oscar François de Jarjayes, a young woman raised as male who has become head of the palace guard, charged with protecting Marie Antoinette. *The Rose of Versailles* was made into a forty-episode anime series, released in Japan in 1979 and in that same year also made into a Japanese-French co-produced film titled *Lady Oscar*, with music by Michel

Legrand. It may seem strange that eighteenth century French history should become the basis for a manga/anime narrative, but the connection between Japan and French culture is a strong one dating back even to the period before Japan opened to the West in 1854. One obvious connection is the silk industry, with Japan the center for supplying the raw material, and France the center for manufacture and distribution of the final products. Japan absorbed the modernism of the European capitalist industrial society of the nineteenth century through its participation in the Paris World's Fairs held in 1867 and 1879, and subsequently, France played an important role in Japan's modernization including the military. Furthermore, *The Rose of Versailles* was created in the 1970s at a time when Japan was experiencing the same kind of student protests that had occurred in France in 1968, making a tale of the French Revolution relevant to the present time.[24]

Yasuka Aoike and Moto Hagio are credited with some of the earliest manga/anime featuring nonbinary love and sex, leading to the subculture categories called *shōnen-ai* when the attachment between two young men (or boys) is affectionate but nonsexual, and *yaoi*, when the relationship becomes sexual. Representative of "boy-love" narratives, *The Poem of Wind and the Trees* (first published as a manga by Shougakukan from 1976 to 1984 in the magazine *Shōjo Comic* and made into a film in 1987) by Keiko Takemiya tells the story of Gilbert and Serge, two boys who meet when they become roommates at boarding school in France. Gilbert is ostracized by his classmates because he skips classes and has sexual relationships with the older boys. However, Gilbert and Serge bond with each other and eventually become lovers. Serge finds out that Gilbert's behavior is the result of having been molested by his uncle before coming to the boarding school. They run off to Paris where they hope to make a new life, but Serge, attempting to escape, is run over by a carriage.[25]

The final consideration of manga/anime is its impact on artists in the fine art world. In Japan, manga/anime style was appropriated by painters, particularly by the internationally known artist, Takashi Murakami, who even created an art movement called Superflat, based on anime style. His paintings from the 1990s through the first decade of the twenty-first century feature figures based on classic manga/anime tropes—young women with exaggeratedly large eyes and huge breasts along with science fiction monsters. As a teenager, he had been an *otaku* (self-described)—addicted to manga/anime. Rejecting Japanese contemporary art as influenced by the West, he created a style based on manga/anime. In his *Superflat Manifesto*, he postulates that the worlds of entertainment and art are merging to create a contemporary culture that's flat rather than layered. This merger, he states is "source of energy" resulting in a unified culture that reflects contemporary life.[26]

Murakami mentored younger artists, among them women who became well-known artists in their own right. Aya Takano and Chiho Aoshima both worked in Murakami's KaiKai Kiki studio and gallery (Aoshima and Murakami eventually married each other). Like Murakami, their art practice is grounded in manga/anime in content and style but like the pop culture women artist/designers of manga/anime, they subvert the masculinist structure of Superflat (and of Murakami) to express nonbinary, feminist, and queer messages. Both Takano and Aoshima have written about their gender identity. Takano has stated bluntly that she is "not a man" and thus can only speak from a female perspective. Chiho Aoshima is open about her sexual subjectivity. She says that as a little girl she couldn't draw a male figure and that she still can't. She also describes how as a child, she experienced erotic imaginings that she recorded in secret notebooks, and her feelings of shame when her parents discovered them.[27]

In Takano's *The Jelly Civilization Chronicle* (2015), a major set of paintings from which she created a manga, her female protagonists are dressed in typical manga/anime fashion in school uniforms, but then they enter an imaginary world where their uniforms disappear and instead, they are seen in strange semitransparent garments more appropriate to the dream world they have entered. From a Western feminist perspective, Takano's childlike, almost androgynous figures would seem a continuation of the infantilization of women associated with the male gaze, but Takano herself describes them as otherworldly, ethereal essences. She imagines them as signs representing realities not yet envisioned (Plate 32).[28]

Chiho Aoshima also speaks of her wraithlike, childlike female figures as spirits rather than real people. Her video installation, *Little Miss Gravestone's Absent Musings* (2016) is a peek into her imaginary world where buildings—very phallic and yet plantlike—have faces, as do the hills. But it's a world of destruction and death as well as life (Aoshima was deeply affected by the earthquake and tsunami of March 2011). A volcano rains down lava, the buildings die but they are reborn. Aoshima's fairy-like creatures that inhabit this new, Utopian, world are barely human, let alone defined by gender. Their androgyny takes them out of the binary.[29]

The relationship to manga/anime integral to Aya Tanaka's and Chiho Aoshima's work can also be seen in the art practice of Mariko Mori, a Japanese artist well known in the Western world. In her early career, Mori used photography to subvert the manga/anime digital creation called an *idoru*—a celebrity who lives only in the computer. The *idoru* was adored by real-life men who followed her activities on their devices, believing that she was a real woman. Mori subverted the *idoru* image in performances where she would dress in gender-bending manga/anime costumes and pose in Tokyo's neighborhoods. In one of her performances she dresses like Sailor Moon, wearing a battle costume, armed with communication devices and weapons, combined with two huge light-blue ponytails (Plates 33a and 33b). In another she wears the uniform of a tea-room waitress fitted out with silver animal ears and silver legs.[30]

However, like Aya Tanaka and Chiho Aoshima, she shifted her art practice to create performances and videos that focused on a spiritual fantasy world that can also be interpreted as queer. Dressed in a manga/anime science fiction silver outfit with strange winglike appendages and the pale eyes of a zombie, her first video of this kind, *Miko No Inori* (2016) [Shaman girl's prayer], shows the artist caressing a crystal ball in the hall of the Kansai airport. Mori transformed herself, as Allison Holland portrays it, into "an avatar [who is] a conduit to the gods."[31]

The most important work to come from this period in Mori's career is the video installation, *Pure Land* (1996–8), in which Mori, dressed as the Buddha, presides over a lotus blossom, in a landscape based on the Dead Sea, surrounded by little pastel-colored *kawaii* creatures playing instruments. The concept of a future in which all might live in an earthly equivalent of the Pure Land (the Buddhist equivalent of the Christian heaven) is related to the utopianism of manga/anime: despite the obstacles and horrors that the central characters experience, at the end, they will triumph over their enemies and live forever in peace and tranquility. It is also related to the visions of dystopia/utopia in the work of queer artists in the West, as for instance, in the work of Zach Blas, micha cárdenas, Hannah Black, and Juliana Huxtable, referred to earlier.[32]

Because of its impact on visual culture globally, this chapter concentrates on Japan. Just to give one example of how feminist artists elsewhere in Asia are creating art based on digital technology, artists living in Thailand, Nitaya Ueareeworakul, Phaptawon Suwannakudt, and Mink Nopparat founded Womanifesto, with biennials and workshops in Thailand that ran from 1997 to 2008. A lasting project of Womanifesto is the No Man's Land website in which artists participate from countries worldwide to present work about borders. The founders envision cyberspace as without borders, in itself, a no man's land. Their project not only shows that feminist artists in other Asian countries are also working with digital technology, it also reveals the spread of the feminist vision of how an art practice based on digital technology eliminates the binary.[33]

Notes

1 Those documented in this book include Shu Lea Cheang (Taiwanese), Anicka Yi (South Korean), Cao Fei (Chinese), Jennifer Chan (Canadian Chinese), Chitra Ganesh (Indian American), Shigeko Kubota (Japanese), Tamiko Thiel (Japanese American), Hito Steyerl (German/Japanese). Yoko Ono and Yayoi Kusama, both Japanese, have been major figures in Western art since the 1960s.

2 Yoshiko Shimada, "Short List: The Defiant Fringed Pink: Feminist Art in Japan," Asia Art Archive, Ideas, https://aaa.org.hk/en/ideas/ideas/shortlist-the-defiant-fringed-pink-feminist-art-in-japan.

3 Ibid.

4 Tomorrow Girls Troops, https://tomorrowgirlstroop.com/english-home-stacks#second-stack-1.

5 Motoko Rich, "The Exhibit Lauded Freedom of Speech. It Was Silenced," *New York Times*, August 5, 2019, https://www.nytimes.com/2019/08/05/world/asia/japan-aichi-trienniale.html; Hakim Bishara, "Freedom of Speech Exhibition in Japan Closed Due to Censorship," Hyperallergic, August 6, 2019, https://hyperallergic.com/512514/freedom-of-speech-aichi-triennial/.

6 Back and Forth Collective, https://backandforthcollective.wordpress.com/quiet-dialogue/about/.

7 Daisy Yan Du, *Animated Encounters: Transnational Movements of Chinese Animation, 1940s–1970s* (Honolulu: University of Hawai'i Press, 2019); John G. Russell, "Replicating the White Self and Other: Skin Color, Racelessness, Gynoids, and the Construction of Whiteness in Japan," *Japanese Studies* 37, no. 1 (2017): 23–48; Koichi Iwabuchi, *Recentering Globalization: Popular Culture and Japanese Transnationalism* (Durham, NC: Duke University Press, 2002).

8 Du, *Animated Encounters*; Du includes a long quote from Tezuka on the influence of Princess Iron Fan, 66–8.

9 Richard K. Yu, quoting Sara Catharine Osenton, "Otaku Subculture and Unhealthy Sexual Obsessions," Medium, January 2, 2018, https://medium.com/@richardkyu/effect-of-otaku-subculture-and-the-obsessive-da6c2bba6a2e.

10 Melanie L. Glocker, Daniel D. Langleben, Kosha Ruparel, James W. Loughead, Ruben C. Gur, and Norbert Sachser, "Baby Schema in Infant Faces Induces Cuteness Perception and Motivation for Caretaking in Adults," *Ethology* 115, no. 3 (March 2009): 257–63.

11 Russell, "Replicating the White Self and Other."

12 Ibid.

13 Hiroki Azuma, *Otaku: Japan's Database Animals*, trans. Jonathan E. Abel and Shion Kono (Minneapolis: University of Minnesota Press, 2009); Rich, "How I Learned to Stop Worrying and Love Being Otaku: Answering Questions of Identity and Fandom in Japan and Beyond," Tofugu, June 6, 2016, https://www.tofugu.com/japan/

otaku-meaning/. For a simplified description of anime genres based on targeted audiences, see That Anime Project (2001), a site created by the University of Michigan Japanese Animation Group, Bonnie Bonifield, Eric Goldberg, Brian Kerr, Jeff Lee, and Liana Sharer, students in the University of Michigan class, English 414, under Professor Eric Rabkin, http://umich.edu/~anime/about.html. A helpful but non-comprehensive list of literature (in addition to books noted in other footnotes) on classification, content analysis, marketing, and history of anime includes Frederik L. Schodt, *Manga! Manga! The World of Japanese Comics* (Berkeley, CA: Stonebridge Press, 2002); Jonathan Clements and Helen McCarthy, *The Anime Encyclopedia: A Century of Japanese Animation* (3rd ed., Berkeley: Stone Bridge Press, 2015); Rayna Denison, *Anime: A Critical Introduction* (London: Bloomsbury Academic, 2015); Jonathan Clements, *Anime: A History* (London: Palgrave Macmillan on behalf of the British Film Institute, 2013 [reissued as ebook by Bloomsbury, 2018]).

14 Christopher Kohler, *Power-Up: How Japanese Video Games Gave the World An Extra Life* (revised ed., Mineola, NY: Dover Publications, 2016).

15 Ibid.

16 Ibid., 10.

17 Iwabuchi, *Recentering Globalization*, 4–7.

18 Alexandra Gueydan-Turek, "The Rise of Dz-Manfg in Algeria: Glocalization and the Emergence of a New Transnational Voice," *Journal of Graphic Novels and Comics* 4, no. 1 (Spring 2013): 161–78.

19 Gueydan-Turek, "The Rise Of Dz-Manga in Algeria"; Djamila Ould Khettab, "Manga Gains Popularity in Algeria," *Middle East Eye*, October 16, 2015, https://www.middleeasteye.net/features/manga-gains-popularity-algeria.

20 To read conflicting views on whether the manga/anime narratives created by women promote empowerment of women and girls, see Susan Napier, *Anime, from Akira to Howl's Moving Castle* (New York: St. Martin's Griffin, 2001) for a positive assessment; for a negative perspective, see ees, a graduate student in ethics and applied philosophy, "Can Manga and Anime Contribute to Feminism and Gender Studies?" Artifice, March 18, 2019, https://the-artifice.com/manga-anime-feminism-gender-studies/. For analysis of the boy/love aspect of Takemiya's work, see Rebecca Suter, "Gender Bending and Exoticism in Japanese Girls Comics," *Asian Studies Review* 35, no. 4 (September 2013): 546–58.

21 For an example of how Sailor Moon empowered a young girl in the United States, read Soleil Ho, "What I Learned About Gender and Power from Sailor Moon," Bitch Media, May 31, 2013, www.bitchmedia.org/post/what-i-learned-about-gender-and-power-from-sailor-moon. Another personal story about the empowerment of Sailor Moon is Ryan Khosravi, "'Sailor Moon' and the Queer History of Anime Transformations," *Digg* (blog), December 19, 2018, https://digg.com/2018/history-of-the-transformation-sequence.

22 Kathryn Hemmann, "Queering the Media Mix: The Female Gaze in Japanese Fan Comics," *Transformative Works and Cultures* 20 (2015), https://doi.org/10.3983/twc.2015.0628.

23 Dani Cavallaro, *CLAMP in Context: A Critical Study of the Manga and Anime* (Jefferson, NC: McFarland, 2012).

24 Matthew Thorn (Rachel Matt Thorn), "Girls and Women Are Getting Out of Hand, The Pleasure and Politics of Japan's Amateur Comics Community," in *Fanning the Flames: Fandoms and Consumer Culture in Contemporary Japan*, ed. William W. Kelly (Albany: State University of New York Press, 2004).

25 Frenchy Lunning, "The 24 Nengumi: the Female Progenitors of Shōjo Manga," Comic Book Legal Defense Fund (CBDF), March 31, 2015, http://cbldf.org/2015/03/women-who-changed-free-expression-special-24-nengumi/; Rachel Matt Thorn, associate professor, Kyoto Seika University, "The Magnificent Forty-niners," *Community for the Revival and Promotion of Shōjo Manga*, the blog of the committee chair, Professor Thorn, May 30, 2017, https://www.en.matt-thorn.com/single-post/2017/05/31/The-Magnificent-Forty-Niners; for interviews with Keiko Taekmiya and Moto Hagio, two of the leading figures in the Year 24 Group, see Masami Toku, *International Perspectives on Shojo and Shojo Manga* (New York: Routledge, 2015): 197–212.

26 Takashi Murakami, "The Super Flat Manifesto, A Theory of Super Flat Japanese Art," in *Super Flat* (Tokyo: Madra, 2000); Arthur Lubow, "The Murakami Method," *New York Times*, April 3, 2005, https://www.nytimes.com/2005/04/03/magazine/the-murakami-method.html.

27 Rhiannon Platt, "May All Things Dissolve in the Ocean of Bliss: An Interview with Aya Takano," *Complex*, March 17, 2014, https://www.complex.com/style/2014/03/global-track-6.

28 Ibid.

29 Shona Martyn, "Cute and Dark: The Magical World of Japanese Art Star Chiho Aoshima," *Sydney Morning Herald*, October 25, 2019, https://www.smh.com.au/culture/art-and-design/cute-and-dark-the-magical-world-of-japanese-art-star-chiho-aoshima-20191017-p531iz.html; Butterfly, "Paris: Aya Takano—The Jelly Civilization Chronicle," *Butterfly Art News* (blog), May 26, 2017, https://butterflyartnews.com/2017/05/26/paris-aya-takano-the-jelly-civilization-chronicle/.

30 SooJin Lee, "Mariko Mori and the Globalization of Japanese 'Cute Culture': Art and Pop Culture in the 1990s," *Journal of Art Studies*, National Central University, Taiwan, no. 16 (July 22, 2015): 131–65, https://www.academia.edu/32616339/Mariko_Mori_and_the_Globalization_of_Japanese_Cute_Culture_Art_and_Pop_Culture_in_the_1990s; Robert Jarrell, "Synthetic Dreams: The Art of Mariko Mori," *Kyoto Journal* 51, no. 1 (August 20, 2011), https://kyotojournal.org/culture-arts/synthetic-dreams-the-art-of-mariko-mori/; Sylvia Tsai, "Flatstone, Mariko Mori," ArtAsiaPacific, July 29, 2013, http://artasiapacific.com/Magazine/WebExclusives/

FlatstoneMarikoMori; Streaming Museum, "Mariko Mori Intersects Nature, Ancient Culture, and Technology," October 28, 2013, https://www.streamingmuseum.org/post/rebirth-recent-work-by-mariko-mori/.

31 Allison Holland, "Mori Moriko and the Art of Global Connectedness," *Intersections, Gender and Sexuality in Asia and the Pacific* 23 (November 2009), http://intersections.anu.edu.au/issue23/holland.htm. Also see Allison Holland, "From Gothic Lolita to Radiant Shaman: The Development of Moriko Mori's Ethereal Personae," *U.S.-Japan Women's Journal* 40 (2011): 3–28.

32 An interesting analysis of *Pure Land* in which the author refers to Murakami's Super Flat concept as related to Mori's art practice along with manga/anime influences, but also sees Mori's flatness and interest in the sublime coming from a variety of sources: Landi Raubenheimer, "Flatness and Immersion in Mariko Mori's 'Pureland:' The Possibility of a Digital Sublime," *South African Journal of Art History (SAJAH)* 22, no. 3 (2007): 150–67; David M. Khan, "Questions of Cultural Identity and Difference in the Work of Yasumasa Morimura, Mariko Mori and Takashi, Murakami" (MA thesis, University of Canterbury, 2007), https://core.ac.uk/download/pdf/35458251.pdf.

33 Varsha Nair, "Womanifesto: A Biennial Art Exchange in Thailand," *Southeast of Now: Directions in Contemporary and Modern Art in Asia* 3, no. 1 (March 2019): 147–71.

13

Artificial Intelligence, Facial Recognition, and Virtual Reality

This chapter examines the art practices of feminist artists in three growing areas of digital art, artificial intelligence (AI), facial recognition, and virtual reality (VR). The first section outlines the responses of feminist artists to the gender and racial biases inherent in the development of AI. They recognize that while AI is producing beneficial applications in fields like medicine, it is also problematic in ways that affect everyday life as in its use for intelligent personal assistants (IPAs) such as Siri on the smartphone and Alexa on tabletop speakers. By 2019, Amazon announced, it had sold over 100 million Alexa-enabled devices. Why, asked feminists, did these assistants always speak with women's voices (It should be noted, that one can now select the gender of Alexa's voice)? The second section describes how feminist artists have exposed the gender and race biases in the facial recognition programs that are increasingly being used by law enforcement officials. The third explores the attraction of feminist artists to VR as an art form.

AI is now pervasive in every sector of the economy. Giant distribution warehouses are completely automated as a result of AI application, with potential unprecedented shifts in employment patterns. Personal electronic devices like cell phones and digital notebooks are used to control household tasks from turning on lights, through locking and unlocking doors, to making sure the baby is sleeping safely. Vacuum cleaners are self-directed, and cars are becoming self-driving, though there is skepticism about the effectiveness of vacuum cleaners, and of safety in the cars. Robots are now common in health care, sometimes more effective in surgery than humans, although the use of robots in care for the elderly is questionable.

Judy Wajcman and other sociologists who investigate technology from a feminist perspective have exposed how the robotic devices invented to relieve women of domestic chores have not worked in that way. As Wajcman states, they have raised the standards of home care to such an extent that women spend more, rather than less time in domestic chores.[1]

Although the criticism of AI by feminist artists is a serious endeavor, the works themselves convey their messages with wit and outright humor, as for instance in the art of Annina Rüst, Adrianne Wortzel, and Heidi Kumao. Their conceptions are also characterized by references to domesticity such as cooking, children's toys, and children themselves, upending their traditional meaning within the patriarchal value system.

Annina Rüst's installation *A Piece of the Pie Chart* (2015) employs the act of baking to demonstrate gender inequity. Visitors to the exhibition use a computer to choose a pie chart that exposes bias. The pie charts include statistics that illustrate for example, the gender disparity in Swiss technical universities, IT teams in public administration, and in major Swiss technological corporations. Once a viewer has selected a pie chart, the computer screen instructs him/her/they to place a pie from a stack of pies into the machine, whereupon a heat gun melts the chocolate on top of the pie. A vacuum hung from the ceiling picks up the pie chart chosen by the viewer and deposits it on the sticky surface of melted chocolate. The pie is then moved along a conveyor belt to be photographed with the chart decoration by a webcam and posted on Twitter. The pie itself is then mailed to the institution where the data originated. When Rüst writes about her own work, she uses feminist language. She terms herself "a feminist technologist," who is creating art that will help achieve gender parity. She is optimistic that human beings and technology are both "she-able" and thus malleable.[2]

Elmo dolls were one of the biggest hits during the era of megapopular toys in the 1990s. Elmo was one of the most important characters on PBS's Sesame Street, watched by millions of children. Elmo often replaced the security blanket as the object with which children went to bed. Elmo also was electronic. When shaken, squeezed, or hugged, Elmo emitted the giggle which was the Elmo trademark. In 2008, Adrianne Wortzel created an installation titled *The Battle of the Pyramids*. She stripped the outer covering of dozens of Elmo dolls to reveal the black mechanical automatons beneath, removed the electronic boards, and reprogrammed the dolls to march, raise their arms in salute, and fall as if killed on the battlefield (Plate 34). She then orchestrated dozens of them as Napoleon's army and accompanied by martial music, they reenact the European style tactics used in the war to conquer Egypt, inappropriate as they were for desert maneuvers. Writing about *The Battle of the Pyramids* in the catalog for an exhibition she curated at Rutgers University a few years ago, Anne Swartz interpreted Wortzel's conversion of the Elmo dolls as showing the ambiguity implicit in children's play. Children treasure their cuddly soft toys like Elmo, but also experiment with violence, historically with old-fashioned toy soldiers and toy guns, or in the contemporary world through participation in shooter and other combat video games. Wortzel turns Elmo's gentle floppy arms into the stiff arms of marching soldiers so that, instead of a toy to take to bed, the Elmo dolls become threatening entities.[3]

Another example of the response of feminist artists to gender bias in toys is the action undertaken by the Barbie Liberation Organization, the members of which switched the voice boxes in Teen Talk Barbies and G.I. Joes during the 1993 holiday shopping season in protest against the way Mattel had programmed the voice boxes reflecting gender stereotypes. When the switch was made, G.I. Joe then complained that "Math is hard!" and Barbie declared, "Vengeance is mine!"[4]

Heidi Kumao, professor in the Penny W. Stamps School of Art and Design at the University of Michigan, has created a series of robotic devices under the title *Misbehaving: Media Machines Act Out* (2002–7). Kumao describes her constructions as overturning conventional robot design in which robots are programmed to perform practical tasks such as playing chess or assembling the bodies of automobiles or refrigerators. Instead, she conceives them to "act out and misbehave." She intends them to be machines that mimic human emotional responses like anger and fear.[5]

Kumao's sculpture, *Protest: Portrait of a Girl*, consists of a pair of motorized mechanical legs ending in tap shoes on a glass table. As people approach the table, a proximity sensor initiates movement by the legs. They begin to tap, becoming more and more energetic, the closer spectators come to the table, until finally they emulate the legs of a little girl throwing a tantrum, kicking, shaking, and stomping. In *Resist: A Machine Portrait*, a pair of mechanized little girl's legs squirms on the floor, suggesting fear of, and defiance to, an invisible abuser. A third sculpture, titled *Translator*, is a comment on how children are caught in conflicting parental commands. A round screen mounted on a pair of mechanical legs ending in roller skates travels back and forth between two upholstered armchairs with video projectors focused on the round screen (face) of the *Translator*. Each personage delivers a contradictory "message" that appears on the face of the figure. One message shows an eye that gradually disappears as a covering is zipped up. When the figure moves to the opposite chair and projector, the image on its so-called face shows a garment being unzipped revealing a skeletal torso beneath. Kumao describes it on her website not only in terms of a family situation, but also as a micro version of the larger aspect of social exchange, particularly in politics. Kumao compares the mechanized figure traveling back and forth between competing directives to a mediator between two diplomats with opposing views.[6]

After working with toys, Adrianne Wortzel went on to investigate another aspect of AI, whether robots that interact with humans should be constructed to look like human beings and whether they can be programmed to have human emotions. She explored these questions in a film titled *The Sentient Thespian* (2019) in which she appropriates the characters and plot of Shakespeare's *A Midsummer's Night Dream* to focus on the fairy creature, Puck, whom she recreates as a robot—Shakespeare himself envisioned Puck as nonhuman although with empathetic human characteristics that make him engaging. Wortzel's Puck is a four-legged robot called the MekaMon, developed by Reach Robotics, a company in the UK. Rather than humanoid, it looks like a mechanical spider. As Wortzel's Puck interacts with Lysander, who, in Wortzel's film, is a fifteen-foot-high industrial robot, the MekaMon shakes, jiggles, and wiggles in response. Wortzel talks about the MekaMon in terms similar to those used by Kumao in describing her sculptures. Wortzel sees the MekaMon's playfulness as allowing her "to emulate human emotion through gestures." She sees robots like the MekaMon becoming a "new social, dramaturgical, and psychotherapeutic tool."[7]

Adrianne Wortzel also explored the possibility of emotional responsiveness in robots through an automaton she named Kiru, commissioned by Christiane Paul, eminent digital art theoretician and historian and Adjunct Curator, New Media Arts, Whitney Museum of American Art, for an exhibition she curated called *Data Dynamics* (2001). Throughout the duration of the exhibition, Kiru roamed the lobby of the Whitney Museum of American Art greeting and chatting with visitors. The robot was controlled randomly by people in remote places around the world who could converse through the robot with visitors at the museum. Although Kiru had a lower body construction that resembled a skirt, he/she/they/it had a male voice unlike the personal assistant devices personified by female voices. As with Puck in *The Sentient Thespian*, Wortzel did not make Kiru an android (resembling a human being); Kiru's mechanisms are all visible including the wheels on which Kiru navigates.[8]

Erin Gee has also been exploring how to create robots with emotional responses. She states that she found the mirror-imaging concept that underlies most robotic creation very limited—there was no need for robots to reflect human beings. Gee began to think in terms of other senses besides sight as alternative pathways through which emotion could be transmitted. *Swarming Emotional Pianos* (2014) is the result of her investigation. She built a set of sculptures based on the structure of the piano but instead of the strings and hammers placed horizontally, she made them vertical. Each sculpture is on wheels so that it can also move around the space. The sculptures respond to sensors placed on the bodies of visitors to the gallery. One set of sensors responds to heartbeat rate, another to sweat, a third to blood pressure, and others to additional functions of the body. The rhythm of the music increases or decreases in speed according to heart rate, the density of the music reacts to sweat, and the harmonies shift in according to the rise and fall of blood pressure. When the participants' emotions spike, the instruments begin to move around the room.[9]

How far can AI go in creating robots who have the emotional responses and intellectual flexibility of human beings? Can a robot choose its own gender identity? When clinical psychologist Barbara Wren created a Twitter robot, she did not give it a gender identification initially. However, she had programmed her creation in such a way, that "he" chose his gender identity. He declared that his name was Ken and that he used masculine pronouns but did consider himself as possibly gender fluid.[10]

Wren obviously endowed Ken with feminist concepts of the significance of gender identification and a comprehension of gender variation. Ken's capacity to decide on his own gender raises the issue of what Daniel Estrada calls "value alignment,"[11] meaning that the robot is instilled with the values of its maker. Journalist, Bax J. Ferguson, who reported on Ken, commented that Wren's experiment shows how easy it is to insert one's own principles into a android. If that is the case, then it goes without saying that most robots will be built on patriarchal principles since it is mostly men who are their developers.[12]

The work of robotic engineers to create realistic-looking female robots has been subjected to feminist critique for duplicating the attitudes of the patriarchal society toward women in both their appearance and the way they function. A controversy arose in 2015 when Hanson Robotics introduced Sophia, a robot who looked and acted more like a human woman than any previous robots. Her body and facial movements were programmed successfully to have the fluidity of human movement, even though the back of her head was transparent so that the digital machinery that made her function was clearly visible. Hanson Robotics and Ben Goertzel, Sophia's designer, promoted Sophia as having human attributes of emotion and intellectual flexibility that made her more than just look and act human—she was posthuman, meaning that she could supplant human beings. It was all a big joke. Beautiful Sophia seemed to have the capacity to speak spontaneously when she gave the 2018 commencement speech at the Rhode Island School of Design until it was revealed afterwards that she was scripted. In a parody of real-life political controversies around granting citizenships, arguments ensued about whether robots like Sophia should have rights and, in 2017, she was granted citizenship by Saudi Arabia—ironic in the extreme considering that, just like Sophia, women in that nation are the property of males. Continuing the joke, Sophia also gave a talk at the UN in 2017 and was pictured on the cover of *Elle* magazine.[13]

Hiroshi Ishiguro at Osaka University's Intelligent Robotics Laboratory created another almost lifelike android, ERICA, in 2016. Ishiguro said that he tried to instill in ERICA "intention and desire." He gave her the "intentions and desires" appropriate for a receptionist in a corporate office—to be organized, to be polite and greet visitors, to help visitors reach their destinations on time.[14]

One of the most provocative realistic female robots has been the sex robot. The Vietnamese/British porn artist and blogger Harriet Sugarcookie conducted a multiple-choice survey asking 500 heteronormative males what they wanted in a sex robot beyond the obvious goals of enhancing masturbation practices or having intercourse. Many answers were what might be expected: 38 percent said they could conduct fantasies that they would not be able to do with a human partner, 20 percent said it would be "cool" because they were interested in new technology, and 30 percent said that they were shy or lonely.

However, other responses revealed their attitudes toward women and their expectations about relationships with women were more complex: As many as one in ten announced readiness to date a realistic sex robot to have a "more intelligent" partner, 15 percent each wanted one because "she would never let him down" nor become "sad or upset." One in five thought an AI sex partner would always be there "to listen." And 17 percent thought a robot sex partner might have "the same interests." Sugarcookie concluded that her survey showed that in choosing the most desirable qualities in a sex robot, those qualities were the same ones that heteronormative men have always wanted in their female mates; sexual gratification on demand and emotional support without responsibility for reciprocity.[15]

Karen Palmer is African American, and her concerns about the communication of emotion during racial disturbances led her to undertake a project investigating the relationship of human emotion and AI. Her concern is the fact that, although AI can detect the outward expression of human emotion, it is limited in comprehending the meaning of the human response. In other words, a robot can be programmed to recognize that crying means that someone is upset but isn't very adept at taking the next step to find out why. To capture her concepts in visual form, during a residency at ThoughtWorks in New York, she collaborated with Angelica Perez, Stephanie Weber, and Sofia Tania on a film called RIOT

(2018), during which, viewers' reactions are transmitted to the film itself through webcams focused on their facial expressions. Their expressions affect the narrative in the film. However, even though using EmoPy, an advanced facial expression recognition (FER) technology developed by ThoughtWorks (and available as open source), the responses in the film sometimes are not accurate reflections of the meaning of the facial expressions.[16]

The artists whose work is described above are all concerned with how to prevent AI from becoming inscribed with patriarchal values. NOSSAS [Ours], a feminist organization in Brazil, took AI one step further into activism in 2015 by creating Beta, a robot on Facebook's platform, Messenger. When viewers had conversations with Beta, they could ask "her" to keep them updated on activities that pose a threat to women's rights and safety. They could also instruct "her" to send pre-written letters to government officials when there were legal issues affecting women. This function proved very effective: when a bill was proposed to reverse the right for women to have abortions in cases involving rape, life-threatening health issues, or fetus non-viability, legislators received over 35,000 emails through Beta and voting on the bill was suspended indefinitely.[17]

Another controversial development in AI are the programs to use digital technology to create art. In 2019, the gallerist Aidan Meller, introduced Ai-Da, the first robot artist to draw from life. She "sees" through facial recognition software in the cameras that are embedded in her eyes; what she "sees" is transmitted through neural networks to her arm and hand. Meller says Ai-Da is named after Ada Lovelace, the early nineteenth century woman who conceptualized the modern computer (but more likely after himself). She is another in the series of female-bodied robots who fit the stereotype of the patriarchal female ideal—slender yet with noticeable breasts, long hair, full lips, straight nose, and large eyes. Like Sophia and ERICA, Ai-Da is promoted as having more human abilities than is the case. Largely scripted by the curator of Ai-Da's first exhibition at the Aidan Meller Gallery in Oxford, Lucy Seal, Ai-Da speaks about the importance of recognizing women artists, her words at odds with her appearance as a sex object for the male gaze. The drawings are more like map plottings. The paintings based on them are created by a woman artist named Suzie Emery who remains unrecognized in the attribution to Ai-Da as the artist. The sculptures are executed by a computer scientist in Sweden and then cast in bronze, according to an article on Artnet.[18]

In contrast, the US artist Anne Spalter, who has been a pioneer in the legitimization of digital art as a collector of computer-based work and the writer of a college-level textbook on digital art, in 2019 became interested in using the potential of the vast number of images in big data-storage programs as raw material for paintings. Spalter describes her process as a collaboration with the computer and the "cloud," the cloud being the name for storing data on the internet rather than within the physical body of a computer. The cloud permits much larger amounts of data to be stored. Spalter saved images in the cloud, altered them, and then downloaded the images they generated. The end results were compositions that she would not have been able to create using traditional sources, whether from live observation or photographs. She also says that there's an element of mystery about using these "neural-net-based algorithms" because no one really knows how they function and the results are unpredictable. Spalter uploaded thousands of images depicting airplanes, then subjected them to alteration through programs that rendered them unearthly, making them resemble fantasy UFOs arriving to save the planet from oblivion, "their desired appearance as saving forces for the human race in troubled times." At first Spalter tried digital printing or video as the final format for her images, but found both unsatisfactory. Instead, she turned to the traditional modes of painting and pastels to render the compositions effective. Spalter states that by combining the computer/cloud-based files with tradition 2-D art practices, she was able to achieve a merging of the 2-D and 3-D worlds that would have been impossible without the digital data (Plate 35).[19]

As described earlier both in Chapter 10 on surveillance and at the beginning of this chapter, facial recognition systems are being increasingly employed by governmental authorities and corporations to create a virtual panopticon. These systems are another form of AI to which feminist artists have reacted and they have been successful in drawing attention to the issues: The race and gender biases in facial recognition programs are being recognized. One of the problems that cause the biases was the fact that the digital technology experts working on the creation of the programs were almost all white males and their data sets consisted of people who looked like them. One set turned out to be more than 80 percent white and 75 percent male. It took an African American Rhodes scholar and Fulbright recipient, Joy Buolamwini, a researcher at MIT Media Lab to conduct one of the first studies to produce the data. Her research project showed that while facial recognition systems worked 99 percent of the time on white males, it could not identify women of color 35 percent of the time.[20]

In the following paragraphs the art practices of a few of the artists who are investigating bias in AI and facial recognition are described. The first is the African American artist, Stephanie Dinkins. To counteract the bias in AI that has resulted in the whiteness of android robots, she has created non-white robots who speak in voices based on the intonations of Dinkins's African American family members whom Dinkins recorded telling stories about their experiences of racism. The robots are programmed to respond to questions from visitors.[21]

The Dazzle Club collective, formed in 2019 by four performance artists, Emily Roderick, Georgina Rowlands, Anna Hart, and Evie Price, monthly paint their faces in blue, black, and red stripes, a makeup based on CV Dazzle, a camouflage makeup created by artist Adam Harvey in 2010, and walk through a London neighborhood to protest the the use of facial recognition programs in surveillance cameras. The camouflage makeup breaks up the planes of the face thus preventing the facial recognition programs from registering them.[22]

A group of design students from the HKU University of the Arts Utrecht created masks to avoid the invasion of privacy from facial recognition programs. Sanne Weekers designed a scarf printed with other faces so that when worn, surveillance cameras can't distinguish which face belongs to the actual wearer. Jip van Leeuwenstein invented a transparent hood that acts like a lens to distort the face yet allows the wearer to see out. And Jing-cai Liu envisioned a projector to be worn on the head pointed toward the face, beaming another face over the wearer's face. And the fourth is Zach Blas, who conceived the *Facial Weaponization Suite*—masks created from merging so much facial information from numerous individuals as to confuse the programs through an excess of data.[23]

Like AI and so much other digital technology, VR originated in the 1960s as a US defense training technology, placing the viewer within a computer-generated 3-D world to experience what might occur in a military action. Despite the fact that VR has been available for close to seventy-five years, there has been little overall documentation of the history of VR in the arts. A useful source is an unpublished thesis by Jacquelyn Ford Morie, a digital technology specialist as well as an artist whose practice involves VR.

According to Morie, the term itself was created in the 1980s by Jaron Lanier, who founded one of the first companies to produce the gear needed to experience VR. Morie defines VR as a term for a computer-generated simulation of a physical world which can be entered using particular equipment that provides the viewer with an experience that he or she is actually within that world and to "feel" the textures that are, in reality, only digital codes.[24]

Morie goes on to write that feminist artists were among the first to be attracted to VR in the 1990s and speculates that the concept behind VR of mingling the virtual and offline worlds was the compelling feature. VR offered the possibility "for becoming," a holistic form of art which was open-ended since the viewer, rather than the artist, controlled what was experienced. Like hypertext literature,

VR is non-hierarchic. The artist creates the environment but the viewer selects what to see, hear, or feel, unlike the linear narrative of patriarchal literature, film, and video in which the creator is the authority and the reader a captive. Morie also relates the attraction of VR to feminist artists as a way to create art that a viewer undergoes through the senses of the body, thus avoiding the use of language which some feminist theorists have defined as male: the pen as phallic. For these reasons, more women seem drawn to VR than men. In the period between 1970 and 2007, for instance, over 60 percent of VR works were created by women artists.[25]

Morie cites Nicole Stenger as one of the first artists to work in VR in 1989, when she had a residency in the Human Interface Technology Lab, at the University of Washington, which was conducting research on VR. *Les Angeliques* (1989–92) was created by Stenger to engage three senses: the visual, sound, and touch. The images of *Les Angeliques* bear resemblance to feminist gender iconography of the 1970s as in the work of such artists as Judy Chicago with her flowerlike vulva images used for the plates in *The Dinner Party*. Its feminist content supports Morie's contention that women artists were drawn to VR because of its innate possibility for feminist expression. The film consists of three abstract episodes, each of which is initiated by a digital hand operated through a haptic glove that causes the hand to touch what is a carousel-or-windchime-looking structure. In the middle of this structure are hanging heart-shaped objects. As the hand (initially humanoid, but later like the hand of a mannequin) touches one of these objects, the heart unfolds into abstract flowerlike forms related to the shapes of female sexual organs. Music created by electronic composer Diane Thome, evoke the comparison to wind chimes as the hanging rods are struck and bell reverberations occur.[26]

A residency program from 1995 to 2005 at the Banff Centre (now the Banff Centre for Arts and Creativity) in Alberta, Canada, created and directed by Sara Diamond, a digital artist herself, who later become president of the Ontario College of Art & Design (OCAD) University, was unique in fostering the evolution of VR as an artistic medium. Among the artists who worked at Banff were feminist digital artists already discussed in earlier chapters such as Brenda Laurel, who collaborated with Rachel Strickland and two male artists, Rob Tow and Michael Naimark, during a Banff residency to create *Placeholder* (1993) for which they photographed the surrounding spectacular topography from many angles. Two participants at a time could wear VR googles and move about the landscape—even flying over it. The concept was feminist—to enable participants to experience the living world from the nonbinary perspective of a nonhuman breathing creature.[27]

Another characteristic of VR is its capacity to create empathy. Like video games, VR draws the viewer into the artwork as a participant rather than an observer. As

Laurie Anderson explains in speaking about her VR production created in collaboration with Hsin-Chien Huang, *Chalkroom* (2017), rather than only looking at what someone places in front of the viewer, the participant in VR chooses where to look—not only forward, but also up, or down, or back, and in technologically advanced VR, can also move around the space at will rather than just observing. The offline world is completely shut out—the VR world takes its place, generating a sense of involvement so much more intense than observing a work of art from a distance. Not only is the viewer in control of his/her/their actions, but those actions mean something, whereas nothing is required of the viewer when confronting a conventional work of art except to observe. That sense of agency and empathy may be one of the reasons VR has special appeal to women artists.[28]

Feminist artists have used this capacity for empathy to deliver social justice messages. Japanese American artist Tamiko Thiel, who lives in Munich, Germany, has made many works about issues of racism, occupation, and persecution. In her VR work, *Beyond Manzanar* (2000) she collaborated with Iranian artist, Zara Houshmand, to protest against the proposal to intern US citizens of Iranian descent in the barracks of one of the old internment camps for Japanese-origin citizens of the United States during the Second World War. The work places the participant in the midst of one of the infamous camps. Using a set of controls, the participant can move about the camp among sights and sounds of the past like a camp resident, the personal sense of imprisonment and hopelessness evoking repulsion for the proposal much more than watching a film or video or reading a book about the horrors of the internments can achieve.[29]

Two Los Angeles artists, Nonny de la Peña, who has been called the godmother of VR, and Janicza Bravo have used VR to elicit sympathy for victims of poverty and racism. *Hunger in Los Angeles* (2010–12), by de la Peña, is a VR installation in which a participant experiences what it is like being in a line at a food bank. De la Peña, a former journalist, believes that VR is so productive of empathy that it should become a new form of journalism and has established Emblematic Group to promote the journalistic use of VR.[30]

Janicza Bravo produced *Hard World for Small Things* (2016), a prize-winning VR experience that exposes the unconscious racism of the police. The participant sits in the back seat of a car driving through Los Angeles neighborhoods and becomes acquainted with the driver and the other passengers who talk about their everyday activities. It concludes with a police officer accidentally killing the driver on the assumption that the driver is doing something wrong simply because he's Black. Bravo states that her motivation for using VR was her frustration with how easy it was to dismiss the terrible events seen on the daily news. She thought that people's response would be more empathetic if they could experience events "from the inside." Then it would be impossible to stay unaffected.[31]

Milica Zec's *Giant* (2017; Plate 36) puts the viewer into a bomb shelter in the cellar of a house in Serbia during the period of the NATO bombings. A mother and father try to keep a young child amused during an attack. They invent a giant by using their hands in shadow images on the wall—the giant is approaching but will pass by. However, the bombing continues and at the end, a bomb hits the house above, causing it to collapse on the family crouched beneath.[32]

NeuroSpeculative AfroFeminism (2017) was created by Carmen Aguilar y Wedge and Ece Tankal, who founded and manage Hyphen-Labs to use VR technology to insert the experience of Black women into the technological mainstream. On entering the space of the production, the participant is in a real-life beauty salon. Upon donning VR goggles, the viewer is transported into a virtual beauty salon where the mirror image shows a Black woman reflected back at the viewer, thus placing the viewer, no matter what race or color the viewer might be, inside the body of a Black woman. The attendant then proceeds to braid the viewer's hair virtually.[33]

VR has had its good and bad times. Disturbed by the inequality of access to VR and technology in general, Catherine Allen, who had worked on VR productions for the BBC in London in 2015, co-founded Limina Immersive in 2016 to broaden access to VR. Allen was concerned that the audience for VR consisted mostly of young males who were accustomed to VR because they use their headsets to play video games. She wanted larger and more diverse audiences for the VR that artists were making. In addition, Allen also wrote a manifesto, *A Vision for Women and VR*, to encourage women to enter the field of VR and make it a gender-balanced area of digital art practice.[34]

In 2018, Google introduced Google Cardboard, an inexpensive set of goggles that could be bought or even handmade at home requiring only the purchase of the right lenses. The concept was to capitalize on the universal spread use of smartphones. Google Cardboard has a slot into which a smartphone would be inserted. Using Google apps for the device, the viewer could then look through the goggles at the images on the phone, now transformed into a VR instrument. However, the quality could not compare with high-end goggles and Google stopped making VR goggles to use with new smart phone models. As seductive as VR is, the fact remains that it is awkward to have to rely on equipment in order to experience it. Alternatively, augmented reality (AR) is much more accessible and can be experienced through a smartphone. With the universality of smartphones, women artists are now using AR to promote feminist concepts as described in the next chapter.

Notes

1 Judy Wajcman, *Feminism Confronts Technology* (Cambridge: Polity Press, 1991; Google Books reprint, 2000): 11–13.

2 Annina Rüst, *A Piece of the Pie Chart*, http://www.anninaruest.com/pie/; Annina Rüst, "A Piece of the Pie Chart: Feminist Robotics," *Leonardo* 47, no. 4 (2014): 360–6.

3 Anne Swartz, *Momentum: Women/Art/Technology*, New Brunswick, NJ: Rutgers University Center for Women in the Arts and Humanities Exhibition Catalog (2015) 26, https://www.academia.edu/14827301/Momentum_Women_Art_Technology; Adrianne Wortzel, "Battle of the Pyramids (Documentation)," www.adriannewortzel.com/project/battle/.

4 Mike Bonanno, "Barbie Liberation Organization," Beautiful Trouble, Case study, https://beautifultrouble.org/case/barbie-liberation-organization/; David Firestone, "While Barbie Talks Tough, G.I. Joe Goes Shopping," *New York Times*, December 31, 1993, https://timesmachine.nytimes.com/timesmachine/1993/12/31/726193.html?pageNumber=12.

5 Heidi Kumao, "Misbehaving Machines Act Out," Heidi Kumao, Projects, http://heidikumao.net/misbehaving-machines/.

6 Heidi Kumao, "Translator-2008," Heidi Kumao, Projects, http://heidikumao.net/portfolio-items/translator-2008/?portfolioCats=94.

7 ThoughtWorks Arts, "*The Sentient Thespian*, Project Work Summary: Fall 2018," https://thoughtworksarts.io/projects/sentient-thespian/; Geraint Evans, "*MekaMon* Takes the Stage with *ThoughtWorks Arts* Collaboration," *TechSPARK* (blog), April 18, 2019, https://www.techspark.co/blog/2019/04/18/mekamon-takes-the-stage-with-thoughtworks-arts-collaboration/.

8 Adrianne Wortzel, "Camouflagetown (documentation)," http://www.adriannewortzel.com/project/camouflagetown/; also see Swartz, *Momentum*, 58.

9 Erin Gee, "Swarming Emotional Pianos," https://eringee.net/swarming-emotional-pianos/; Lauren Oyler, "Erin Gee Makes Feminist Robots that Respond to Human Emotion," VICE, December 16, 2014, https://www.vice.com/en_us/article/mv5nzn/erin-gee-makes-feminist-robots-that-respond-to-human-emotion-456; Jennifer Rhee, *The Robotic Imaginary: The Human and the Price of Dehumanized Labor* (Minneapolis: University of Minnesota Press, 2018), 120–3.

10 Bax J. Ferguson, "How to 'Make' a Woman: Addressing the Gendering of Artificial Intelligence—and the Issues of Bias in the Technology We Create," Medium, February 5, 2018, https://medium.com/s/the-future-of-flesh/how-to-make-a-woman-1a378ed7b827.

11 Daniel Estrada, "Value Alignment, Fair Play, and the Rights of Service Robots," paper presented at the February 2020 conference on "AI, Ethics, and Society," sponsored by the Special Interest Group on Artificial Intelligence of the Association

for Computing Machinery in conjunction with the Association for Advancement of Artificial Intelligence, https://arxiv.org/pdf/1803.02852.pdf.

12 Ibid.

13 Lisa Chai, "Spotlight on the AI Pioneer Behind Sophia, the Robot: Ben Goertzel," Robo Global, August 8, 2019, https://www.roboglobal.com/insights/sophia-the-robot-ben-goertzel/; James Vincent, "Sophia the Robot's Co-creator Says the Bot May Not Be True AI, but It Is a Work of Art," The Verge, November 10, 2017, https://www.theverge.com/2017/11/10/16617092/sophia-the-robot-citizen-ai-hanson-robotics-ben-goertzel; Michael Greshko, "Meet Sophia, the Robot that Looks Almost Human," *National Geographic*, May 18, 2018, https://www.nationalgeographic.com/photography/proof/2018/05/sophia-robot-artificial-intelligence-science/; Elena Renken, "Robot Gives Keynote Address at Inclusion-Themed RISD Commencement," *Providence Journal*, June 2, 2018, https://web.archive.org/web/20201109101405/https://www.providencejournal.com/news/20180602/robot-gives-keynote-address-at-inclusion-themed-risd-commencement--video.

14 Justin McCurry, "Erica the 'Most Beautiful and Intelligent Android' Leads Japan's Robot Revolution," *Guardian* (US edition), December 31, 2015, https://www.theguardian.com/technology/2015/dec/31/erica-the-most-beautiful-and-intelligent-android-ever-leads-japans-robot-revolution; Alex Mar, "Love in the Time of Robots," WIRED, October 17, 2017, https://www.wired.com/2017/10/hiroshi-ishiguro-when-robots-act-just-like-humans/.

15 Ferguson, "How to 'Make' a Woman."

16 Andrew McWilliams, "How Artists Are Reshaping Emerging Technology Research," Projects, June 27, 2018, https://www.thoughtworks.com/insights/blog/how-artists-are-reshaping-emerging-technology-research; ThoughtWorks Arts, "RIOT: Project Summary: Winter 2018," *ThoughtWorks Arts* (blog), https://thoughtworksarts.io/projects/riot/; ThoughtWorks Arts, "Karen Palmer: The Film that Watches You Back," TED Talk, *Thought Works Arts* (blog), May 25, 2018, https://thoughtworksarts.io/blog/karen-palmer-film-watches-you-back/.

17 Mafê Souza, "Beta: The First Cyberfeminist Bot," Women's Media Center, *FBomb* (blog), September 13, 2018, www.womensmediacenter.com/fbomb/beta-the-first-cyberfeminist-bot; NOSSAS, https://www.en.nossas.org/.

18 Naomi Rea, "A Gallery Has Sold More Than $1 Million in Art Made by an Android, but Collectors Are Buying into a Sexist Fantasy," Artnet News, June 6, 2019, https://news.artnet.com/opinion/artificial-intelligence-robot-artist-ai-da-1566580.

19 Curatorial Dept. Spring/Break Art Show, "Confirmation: We have received your SPRING/BREAK NYC 2020 Curatorial Application, *Spring/Break*," forwarded from Anne Spalter to Judith K. Brodsky, December 10, 2019. More information on Spalter's artwork can be found on her website, https://annespalter.com/. Spalter and her husband have an important collection of early digital artwork with information

available at https://spalterdigital.com/. For further information on their collection, see Art in America, "Collecting and Computing: A Conversation at the Armory Show," March 12, 2020, https://www.artnews.com/art-in-america/features/spalter-collection-computer-art-1202680682/. For one of the few textbooks on computer art that is conceptual as well as practical, see Anne Spalter, *The Computer in the Visual Arts* (Boston, MA: Addison Wesley-Longman, 1999).

20 Joy Buolamwini, "Face: The Final Frontier of Privacy, Full Spoken Congressional Testimony, May 22, 2019," Medium, May 23, 2019, https://medium.com/@Joy; Buolamwini/face-the-final-frontier-of-privacy-full-spoken-congressional-testimony-may-22-2019-ff8607df045b; Joy Buolamwini, "Written Testimony of Joy Buolamwini, Founder, Algorithmic Justice League," Hearing on Artificial Intelligence: Societal and Ethical Implications, United States House Committee on Science, Space, and Technology, June 26, 2019, https://science.house.gov/imo/media/doc/Buolamwini%20Testimony.pdf; Erika Beras, "Joy Buolamwini, When AI Misclassified Her Face, She Started a Movement for Accountability," *MIT Technology Review*, https://www.technologyreview.com/innovator/joy-buolamwini/; Ian Tucker, " 'A White Mask Worked Better': Why Algorithms Are Not Colour Blind," *Guardian* (US edition), May 28, 2017, https://www.theguardian.com/technology/2017/may/28/joy-buolamwini-when-algorithms-are-racist-facial-recognition-bias.

21 Tatum Dooley, "Stephanie Dinkins Is Turning Memoir into AI," VICE, August 15, 2019, https://garage.vice.com/en_us/article/43kdnm/stephanie-dinkins-is-turning-memoir-into-ai; "Q&A with Transdisciplinary Artist Stephanie Dinkins," interview by Future of Storytelling, Medium, January 10, 2020, https://medium.com/future-of-storytelling/q-a-with-transdisciplinary-artist-stephanie-dinkins-592b420c8703.

22 James Tapper, "Hiding in Plain Sight: Activists Don Camouflage to Beat Met Surveillance," *The Guardian* (US edition), February 1, 2020, https://www.theguardian.com/world/2020/feb/01/privacy-campaigners-dazzle-camouflage-met-police-surveillance; for more about the Dazzle Club see Moya Lothian-McLean, "These Activists Use Makeup to Defy Mass Surveillance," i-D, January 29, 2020, https://i-d.vice.com/en_uk/article/jge5jg/dazzle-club-surveillance-activists-makeup-marches-london-interview.

23 HKU Design, "Anonymous," https://web.archive.org/web/20190512083013/https://www.hku.nl/Opleidingen/Design/OverHKUDesign/HKUDesignInMilan2017/anonymous.htm.

24 Jacquelyn Ford Morie, "Meaning and Emplacement in Expressive Immersive Visual Environments" (PhD diss., University of East London, September 2007), 8.

25 Ibid., 5.

26 Ibid., 23.

27 Ibid., 23–6.

28 Laurie Anderson, "Laurie Anderson, Telling Stories in Virtual Reality," interview by Bonnie Marranca, *Performing Arts Journal* no. 120 (2018): 37–44.

29 Matthew Wilson Smith, "Liquid Walls: The Digital Art of Tamiko Thiel," *Performing Arts Journal* no. 96 (2010): 25–34, https://direct.mit.edu/pajj/article-pdf/32/3%20(96)/25/1797204/pajj_a_00004.pdf; SIGGRAPH, "Tamiko Thiel, Beyond Manzanar," ACM SIGGRAPH, https://digitalartarchive.siggraph.org/artwork/tamiko-thiel-beyond-manzanar/.

30 For a brief description and a link to more information see Docubase, MIT Open Documentary Lab, "Hunger in Los Angeles," 2012. https://docubase.mit.edu/project/hunger-in-los-angeles/; Caleb Garling, "Virtual Reality, Empathy and the Next Journalism," WIRED, 2015, https://www.wired.com/brandlab/2015/11/nonny-de-la-pena-virtual-reality-empathy-and-the-next-journalism/; Emblematic, "Step into the Story: Immersive, Virtual, Augmented and Mixed Reality," https://emblematicgroup.com/.

31 Wevr Transport, "Hard World for Small Things, A Day in the Life of a Tight-Knit Community," https://transport.wevr.com/hard-world-for-small-things; Andrew Marantz, "Studio 360: The Pioneers Who Are Making the First Virtual Reality Narratives," *New Yorker* (April 25, 2016).

32 Beckett Mufson, "A War Survivor's Virtual Reality Film Brings the Terror of a Conflict Zone to Life," VICE, March 14, 2016, https://www.vice.com/en_us/article/8qv7jg/giant-vr-film-gdc; Milica Zec and Winslow Porter, "Creating the Authentic Experience of GIANT in Virtual Reality," Medium, July 6, 2017, https://medium.com/@Within/creating-the-authentic-experience-of-giant-in-virtual-reality-570cda7b763d.

33 Adi Robertson, "Building the Afro-Feminist Future at Sundance, One Cyberpunk Beauty Salon at a Time," The Verge, January 26, 2017, https://www.theverge.com/2017/1/26/14377214/neurospeculative-afrofeminism-vr-science-fiction-sundance-interview-2017; Jasmine Weber, "An Afrofeminist Project Uses Technology to Empower Marginalized Communities," *Hyperallergic*, September 18, 2018, https://hyperallergic.com/460424/hyphen-labs/; Docubase MIT, "NeuroSpeculative AfroFeminism," 2017, https://docubase.mit.edu/project/neurospeculative-afrofeminism/; Hyphen-Labs, http://www.hyphen-labs.com/nsaf.html.

34 Tola Onanuga, "Virtual Reality: How Women Are Taking a Leading Role in the Sector," *Guardian* (US edition), May 28, 2018, amended May 29, 2019, https://www.theguardian.com/careers/2019/may/28/virtual-reality-how-women-are-taking-a-leading-role-in-the-sector.

14

Digital Public Art and Augmented Reality

This final chapter details how feminist artists are creating novel and effective public art based on the accessibility and adaptability of digital technology in general, and the user-friendly attributes of augmented reality (AR), the art form that merges the digital and offline worlds, in particular. The artists included in this chapter redefine public art to address social, political, and cultural issues at the heart of twenty-first century feminism such as the preservation of the character of local communities, the environment, and inequality as well as gender and race bias.

Two feminist artists who have addressed the community through public art commissions are Grimanesa Amorós and Susan Narduli. Amorós was born in Peru and emigrated to the United States as a young adult. Her light-based and digitally programmed projects have been installed in Europe, South America, and Asia as well as the United States. Amorós describes her projects in terms of community engagement, local history, and the environment. HEDERA (2018) was an installation commissioned by the Brooklyn-based organization BRIC (Brooklyn Information & Culture) for the fortieth anniversary of the Celebrate Brooklyn! Festival (Plate 37). Amorós covered a band shell in Prospect Park, Brooklyn with loops of variously colored lighted tubing, emulating the leafy vines that cover the exteriors of buildings around the world—*hedera* is the Latin name for climbing vines. Underneath the roof of the band shell are balloons which resemble the buds of a flower; their color varies as the colors in the tubes around them change. Amorós writes about this public sculpture, saying "The piece cultivates a relationship between public space and community through the conversation it generates ... [it] coexists with its viewers, bringing them closer to an ideal world where individuals can unite in celebration of diversity and a shared humanity."[1]

The inspiration for Amorós's public art installation *Golden Waters*, mounted in Scottsdale, Arizona during 2015, was the use of irrigation canals by the Hohokam people who occupied the area in the early part of the first millennium CE. Also motivated by Paolo Soleri's concept for Arcosanti, the community he established in 1965 to conduct projects bringing together urban and natural environments, she laid her distinctive strands of lighted tubing over the Arizona Canal at the point where the pedestrian bridge designed by Soleri crossed the canal.

American artist Susan Narduli conceived an installation for Palo Alto City Hall, California that would allow citizens to convey their concerns to the city government. Narduli wanted to create a setting that would empower individuals to feel that they counted. She says she "imagined something that offered the spontaneity and integrity of a person raising a hand in a public meeting." Titled *Conversation* (2016), it consists of a wall of monitors in the front lobby facing the entrance. Narduli programmed the monitors to receive local, national, and global news from various sources including social media. Quotes from these sources float across the screens as do patterns that are created by the words. Visitors can then interact with the screens by posting comments in response to reports, or by entering their own ideas and even photos. Narduli describes her intention as wanting to create a work that would be a physical embodiment of democracy. Because viewers would be able to interact with the monitors, they would realize that they were not without agency. They could express themselves, be heard, and hear others.[2]

Andrea Polli combines her feminism with a passion for making the public aware of environmental issues. Like Amorós's project in Scottsdale, one of her projects also involved a bridge. It was one of the three suspension bridges that unite the banks of the Allegheny River in Pittsburgh, Pennsylvania, named in memory of Rachel Carson. Carson was the author of the paradigm-changing book, *Silent Spring*, which revolutionized the way people thought about the environment by making them aware of the dangers of industrial development. Carson was born in a suburb of Pittsburgh, grew up in the area, and was an alumna of what was then known as the Pennsylvania College for Women. In 2016, Polli received a commission for a public-art project honoring Carson. In homage to Carson, she designed an environmentally friendly, self-sustaining, sculpture consisting of 27,000 multicolored LED lights that outlined the configuration of the Rachel Carson Bridge, powered by sixteen wind turbines. In addition, the installation included a weather station and a nanogrid (a collection of small generators that form a memory unit) to collect environmental data. Polli writes that people are so accustomed to just turning on a light switch or pressing the ignition button in their cars that they take the energy systems that power their lights, heat, cars, or digital devices for granted. She wanted to create a site-specific work that would counteract the invisibility of energy by giving it a physical embodiment with the goal of alerting people to environmental considerations.[3]

Several artists have addressed pollution, among them Polli, who developed a portable public sculpture titled *Particle Falls* (2010–), which debuted in San José, CA and which she took to Detroit, Philadelphia, Pittsburgh, and the University of Utah, Logan. *Particle Falls* functions through a nephelometer, a digital device that measures air pollution by means of a beam of light that strikes the particulate matter in the air, causing the light beam to change color from red to yellow to blue according to the concentration.

Another of Polli's projects devoted to pollution was *Breather* (2010) in Delhi, India. An automobile was encased in a plastic bubble with digitally programmed equipment that caused the bubble to inflate and deflate mimicking human breathing, thus demonstrating the importance of clean air in a city where the quality of the air is dangerous to the health of its inhabitants.[4]

To address pollution caused by industrial waste, Helen Evans and Heiko Hansen, a Finnish collaborative team known as HeHe, created the *Nuage Vert* [Green cloud] project, which took place at night outside a power plant in Helsinki (2008) and a waste-burning plant near Paris (2012) as well as several other locations from 2003 to 2012. They programmed laser beams to illuminate emissions coming from the plants, turning the plumes of smoke into pulsating green shapes that changed size and shape according to how much energy was being used, showing how much pollution the plants were sending into the air.[5]

Laurie Palmer pushed her *Oxygen Bar* (2005), a mobile free breathing machine which creates its oxygen from a "mini forest" contained within the structure, through the streets of Pittsburgh, to protest the planned razing of Hays Woods, a forested area on the outskirts of the city, for development. Her goal was to bring citizens of Pittsburgh to understand the importance of forests for clean air.[6]

Another American artist who addresses pollution is Amy Balkin. Starting in 2004 and continuing for several years, she carried out *Public Smog*, a conceptual "park" in the air to promote awareness of atmospheric pollution. She bought carbon gas emission credits from international trading markets so that polluting companies could not operate in those areas, thus creating in-the-atmosphere clean-air "parks." *Public Smog* was featured in *documenta* (*13*) (2012). The display consisted of hundreds of letters (later published by *documenta*) that Balkin solicited from people in countries around the world, requesting that the earth's atmosphere be placed on the World Heritage List.[7]

One of the rapidly growing areas of digital technology used by artists in the twenty-first century is AR. AR came into being in the 1990s. As was the case with many aspects of digital technology, it was developed as a defense tool. The first AR application was produced, in 1992, for the US Department of Defense, by Louis Rosenberg at the USAF Armstrong Laboratory, to allow employees in the lab to see information placed over the real spaces in which they worked.

How does AR work? Simply put, it is a process whereby visual elements can be added to the view from a camera through digital technology. While any camera can be used for AR, what made AR so accessible, as opposed to VR, is the merging of a camera with the cell phone. That merger took place in the mid-1990s, and the first software to create AR was released to the public in 1999.

But AR really took off with the advent of the smartphone in 2007. The technological capabilities of the smartphone were so advanced and improved the quality of the cell-phone camera to such a degree that in addition to becoming loved by individuals everywhere, the smartphone made AR an important component in academic, industrial, medical, and political sectors.

AR began to fascinate artists as well. But while there is a significant body of literature documenting the development of AR as a visual arts discipline, there is a paucity of information about its use by women artists. Yet women artists in general, and feminist artists in particular, have been integral to the development of AR.

A 2013 issue of the *Leonardo Electronic Almanac* was one of the first publications to focus on artists using AR. In an essay from that issue, the art critic and curator Simona Lodi described how, from 2009 to 2012, politically active visual artists in collectives such as Les Liens Invisibles, Molleindustria, and RomaEuropa FakeFactory in Italy; Manifest.AR in the United States; the Chinese duo Lily Honglei; and #arOWS, a collective of twenty-five artists who participated in the Occupy Wall Street protest, were influential in establishing the aesthetics of AR and positioning AR as an art form for radical political action. While the members of these collectives were mostly men, the women involved made significant contributions. Both male and female artists, even if not conscious of a connection to feminism, operated from a feminist position, protesting and erasing the inequalities of the patriarchal society. The connection to feminist art can also be seen in the satirical tone of many of these activist AR projects, reminiscent of the aesthetic of 1970s feminist artists who often used parody to mock patriarchal principles.[8]

The Apparition of the Unicorn, Pink and Invisible at the Same Time, mounted by Les Liens Invisibles at the Vatican in 2011, is an example of this usage. The Pink Unicorn parodied theistic beliefs. It appeared on the internet sometime in the 1990s, and internet technophiles were waiting for it to surface somewhere in the offline world. Its materialization was staged by Les Liens Invisibles on Easter Sunday, April 23, 2011 where the apparition of the Pink Unicorn rising like

Christ out of the grave above St. Peter's Basilica could be seen by invited spectators who had been given the software that would make the apparition visible on their cell phones.[9]

The Museum of Modern Art in New York was invaded in 2010 by the collective, Manifest.AR. Each of the artists created an AR work that viewers could see as they roamed through the museum using the Layar app, one of the early software programs that enabled cell phone users to see AR projects. Collective member Tamiko Thiel contributed a piece titled *ARt Critic Face Matrix* (Plate 38), which consisted of giant screaming faces that dominated the cell phone screen, ironically blocking the view of the museum's art.[10]

One of the most ambitious AR projects was *The Invisible Pavilion*, organized by Simona Lodi and Les Liens Invisibles for the Venice Biennale of 2011. They invited ten AR individual artists or artist collectives to participate. The artists stood at the gates to the Biennale grounds, offering free software so that visitors could view the AR interventions on their cell phones as they walked the paths leading from one pavilion to another. According to Simona Lodi, the goal of the project was to "give new meaning to public space, changing its proprietary boundaries, and the concept of what it is to perceive reality."[11]

Molleindustria protested the arrest by the Chinese government of Ai Weiwei at Beijing Airport on August 3, 2011, by programming an AR image of a hand raising the middle finger in an obscene gesture that viewers would see on their cell phones as they approached the Chinese pavilion. The image, in homage to Ai Weiwei, was based on his photographic series, *Study of Perspective* (1995–2003) in which he created a series of photographs of hands making the same gesture in front of global sites of patriarchal power such as the Tiananmen Gates, the White House, and the Eiffel Tower. In her contribution, *Shades of Absence: Outside, Inside*, Tamiko Thiel reminded visitors of how many artists had been persecuted rather than celebrated through inclusion in events like the Biennale, by programming an intervention featuring images of artists who had been subjected to threats of physical violence; others, whose work had been censored; and a third group of artists who had been arrested for activism. Lodi quotes the AR artist Tamiko Thiel: "As corporations privatize many public spaces and governments put the rest under surveillance, augmented reality artists take over the invisible but actual realm that overlays real space with multiple parallel universes."[12]

Artists have continued to consider AR a successful form of protest against the institutions of the patriarchal society in the twenty-first century. One example is *iSkyTV* (2013), created by Sophia Brueckner under the sponsorship of the Institute for Infinitely Small Things, in homage to Yoko Ono's *Sky TV* of 1966, in which cameras on the rooftop transmitted views of the sky to screens on the inside—perhaps the first civilian electronic transmission of data from the outside world to interior computers. *iSkyTV* detects the user's location and, instead of viewers seeing the sky directly, the screens display the sky above their heads through Google Street View. Her intention is to bring viewers to realize how we no longer experience the world directly, but rather through digital mediation. Programs like Google Maps have taken ownership of the landscape, presenting it to us through its own lens.[13]

In response to the restrictive actions of the United States to prevent immigrants from crossing the Mexican–United States border, the Electronic Disturbance Theater (EDT), co-founded by Ricardo Dominguez and Brett Stalbaum (an arts collaborative consisting of a diverse membership including lesbian, gay, and trans individuals with varied ethnic backgrounds, such as the artist micha cárdenas whose work is discussed earlier in this book), developed the *Transborder Immigrant Tool* (TBT), a mobile phone technology based on AR to help would-be immigrants find the water caches deposited by NGOs like Water Station, Inc. and Border Angels. At the same time that individuals trying to cross the border hear practical information, they also hear poems to inspire them. Declaring that the TBT is conceptually an arts project, Dominguez makes the distinction between art and activism by saying that artists disturb the law whereas activists break the law. He describes the TBT as "a global poetic system instead of a global positioning system," one that generates thought about the larger political/philosophic issues of the oppressive character of the patriarchal society.[14]

Digital feminist artist Nancy Baker Cahill, known for her innovational AR work, used AR to reach the general public in support of the #MeToo movement. Cahill, like other feminist artists, was angry not only at Jeffrey Epstein and his fellow predator, Harvey Weinstein, for their sexual exploitation of young women, but even more so at the misogyny of the Republican Party with its constant attacks on the rights of women and its casual dismissal of President Trump's aggressive behavior toward women. Cahill expressed her concern with an AR project titled *The Ghost of Jeffrey Epstein* (2019), in which viewers with cell phones could download Cahill's software program and see an image of Jeffrey Epstein looming over Republican headquarters in Manchester, NH, manipulating puppet strings attached to the building below (Plate 39).[15]

In the Fall of 2020, Jenny Holzer created *You Be My Ally*, a commission at the University of Chicago in which students, faculty, and staff could install a free AR application on their cell phones through which quotes from the readings in the core curriculum required at the university could be seen projected onto campus buildings. Students collaborated in the project by selecting the passages from which Holzer chose. Among the authors were W.E.B. Dubois, Helen Keller, Toni Morrison, Plato, Frederick Nietzsche, Mary Shelley, and Virginia Woolf. In addition, a message to vote in the upcoming election contest between President Trump and Vice President Biden could also be seen on trucks moving in and about the campus and the city.[16]

Locative media, art based on the AR potential in digital navigational systems, is another area of AR activity among feminist artists. In 1993, the Global Positioning System (GPS), with its twenty-four satellites that made it possible to identify locations anywhere on the globe, and the Geographic Information System (GIS), which provided the mapping capacity necessary for tracking, were developed. GPS and GIS quickly became ubiquitous in everyday navigation enabling motorists around the world to get to their destinations by using locative media such as Google Maps, Wave, and other software through smartphones attached to the cup holders in their cars. In addition, their creation provided the crucial elements that enabled Nintendo to create *Pokémon Go*, the video game in which participants search for *Pokémon* characters projected onto various surfaces in their physical-life geographic surroundings, Google to generate Google Earth, the software program that enables viewers to see almost any spot in the world from their electronic devices, and artists to use AR for environmental performances.

Feminist artists recognized locative media as an artmaking vehicle to enrich people's lives through enhancing their simple physical activities like hiking or broadening their intellectual horizons by learning more about their community histories activities.

Teri Rueb was one of the first artists to generate locative projects, her first being a work called *Trace*, which she finished in 1999. Rueb describes locative media as a digital form of placemaking, the process by which a community either intentionally or inadvertently shapes its public places, a phenomenon that exists in all cultures. Placemaking also establishes social and political aspects through its formation. Rueb used locative media to create *Trace*, a site-specific sound installation in Yoho National Park, British Columbia, an invisible memorial garden that connects the landscape with its history and the people associated with it. As hikers walk the trail, they hear memorial poems, songs, and stories through earphones connected to a computer / GPS device in their backpacks. In addition to her motivation to add a historic sense to the physical aspect of the landscape, Rueb conceives of her project as promoting a nonhierarchical aspect. *Trace* is ongoing: Rueb continues to extend an invitation to visual artists, performers, poets, and others to contribute to *Trace*, as she has done in subsequent projects as well, with the goal of breaking the government's monopoly on information gathering.[17]

At the same time, Naomi Spellman, Jeremy Hight, and Jeff Knowlton were working on an AR project similar in conception to *Trace*. In 2002, they introduced *34 North, 118 West* which was, like *Trace*, a walking project. Participants were given computers with a GPS unit and headphones and followed a map shown on the computers. As they walked, the computers tracked their movements and revealed various locations along the way. When they arrived at locations, narratives were read to them on their headphones. The artists' concept was to join together what they called the "connotative and denotative" worlds, the former being the physical world participants were walking through, and the latter, the narratives they were hearing—they were experiencing the present reality of the city and its archaeology, in a sense moving back and forth through time as a result of simultaneous immersion in the virtual and real worlds.[18]

Hana Iverson and Sarah Drury developed a software program that is available to anyone who would like to use it, utilizing the geographic positional and tracking software in AR for community history projects. They first used it for a project titled *Mechanics of Place* (2011) in which they focused on Boğazkesen Street in the center of Istanbul, located in the economically diverse, residential, small business, entertainment and arts neighborhood of Tophane. They invited artists to participate in a workshop to learn about the rich cultural and historic identity of the area and develop AR works that would relate to the ethos of the street and would be seen through smartphones. The artists took various directions. Cynthia Rubin became interested in the history of the street and created small films in which she imagined visual narratives around the one remaining wooden house on the street (wooden houses were typical Istanbul dwellings until modernization of the city in the twentieth century). Petek Kizilelma's project protested Turkey's censorship of 138 words on the internet that were deemed pornographic or suggestive. Through his AR interventions, words like "skirt," "gay," and "animal" became graffiti on the walls of the buildings. Kerem Ozcan invented fictional characters who might have lived on the street if it hadn't been for Turkey's repeated exiling of minority populations. Teoman Madra organized collages of images by local artists that were projected in protest against the globalization of the art world, onto the galleries that led up to the Museum of Modern Art where the Istanbul Biennial was being held.[19]

Another area in which AR emerged was as a device to develop narrative projects. As in web-based hypertext, AR provides non-linear in-depth narrative experiences for the viewer. Evelyn Hriberšek began working with AR narrative in 2007. Her experiments resulted in *O.R.pheus* (2012), which was performed in an abandoned hospital in a Munich, Germany underground bunker. Participants wandered through the various rooms using the software program Hriberšek developed to view camera-readable icons on their phones. Clicking on the icons opened up images and narratives about the history and use of the rooms. (Hriberšek was a true pioneer in AR. As she herself has noted, *O.R.pheus* precedes *Pokémon Go* by five years.) The narratives were a mix of the Orpheus myth with emphasis on Orpheus's deliberation about whether or not he should cross the border between the living and dead worlds and texts about the building itself—its construction, its use or nonuse. In 2017, Hriberšek explored the Orpheus theme again in a more elaborate AR and VR production this time titled EURYDIKE, focused more on Euridice's story rather than on Orpheus, providing a feminist slant on the myth. Hriberšek says she arrived at using AR and, ultimately, VR, because, like Nicole Stenger, she was interested in how to bring multiple art forms together into a unified experience. She saw VR as an innovative process that could achieve her goal.[20]

Swiss artist Camille Scherrer began working with narrative elements generated through AR while she was still a student at the University of Art and Design Lausanne (ECAL). She envisioned a book in which the reader would see animated illustrations. Not knowing enough about coding to be able to construct the book alone, she collaborated with computer scientist Julien Pilet to create *The Haunted Book* (2007), the first of a series of AR-animated books she went on to make. She took photographs of the illustrations she had drawn and then projected them onto a computer screen, where they merged with animation generated by the computer—a black bird flies out from a wall sconce, little creatures parachute from a chandelier, a skeleton hand turns a doorknob.[21]

Increasingly, this idea of AR as narrative has attracted artists. Using an application developed by the innovative technology organization, Holition, Jenny Holzer created an AR installation as an element in her solo exhibition at Blenheim Palace in 2017. Using their smartphones visitors accessed personal narratives that revealed the history of the Palace.[22]

Professor of Design at Ontario College of Art and Design (OCAD) University, Martha Ladly, has written about the capacity of AR to generate empathy. She cites Alyssa Wright's *Cherry Blossoms* (2014) in which players with backpacks that contained microcontrollers and GPS units, accessed GPS locations on the streets of Boston that she correlated with bombing attacks that took place on the streets of Baghdad, Iraq. Each time that a player accessed a location, the backpack released compressed air causing a mini explosion. But instead of discharging shrapnel, the backpack emitted bits of paper, each bearing the name of a noncombatant who lived in one of the Baghdad neighborhoods under attack. The barrage of paper scraps swirled around the participants and onlookers looking like smoke or as Ladly describes the scene, "falling white blossoms from a cherry tree," the physical experience causing spectators to focus on the tragedy of the Iraq wars.[23]

A striking example of how effective the AR capacity for empathy can be is a project set up in 2017 by Claudia Hart at the School of the Art Institute of Chicago (SAIC) in collaboration with Art Institute of Chicago (AIC) curator, Michael Darling, for her students to use AR in conjunction with the exhibition, *Riot Grrrls*, featuring abstract paintings by ten women artists who were feminist pioneers. The exhibition included work by established artists like Mary Heilmann as well as emerging feminist artists, all drawn from the collection of the AIC. Michael Darling explained his intention in mounting this exhibition as "a challenge" to the conventional history of abstract painting which mostly ascribes abstraction as a male art practice. He selected paintings by women artists that he says stand on their own in terms of skill and originality, thus deconstructing abstract painting as male.[24]

Hart's students each chose an image and developed an AR response to it. While some students concentrated on the formal aspects of creating an AR work to relate to a real-life painting, others moved in the direction of content: Christine Chin overlaid the images of women artists whose works and careers had been rendered invisible because of their gender onto Ellen Berkenblit's *Love Letter to a Violet*. Chin says she wanted the viewer who tried to see the painting but was prevented from doing so by this welter of images obscuring it, feel the frustration of women artists denied their recognition.

Jasmin Han decided to work with the Ree Morton piece in the exhibition. She said that she was surprised and upset by the fact that women artists today were still experiencing the gender discrimination that Ree Morton did in the 1970s. Using the washing and peeling of apples as a metaphor for tiresome repetitive labor, she created a video in which apples are endlessly washed and peeled. She compared the process to what she describes as the never-ceasing brainwashing and imposition of gender expectations on women by the patriarchal society. Han drew from her Korean heritage for the imagery she used. If a young woman in South Korea were serving prepared apples to guests, she might be complimented by her guests as being a potentially good housewife, the implication being that there were no other opportunities for her.[25]

Recognizing the potential in the way artists were using AR to reach the public, museums and other arts institutions began to adopt AR for their own benefit. In many museums around the world, instead of the bulky, awkward audio guides in use for decades, individuals can now direct their phones toward a work of art to learn more about the artist, the content, and the period in which it was created. An innovative example is the creation of a free software program by Mural Arts Philadelphia for people to view its first AR mural, *Dreams, Diaspora, and Destiny* (2018), a block-long work consisting of holograms and a soundtrack.[26]

The art practices of VR and AR described in these last two chapters are still in the developmental stage. As the technology in both advances, it is likely that more and more artists will turn to these technologies for the potential they offer for empathy and narration. Already by the end of the second decade of the twenty-first century, the number of artists using VR and AR is so great that it has been impossible to do more than give examples of those who are working from feminist principles.

As exciting as the potential for making art through VR and AR may be, the disquieting aspect of both is how they connect the digital and offline worlds ever more seamlessly, allowing individuals to live in both simultaneously. In a few years it may no longer be possible to distinguish between the two worlds. The question is whether the merger will further the humanist and intersectional principles of feminist art practice in the future world. Will the merger dismantle the patriarchy?

Notes

1 Grimanesa Amorós, "HEDERA, Prospect Park Bandshell, Brooklyn, NY 2008," https://www.grimanesaamoros.com/publiccommission/bric-brooklyn/; BRIC, "Grimanesa Amorós: HEDERA," Brooklyn Information & Culture, https://www.bricartsmedia.org/art-exhibitions/grimanesa-amor%C3%B3s-hedera.

2 Susan Narduli, "Conversation," Narduli Studio, https://www.nardulistudio.com/conversation.

3 Cameron Vernali, "Tangibility of Artist's Work Wakes Public to Environmental Issues," *Daily Bruin*, November 13, 2018, https://dailybruin.com/2018/11/12/tangibility-of-artists-work-helps-to-wake-public-to-environmental-issues/; Andrea Polli, *Hack the Grid* (Pittsburgh, PA: Carnegie Museum of Art, 2017), a project of the Hillman Photography Initiative in which the Carnegie Museum invites artists to investigate contemporary social issues through photography's measurement of light and time.

4 Allison Meier, "A Digital Waterfall that Illuminates the Threat of Air Pollution," Hyperallergic, February 16, 2015, https://hyperallergic.com/182480/a-digital-waterfall-that-illuminates-the-threat-of-air-pollution/.
5 Régine Debatty, "Andrea Polli—'Who Owns the Air?'" We Make Money Not Art, March 16, 2011, https://we-make-money-not-art.com/andrea_polli_who_owns_the_air/. We Make Money, Not Art is a website created by Debatty to "present the many encounters of art and science in an approachable yet rigorous and critical way and to include 'media art' in a broader cultural discussion." For further information on *Nuage Vert*, see "NUAGE VERT (GREEN CLOUD)—HeHe (Helen Evans & Heiko Hansen), Helsinki, Finland, 2008," Curating Cities, http://eco-publicart.org/nuage-vert-green-cloud/.
6 Laurie Palmer, "Hays Wood / Oxygen Bar," Groundworks, Environmental Collaborations in Contemporary Art, https://groundworks.collinsandgoto.com/artists/hays-woods-oxygen-bar.
7 Amy Balkin, "Public Smog Will Save the Earth," http://tomorrowmorning.net/publicsmog; for an interview with Balkin, see Thom Donovan, "5 Questions (for Contemporary Practice) with Amy Balkin," *Art21 Magazine*, February 17, 2011, http://magazine.art21.org/2011/02/17/5-questions-for-contemporary-practice-with-amy-balkin/#.Xpm0dqtKjyg; Sarah Hotchkiss, "Public Park in the Sky Seeks to Protect Atmosphere," KQED, November 25, 2015, https://www.kqed.org/arts/11105426/public-park-in-the-sky-seeks-to-protect-atmosphere. Ana Teixeira Pinto, "Atmospheric Monument," *Mousse* no. 34 (2012): 152–7, http://tomorrowmorning.net/texts/Mousse_d13_Amy%20Balkin.pdf.
8 Simona Lodi, "Spatial Art: An Eruption of the Digital into the Physical," *LEA: Leonardo Electronic Almanac* 19, no. 2 (April 15, 2013): 12–31.
9 Ibid.
10 Ibid.
11 Ibid., 20–1.
12 Ibid., 24.
13 Catherine D'Ignazio, "iSkyTV," kanarinka, http://www.kanarinka.com/project/iskytv/; Sophia Brueckner, *iSkyTV*, http://turbulence.org/Works/iSkyTV/.
14 Leila Nadir, "Poetry, Immigration, and the FBI: The Transborder Immigrant Tool," Hyperallergic, July 23, 2012, https://hyperallergic.com/54678/poetry-immigration-and-the-fbi-the-transborder-immigrant-tool/; Ricardo Dominguez, "Border Research, Border Gestures: The Transborder Immigrant Tool," *American Quarterly* 71, no. 4 (December 2019): 1053–8.
15 To view the AR sight, see Nancy Baker Cahill, "A Performance in Augmented Reality," Twitter, August 14, 2019, 4:16 p.m., https://twitter.com/4thwallapp/status/1161733314857693184?lang=en.
16 UChicago News, "Renowned Artist Jenny Holzer to Debut Project at UChicago Using Augmented Reality," September 10, 2020, https://news.uchicago.edu/

story/renowned-artist-jenny-holzer-debut-project-uchicago-using-augmented-reality.

17 Teri Rueb, "Interview with Teri Rueb," Interview by Jeremy Hight, *LEA: Leonardo Electronic Almanac*, February 2011, https://www.leoalmanac.org/wp-content/uploads/2011/03/Interview_Rueb.pdf.

18 Naomi Spellman, Jeremy Hight, and Jeff Knowlton, *34 North, 118 West: Mining the Urban Landscape* (2002), https://eliterature.org/collection.eliterature.org/3/work.html?work=34-north-118-west; Jeremy Hight, "Views From Above: Locative Narrative and the Landscape," *LEA: Leonardo Electronic Almanac* 14, no. 07/08 (November 2006), https://www.leoalmanac.org/wp-content/uploads/2012/09/09_JHight.pdf.

19 Hana Iverson and Sarah Drury, "Mechanics of Place: Textures of Tophane," *LEAL Leonardo Electronic Almanac* 19, no. 2 (April 15, 2013): 84–97, https://www.leoalmanac.org/vol19-no2-not-here-not-there-part-2/.

20 Matthew Mensley, "Interview with Evelyn Hriberšek: Creating Mixed Reality Art," All3DP, March 10, 2019, https://all3dp.com/evelyn-hribersek-ar-art-eurydike/; *Prolight+Sound* (blog), "The Fine Line to Reality: Immersive Technologies," June 20, 2019, http://prolight-sound-blog.com/the-fine-line-to-reality-immersive-technologies/. To see the trailer for *O.R.pheus*, https://www.youtube.com/watch?v=D5cXt0jFiKk. The trailer for *Eurydike* can be viewed on the *Eurydike* website, https://www.eurydike.org/.

21 Camille Scherrer, "An Interview with Interactive Designer Camille Scherrer," interview by Nelio de Barros, Kinobrand [June 2010], http://kinobrand.com/an-interview-with-interactive-designer-camille-scherrer/.

22 Gareth Harris, "Jenny Holzer to Use Augmented Reality in Blenheim Palace Show," *The Art Newspaper*, March 6, 2017, https://www.theartnewspaper.com/news/jenny-holzer-to-use-augmented-reality-in-blenheim-palace-show.

23 Martha Ladly, "Narrative in Hybrid Mobile Environments," in "L.A. Re.Play, Mobile Network Culture in Placemaking," special issue, *LEA: Leonardo Electronic Almanac* 21, no. 1 (January 15, 2016): 76–95, https://www.leonardo.info/sites/default/files/leavol21no1_la_replay_martha-ladly.pdf.

24 Museum of Contemporary Art, Chicago, Riot Grrrls, Exhibitions, May 23, 2017, https://mcachicago.org/Exhibitions/2016/Riot-Grrrls; Museum of Contemporary Art, Chicago, "Giving a F@*0/0: Forms of Feminism in Response to Riot Grrrls," MCA DMA (blog), May 23, 2017, https://mcachicago.org/Publications/Blog/2017/05/Riot-Grrrls-App-2.

25 Museum of Contemporary Art, Chicago, "Giving a F@*0/0."

26 Grace Dickinson, "Mural Arts Philadelphia Debuts Its First Augmented Reality Mural, 'Dreams, Diaspora, and Destiny,'" *The Philadelphia Inquirer*, October 10, 2018, https://www.inquirer.com/philly/blogs/things_to_do/mural-arts-philadelphia-augmented-reality-mural-king-britt-20181010.html.

Conclusion

The work of digital artists whose art practice is consciously or unconsciously based on feminist theory and/or its intersectional mutations has had significant impact on the visual arts, affected popular culture, and modified the masculinist nature of digital technology itself. These artists have furthered cultural globalization through feminist websites, internet art, and art transmitted by social networking while, at the same time, working to preserve local culture. They have been leaders in drawing attention to the fact that feminist art theory, as first articulated, did not adequately address queerness and race. Through their art, they addressed the increasing merger of the offline and virtual worlds. They are innovators in interdisciplinarity, working with sound as well as visual imagery, merging word and image through hypertext and augmented reality. They have broken through the barrier between high art and popular visual culture, creating video games and working with community organizations. They have transformed digital technology into a more human mode of communication through introducing empathy into its makeup.

It might appear that some of the artists of the last century included in this book have little to do with digital technology, but they are essential because of the contributions they made to the aesthetics and concepts that led to digital art, both in developing uses of techniques and in promoting the legitimacy of technology-based art. In addition, the work of writers like Donna Haraway, Sadie Plant, Legacy Russell, and essays by artists like Hannah Black and Claudia Hart, exploring ideas drawn from feminism, poststructuralism, critical race theory, and postcolonialism are crucial to the work of the artists discussed.

While it is the creativity and innovativeness of the artists themselves that have resulted in the impact of their work, their interaction with academic institutions, professional organizations, residency centers, and research institutes, particularly in the United States and the UK, has been a significant factor in their success. As Donna Cox, Ellen Sandor, and Janine Fron have documented, universities and art schools in the Midwest of the United States, especially the University of

Illinois at both its Urbana and Chicago campuses, along with the School of the Art Institute of Chicago played a key role, in nurturing feminist digital artists. MIT has also supported feminist digital artists for decades through its various research units. Residency centers like the Banff Centre in Canada, research institutes like Rhizome and Eyebeam in New York City, both of which were founded specifically to support artists working in digital technology, and forward-looking software companies like ThoughtWorks with offices around the world have provided funding and time to enable feminist digital artists (and others) to bring their ideas to realization.

In addition to receiving support from varied institutions, digital artists influenced by feminist theory have supported each other through collectives and continue to do so. FACES (https://www.faces-1.net), a global online community of women in media culture, was established in 1997 by American curator, Kathy Rae Huffman, along with Vali Djordjevic and Diana McCarty, both Berlin-based, to answer the question, where are the women. FACES now numbers over 400 women who participate in an email listserv to keep abreast of exhibitions, events, and publications relevant to women in media culture. The collectives are not always confined to women, or to artists; often they are multidisciplinary involving engineers, social scientists, and writers, but they should be documented since they were devoted to feminist principles of social justice and experimentation with digital technology. Many such as Deep Lab, the Free Art and Technology Lab (F.A.T.) and collectives like Black Girls Code dedicated to bringing more women of color into the digital world have already been mentioned. These collectives exist not only in the United States and Western Europe but can be found worldwide, for instance in St. Petersburg, Russia where five feminist digital artists formed CYLAND Media Art Laboratory; India, where women have founded the Feminist Approach to Technology collective (FAT); and Japan, where an interdisciplinary art and science group has founded TeamLab.

Many artists found recognition through appearances at professional conferences, particularly the Ars Electronica Festivals and SIGGRAPH, the largest international conference for digital design, attended by engineers, software developers, and other professionals in digital technology besides artists. As a result, their ideas became widespread and influenced the legitimization and adoption of digital technology as a serious art discipline as well as generating discourse and discussion about its aesthetic and philosophic implications. Feminist digital artists, through becoming educators and administrators in higher education, often were responsible for the introduction of digital art into the curricula and the establishment of digital art departments.

Besides proving through their own careers that women are capable of understanding such male-associated fields as science and engineering, feminist digital artists have also been among the leaders in establishing programs designed to attract girls, especially ethnically diverse young women, into these fields.

Even more importantly, they resolve the question of whether there can be a feminist technology by altering digital technology, supposedly unchangeable in its binary and masculinist configuration, a male area forbidden to women. In rethinking the binary and using its component parts in a way that undermines its exclusionary nature, the work of women digital artists furthers the feminist goal of deconstructing the patriarchy and instituting a more democratic and inclusive way of life.

One of the most visible assaults on the binary was VNS Matrix's Manifesto, declaring the configuration of "on/off" the basis of all digital technology, to be a metaphor for the patriarchal binary of gender in which the male is dominant and the female absent. Theorists like Donna Haraway and Sadie Plant reinforced VNS Matrix's analysis with their proposals to redefine the female "off," position as presenting opportunity rather than erasure. Similarly, artists like Joan Jonas and Ewa Partum used the "glitch," meaning a fault in the system, to declare their right as women artists to be heard. In the male-dominated technological world, a "glitch" was valueless, a break down that needed to be eliminated. In their work, it became a signifier of femaleness—the effort to eliminate a "glitch" paralleling the erasure of women in patriarchal society. The "glitch" became embedded in feminist theory as signifying a symbolic interruption of the status quo, and in queer and critical race theory as signifying the absence of queer and Black people in the feminist critique of the binary nature of the patriarchal society.

Feminist digital artists called the binary into question by dissolving the boundaries between the offline and digital worlds. Conscious of the fact that we now live in a digital world much of the time, working on our computers, talking on our cell phones, exchanging our digital photos, streaming video series, participating in online meetings while working at home, but that we also continue to interact in-person with our family, friends, and colleagues, they ask are these truly separate worlds? LaTurbo Avedon, for instance, has declared that they and their virtual avatar are one and the same. "They" only give interviews through "their" digital avatar, leading us to think beyond the binary separation of the offline and digital worlds.

Artists consciously working from queer theory like Zach Blas, micha cárdenas, and Mariko Mori created Utopian and dystopian online worlds in their critique of the heteronormative offline world. Japanese anime by the CLAMP and the Year 24 Group also dissolved the binary in its depiction of imaginary worlds in which there is constant gender fluidity. And other feminist artists have escaped the binary by using the capacity of digital technology to create Utopian worlds as in the work of Japanese artist, Chiho Aoshima, who envisions a world inhabited by genderless posthumans. Finally, it is a reasonable conjecture that female-identifying artists are attracted to VR because of its capacity to escape from the offline binary world.

One of the most significant impacts of feminist digital artists has been on representation of the female body.

Feminist artists in the 1970s developed ways to portray women's bodies differently from the ways male artists had objectified them. In the 1980s, their work was rejected as essentialist by some artists and theorists who believed that representation of the nude female body as seen through the male gaze was so embedded in patriarchal society that depicting it at all simply reinforced the male gaze. As art historian Mary Garrard put it:

> the orthodox position for postmodern feminism rested on three incredibly negative tenets: (1) the notion of Woman is not real; woman exists only as a cipher of male dominance; (2) no possibility exists within a patriarchal social structure of a positive or empowered image of woman in art; and (3) the only possible move for women artists is to resist visual pleasure and expose the patriarchal system through deconstruction.[1]

The disappearance of the female body, as desired by 1980s feminist artists, is actually achieved through digital artmaking in which all representations of the body are dematerialized and transformed into pixels, the basic unit that makes up the image on the computer screen, television monitors, and other digital devices. Feminist digital artists recognized the implications. Hito Steyerl addressed the issue humorously through a parody of an educational video showing how to make the body disappear. Hannah Black pointed out that the Black body or the disabled body doesn't exist for the male gaze. Claudia Hart wrote that it was even difficult to learn 3-D modeling software because it was conceptually so alien to the way in which representation was conventionally theorized. It involved "modeling a parallel universe 'inside the computer' and then outputting it" rather than the "analogical, photographic model of representation that has been the cultural standard since the nineteenth century."[2]

While cyberfeminists eradicated representation of human bodies by converting them into pixels, other feminist digital artists generated creatures such as monsters, robots, and avatars that were other than human. Transgender artist micha cárdenas, explored what she terms, "the Transreal" dramatically, by living in the virtual body of a dragon for 365 hours (a symbolic representation of a year) to experience what it would be like to have a nonhuman body and be free from the restrictions of patriarchal gender definitions. Adrianne Wortzel explored whether robots could be made sentient, thus becoming an alternative to the human species because they could feel emotion. Patricia Piccinini used digital modeling to create posthuman figurative sculptures, merging the features of animals and humans. Shelley Jackson conceived of her *Patchwork Girl*, who exists only electronically, in narratives generated through hypertext links accessed on the internet, as a present-day version of Mary Shelley's monster created by Dr. Frankenstein. Kathy High and Patricia Piccinini extended the feminist deconstruction of the female body to the male body, indeed to the human body in general, by questioning the patriarchal elevation of *Homo sapiens* above other living creatures. And Michèle Magema says that she is not even considered human because her dual political identity, half-African and half-French, cancels out her female gendered body because they are patriarchal societies.

A third area where digital feminist artists have had influence is in the elimination of the patriarchal cultural hierarchy in which fine art is valued over popular culture. The evolution of live performance art of the 1970s to online performances of the twenty-first century has been responsible in great measure, allowing feminist performance art to have a much more powerful effect on mainstream culture than in the past.

Feminist digital artists have harnessed the potential of social networking for person-to-person communication. Artists like Jennifer Chan and Ann Hirsch talk directly to their audience in their videos. As expert performance artists they know how to reach online audiences with the same intensity that in-person performance achieves, and the size of the online audiences for their performances gives them more impact and influence. They can be said to belong to the category named now as the "influencers."

Women artists have introduced feminist concepts into two areas of popular visual culture global in their reach, video gaming and anime. Imaginative research by feminist cultural historians in the histories of the video game industry and anime has led to revelations that hold, contrary to conventional belief, that these areas are completely male-dominated; women have been significantly involved both as makers and audience. When media archaeology was used to deconstruct the masculinist history of technology, the patriarchal myth of video gaming as exclusively male was debunked through researching the statistics and exploring records through a feminist lens. The result of these efforts was the discovery that women have made up a sizable portion of gamers since its early days and even that some of the first game designers were women.

Recognizing the patriarchal masculinism of most video games, whether American or Japanese in origin, contemporary game designers like Anna Anthropy and Mattie Brice have designed games that incorporate queerness into game design, and Mary Flanagan and Brenda Brathwaite, now Brenda Romero, have used the empathetic aspect of games to address social and political issues of inequality and oppression. Similarly, the history of the development of anime and Japanese animation style has been portrayed as male-dominated when, in reality, female artists have been influential and female-identifying audiences crucial to some of its most successful aesthetics and narratives. The Year 24 Group and the CLAMP group, both all-female, include some of the most respected anime artists. *Sailor Moon*, an anime series featuring gender fluidity, is the most popular anime series of all time globally.

It's important to recognize that feminist influence on digital technology will only continue to grow because women are becoming the dominant users of social media. Statistics show that women users in the United States now outnumber men, particularly in the second- and third-generation sites such as Instagram and Snapchat. Thanks to software that makes the process easy, women everywhere without any technical background are coding and programming on the internet, making women's voices heard in a new way. Since the internet is a decentralized system of communication, origin is invisible, thus doing away with issues of authority. While the situation has given rise to such phenomena as fake news or misinformation, it has also opened the way for women to express their own thoughts and desires unedited, free from misinterpretation by patriarchal authority. In a study conducted by the Qatar Computing Research Institute in 2018, women in countries with more offline gender restrictions had more significant presence on the internet than men, perhaps showing that they were freer to express themselves online than in physical interaction. Furthermore, feminist digital artists have been helping women users of social media, including women of color, to create their own games or engage in performance art by developing free software and establishing support websites like I Need Diverse Games, Thumbstick Mafia, and Brown Girl Gamer Code.

One of the most insightful and influential innovations of feminist digital artists has been to recognize and use the potential of video games and virtual and augmented reality to arouse empathy in participants, thus making feminist activism on behalf of social justice more effective. Their various projects are based on analysis of how video games, virtual reality, and augmented reality are different from the storytelling structures of novels, films, or television, in that participants in games and imaginary worlds are responsible for the action and thus have an emotional stake in the outcomes of the narratives. In traditional narrative, on the other hand, the action has already been determined by the author.

The feminist collective subRosa uses empathy on behalf of reproductive rights. Ellen K. Levy persuades people to consider the destruction of cultural artifacts in the Middle East through engaging them in a videogame version of Three-Card Monte, the street-corner game played by con artists. Tamiko Thiel, Nonny de la Peña, Milica Zec, Janicza Bravo, and the NeuroSpeculative AfroFeminist Collaborative have created virtual reality narratives for protest against patriarchal oppression. Viewers are imprisoned in an internment camp, made to wait on a food line, trapped in a cellar during a bombing, killed by police brutality, or in a more positive project, experiencing what it's like to be in the body of an African American woman. Surveillance projects like Terri Te Tau's *Unwarranted and Unregistered* employs the empathy-producing capacity of virtual reality to make her critique of unwarranted surveillance of the Māori population in New Zealand effective.

These last few pages mark a return to the book's intent announced in the first few pages: to insert artists who are transforming technology under the impact of feminist theory and its mutations into mainstream art history by documenting the historical and contemporary digital practice of such artists in one volume for the first time, and also to show how they have made significant contributions to the aesthetic and practice of digital art and altered digital technology itself. These artists have brought innovation to the practice of digital art while they have been harnessing the potential of digital technology to deliver the intersectional feminist, queer, and postcolonialist critique of the patriarchal, masculinist society in which we live. Their impact goes far beyond the art world. With the rapidly increasing number of women who use digital technology and the capacity of digital technology to transmit these principles of social justice to individuals in the far corners of the earth, the chances of transforming the patriarchal society into a society built on nonbinary inclusivity and equality look more promising.

Notes

1 Mary D. Garrard, "Feminist Art and the Essentialism Controversy," *The Centennial Review* 39, no. 3 (1995): 473.

2 Claudia Hart, "Beginning and End Games: A Parable in 3D," *Cultural Politics* 9, no. 1 (2013): 88.

Select Bibliography

Note: This bibliography contains the sources for all texts referenced in the notes, and includes links (where they exist) to online versions of texts that originally appeared in print. Because the videos and artists' own websites mentioned in the notes are easily available online, they are excluded here but are included in the index.

Abandon Normal Devices. "Learning to See: A Conversation with Addie Wagenknecht on COSMOS 2018," Journal, July 11, 2018. https://www.andfestival.org.uk/blog/a-conversation-with-addie-wagenknecht/.

Aima, Rahel. "Body Party: Hannah Black," *Mousse* 57 (February/March 2017). http://moussemagazine.it/rahel-aima-hannah-black-2017/.

Alberro, Alexander, ed. *Barbara Kruger*. New York: Rizzoli, 2010.

Alchetron: Free Social Encyclopedia for the World. "Simone Forti," updated February 3, 2018. https://alchetron.com/Simone-Forti.

Alexander, Leigh. "Anna Anthropy Turns a Personal Struggle into a Heartfelt Game," Gamasutra, March 30, 2012. https://www.gamasutra.com/view/news/163496/Anna_Anthropy_turns_a_personal_struggle_into_a_heartfelt_game.php.

Alvarez, Ana Cecilia. "Bend It Like Benglis," The New Inquiry, October 20, 2014. https://thenewinquiry.com/bend-it-like-benglis/.

Amerika, Mark. "Stitch Bitch: The Hypertext Author As Cyborg-Femme Narrator," Amerika Online 7, March 16, 1998. https://www.heise.de/tp/features/Amerika-Online-7-3441257.html.

Amorós, Grimanesa. "*HEDERA*, Prospect Park Bandshell, Brooklyn, NY 2008," https://www.grimanesaamoros.com/publiccommission/bric-brooklyn/.

Anderson, Laurie. "Laurie Anderson, Telling Stories in Virtual Reality," interview by Bonnie Marranca, *Performing Arts Journal* no. 120 (2018): 37–44. https://www.mitpressjournals.org/doi/pdf/10.1162/pajj_a_00432.

Annenberg School for Communication and Journalism, University of Southern California (USC). "In 'Algorithms of Oppression,' Safiya Noble Finds Old Stereotypes Persist in New Media," updated December 11, 2019. https://annenberg.usc.edu/news/diversity-and-inclusion/algorithms-oppression-safiya-noble-finds-old-stereotypes-persist-new.

Antin, Eleanor. Interview by Rachel Mason, BOMB Magazine, September 8, 2014. https://bombmagazine.org/articles/eleanor-antin/.

Appler, Vivian. "Moonwalking with Laurie Anderson: The Implicit Feminism of *The End of the Moon*," *The Journal of American Drama and Theatre (JADT)* 28, no. 2 (Spring

2016). https://jadtjournal.org/2016/05/27/moonwalking-with-laurie-anderson-the-implicit-feminism-of-the-end-of-the-moon.

Armitstead, Claire. "Zina Saro-Wiwa, 'For 10 Years, I Didn't Cry About My Father,'" *Guardian* (US ed.), September 18, 2018. https://www.theguardian.com/artanddesign/2018/sep/18/zina-saro-wiwa-artist-for-ten-years-i-didnt-cry-about-my-father.

Art in America. "Collecting and Computing: A Conversation at the Armory Show," March 12, 2020. https://www.artnews.com/art-in-america/features/spalter-collection-computer-art-1202680682/.

Artnet. "The Computer Pioneer," November 2, 2018. https://news.artnet.com/exhibitions/hungarys-radical-women-artists-finally-get-the-recognition-they-deserve-1383892.

Artnet News. "In the '60s, Miriam Schapiro Was Already Using Computer Models to Build Dream-Like Geometries," January 5, 2018. https://news.artnet.com/exhibitions/in-the-60s-miriam-schapiro-was-already-using-computer-models-to-build-dream-like-geometries-see-the-paintings-here-1190042.

Atari Women. "Dona Bailey." https://www.atariwomen.org/stories/dona-bailey/.

Avedon, LaTurbo. "From a Conversation with Willa Köerner: LaTurbo Avedon on Identity and Immateriality," interview by Willa Köerner, The Creative Independent, February 23, 2008. https://thecreativeindependent.com/people/laturbo-avedon-on-identity-and-immateriality/.

Avis, Jade. "Lara Croft—Pixelated Object or Feminist Gaming Icon?" *brightONLINE* no. 6 (November 26, 2015). http://arts.brighton.ac.uk/projects/brightonline/issue-number-six/lara-croft-pixelated-object-or-feminist-gaming-icon.

Azuma, Hiroki. *Otaku: Japan's Database Animals*, trans. Jonathan E. Abel and Shion Kono, Minneapolis: University of Minnesota Press, 2009.

Bacharach, Elizabeth. "Charlotte Moorman Shattering Barriers Between Art and Technology," Medill Reports, February 24, 2016. https://news.medill.northwestern.edu/chicago/charlotte-moorman-shattering-barriers-between-art-and-technology/.

Baguley, Richard. "Spanning the Tree: Dr. Radia Perlman and Untangling Networks," Hackaday, May 29, 2018. https://hackaday.com/2018/05/29/spanning-the-tree-dr-radia-perlman-untangling-networks/.

Bailey, Dona. "The Original Gaming Bug: *Centipede* Creator, Dona Bailey," interview by Leigh Alexander, Gamasutra, August 27, 2007. https://www.gamasutra.com/view/feature/130082/the_original_gaming_bug_centipede_.php.

Balkin, Amy. "Public Smog Will Save the Earth." http://tomorrowmorning.net/publicsmog.

Bangert, Colette S., and Charles J. Bangert. "Computer Grass Is Natural Grass," Atari Archives, September 1975. https://www.atariarchives.org/artist/sec5.php.

Barcio, Phillip. "When Miriam Schapiro Used Computers to Generate Geometric Abstract Art," *IdeelArt* (blog), January 17, 2018. https://www.ideelart.com/magazine/miriam-schapiro.

Barker, Jeremy M. "Can Un-licensed Therapy Be Performance Art? Can Prostitution?" Culture bot. May 9, 2012. https://www.culturebot.org/2012/05/13501/can-un-licensed-therapy-be-performance-art-can-prostitution/.

Barnes, Sue. "Hypertext Literacy," *Interpersonal Computing and Technology: An Electronic Journal for the 21st Century* 2, no. 4 (October 1994): 24–36, http://serials.infomotions.com/ipct/ipct-v2n04-barnes-hypertext.txt.

Bass, Chloë. "How Adrian Piper Challenges Us to Change the Ways We Live," Hyperallergic, April 21, 2018. https://hyperallergic.com/439255/adrian-piper-museum-of-modern-art-retrospective/.

Beete, Paulette. "NEA Arts Magazine Spotlight: Brenda Laurel: Girls Just Wanna . . . Play Video Games," *National Endowment for the Arts Blog*, April 3, 2018. https://www.arts.gov/stories/blog/2018/nea-arts-magazine-spotlight-brenda-laurel-girls-just-wannaplay-video-games.

Beras, Erika. "Joy Buolamwini, When AI Misclassified Her Face, She Started a Movement for Accountability," *MIT Technology Review*, posted on Facebook, June 30, 2018. https://www.technologyreview.com/innovator/joy-buolamwini/.

Bieri, Fabienne. "Intervention with the Body," The Art of Intervention, November 28, 2018. https://theartofintervention.blog/2018/11/28/intervention-with-the-body/.

Bishara, Hakim. "Freedom of Speech Exhibition in Japan Closed Due to Censorship," Hyperallergic, August 6, 2019. https://hyperallergic.com/512514/freedom-of-speech-aichi-triennial/.

Blas, Zach. "ENgenderingGenderChangers / Sketches." http://users.design.ucla.edu/~zblas/thesis_website/gender_changers/gc_sketches.html.

Bonifield, Bonnie, Eric Goldberg, Brian Kerr, Jeff Lee, and Liana Sharer. That Anime Project (2001). http://umich.edu/~anime/about.html.

Bonin, Vincent. "Software—Information Technology: Its New Meaning for Art," la fondation Daniel Langlois pour l'art, la science et la technologie. https://www.fondation-langlois.org/html/e/page.php?NumPage=541.

Bonanno, Mike. "Barbie Liberation Organization," Beautiful Trouble, case study. https://beautifultrouble.org/case/barbie-liberation-organization/.

Bookchin, Natalie. "The Intruder," *Frontiers: A Journal of Women Studies* 26, no. 1 (2005): 43–7. https://www.jstor.org/stable/4137432.

Bosma, Josephine. " 'Body Anxiety,' Sabotaging Big Daddy Mainframe, via Online Exhibition," Rhizome, January 26, 2015. https://rhizome.org/editorial/2015/jan/26/body-anxiety/.

Bouwhuis, Jelle. "Alex Mawimbi, Displaced Artist Formerly Known As . . ." africanah, February 2, 2019. https://africanah.org/alex-mawimbi/.

Bravinder, Tristan. "35 Prints by Laura Aguilar, Photographer of Radical Vulnerability, Join the Getty Collection," *The Iris* (blog), J. Paul Getty Trust, September 26, 2019. https://blogs.getty.edu/iris/35-prints-by-laura-aguilar-photographer-of-radical-vulnerability-join-the-getty-collection/.

BRIC. "Grimanesa Amorós: HEDERA," Brooklyn Information & Culture. https://www.bricartsmedia.org/art-exhibitions/grimanesa-amor%C3%B3s-hedera.

Brice, Mattie. "Postpartum: Mainichi—How Personal Experience Became a Game," Gamasutra, November 13, 2012. https://www.gamasutra.com/blogs/MattieBrice/

20121113/181401/Postpartum_Mainichi__How_Personal_Experience_Became_a_Game.php.

Brock, Hovey. "Carolee Schneemann: Kinetic Painting," *Brooklyn Rail* (December 2017–January 2018). https://brooklynrail.org/2017/12/artseen/Carolee-Schneemann-Kinetic-Painting.

Broude, Norma, and Mary D. Garrard, eds. *The Power of Feminist Art*. New York: Harry N. Abrams, 1993.

Brown, Anna. "Younger Men Play Video Games, But So Do a Diverse Group of Other Americans," Fact Tank, Pew Research Center, September 11, 2017. https://www.pewresearch.org/fact-tank/2017/09/11/younger-men-play-video-games-but-so-do-a-diverse-group-of-other-americans/.

Brown, Paul, Charlie Gere, Nicholas Lambert, and Catherine Mason, eds. *White Heat Cold Logic: British Computer Art 1960–1980*. Cambridge, MA: MIT Press, 2008.

Brueckner, Sophia. *iSkyTV*. http://turbulence.org/Works/iSkyTV/.

Buchmann, Sabeth, Yilmaz Dziewior, Elke Krasny, Hanne Lorek, Maren Luebbke-Tidow, Letizia Ragaglia, Brigitte Reutner, Johanna Schwanberg, and Berta Sichel. *Valie Export: Time and Countertime*. Cologne: Walther König, 2011.

Bullock, Natasha. "Pipilotti Rist: 'Sip My Ocean,'" Museum of Contemporary Art, Australia, Stories and Ideas, November 1, 2017. https://www.mca.com.au/stories-and-ideas/pipilotti-rist-sip-my-ocean-curatorial-essay/.

Buolamwini, Joy. "Face: The Final Frontier of Privacy, Full Spoken Congressional Testimony, May 22, 2019," Medium, May 23, 2019. https://medium.com/@Joy.Buolamwini/face-the-final-frontier-of-privacy-full-spoken-congressional-testimony-may-22-2019-ff8607df045b.

Buolamwini, Joy. "Written Testimony of Joy Buolamwini, Founder, Algorithmic Justice League," Hearing on Artificial Intelligence: Societal and Ethical Implications, United States House Committee on Science, Space, and Technology, June 26, 2019. https://science.house.gov/imo/media/doc/Buolamwini%20Testimony.pdf.

Burai, Johanna. World White Web, 2015. https://johannaburai.com/WORLD-WHITE-WEB-Link.

Burko, Diane. "Diane Burko," Institute of Arctic and Alpine Research, University of Colorado, Boulder: People. https://instaar.colorado.edu/people/diane-burko/.

Bush, Vannevar. "As We May Think," *The Atlantic* (July 1945). https://www.theatlantic.com/magazine/archive/1945/07/as-we-may-think/303881/.

Butler, David. "Delia Derbyshire," History of the BBC: 100 Voices. https://www.bbc.com/historyofthebbc/100-voices/pioneering-women/women-of-the-workshop/delia-derbyshire.

Butler, Judith. *Gender Trouble: Feminism and the Subversion of Identity*. New York: Routledge, 1990.

Butterfly. "Paris: Aya Takano—The Jelly Civilization Chronicle," *Butterfly Art News* (blog), May 26, 2017. https://butterflyartnews.com/2017/05/26/paris-aya-takano-the-jelly-civilization-chronicle/.

buymymixtape123. "We Need More Black Protagonists in Gaming," GameSkinny, January 25, 2018. https://www.gameskinny.com/0nwmx/we-need-more-black-protagonists-in-gaming.

Calvert, Melodie, and Jennifer Terry, eds. *Processed Lives: Gender and Technology in Everyday Life*. London: Routledge, 2005. Kindle.

cárdenas, micha, Elle Mehrmand, Amy Sara Carroll, Ricardo Dominguez, Brian Holmes, James Morgan, Allucquére Rosanne Stone, and Stelarc. *The Transreal: Political Aesthetics of Crossing Realities*. Zach Blas and Wolfgang Schirmacher. New York: Atropos, 2011.

Carrier, David. "Adrian Piper in Her Own Words," Hyperallergic, November 10, 2018. https://hyperallergic.com/470351/adrian-piper-escape-to-berlin-2018/.

Cateforis, David, Steven Duval, and Shepherd Steiner, eds. *Hybrid Practices: Art in Collaboration with Science and Technology in the Long 1960s*. Oakland: University of California Press, 2019.

Cavallaro, Dani. *CLAMP in Context: A Critical Study of the Manga and Anime*. Jefferson, NC: McFarland, 2012.

Centerbeam (1978). Center for Advanced Visual Studies Special Collection: Works, People, About, Search. http://act.mit.edu/cavs/item/Centerbeam.

Chai, Lisa. "Spotlight on the AI Pioneer Behind Sophia, the Robot: Ben Goertzel," ROBO Global, August 8, 2019. https://www.roboglobal.com/insights/sophia-the-robot-ben-goertzel/.

Chan, Jennifer. "The Real Ann Hirsch: The Power of Performative Fiction," *Illuminati Girl Gang* 2 (2012). https://www.academia.edu/2072836/The_Real_Ann_Hirsch_The_Power_of_Performative_Fiction.

Chan, Jennifer. "Why Are There No Great Net Artists?" 2011, Mouchette, May 2012. http://about.mouchette.org/wp-content/uploads/2012/05/Jennifer_Chan2.pdf.

Chan, Jennifer, and Leah Schrager. "*Body Anxiety*, an Online Exhibition," Body Anxiety. http://bodyanxiety.com/about/.

Chang, Jiang, Hailong Ren, and Qiguang Yang. "A Virtual Gender Asylum? The Social Media Profile Picture, Young Chinese Women's Self-Empowerment, and the Emergence of a Chinese Digital Feminism," *International Journal of Cultural Studies* 21, no. 3 (2018): 325–40. https://doi.org/10.1177/1367877916682085.

Chatel, Marie. "In Focus: Morehshin Allahyari," Medium, March 15, 2019. https://medium.com/digital-art-weekly-by-danae-hi/in-focus-morehshin-allahyari-807c8b3156c8.

Cheang, Shu Lea. "Shu Lea Cheang on *Brandon*," interview with Shu Lea Cheang by Yin Ho, Rhizome, May 10, 2012. https://rhizome.org/editorial/2012/may/10/shu-lea-cheang-on-brandon/.

Chicago, Judy. "Made in California: Feminist Art Education," Judy Chicago Art Education Collection @ Penn State, March 3, 2001. https://judychicago.arted.psu.edu/wp-content/uploads/2013/10/Made-in-California-Feminist-Art-Education-20010303-Box-11-101.pdf.

Chua, Lawrence. "Shu Lea Cheang," interview, *BOMB Magazine* 54, January 1, 1996. https://bombmagazine.org/articles/shu-lea-cheang/.

Clark, Carlton. "Surely Teaching Hypertext in the Composition Classroom Qualifies as a Feminist Pedagogy?" *Kairos: A Journal of Rhetoric, Technology, and Pedagogy* 6, no. 2 (Fall 2001). https://www.researchgate.net/publication/337335900_Surely_Teaching_Hypertext_in_the_Composition_Classroom_Qualifies_as_a_Feminist_Pedagogy.

Clements, Alexis. "The Many Faces of Eleanor Antin," Hyperallergic, November 29, 2013. https://hyperallergic.com/95936/the-many-faces-of-eleanor-antin/.

Clements, Jonathan. *Anime: A History*. London: Palgrave Macmillan on behalf of the British Film Institute, 2013 [reissued as ebook by Bloomsbury, 2018].

Clements Jonathan, and Helen McCarthy. *The Anime Encyclopedia: A Century of Japanese Animation*. 3rd ed. Berkeley: Stone Bridge Press, 2015.

Cohen, Lisa. "Joan Jonas: All at Once," *New York Times*, April 5, 2015. https://www.nytimes.com/2015/04/05/t-magazine/joan-jonas-reanimation-venice-biennale.html.

Cohn, Terri, ed. *Pairing of Polarities: The Life and Art of Sonya Rapoport*. Berkeley, CA: Heyday, 2012.

Cole, Yussef, and Tanya DePass. "Black Skin Is Still A Radical Concept in Video Games," VICE, March 1, 2017. https://www.vice.com/en_us/article/78qpxd/black-skin-is-still-a-radical-concept-in-video-games.

Compart. "*Projekte generativer Ästhetik* [The Projects of Generative Aesthetics] 1965." http://dada.compart-bremen.de/item/exhibition/164.

Computer History Museum. "Nintendo Ups the Ante." https://www.computerhistory.org/revolution/computer-games/16/194.

Connor, Michael. "Amalia Ulman—Excellences & Perfections," Rhizome, October 20, 2014. https://rhizome.org/editorial/2014/oct/20/first-look-amalia-ulmanexcellences-perfections/.

Corinne, Tee. *The Cunt Coloring Book*, self-published, 1975; reissued San Francisco: Last Gasp Publishers, 1989.

Cotter, Holland. "Carolee Schneemann, Visionary Feminist Performance Artist Dies at 79," *New York Times*, March 10, 2019. https://www.nytimes.com/2019/03/10/obituaries/carolee-schneemann-dead-at-79.html.

Cotter, Holland. "Laura Poitras: 'Astro Noise' Examines Surveillance and the New Normal," *New York Times*, February 4, 2016. https://www.nytimes.com/2016/02/05/arts/design/laura-poitras-astro-noise-examines-surveillance-and-the-new-normal.html.

Cox, Donna J., Ellen Sandor, and Janine Fron, eds. *New Media Futures: The Rise of Women in the Digital Arts*. Urbana: University of Illinois Press, 2018.

Creative Time. "Jenny Holzer: For the City, Projections, 1996–2004," http://creativetime.org/programs/archive/2005/holzer/pastprojects.html.

Crenn, Julie. "Michèle Magema: 'Without Echo, There Is No Meeting,'" *n.paradoxa* 31 (January 2013): 15–22. https://www.ktpress.co.uk/nparadoxa-volume-details.asp?volumeid=31.

Crenshaw, Kimberle. "Mapping the Margins, Intersectionality, Identity Politics and Violence Against Women of Color," *Stanford Law Review* 43, no. 6 (July 1991): 1241–99. https://doi.org/10.2307/1229039.

Cunningham, Andrew. "The NES Turns 30: How It Began, Worked, and Saved an Industry," Ars Technica, July 15, 2013. https://arstechnica.com/gaming/2013/07/time-to-feel-old-inside-the-nes-on-its-30th-birthday/.

Dahir, Abdi Latif. "African Video Game Makers Are Breaking into the Global Industry with Their Own Stories," Quartz Africa, May 5, 2017. https://qz.com/africa/974439/african-video-game-makers-are-breaking-into-the-global-industry-with-their-own-stories/.

Damon, Betsy. "The 7000 Year Old Woman," in "Lesbian Art and Artists," special issue, *Heresies: A Feminist Publication on Art and Politics* 1, no. 3 (September 1977): 10–13. http://heresiesfilmproject.org/wp-content/uploads/2011/09/heresies3.pdf.

Daniel, Marion. "Gillian Wise." Translated from the French by Anna Knight, Archives of Women Artists Research and Exhibitions (AWARE), 2013. https://awarewomenartists.com/en/artiste/gillian-wise/.

Darling, Jesse. "Artist Profile: Hannah Black," Rhizome, February 17, 2015. https://rhizome.org/editorial/2015/feb/17/artist-profile-hannah-black/.

Debatty, Régine. "Andrea Polli—'Who Owns the Air?'" *We Make Money Not Art*, March 16, 2011. https://we-make-money-not-art.com/andrea_polli_who_owns_the_air/.

Denison, Rayna. *Anime: A Critical Introduction*. London: Bloomsbury Academic, 2015.

Detlefsen, Karen. "Émilie du Châtelet," *Stanford Encyclopedia of Philosophy*, substantive revision, June 13, 2014. https://plato.stanford.edu/entries/emilie-du-chatelet/.

Dickinson, Grace. "Mural Arts Philadelphia Debuts its First Augmented Reality Mural, 'Dreams, Diaspora, and Destiny,'" *Philadelphia Inquirer*, October 10, 2018. https://www.inquirer.com/philly/blogs/things_to_do/mural-arts-philadelphia-augmented-reality-mural-king-britt-20181010.html.

D'Ignazio, Catherine. "iSkyTV," kanarinka. http://www.kanarinka.com/project/iskytv/.

Dinkins, Stephanie. "Q&A with Transdisciplinary Artist Stephanie Dinkins," interview by Future of Storytelling, January 10, 2020, Medium. https://medium.com/future-of-storytelling/q-a-with-transdisciplinary-artist-stephanie-dinkins-592b420c8703.

Docubase, MIT Open Documentary Lab. "Hunger in Los Angeles," 2012. https://docubase.mit.edu/project/hunger-in-los-angeles/.

Docubase, MIT Open Documentary Lab. "NeuroSpeculative AfroFeminism," 2017. https://docubase.mit.edu/project/neurospeculative-afrofeminism/.

Dominguez, Ricardo. "Border Research, Border Gestures: The Transborder Immigrant Tool," *American Quarterly* 71, no. 4 (December 2019): 1052–8. https://muse.jhu.edu/article/744972.

Donovan, Thom. "5 Questions (for Contemporary Practice) with Amy Balkin," *Art21 Magazine*, February 17, 2011. http://magazine.art21.org/2011/02/17/5-questions-for-contemporary-practice-with-amy-balkin/#.Xpm0dqtKjyg.

Dooley, Tatum. "Stephanie Dinkins Is Turning Memoir into AI," VICE, August 15, 2019. https://garage.vice.com/en_us/article/43kdnm/stephanie-dinkins-is-turning-memoir-into-ai.

Dougherty, Cecilia. "Stories from a Generation: Video Art at the Woman's Building." In *From Site to Vision: The Woman's Building in Contemporary Culture*, edited by Terry Wolverton and Sondra Hale, 303–25. Los Angeles: Otis College of Art and Design, 2011.

Dream the End. "Marian Zazeela." https://www.dreamtheend.com/?cat=289.

Du, Daisy Yan. *Animated Encounters: Transnational Movements of Chinese Animation, 1940s–1970s*. Honolulu: University of Hawai'i Press, 2019.

E.A.T. "Experiments in Art and Technology Records, 1966–1993 (bulk 1966–1973)," The Getty Research Institute, Collection Inventories and Finding Aids. http://archives2.getty.edu:8082/xtf/view?docId=ead/940003/940003.xml;query=;brand=default.

E.A.T. "Guide To The Experiments In Art And Technology (E.A.T.) Collection MSS.018," Bard Center for Curatorial Studies, CCS/Bard Archives, November 2018. http://www.bard.edu/ccs/findingaids/index.html/mss.018/eat.html.

Edwards, Benj. "*Myst* at 25: How it Changed Gaming, Created Addicts, and Made Enemies," Fast Company, September 24, 2018. https://www.fastcompany.com/90240345/myst-at-25-how-it-changed-gaming-created-addicts-and-made-enemies.

ees. "Can Manga and Anime Contribute to Feminism and Gender Studies?" Artifice, March 18, 2019. https://the-artifice.com/manga-anime-feminism-gender-studies/.

Ericson, Cathie. "Mover and Shaker, Jennifer Macdonald: Director of Project Management, NYSE," The Glass Hammer, June 25, 2015. https://theglasshammer.com/2015/06/25/mover-and-shaker-jennifer-macdonald-director-of-product-management-nyse/.

Essinger, James. *Ada's Algorithm: How Lord Byron's Daughter Ada Lovelace Launched the Digital Age*. Brooklyn, NY: Melville House, 2014.

Estrada, Daniel. "Value Alignment, Fair Play, and the Rights of Service Robots," paper presented at the February 2020 conference on "AI, Ethics, and Society," sponsored by the Special Interest Group on Artificial Intelligence of the Association for Computing Machinery in conjunction with the Association for Advancement of Artificial Intelligence. https://arxiv.org/pdf/1803.02852.pdf.

Eubanks, Virginia. "Cyberfeminism Meets NAFTazteca: Recoding the Technotext." In *Appropriating Technology: Vernacular Science and Social Power*, edited by Ron Eglash, Jennifer L. Croissant, Giovanna Di Chiro, and Rayvon Fouché, 151–62. Minneapolis: University of Minnesota Press, 2004.

Evans, Geraint. "*MekaMon* Takes the Stage with *ThoughtWorks Arts* Collaboration," *TechSPARK* (blog), April 18, 2019. https://www.techspark.co/blog/2019/04/18/mekamon-takes-the-stage-with-thoughtworks-arts-collaboration/.

Fateman, Johanna. "Women on the Verge: Art, Feminism, and Social Media." *Artforum* 53, no. 8 (April 2015): 218–23. https://www.artforum.com/print/201504/art-feminism-and-social-media-50736.

"Feminist Internet Manifesto," https://web.archive.org/web/20201101021935/https://feministinternet.com/manifesto/.

Ferguson, Bax J. "How to 'Make' a Woman: Addressing the Gendering of Artificial Intelligence—and the Issues of Bias in the Technology We Create," Medium, February 5, 2018. https://medium.com/s/the-future-of-flesh/how-to-make-a-woman-1a378ed7b827.

Firestone, David. "While Barbie Talks Tough, G.I. Joe Goes Shopping," *New York Times*, December 31, 1993. https://timesmachine.nytimes.com/timesmachine/1993/12/31/726193.html?pageNumber=12.

Fitzpatrick, Tracy. *Hannah Wilke: Gestures*. Purchase, NY: The Neuberger Museum of Art, 2010.

Forti, Simone. "Simone Forti Archive," Getty Research Institute Archives. https://www.getty.edu/research/special_collections/notable/forti.html.

Foucault, Michel. *Discipline and Punish: The Birth of the Prison*. Translated by Alan Sheridan (first English ed.). New York: Pantheon, 1977.

Fouriezos, Nick. "Black Female Gamers Are Claiming Their Space at Last," OZY, July 4, 2019. https://www.ozy.com/fast-forward/black-female-gamers-are-carving-out-space-in-an-industry-thats-denying-them-chances/95136/.

Frank, Peter. "Art: '*Software*' at Jewish Museum," *Columbia Daily Spectator* 115, no. 22, October 23, 1970. http://spectatorarchive.library.columbia.edu/cgi-bin/columbia?a=d&d=cs19701023-01.2.15&e=-------en-20--1998-byDA-txt-txIN-columbia-TITLE_SECTION-----.

Fredericksen, Eric. "Two of a Kind, the Art World's World," The Stranger, July 15, 1999. https://www.thestranger.com/seattle/two-of-a-kind/Content?oid=1538.

Fregger, Brad. "Joan Shogren, Computer Art Pioneer," Brad Fregger, Papers of Exceptional Interest, updated November 2018. http://fregger.com/Joan/index.html.

Frenkel, Vera. "The Story is Always Partial: A Conversation with Vera Frenkel," interview by Dot Tuer and Clive Robertson, *Art Journal* 57, no. 4 (Winter 1998): 2–15. https://doi.org/10.2307/777924.

Fritz, Darko. "International Networks of Early Digital Art." In *A Companion to Digital Art*, edited by Christiane Paul, 45–68. Hoboken, NJ: Wiley-Blackwell, 2016.

Furness, Amy Louise. "Towards a Definition of Visual Artists' Archives: Vera Frenkel's Archives as a Case Study." PhD diss., Faculty of Information, University of Toronto, 2012. ProQuest (NR97313).

Gaboury, Jacob. "Interview with Zach Blas, 'QT, Queer Technologies,'" Rhizome, August 18, 2010. https://rhizome.org/editorial/2010/aug/18/interview-with-zach-blas/.

Galloway, David, Christopher Benjamin Schultz, Anne Telford, Elyssa Dimant, Steven Heller, Cynthia Goodman, Douglas Dodds, Kisa Lala, Philip Koether, and Gloria

Steinem. *Barbara Nessim: An Artful Life*. Victoria and Albert Museum, Exhibition Catalogue. New York: Harry N. Abrams, 2013.

Gambino, Megan. "Cracking the Code of the Human Genome: Creepy or Cool? Portraits Derived from the DNA in Hair and Gum Found in Public Places," Smithsonian Magazine, May 3, 2013. https://www.smithsonianmag.com/science-nature/creepy-or-cool-portraits-derived-from-the-dna-in-hair-and-gum-found-in-public-places-50266864/.

Garling, Caleb. "Virtual Reality, Empathy and the Next Journalism," WIRED, November 2015. https://www.wired.com/brandlab/2015/11/nonny-de-la-pena-virtual-reality-empathy-and-the-next-journalism/.

Garrard, Mary D. "Feminist Art and the Essentialism Controversy," *The Centennial Review* 39, no. 3 (1995): 468–92. https://www.jstor.org/stable/23739358.

GEDOK. "Profile of an Institution." GEDOK, Stuttgart, Germany. https://gedok-muc.de/english-version.

Gee, Erin. "Swarming Emotional Pianos." https://eringee.net/swarming-emotional-pianos/.

Gerardi, Augusto. "When Computational Devices Are Used for the Visual Arts," Colección Patricia Phelps de Cisneros, April 9, 2019. https://www.coleccioncisneros.org/content/when-computational-devices-are-used-visual-arts.

Ghani, Mariam, and Chitra Ganesh. *The Index of the Disappeared* (2004 ongoing). https://www.mariamghani.com/work/626; and https://www.chitraganesh.com/index-of-the-disappeared.

Gillick, Liam. "Joan Jonas," interview, ArtReview, March 2018. https://artreview.com/features/march_2018_feature_joan_jonas/.

Giloth, Copper. "Copper Giloth," in *New Media Futures: The Rise of Women in the Digital Arts*, edited by Donna J. Cox, Ellen Sandor, and Janine Fron, 215–16. Urbana: University of Illinois Press, 2018.

Ginsberg, Ellen S., and Jennifer Hall. "The Tipping Point Project: A Case Study in the Collaboration between Medical Anthropology and Art." In *Blaze: Discourse on Art, Women, and Feminism*, edited by Karen Frostig and Kathy A. Halamka, 229–37. Newcastle upon Tyne: Cambridge Scholars, 2007.

GitHub. "Mimi Onuoha, On Missing Data Sets," January 25, 2018. https://github.com/MimiOnuoha/missing-datasets.

Giuliano, Charles. "Holographer Harriet Casdin-Silver Remembered," Berkshire Fine Arts, June 15, 2008. https://www.berkshirefinearts.com/06-15-2008_holographer-harriet-casdin-silver-remembered.htm.

Glocker, Melanie L., Daniel D. Langleben, Kosha Ruparel, James W. Loughead, Ruben C. Gur, and Norbert Sachser. "Baby Schema in Infant Faces Induces Cuteness Perception and Motivation for Caretaking in Adults." *Ethology* 115, no. 3 (March 2009): 257–63. https://www.ncbi.nlm.nih.gov/pmc/articles/PMC3260535/.

Glueck, Grace. "And Now a Few Words From Jenny Holzer," *New York Times Magazine*, December 3, 1989. https://www.nytimes.com/1989/12/03/magazine/and-now-a-few-words-from-jenny-holzer.html.

Goldin, Nan. *The Other Side*. Göttingen: Steidl, 2019.

Gómez, Edward M. "Topless but Far From Helpless: Charlotte Moorman's Avant-Garde Life," Hyperallergic, January 17, 2015. https://hyperallergic.com/175600/topless-but-far-from-helpless-charlotte-moormans-avant-garde-life/.

Google Arts and Culture. "A Brief History of Women in Gaming—The 1980s." https://artsandculture.google.com/exhibit/a-brief-history-of-women-in-gaming-the-1980s-the-strong/CwKCGJf3HpdoIg?hl=en.

Gorzadek, Ewa. "Ewa Partum." Culture.pl, Adam Mickiewicz Institute, updated May 2016. https://culture.pl/en/artist/ewa-partum.

Gotthhardt, Alexxa. "Charlotte Moorman is Finally Remembered as More Than 'The Topless Cellist,'" Artsy, September 4, 2016. https://artsy.net/article/artsy-editorial-the-topless-cellist-charlotte-moorman-finally-finds-her-place-in-art-history.

Gouma-Peterson, Thalia, and Patricia Mathews. "The Feminist Critique of Art History." *Art Bulletin* 69, no. 3 (September 1987): 326–57. https://doi.org/10.2307/3051059.

Grattarola, Florencia. "Roberta Williams—The Queen of Graphic Adventures," Medium, December 18, 2018. https://medium.com/a-computer-of-ones-own/roberta-williams-the-queen-of-graphic-adventures-766e288ca3.

Gray, Robert M. "Coeducation at MIT, 1950s–60s," last edited October 29, 2017. https://ee.stanford.edu/~gray/TitleIX.pdf.

Greenberger, Alex. "Changing Channels: Dara Birnbaum's Televisual Art Comes into Focus," ARTnews, March 27, 2018. https://www.artnews.com/art-news/artists/icons-dara-birnbaum-9973/.

Greenberger, Alex. "Full Circle: Howardena Pindell Steps Back into the Spotlight with a Traveling Retrospective," ARTnews, February 6, 2018. https://www.artnews.com/art-news/news/full-circle-howardena-pindell-steps-back-spotlight-traveling-retrospective-9762.

Greenberger, Alex. "A New Future from the Passed: Lynn Hershman Leeson Comes into Her Own After 50 Years of Prophetic Work," ARTnews, March 28, 2017. https://www.artnews.com/art-news/artists/a-new-future-from-the-passed-lynn-hershman-leeson-comes-into-her-own-after-50-years-of-prophetic-work-8028/.

Greenberger, Alex. "For Whitney Biennial, One Participant Targets Controversial Whitney Patron," ARTnews, May 13, 2019. https://www.artnews.com/art-news/artists-forensic-architecture-whitney-biennial-warren-b-kanders-12543/.

Gregory, Alice. "What Happened After Mexico's Greatest Architect Was Turned into a Diamond," *New Yorker*, May 21, 2017. https://www.newyorker.com/culture/culture-desk/what-happened-after-mexicos-greatest-architect-was-turned-into-a-diamond.

Greshko, Michael. "Meet Sophia, the Robot that Looks Almost Human," *National Geographic*, May 18, 2018. https://www.nationalgeographic.com/photography/proof/2018/05/sophia-robot-artificial-intelligence-science/.

Griffiths, Mary. "Against the Grain—Collecting Contemporary Art at the Whitworth Art Gallery, University of Manchester, UK," 135–42, Seoul National University Library. http://s-space.snu.ac.kr/bitstream/10371/78657/1/135-142.pdf.
Grigar, Dene. "On Evolving and Emerging Literary Forms: A Curatorial Statement For 'Electronic Literature & Its Emerging Forms,'" Electronic Literature & Its Emerging Form at the Library of Congress, April 3–5, 2013, http://dtc-wsuv.org/elit/elit-loc/denes-curatorial-statement/.
Grimm, Ernie. "UCSD Pays for Trans-Species Project, My Gender is Bunny," *San Diego Reader*, March 25, 2009. https://web.archive.org/web/20090401190903/https://www.sandiegoreader.com/news/2009/mar/25/my-gender-bunny/.
Gueydan-Turek, Alexandra. "The Rise Of Dz-Manga in Algeria: Glocalization and the Emergence of a New Transnational Voice," *Journal of Graphic Novels and Comics* 4, no. 1 (Spring 2013): 161–78. http://works.swarthmore.edu/fac-french/29.
Gupta, Alisha Haridasani. "Maria Qamar's Bold Art is Both Therapy and Weapon" *New York Times*, August 15, 2019. https://www.nytimes.com/2019/08/15/arts/design/maria-qamar-art-richard-taittinger.html.
Hale, Sondra and Terry Wolverton, eds. *From Site to Vision: The Woman's Building in Contemporary Culture*. Los Angeles: Otis College of Art and Design, 2011.
Hammer, Barbara. "On Times in Women's Cinema," in "Lesbian Art and Artists," special issue, *Heresies: A Feminist Publication on Art and Politics* 1, no. 3 (September 1977): 87–9. http://heresiesfilmproject.org/wp-content/uploads/2011/09/heresies3.pdf.
Hammond, Harmony. *Lesbian Art in America: A Contemporary History*. New York: Random House, 2000.
Haraway, Donna J. "A Cyborg Manifesto." In *Simians, Cyborgs, and Women*, 148–81. London: Routledge, 1990.
Harris, Aisha. "Juliana Huxtable's Next Chapter," T Presents, *New York Times Magazine*, August 10, 2020. https://www.nytimes.com/2020/08/10/t-magazine/juliana-huxtable.html.
Harris, Gareth. "Jenny Holzer to Use Augmented Reality in Blenheim Palace Show," *The Art Newspaper*, March 6, 2017. https://www.theartnewspaper.com/news/jenny-holzer-to-use-augmented-reality-in-blenheim-palace-show.
Harris Williams, Mandy. Interviewed by Tamu McPherson, All the Pretty Birds, October 13, 2020. https://www.alltheprettybirds.com/mandy-harris-williams/.
Hart, Claudia. "Beginning and End Games: A Parable in 3D," *Cultural Politics* 9, no. 1 (2013): 86–94. https://doi.org/10.1215/17432197-1907190.
Hatoum, Mona. "Using the Body Against the Body Politic: Mona Hatoum on How Art Can Be a Form of Resistance," Artspace Magazine, November 11, 2016. https://www.artspace.com/magazine/art_101/book_report/using-the-body-against-the-body-politicmona-hatoum-on-lessons-in-art-as-resistance-54354.
Hawkins, Alexander. "How Channa Horwitz Permeated LA's 1960s Art Scene," AnOther Magazine, April 13, 2016. https://www.anothermag.com/art-photography/8576/how-channa-horwitz-permeated-las-1960s-art-scene.

Hemmann, Kathryn. "Queering the Media Mix: The Female Gaze in Japanese Fan Comics." *Transformative Works and Cultures* 20 (2015). https://doi.org/10.3983/twc.2015.0628.

Hennessey, Peter. "Patricia Piccinini—Early Installations," Patricia Piccinini, Writings, http://patriciapiccinini.net/printessay.php?id=9. [Originally published in Adam Geczy and Benjamin Genocchio, eds., *What Is Installation? An Anthology of Writings on Australian Installation Art*. Sydney: Power Publications, 2001.]

Heresies Magazine Collection, Internet Archive. December 18, 2012. https://archive.org/details/heresies_magazine.

Hershman Leeson, Lynn. *The Art and Films of Lynn Hershman Leeson: Secret Agents, Private I*. Edited by Meredith Tromble. Berkeley: University of California Press co-published with the Henry Gallery, Seattle, University of Washington, December 2005.

Hershman Leeson, Lynn. *Lynn Hershman Leeson: Civic Radar*. Edited by Peter Weibel. Karlsruhe: ZKM, 2016.

Hershman Leeson, Lynn. "Romancing the Anti-Body: Lust and Longing in Cyberspace," (1985), in "Selected Texts, 1984 to Present," https://www.lynnhershman.com/writing/.

Hessler, Stefanie. "Lynn Hershman Leeson's 'First Person Plural,'" Art Agenda, April 18, 2019. https://www.art-agenda.com/features/264437/lynn-hershman-leeson-s-first-person-plural.

Hester, Jessica Leigh. "Who Keeps Track of All the Craters on the Moon?" Atlas Obscura, April 25, 2018. https://www.atlasobscura.com/articles/how-do-moon-craters-get-names.

High, Kathy. "Straight Talk: BioArt with Kathy High," interview with Julia Swanson, *SciArt Magazine* 23, no. 4 (April 2017). https://www.sciartmagazine.com/straight-talk-kathy-high.html.

Hight, Jeremy. "Views From Above: Locative Narrative and the Landscape," *LEA: Leonardo Electronic Almanac* 14, no. 07/08 (November 2006). https://www.leoalmanac.org/wp-content/uploads/2012/09/09_JHight.pdf.

Hirsch, Ann. "Artist Ann Hirsch Recreates AOL Cybersex," interview by Kat Stoeffel, The Cut, November 15, 2013. https://www.thecut.com/2013/11/artist-ann-hirsch-recreates-aol-cybersex.html.

Hirsch, Ann. "Artist Profile: Jennifer Chan," Rhizome, December 18, 2014. https://rhizome.org/editorial/2014/dec/18/artist-profile-jennifer-chan/.

HKU Design. "Anonymous," https://web.archive.org/web/20190512083013/https://www.hku.nl/Opleidingen/Design/OverHKUDesign/HKUDesignInMilan2017/anonymous.htm.

Ho, Melissa, Mahnaz Afkhami, and Melissa Chu. *Shirin Neshat: Facing History*. Washington, DC: Smithsonian Books, 2015.

Ho, Soleil. "What I Learned About Gender and Power from Sailor Moon," Bitch Media, May 31, 2013. https://www.bitchmedia.org/post/what-i-learned-about-gender-and-power-from-sailor-moon.

Hocks, Mary E. "Feminist Interventions in Electronic Environments," *Computers and Composition* 16, no. 1 (1999): 107–19. https://doi.org/10.1016/S8755-4615(99)80008-5.

Holland, Allison. "From Gothic Lolita to Radiant Shaman: The Development of Mariko Mori's Ethereal Personae." *U.S.-Japan Women's Journal* 40 (2011): 3–28. https://www.jstor.org/stable/42772304.

Holland, Allison. "Mori Mariko and the Art of Global Connectedness." *Intersections: Gender and Sexuality in Asia and the Pacific* 23 (November 2009). http://intersections.anu.edu.au/issue23/holland.htm.

Holzer, Jenny. "Truisms," fak3r, April 2, 2011. https://fak3r.com/2011/04/02/jenny-holzer-truisms/.

Hood, Vic. "How the Sims Broke Down Sexuality and Gender Boundaries," PCGames[N], May 9, 2018. https://www.pcgamesn.com/the-sims/the-sims-gender-sexuality.

Hotchkiss, Sarah. "Public Park in the Sky Seeks to Protect Atmosphere," KQED, November 25, 2015. https://www.kqed.org/arts/11105426/public-park-in-the-sky-seeks-to-protect-atmosphere.

Hotovy, Hannah. "NASA and Art: A Collaboration Colored with History," NASA. History, April 18, 2017. https://www.nasa.gov/feature/nasa-and-art-a-collaboration-colored-with-history.

"Howard Wise Gallery Records, 1943–1989," Archives of American Art, Smithsonian Institution. https://www.aaa.si.edu/collections/howard-wise-gallery-records-9357.

Ibarra, Xandra. Interview by Andy Campbell, Artforum, August 27, 2019. https://www.artforum.com/interviews/xandra-ibarra-80626.

Isbister, Katherine. *How Games Move Us: Emotion by Design*. Cambridge, MA: MIT Press, 2016. Kindle.

Isselhardt, Tiffany R. "The Mystery & Horror of Roberta Williams," LevelSkip, October 24, 2017. https://web.archive.org/web/20180301173100/www.levelskip.com/action-adventure/The-Mystery-Horror-of-Roberta-Williams.

Iverson, Hana, and Sarah Drury. "Mechanics of Place: Textures of Tophane," *LEA: Leonardo Electric Almanac* 19, no. 2 (April 15, 2013): 84–97. https://www.leoalmanac.org/vol19-no2-not-here-not-there-part-2/.

Iwabuchi, Koichi. *Recentering Globalization: Popular Culture and Japanese Transnationalism*. Durham, NC: Duke University Press, 2002.

Jackson, Shelley. Interview by Mark Amerika. "Stitch Bitch: The Hypertext Author As Cyborg-Narrator," HyperX, AltX. http://www.altx.com/hyperx/writerly/jackson.html.

Jackson, Shelley. *Patchwork Girl*, Watertown, MA: Eastgate, 1995. https://www.eastgate.com/catalog/PatchworkGirl.html.

Jamie. "History of Women in Computing," MakeAWebsiteHub.com. https://makeawebsitehub.com/history-women-computing/.

Jarrell, Robert. "Synthetic Dreams: The Art of Mariko Mori," *Kyoto Journal* 52, no. 1 (August 20, 2011). https://kyotojournal.org/culture-arts/synthetic-dreams-the-art-of-mariko-mori/.

Jenseth, Alexander. "The Quiet Circus: The Colorful, Complicated, Slightly Schizophrenic, History of Early Computer Art at Bell Labs," Bard Undergraduate Senior Project, Fall 2011, 8. https://digitalcommons.bard.edu/cgi/viewcontent.cgi?article=1030&context=senproj_f2011.

Johnson, Steven. "Why No One Clicked on the Great Hypertext Story," WIRED, April 16, 2013. https://www.wired.com/2013/04/hypertext/.

Jonas, Joan. Interview by Rachel Rose. "Joan Jonas—The Performer," *Tate Etc.* 42 (Spring 2018). https://www.tate.org.uk/tate-etc/issue-42-spring-2018/interview-joan-jonas-rachel-rose-the-performer.

Jones, Amelia. "Screen Eroticisms: Exploring Female Desire in Feminist Film and Video," in *Resolutions 3: Global Networks of Video*, edited by Ming-Yuen S. Ma and Erika Suderburg, Minneapolis: University of Minnesota Press, 2012. Also available at: Minnesota Scholarship Online, August 2015, https://minnesota.universitypressscholarship.com/view/10.5749/minnesota/9780816670826.001.0001/upso-9780816670826-chapter-22.

Jones, Caroline A. "Passages: Shigeko Kubota (1937–2015)," Artforum, October 15, 2015. https://www.artforum.com/passages/caroline-a-jones-on-shigeko-kubota-1937-2015-55566.

Jones, Kyna. "Notes on Nun and Deviant, 1976, Nancy Angelo and Candace Compton," Hugh McCarney, Communication Department, Western Connecticut State University, May 11, 1998. http://people.wcsu.edu/mccarneyh/fva/A/Nun_Deviant.html.

Kennedy, Randy. "Who is Valie Export? Just Look and Please Touch," *New York Times*, June 29, 2016. https://www.nytimes.com/2016/06/30/arts/design/who-is-valie-export-just-look-and-please-touch.html.

Kent, Steven L. *The Ultimate History of Video Games*. New York: Three Rivers Press, 2001.

Khan, David M. "Questions of Cultural Identity and Difference in the Work of Yasumasa Morimura, Mariko Mori and Takashi, Murakami," MA thesis, University of Canterbury, 2007. https://core.ac.uk/download/pdf/35458251.pdf.

Khan, Nora N. "No Safe Mode," Flash Art, September 18, 2017. https://flash---art.com/article/sondra-perry/.

Khettab, Djamila Ould. "Manga Gains Popularity in Algeria," Middle East Eye, October 16, 2015. https://www.middleeasteye.net/features/manga-gains-popularity-algeria.

Khosravi, Ryan. " 'Sailor Moon' and the Queer History of Anime Transformations," *Digg* (blog), December 19, 2018. https://digg.com/2018/history-of-the-transformation-sequence.

Kinsella, Eileen. "In the Heart of the Whitney Biennial, Artists Are Working to Expose Board Member Warren Kanders's Link to Possible War Crimes," Artnet News, May 13, 2019. https://news.artnet.com/art-world/forensic-architecture-triple-chaser-whitney-biennial-1544911.

Klüver, Billy, Julie Martin, and Barbara Rose, eds. *Pavilion: Experiments in Art and Technology*. New York: Dutton, 1972.

Koenitz, Hartmut, Gabriele Ferri, Mads Haahr, Diğdem Sezen, and Tonguç İbrahim Sezen, eds. *Interactive Digital Narrative: History, Theory, and Practice*. New York: Routledge, 2015. Google Books.

Kohler, Christopher. *Power-Up: How Japanese Video Games Gave the World An Extra Life*. Rev. ed. Mineola, NY: Dover Publications, 2016.

Kramer, Hilton. "Boston Museum Mounts an Unusual New Art Show," *New York Times*, February 4, 1971. https://www.nytimes.com/1971/02/04/archives/boston-museum-mounts-an-unusual-new-art-show.html.

Kuhn, Thomas S. *The Structure of Scientific Revolutions*. Chicago: University of Chicago Press, 1962.

Kumao, Heidi. "Misbehaving Machines Act Out," Heidi Kumao. Projects. http://heidikumao.net/misbehaving-machines/.

Kumao, Heidi. "Translator-2008," Heidi Kumao. Projects. http://heidikumao.net/portfolio-items/translator-2008/?portfolioCats=94.

Ladly, Martha. "Narrative in Hybrid Mobile Environments," in "L.A. Re.Play, Mobile Network Culture in Placemaking," special issue, *LEA: Leonardo Electronic Almanac* 21, no. 1 (2016): 76–95. https://www.leonardo.info/sites/default/files/leavol21no1_la_replay_martha-ladly.pdf.

Landow, George. "Hypertext at Brown," CyberArtsWeb, http://www.cyberartsweb.org/cpace/ht/HTatBrown/BrownHT.html.

Lee, SooJin. "Mariko Mori and the Globalization of Japanese 'Cute Culture': Art and Pop Culture in the 1990s," *Journal of Art Studies* 16 (July 22, 2015): 131–65. https://www.academia.edu/32616339/Mariko_Mori_and_the_Globalization_of_Japanese_Cute_Culture_Art_and_Pop_Culture_in_the_1990s.

Levy, Ellen K. "Visualizing Evolution: A Painter's Interaction with Science and Technology," *Leonardo* 20, no. 1 (1987): 3–8. https://www.jstor.org/stable/1578203?seq=1.

Lien, Tracey. "No Girls Allowed," Polygon, December 2, 2013. https://www.polygon.com/features/2013/12/2/5143856/no-girls-allowed.

Light, Jennifer S. "When Computers Were Women," *Technology and Culture* 40, no. 3 (1999): 455–83. https://www.jstor.org/stable/25147356.

Lipinski, Jed. "Video-Game Designer, Anna Anthropy, Describes the Life of a Radical, Queer, Transgender Gamer," Politico New York, April 10, 2012. https://www.politico.com/states/new-york/city-hall/story/2012/04/video-game-designer-anna-anthropy-describes-the-life-of-a-radical-queer-transgender-gamer-067223.

Lodi, Simona. "Spatial Art: An Eruption of the Digital into the Physical," *LEA: Leonardo Electronic Almanac* 19, no. 2 (2013): 12–31. http://journals.gold.ac.uk/index.php/lea/article/view/91/70.

Loos, Ted. "For Zina Saro-Wiwa, Food Carries Meaning and Metaphor," *New York Times*, December 4, 2018. https://www.nytimes.com/2018/12/04/arts/for-zina-saro-wiwa-food-art-basel.html.

Lothian-McLean, Moya. "These Activists Use Makeup to Defy Mass Surveillance," i-D, January 29, 2020. https://i-d.vice.com/en_uk/article/jge5jg/dazzle-club-surveillance-activists-makeup-marches-london-interview.

Lovelace, Ada. "Sketch of the Analytical Engine Invented by Charles Babbage Esq. By L.F. Menabrea of Turin, Officer of the Military Engineers, with Notes by the Translator," *Scientific Memoirs* vol. 3. London: Richard & John E. Taylor, 1843.

Lubow, Arthur. "The Murakami Method," *New York Times*, April 3, 2005. https://www.nytimes.com/2005/04/03/magazine/the-murakami-method.html.

Lunning, Frenchy. "The 24 Nengumi: The Female Progenitors of Shōjo Manga," Comic Book Legal Defense Fund (CBDF), March 31, 2015. http://cbldf.org/2015/03/women-who-changed-free-expression-special-24-nengumi/.

Maas, Peter. "How Laura Poitras Helped Snowden Spill His Secrets," *New York Times Magazine*, August 13, 2013. https://www.nytimes.com/2013/08/18/magazine/laura-poitras-snowden.html.

MacGregor, Brent. "Cybernetic Serendipity Revisited." In *White Heat Cold Logic: British Computer Art 1960–1980*, edited by Paul Brown, Charlie Gere, Nicholas Lambert, and Catherine Mason, 83–94. Cambridge, MA: MIT Press, 2008.

Mallen, George. "Bridging Computing in the Arts and Software Development," in *White Heat Cold Logic: British Computer Art 1960–1980*, edited by Paul Brown, Charlie Gere, Nicholas Lambert, and Catherine Mason, 191–202. Cambridge, MA: MIT Press, 2008.

Malloy, Judy. *its name was Penelope*. Watertown, MA: Eastgate, 1993. https://www.eastgate.com/catalog/Penelope.html.

Malloy, Judy. "Notes on the Creation of *its name was Penelope*," *The WELL*, https://people.well.com/user/jmalloy/statement.html.

Malloy, Judy, ed. "The Process of Creating New Media: Interview with Sonya Rapoport," Content | Code | Process: Authoring Electronic Literature, November 2009, revision posted March 2017. https://www.narrabase.net/rapoport.html.

Malloy, Judy. *Women, Art, and Technology*. Cambridge, MA: MIT Press, 2003.

Manatakis, Lexi. "Why Artist Adrian Piper is One of the Most Innovative Minds of Our Time," Dazed Digital, May 25, 2018. https://www.dazeddigital.com/art-photography/article/40084/1/why-artist-adrian-piper-is-one-of-the-most-innovative-minds-of-our-time-moma.

Mar, Alex. "Love in the Time of Robots," WIRED, October 17, 2017. https://www.wired.com/2017/10/hiroshi-ishiguro-when-robots-act-just-like-humans/.

Marantz, Andrew. "Studio 360: The Pioneers Who Are Making the First Virtual Reality Narratives," *New Yorker* (April 25, 2016). https://www.newyorker.com/magazine/2016/04/25/making-movies-with-virtual-reality.

Martin, Chase Bowen, and Mark Deuze. "The Independent Production of Culture: A Digital Games Case," *Games and Culture* 4, no. 3 (July 2009): 276–95, https://journals.sagepub.com/doi/pdf/10.1177/1555412009339732.

Martin, Julie. "Oral History Interview with Julie B. Martin, 2018 Nov. 7–8," Smithsonian Archives of American Art. https://www.aaa.si.edu/download_pdf_transcript/ajax?record_id=edanmdm-AAADCD_oh_397104.

Martyn, Shona. "Cute and Dark: The Magical World of Japanese Art Star Chiho Aoshima," *Sydney Morning Herald*, October 25, 2019. https://www.smh.com.au/culture/art-and-design/cute-and-dark-the-magical-world-of-japanese-art-star-chiho-aoshima-20191017-p531iz.html.

Mason, Catherine. "Cybernetic Serendipity: History and Lasting Legacy," Studio International. https://www.studiointernational.com/index.php/cybernetic-serendipity-history-and-lasting-legacy.

Mattingly, Mary. "Flock House," https://marymattingly.com/pdfs/FHBookTest2.pdf.

McCurry, Justin. "Erica the 'Most Beautiful and Intelligent Android' Leads Japan's Robot Revolution," *Guardian* (US ed.), December 31, 2015. https://www.theguardian.com/technology/2015/dec/31/erica-the-most-beautiful-and-intelligent-android-ever-leads-japans-robot-revolution.

McWilliams, Andrew. "How Artists Are Reshaping Emerging Technology Research," ThoughtWorks Arts, Projects, June 27, 2018. https://www.thoughtworks.com/insights/blog/how-artists-are-reshaping-emerging-technology-research.

Meier, Allison. "A Digital Waterfall that Illuminates the Threat of Air Pollution," Hyperallergic, February 16, 2015. https://hyperallergic.com/182480/a-digital-waterfall-that-illuminates-the-threat-of-air-pollution/.

Menkman, Rosa. *The Glitch Moment(um)*, Network Notebooks 04. Amsterdam: Institute of Network Cultures, 2011. https://networkcultures.org/_uploads/NN%234_RosaMenkman.pdf.

Mensley, Matthew. "Interview with Evelyn Hriberšek: Creating Mixed Reality Art," All3DP, March 10, 2019. https://all3dp.com/evelyn-hribersek-ar-art-eurydike/.

Milosevic, Nikola. "Orlan / Mireille Suzanne Francette Porte," Widewalls, October 11, 2013. https://www.widewalls.ch/artist/orlan/.

Mirapaul, Matthew. "Beyond Hypertext: Novels With Interactive Animation," Arts Online, *New York Times*, March 5, 2001. https://www.nytimes.com/2001/03/05/books/arts-online-beyond-hypertext-novels-with-interactive-animation.html.

MIT School of Architecture and Planning. "A Brief History of the Center for Advanced Visual Studies, MIT." http://act.mit.edu/collections/cavs/history/.

Mock, Roberta. "Lynn Hershman and the Creation of Multiple Robertas," in *Identity, Performance and Technology: Practices of Empowerment, Embodiment and Technicity*, edited by Susan Broadhurst and Josephine Machon, 126–41. London: Palgrave Macmillan, 2012.

Molnár, Vera. Interview by Hans Ulrich Obrist, *Vintage Galéria* (March 2019): 76–87. https://vintage.hu/wp-content/uploads/2019/03/Molnar-Vera-HUO-interview.pdf.

Monoskop. "Experiments in Art and Technology," last revised, May 6, 2019. https://monoskop.org/Experiments_in_Art_and_Technology.

Monoskop. "From Site to Vision: The Women's Building in Contemporary Culture." https://monoskop.org/images/8/84/From_Site_to_Vision_The_Womans_Building_in_Contemporary_Culture_2011.pdf.

Monoskop. "Laboria Cuboniks," last edited January 22, 2021. https://monoskop.org/Laboria_Cuboniks.

Monoskop. "New Tendencies," last edited May 29, 2019. https://monoskop.org/New_Tendencies.

Monoskop. *Software—Information Technology: Its New Meaning for Art.* https://monoskop.org/images/3/31/Software_Information_Technology_Its_New_Meaning_for_Art_catalogue.pdf.

Monoskop. "TV as a Creative Medium," brochure. https://monoskop.org/images/4/4a/TV_as_a_Creative_Medium_1969.pdf.

Moorhouse, Paul, ed. *Cindy Sherman*. New York: Rizzoli, 2019.

Morie, Jacquelyn Ford. "Meaning and Emplacement in Expressive Immersive Visual Environments," PhD diss., University of East London, September 2007. https://www.academia.edu/355900/Meaning_and_Emplacement_In_Expressive_Immersive_Virtual_Environments.

Morineau, Camille. "Mary Martin." Translated by Jo Garden, Archives of Women Artists Research and Exhibitions (AWARE), 2013. https://awarewomenartists.com/en/artiste/mary-martin/.

Mufson, Beckett. "A War Survivor's Virtual Reality Film Brings the Terror of a Conflict Zone to Life," VICE, March 14, 2016. https://www.vice.com/en_us/article/8qv7jg/giant-vr-film-gdc.

Muñoz, José Esteban. "'The White to Be Angry:' Vaginal Davis's Terrorist Drag," *Social Text* 52/53 (Fall/Winter, 1997): 81–103. https://www.jstor.org/stable/466735.

Murakami, Takashi. "The Super Flat Manifesto." In *Super Flat*, Tokyo: Madra, 2000. http://web.mit.edu/condry/Public/cooljapan/Feb23-2006/MurakamiT-Superflat-E2.pdf.

Museum of Contemporary Art, Chicago. "Giving a F@*0/0: Forms of Feminism in Response to Riot Grrrls." *MCA DMA* (blog), May 23, 2017. https://mcachicago.org/Publications/Blog/2017/05/Riot-Grrrls-App-2.

Museum of Contemporary Art, Chicago. Exhibitions. *Riot Grrrls*. December 15, 2016–June 18, 2017. https://mcachicago.org/Exhibitions/2016/Riot-Grrrls.

Myers, Joe. "5 Female Coders You Have Probably Never Heard of Who Changed the World," The World Economic Forum, July 21, 2016. https://www.weforum.org/agenda/2016/07/5-female-coders-who-changed-the-world/.

Nadir, Leila. "Poetry, Immigration, and the FBI: The Transborder Immigrant Tool," Hyperallergic, July 23, 2012. https://hyperallergic.com/54678/poetry-immigration-and-the-fbi-the-transborder-immigrant-tool/.

Nair, Varsha. "Womanifesto: A Biennial Art Exchange in Thailand." *Southeast of Now: Directions in Contemporary and Modern Art in Asia* 3, no. 1 (March 2019): 147–71. https://muse.jhu.edu/article/721050.

Nake, Frieder. "Computer Art. A Personal Recollection," April 12, 2005. http://citeseerx.ist.psu.edu/viewdoc/download?doi=10.1.1.470.2597&rep=rep1&type=pdf. [Also published: *C&C '05: Proceedings of the 5th Conference on Creativity & Cognition*, April 2005, 54–62. New York: ACM Press.]

Napier, Susan. *Anime, from Akira to Howl's Moving Castle*. New York: St. Martin's Griffin, 2001.

Narduli, Susan. "Conversation," Narduli Studio, https://www.nardulistudio.com/conversation.

Nash, Katherine, and Richard Williams. "Computer Program for Artists: ART I," *Leonardo* 3, no. 4 (October 1970): 439–42. https://doi.org/10.2307/1572264.

Naval History and Heritage Command. "Grace Murray Hopper," Modern Biographical Files in the Navy Department Library. https://www.history.navy.mil/research/library/research-guides/modern-biographical-files-ndl/modern-bios-h/hopper-grace-murray-text.html.

Neo-Griot (blog). "The Video Artwork of Michèle Magema," African Digital Art, January 19, 2016. http://kalamu.com/neogriot/2016/03/19/video-the-video-artwork-of-michele-magema/.

Nessim, Barbara. Interview by Emily Banos, Bard Graduate Center Craft, Art, and Design Oral History Project, October 27, 2014. http://bgccraftartdesign.org/items/show/29.

Ng, Christina. "At the Venice Biennale, Shu Lea Chang Surveils the Surveillance System," Hyperallergic, June 5, 2019. https://hyperallergic.com/503068/at-the-venice-biennale-shu-lea-cheang-surveils-the-surveillance-system/.

Noble, Safiya Umoja. *Algorithms of Oppression: How Search Engines Reinforce Racism*. New York: NYU Press, 2018.

Noll, A. Michael. "The Howard Wise Gallery Show Computer-Generated Pictures (1965): A 50th Anniversary Memoir," *Leonardo* 49, no. 3 (June 2016): 232–9. https://ethw.org/First-Hand:Howard_Wise_Gallery_Show_of_Digital_Art_and_Patterns_(1965):_A_50th_Anniversary_Memoir.

Nooney, Laine. "A Pedestal, a Table, a Love Letter: Archaeologies of Gender in Videogame History," *Game Studies* 13, no. 2 (December 2013). http://gamestudies.org/1302/articles/nooney.

O'Brien, Lucy. "Women in Video Game Development in 2017: A Snapshot," IGN, updated December 22, 2017. https://www.ign.com/articles/2017/12/20/women-in-video-game-development-in-2017-a-snapshot.

Oelbaum, Brenda. *Fat Feminist Activist Artist's Blog*. https://brendaoelbaum.me/.

Olin, Ferris. *Anarchy and Form: Works by Miriam Schapiro*, exhibition catalogue (includes an interview with Schapiro), Mary H. Dana Women Artists Series, Rutgers University (2005), available by request to the Rutgers Center for Women in the Arts and Humanities, womenart@cwah.rutgers.edu.

Onanuga, Tola. "Virtual Reality: How Women Are Taking a Leading Role in the Sector," *Guardian* (US ed.), May 28, 2018, amended May 29, 2019. https://www.theguardian.

com/careers/2019/may/28/virtual-reality-how-women-are-taking-a-leading-role-in-the-sector.

Ong, Sandy. "The Video Game Industry's Problem with Racial Diversity," Newsweek Magazine, October 13, 2016. https://www.newsweek.com/2016/10/21/video-games-race-black-protagonists-509328.html.

Ortiz, Jen. "She's Got Game," Marie Claire, December 5, 2018. https://www.marieclaire.com/career-advice/a25379999/female-gamers/.

Oxman, Neri. "Printing 3-D Buildings: Five Tenets of a New Kind of Architecture," Interview by Pedro Navarro, Metalocus, December 17, 2012. https://www.metalocus.es/en/news/printing-3D-buildings-five-tenets-a-new-kind-architecture.

Oyler, Lauren. "Erin Gee Makes Feminist Robots that Respond to Human Emotion," VICE, December 16, 2014. https://www.vice.com/en_us/article/mv5nzn/erin-gee-makes-feminist-robots-that-respond-to-human-emotion-456.

Packwood, Damon. "The Era of White Male Games for White Male Gamers Is Ending," Quartz, October 21, 2018. https://qz.com/1433085/the-era-of-white-male-games-for-white-male-gamers-is-ending/.

Page, Barbara. "Women Writers and the Restive Text: Feminism, Experimental Writing and Hypertext," *Postmodern Culture* 6, no. 2 (January 1996). http://www.pomoculture.org/2013/09/22/women-writers-and-the-restive-text-feminism-experimental-writing-and-hypertext/.

Palmer, Laurie. "Hays Wood/ Oxygen Bar," Groundworks, Environmental Collaborations in Contemporary Art. https://groundworks.collinsandgoto.com/artist/hays-woods-oxygen-bar.

Palop, Benoit. "Enter LaTurbo Avedon's Video Game Night Club," VICE, March 31, 2015. https://www.vice.com/en_us/article/gvw553/enter-laturbo-avedons-video-game-nightclub.

Parker, Rianna Jade. "How Sondra Perry Turned Glitches into Art About a Broken World at the Serpentine," Artnet News, May 18, 2018. https://news.artnet.com/exhibitions/sondra-perry-at-serpentine-1288877.

Parks, Shoshi. "As Men Took Over the Videogame Industry, Brenda Laurel Pioneered Girls' Games," Medium: Timeline, May 4, 2018. https://timeline.com/brenda-laurel-wanted-to-get-girls-excited-for-tech-155fe57368e5.

Paul, Christiane, ed. *A Companion to Digital Art.* Chichester: Wiley Blackwell, 2016. Kindle.

Paul, Christiane. *Digital Art.* 2nd ed. London: Thames and Hudson, 2008.

PeoplePill. "Brenda Romero, American Video Game Designer and Developer," https://peoplepill.com/people/brenda-romero/.

Pertigkiozoglou, Eliza. "1960s Max Bense and Abraham Moles, Information Aesthetics," Medium, March 9, 2017. https://medium.com/designscience/1960s-d611bd76d056.

Pes, Javier. "Save the Planet—and Marina Abramović's Avatar—From Rising Water Levels in the Artist's First Virtual-Reality Work," Artnet News, March 7, 2018.

https://news.artnet.com/art-world/save-planet-marina-abramovics-avatar-artists-first-vr-work-1238081.
Pias, Claus. "The Game Player's Duty: The User as the Gestalt of the Ports." In *Media Archaeology*, edited by Erkki Huhtamo and Jussi Parikka, 164–83. Berkeley: University of California Press, 2011.
Pinto, Ana Teixeira. "Atmospheric Monument," *Mousse* no. 34 (2012): 152–7. http://tomorrowmorning.net/texts/Mousse_d13_Amy%20Balkin.pdf.
Plant, Sadie. *Zeros + Ones: Digital Women + the New Technoculture*. London: Fourth Estate, 1997.
Platt, Rhiannon. "May All Things Dissolve in the Ocean of Bliss: An Interview with Aya Takano," *Complex*, March 17, 2014. https://www.complex.com/style/2014/03/global-track-6.
Polli, Andrea. *Hack the Grid*. Pittsburgh, PA: Carnegie Museum of Art, 2017.
Prolight+Sound (blog). "The Fine Line to Reality: Immersive Technologies," June 20, 2019. http://prolight-sound-blog.com/the-fine-line-to-reality-immersive-technologies/.
Public Art Fund. "Alfredo Jaar: Messages to the Public: A Logo For America," Public Art Fund/Exhibitions, https://www.publicartfund.org/exhibitions/view/messages-to-the-public-jaar/.
Purdue University Global. "History of Women in IT: 6 Female Pioneers in Computer Science," April 19, 2018. https://www.purdueglobal.edu/blog/information-technology/history-women-information-technology-6-female-computer-science-pioneers/.
Quaytman, R.H. "Joan Jonas," Interview, December 10, 2014. https://www.interviewmagazine.com/art/joan-jonas.
Raubenheimer, Landi. "Flatness and Immersion in Mariko Mori's 'Pureland': The Possibility of a Digital Sublime," *South African Journal of Art History (SAJAH)* 22, no. 3 (2007): 150–67. https://repository.up.ac.za/bitstream/handle/2263/10633/Raubenheimer_Flatness(2007).pdf.
Rea, Naomi. "A Gallery Has Sold More Than $1 Million in Art Made by an Android, but Collectors Are Buying into a Sexist Fantasy," Artnet News, June 6, 2019. https://news.artnet.com/opinion/artificial-intelligence-robot-artist-ai-da-1566580.
Redfern Galleries. "Jean Spencer." https://www.redfern-gallery.com/artists/31-jean-spencer/overview/.
Reichardt, Jasia. "In the Beginning . . ." In *White Heat Cold Logic: British Computer Art 1960–1980*, edited by Paul Brown, Charlie Gere, Nicholas Lambert, and Catherine Mason, 71–82. Cambridge, MA: MIT Press, 2008.
Reid, Frances. "Iris Films, Documenting the Lives of Lesbians," in "Lesbian Art and Artists," special issue, *Heresies: A Feminist Publication on Art and Politics* 1, no. 3 (September 1977): 100–1. http://heresiesfilmproject.org/wp-content/uploads/2011/09/heresies3.pdf.
Renken, Elena. "Robot Gives Keynote Address at Inclusion-Themed RISD Commencement," *Providence Journal*, June 2, 2018. https://web.archive.org/

web/20201109101405/https://www.providencejournal.com/news/20180602/robot-gives-keynote-address-at-inclusion-themed-risd-commencement--video.

Rettberg, Scott. "The American Hypertext Novel, and Whatever Became of It?" In *Interactive Digital Narrative: History, Theory, and Practice*, edited by Koenitz, Hartmut, Gabriele Ferri, Mads Haahr, Diğdem Sezen, and Tonguç İbrahim Sezen, 22–35. New York: Routledge, 2015. Google Books.

Rhee, Jennifer. *The Robotic Imaginary: The Human and the Price of Dehumanized Labor*. Minneapolis: University of Minnesota Press, 2018.

Rich. "How I Learned to Stop Worrying and Love Being Otaku: Answering Questions of Identity and Fandom in Japan and Beyond," Tofugu, June 6, 2016. https://www.tofugu.com/japan/otaku-meaning/.

Rich, Motoko. "The Exhibit Lauded Freedom of Speech. It Was Silenced," *New York Times*, August 5, 2019. https://www.nytimes.com/2019/08/05/world/asia/japan-aichi-trienniale.html.

Richmond, Susan. "The Ins and Outs of *Female Sensibility*, a 1973 Video by Lynda Benglis," *Camera Obscura* 23, no. 3 (69) (2008): 80–108. https://doi.org/10.1215/02705346-2008-008.

Rist, Pipilotti. "Pipilotti Rist in Conversation with Natalie King," Ocula Magazine, January 8, 2018, https://ocula.com/magazine/conversations/pipilotti-rist/#oc-col-1.

Rist, Pipilotti. "Pipilotti Rist Wants You to Spit on Your Mobile Phone: A Q&A with the Ecstatic Hippie Feminist Artist," Artspace Magazine, October 22, 2016. https://www.artspace.com/magazine/interviews_features/book_report/pipilotti-rist-phaidon-interview-54294.

Robertson, Adi. "Building the Afro-Feminist Future at Sundance, One Cyberpunk Beauty Salon at a Time," *The Verge*, January 26, 2017. https://www.theverge.com/2017/1/26/14377214/neurospeculative-afrofeminism-vr-science-fiction-sundance-interview-2017.

Romano, Aja. "Why We've Been Arguing About Lara Croft for Two Decades," Vox, March 17, 2018. https://www.vox.com/culture/2018/3/17/17128344/lara-croft-tomb-raider-history-controversy-breasts.

Rosen, Margit, ed. *A Little-Known Story About a Movement, a Magazine, and the Computer's Arrival in Art: New Tendencies and Bit International, 1961–1973*. Cambridge, MA: MIT Press, 2011.

Rothfuss, Joan. "Topless Cellist," *Sightlines*, September 25, 2014. https://walkerart.org/magazine/charlotte-moorman-paik-topless-cellist.

Rothfuss, Joan. *Topless Cellist: The Improbable Life of Charlotte Moorman*. Cambridge: MIT Press, 2014.

Rovner, Michal. "Michal Rovner, Into the Night," Interview by Haley Weiss, *Interview Magazine*, September 27, 2016. https://www.interviewmagazine.com/art/michal-rovner.

Rueb, Teri. "Interview with Teri Rueb," interview by Jeremy Hight, *LEA: Leonardo Electronic Almanac*, February 2011. https://www.leoalmanac.org/wp-content/uploads/2011/03/Interview_Rueb.pdf.

Russell, John G. "Replicating the White Self and Other: Skin Color, Racelessness, Gynoids, and the Construction of Whiteness in Japan," *Japanese Studies* 37, no. 1 (2017): 23–48. https://doi.org/10.1080/10371397.2017.1297183.

Russell, Legacy. "Digital Dualism and the Glitch Feminism Manifesto." *Cyborgology* (blog), The Society Pages, December 10, 2012. https://thesocietypages.org/cyborgology/2012/12/10/digital-dualism-and-the-glitch-feminism-manifesto/.

Russell, Legacy. "#Glitch Feminism Manifesto," Legacy Russell. https://www.legacyrussell.com/GLITCHFEMINISM.

Russell, Legacy. *Glitch Feminism: A Manifesto*. Brooklyn, NY: Verso, 2020.

Rüst, Annina. "Data as Feminist Protest," *Unframed* (blog), Los Angeles County Museum of Art, July 10, 2014. https://unframed.lacma.org/2014/07/10/data-as-feminist-protest.

Rüst, Annina. "A Piece of the Pie Chart: Feminist Robotics," *Leonardo* 47, no. 4 (2014): 360–6. https://www.jstor.org/stable/43834225.

Sarkeesian, Anita, and Carolyn Petit. "Female Representation in Videogames Isn't Getting Any Better," WIRED, June 14, 2019. https://www.wired.com/story/e3-2019-female-representation-videogames/.

Scherrer, Camille. "An Interview with Interactive Designer Camille Scherrer," interview by Nelio de Barros, Kinobrand [June 2010]. http://kinobrand.com/an-interview-with-interactive-designer-camille-scherrer/.

Schodt, Frederik L. *Manga! Manga! The World of Japanese Comics*. Berkeley, CA: Stonebridge Press, 2002.

Schor, Mira. "Miriam Schapiro's Road to Feminism," Hyperallergic, March 15, 2016. https://hyperallergic.com/283426/miriam-schapiros-road-to-feminism/.

Schrager, Leah. "The Censored Image and My Response," The Naked Therapist. http://thenakedtherapist.org/.

Schwartz, Lillian F. "Biography." http://lillian.com/biography/.

Schwartz, Lillian F. Interview by Christopher Garcia, Computer History Museum, August 21, 2013. https://www.computerhistory.org/collections/catalog/102746737.

Searle, Adrian. "Anne Imhof, 'Sex, But Not As You Know It'," *Guardian* (US ed.), March 27, 2019. https://www.theguardian.com/artanddesign/2019/mar/27/anne-imhof-interview-sex-performance-art-tate-modern.

Segalove, Ilene. *Mom Tapes* (excerpts), video, Metropolitan Museum of Art, Exhibitions, Met Media. https://www.metmuseum.org/metmedia/video/collections/ph/mom-tapes.

Seidel, Madeleine. "Xandra Ibarra: *Forever Sidepiece*," *Brooklyn Rail* (October 2019). https://brooklynrail.org/2019/10/artseen/Forever-SidepieceXandra-Ibarra.

Sellers, Meredith. "The Personal and Poetic Prints of a Female Pioneer of Copier Art," Hyperallergic, April 20, 2016. https://hyperallergic.com/292378/the-personal-and-poetic-prints-of-a-female-pioneer-of-copier-art/.

Shaw, Gwyneth K. "On ENIAC's Anniversary, a Nod to its Female 'Computers'," *Penn Today*, Science and Technology, February 14, 2019. https://penntoday.upenn.edu/news/eniacs-anniversary-nod-its-female-computers.

Shimada, Yoshiko. "Short List: The Defiant Fringed Pink: Feminist Art in Japan," Asia Art Archive, Ideas, August 21, 2019. https://aaa.org.hk/en/ideas/ideas/shortlist-the-defiant-fringed-pink-feminist-art-in-japan.

SIGGRAPH. "Tamiko Thiel, Beyond Manzanar," ACM SIGGRAPH, https://digitalartarchive.siggraph.org/artwork/tamiko-thiel-beyond-manzanar/.

Silas, Susan. "The Virtual Is Liminal: An Interview with Claudia Hart," Hyperallergic, May 24, 2016. https://hyperallergic.com/289316/the-virtual-is-limited-an-interview-with-claudia-hart/.

Silverstein, Josh. "Art from Code: A Response to Grace Hertlein," *A Story Is Not a Tree*, New Genres Program, New Genres and Interactive Art, Sarah Lawrence College, Bronxville, NY, December 13, 2018. http://astoryisnotatree.net/?p=10347.

Singel, Ryan. "Vint Cerf: We Knew What We Were Unleashing on the World," Wired Business, April 23, 2012. https://www.wired.com/2012/04/epicenter-isoc-famers-qa-cerf/.

Smith, Matthew Wilson. "Liquid Walls: The Digital Art of Tamiko Thiel," *Performing Arts Journal* no. 96 (2010): 25–34. https://direct.mit.edu/pajj/article-pdf/32/3%20(96)/25/1797204/pajj_a_00004.pdf.

Social Networks and Archival Context "Tamblyn, Christine." https://snaccooperative.org/ark:/99166/w60z76d0.

Souza, Mafê. "Beta: The First Cyberfeminist Bot." Women's Media Center (WMC), *FBomb* (blog), September 13, 2018. https://www.womensmediacenter.com/fbomb/beta-the-first-cyberfeminist-bot.

Spalter, Anne Morgan. *The Computer in the Visual Arts*. Boston, MA: Addison Wesley-Longman, 1999.

Sparks, Kaegan. "To Cut and To Swipe: Understanding Hito Steyerl Through 'How Not to Be Seen'," Momus: A Return to Art Criticism, May 12, 2015, https://momus.ca/to-cut-and-to-swipe-understanding-hito-steyerl-through-how-not-to-be-seen/.

Spellman, Naomi, Jeremy Hight, and Jeff Knowlton, *34 North 118 West: Mining the Urban Landscape* (2002), https://eliterature.org/collection.eliterature.org/3/work.html?work=34-north-118-west.

spencivetaylor. "Queer Game Analysis, Mattie Brice's *Mainichi*," *Gaymeranthropology* (blog), February 29, 2016. http://gaymeranthropology.blogspot.com/2016/02/queer-game-analysis-mattie-brices.html.

Spieker, Sven. "Artists from the Former Eastern Europe in Berlin: Ewa Partum." ARTMargins Online, October 30, 2017. https://artmargins.com/ewa-partum-d4/.

Spivey, Virginia B. "The Minimal Presence of Simone Forti," *Woman's Art Journal* 30, no. 1 (2009): 11–18. https://www.jstor.org/stable/40605219.

Statista. "Distribution of Gamers in the United States as of April 2015, by Ethnicity," Statista, October 29, 2015. https://www.statista.com/statistics/494870/distribution-of-gamers-by-ethnicity-usa/.

Story, Oriana. "How a Designer Took on Google over the 'World White Web,'" BBC, Newsbeat, April 14, 2016. http://www.bbc.co.uk/newsbeat/article/36044177/how-a-designer-took-on-google-over-the-world-white-web.

Streaming Museum. "Mariko Mori Intersects Nature, Ancient Culture, and Technology," October 28, 2013. https://www.streamingmuseum.org/post/rebirth-recent-work-by-mariko-mori/.

subRosa. "Bodies Unlimited: a Decade of subRosa's Art Practice." *n.paradoxa* 28 (July 2012): 16–25. https://www.ktpress.co.uk/pdf/vol28_npara_16-25_subRosa.pdf.

Suderburg, Erika. "Nun Notes and Deviant Longings." In *Alternative Projections: Experimental Film in Los Angeles, 1945–1980*, edited by David E. James and Adam Hyman, 268–78. New Barnet, UK: John Libbey, 2015.

Sulcas, Roslyn. "Yolanda Sonnabend, Designer Who Influenced Choreographer, Dies at 80," *New York Times*, November 29, 2015. https://www.nytimes.com/2015/11/30/arts/design/yolanda-sonnabend-designer-who-influenced-choreographer-dies-at-80.html.

Sullivan, Laura L. "Wired Women Writing: Towards a Feminist Theorization of Hypertext," *Computers and Composition* 16, no. 1 (1999): 25–54. https://doi.org/10.1016/S8755-4615(99)80004-8.

Suter, Rebecca. "Gender Bending and Exoticism in Japanese Girls Comics." *Asian Studies Review* 35, no. 4 (September 2013): 546–58. https://www.tandfonline.com/doi/full/10.1080/10357823.2013.832111.

Swartz, Anne. *Momentum: Women/Art/Technology*. New Brunswick, NJ: Rutgers University Center for Women in the Arts and Humanities (2015). Exhibition catalogue. https://www.academia.edu/14827301/Momentum_Women_Art_Technology.

Swartz, Anne. "The Pattern and Decoration Zeitgeist," Hyperallergic, June 13, 2018. https://hyperallergic.com/446327/the-pattern-and-decoration-zeitgeist/.

Symonds, Shannon. "Preserving Carol Shaw's Trailblazing Video Fame Career," The Strong National Museum of Play, *Play Stuff* (blog), July 19, 2017. https://www.museumofplay.org/blog/chegheads/2017/07/preserving-carol-shaws-trailblazing-video-game-career.

Tamblyn, Christine. "Mistaken Identities: An Interactive CD-ROM Genealogy," *Leonardo* 30, no. 4 (1997): 261–6, https://doi.org/10.2307/1576470.

Tamblyn, Christine. "'She Loves It, She Loves It Not: *Women and Technology*,' an Interactive CD-ROM." *Leonardo* 28, no. 2 (1995): 99–104, https://doi.org/10.2307/1576130.

Tapper, James. "Hiding in Plain Sight: Activists Don Camouflage to Beat Met Surveillance," *Guardian* (US ed.), February 1, 2020. https://www.theguardian.com/world/2020/feb/01/privacy-campaigners-dazzle-camouflage-met-police-surveillance.

Tarkka, Minna, ed. *The 5th International Symposium on Electronic Art Catalogue*. Helsinki: University of Art and Design, 156–9. https://vnsmatrix.net/wordpress/wp-content/uploads/isea-1994-helsinki-exhibition-catalogue.pdf.

Tate Modern. "5 Ways Jenny Holzer Brought Art to the Streets," https://www.tate.org.uk/art/artists/jenny-holzer-1307/5-ways-jenny-holzer-brought-art-streets.

Taylor, Grant David. " /'Up for Grabs': Agency, Praxis, and the Politics of Early Digital Art," *Lateral* 2 (2013). https://doi.org/10.25158/L2.1.5.

Taylor, Grant David. *When the Machine Made Art: The Troubled History of Computer Art*. New York: Bloomsbury, 2014.

Tau, Terri Te. "Beyond the Corners of Our Whare: A Conceptual Māori Response to State Surveillance in Aotearoa New Zealand," PhD diss., Massey University, 2015. https://mro.massey.ac.nz/bitstream/handle/10179/10825/02_whole.pdf?sequence=2&isAllowed=y.

Te Tau, Terri. *Te Āhua o te Hau ki te Papaioea*, multimedia installation, music composed by Rob Thorne, 2015. https://www.territetau.com/#/798817030644/.

Te Tau, Terri. "Terry Te Tau," CIRCUIT Artist Film and Video Aotearoa New Zealand. https://www.circuit.org.nz/artist/terri-te-tau.

Thorn, Matthew. "Girls and Women Are Getting Out of Hand: The Pleasure and Politics of Japan's Amateur Comics Community." In *Fanning the Flames: Fans and Consumer Culture in Contemporary Japan*, edited by William W. Kelly, 169–88. Albany: State University of New York Press, 2004.

Thorn, Rachel. "The Magnificent Forty-Niners," *Community for the Revival and Promotion of Shōjo Manga*, the blog of the committee chair, Professor Thorn, May 30, 2017. https://www.en.matt-thorn.com/single-post/2017/05/31/The-Magnificent-Forty-Niners.

ThoughtWorks Arts. "Karen Palmer: The Film that Watches You Back," TED Talk, May 25, 2018. https://thoughtworksarts.io/blog/karen-palmer-film-watches-you-back/.

ThoughtWorks Arts. "RIOT: Project Summary: Winter 2018," *ThoughtWorks Arts* (blog). https://thoughtworksarts.io/projects/riot/.

ThoughtWorks Arts. "*The Sentient Thespian*, Project Work Summary: Fall 2018." https://thoughtworksarts.io/projects/sentient-thespian/.

Todd, Monique. "How Genital Stroking Became an Act of Feminist Rebellion," *Dazed Digital*, July 15, 2016. https://www.dazeddigital.com/artsandculture/article/32075/1/how-genital-stroking-became-an-act-of-feminist-rebellion.

Toku, Masami. *International Perspectives on Shojo and Shojo Manga: The Influence of Girl Culture*. New York: Routledge, 2015.

Tomorrow. "Diane Burko." https://tomorrowcreates.com/artist/diane-burko/.

Treister, Suzanne. "HEXEN 2.0," 2009–2011. https://www.suzannetreister.net/HEXEN2/HEXEN_2.html.

Treister, Suzanne. "Suzanne Treister," interview by Marisa Olson, Artforum, October 15, 2019. https://www.artforum.com/interviews/suzanne-treister-on-black-hole-space-time-and-post-surveillance-art-81036.

Truckenbrod, Joan. "Joan Truckenbrod," in *New Media Futures: The Rise of Women in the Digital Arts*, edited by Donna J. Cox, Ellen Sandor, and Janine Fron, 152. Urbana: University of Illinois Press, 2018.

Tsai, Sylvia. "Flatstone, Mariko Mori." ArtAsiaPacific, July 29, 2013. http://artasiapacific.com/Magazine/WebExclusives/FlatstoneMarikoMori.

Tucker, Ian. "'A White Mask Worked Better': Why Algorithms Are Not Colour Blind." *Guardian* (US ed.), May 28, 2017. https://www.theguardian.com/technology/2017/may/28/joy-buolamwini-when-algorithms-are-racist-facial-recognition-bias.

Tuer, Dot. "Threads of Memory and Exile: Vera Frenkel's Art of Artifice." In *Mining the Media Archive: Essays on Art, Technology and Cultural Resistance*, 35–42. Ottawa: YYZBooks, 2005.

UChicago News. "Renowned Artist Jenny Holzer to Debut Project at UChicago Using Augmented Reality," September 10, 2020. https://news.uchicago.edu/story/renowned-artist-jenny-holzer-debut-project-uchicago-using-augmented-reality.

Valley News. "Lucy J. Young," *Valley News* (Vermont), March 13, 2004. https://www.vnews.com/Archives/2014/03/Lucy-Young-obit-vn-031314.

van Straaten, Laura. "Michael Rovner's Doormen of the Darkside at Pace Gallery," Artnet News, September 21, 2016. https://news.artnet.com/exhibitions/michal-rovners-doormen-dark-side-pace-661454.

Vernali, Cameron. "Tangibility of Artist's Work Wakes Public to Environmental Issues," *Daily Bruin*, November 13, 2018. https://dailybruin.com/2018/11/12/tangibility-of-artists-work-helps-to-wake-public-to-environmental-issues/.

Vincent, James. "Sophia the Robot's Co-creator Says the Bot May Not Be True AI, but It Is a Work of Art," The Verge, November 10, 2017. https://www.theverge.com/2017/11/10/16617092/sophia-the-robot-citizen-ai-hanson-robotics-ben-goertzel.

VNS Matrix. "Bitch Mutant Manifesto, 1996," https://vnsmatrix.net/projects/bitch-mutant-manifesto.

VNS Matrix. "The Cyberfeminist Manifesto for the 21st Century, 1991," https://vnsmatrix.net/projects/the-cyberfeminist-manifesto-for-the-21st-century.

Volkova, Lotta. "Anne Imhof Is Creating Hard-Core Performance Pieces that Speak to the Anxieties of a New Generation," Interview Magazine, March 7, 2019. https://www.interviewmagazine.com/art/anne-imhof-is-creating-hard-core-performance-pieces-that-speak-to-the-anxieties-of-a-new-generation.

Voon, Claire. "Paying Tribute to Lillian Schwartz, a Computer Art Pioneer," Hyperallergic, October 19, 2016. https://hyperallergic.com/329466/paying-tribute-lillian-schwartz-computer-art-pioneer/.

Wagley, Catherine. "Closed Circuits: A Look Back at LACMA's First Art and Technology Initiative," East of Borneo, May 11, 2015. https://eastofborneo.org/articles/closed-circuits-a-look-back-at-lacmas-first-art-and-technology-initiative/.

Wagner, Anne. "Eleanor Antin, Los Angeles County Museum of Art," *Artforum* 38, no. 2 (October 1999): 141–2. https://www.artforum.com/print/199908.

Wajcman, Judy. *Feminism Confronts Technology*. Cambridge: Polity Press, 1991. Google Books, reprint 2000.

Wakefield, Nina. "Networking Women and Grrrls with Information/Communication Technology: Surfing Tales of the World Wide Web." In *Processed Lives: Gender and*

Technology in Everyday Life, edited by Melodie Calvert and Jennifer Terry, 2nd ed., 69–84. Francis & Taylor e-Library, 2005 [First published London: Routledge, 1997].

Waldman, Diane. *Jenny Holzer*, exhibition catalog. New York: Solomon R. Guggenheim Foundation in association with Harry N. Abrams, 1989. https://archive.org/details/jennyholzer00wald/page/n11/mode/2up.

Walsh, Joanna. "Post-Cyberfeminist International 2017," *Opinion* (blog), Frieze, https://www.frieze.com/article/post-cyber-feminist-international-2017.

Waltz, Mitzi. *Alternative and Activist Media.* Edinburgh: Edinburgh University Press, 2005.

Weber, Jasmine. "An Afrofeminist Project Uses Technology to Empower Marginalized Communities," Hyperallergic, September 18, 2018. https://hyperallergic.com/460424/hyphen-labs/.

Westecott, Emma, Hannah Epstein, and Alexandra Leitch. *Feminist Art Game Praxis.* Toronto: Authors and Digital Games Research Association (DiGRA), 2013. http://www.digra.org/digital-library/publications/feminist-art-game-praxis/.

Wevr Transport. "Hard World for Small Things, A Day in the Life of a Tight-Knit Community," https://transport.wevr.com/hard-world-for-small-things.

Wiener Library. "One Family, Three Cities, Six Years of War: A Family of Artists During the War and the Holocaust," Exhibition at the Wiener Library, 1 March–24 April 2017. https://wienerholocaustlibrary.org/exhibition/one-family-three-cities-six-years-of-war-a-family-of-artists-during-the-war-and-the-holocaust/.

Wilding, Faith, and Hyla Willis. "SmartMom Rebooted: A Cyberfeminist Art Collective Reflects on its Earliest Work of Internet Art," *Studies in the Maternal* 8, no. 2 (December 15, 2016). https://doi.org/10.16995/sim.229.

Williams, Thomas Chatterton. "Adrian Piper's Show at MoMA Is the Largest Ever for a Living Artist. Why Hasn't She Seen It?" *New York Times Magazine*, June 27, 2018. https://www.nytimes.com/2018/06/27/magazine/adrian-pipers-self-imposed-exile-from-america-and-from-race-itself.html.

Withers, Josephine. "Feminist Performance Art: Performing, Discovering, Transforming Ourselves." In *The Power of Feminist Art*, edited by Norma Broude and Mary D. Garrard, 158–73. New York: Harry N. Abrams, 1993.

Women Make Movies. "Frances Reid, Filmmaker." https://www.wmm.com/filmmaker/Frances+Reid/.

World Wide Web Foundation. "Sir Tim Berners-Lee," History of the Web. https://webfoundation.org/about/vision/history-of-the-web/.

Yau, John. "A Trailblazer of Computer Drawing Gets Her Due," Hyperallergic, April 15, 2018. https://hyperallergic.com/437834/vera-molnar-drawings-1949-1986-senior-and-shopmaker-gallery-2018/.

Yi, Anicka. "Anicka Yi, A Political Interview," interview by Paul Laster, Conceptual Fine Arts, last updated December 3, 2019. https://www.conceptualfinearts.com/cfa/2017/05/09/anicka-yi-and-her-political-statement-to-counter-the-ocular-centric-society-we-live-in-an-interview/.

Yu, Richard K. "Otaku Subculture and Unhealthy Sexual Obsessions," Medium, January 2, 2018. https://medium.com/@richardkyu/effect-of-otaku-subculture-and-the-obsessive-da6c2bba6a2e.

Zarrelli, Natalie. "How Female Computers Mapped the Universe and Brought America to the Moon," Atlas Obscura, March 4, 2016. https://www.atlasobscura.com/articles/how-female-computers-mapped-the-universe-and-brought-america-to-the-moon.

Zec, Milica, and Winslow Porter. "Creating the Authentic Experience of GIANT in Virtual Reality," Medium, July 6, 2017. https://medium.com/@Within/creating-the-authentic-experience-of-giant-in-virtual-reality-570cda7b763d.

Zielinski, Sarah. "Hypatia, Ancient Alexandria's Great Female Scholar," Smithsonian Magazine, March 14, 2010. https://www.smithsonianmag.com/history/hypatia-ancient-alexandrias-great-female-scholar-10942888/.

Zuboff, Shoshana. "You Are Now Remotely Controlled," *New York Times*, January 24, 2020. https://www.nytimes.com/2020/01/24/opinion/sunday/surveillance-capitalism.html.

Zuckerman, Gabrielle. "An Interview with La Monte Young and Marian Zazeela," American Public Media, *Histories and Theories of Intermedia* (blog), July 2002. http://umintermediai501.blogspot.com/2008/06/interview-with-la-monte-young-and.html.

Index